FOOD FIGHT INC.

Napkin Sketches to Retail Shelves:
An Entrepreneur's Odyssey
of Triumphs and Lemons

MIROLAND IMPRINT 11

Canada Council **Conseil des Arts**
for the Arts **du Canada**

ONTARIO ARTS COUNCIL
CONSEIL DES ARTS DE L'ONTARIO

an Ontario government agency
un organisme du gouvernement de l'Ontario

Canadä

Guernica Editions Inc. acknowledges the support of the Canada Council
for the Arts and the Ontario Arts Council. The Ontario Arts Council
is an agency of the Government of Ontario.

We acknowledge the financial support of the Government of Canada.

FOOD FIGHT INC.

Napkin Sketches to Retail Shelves:
An Entrepreneur's Odyssey
of Triumphs and Lemons

Bruno J. Codispoti

www.foodfightinc.ca

MiroLand
p u b l i s h e r s

MIROLAND (GUERNICA)
TORONTO • BUFFALO • LANCASTER (U.K.)
2017

Connie McParland, series editor
Michael Mirolla, editor
David Moratto, cover and interior book design
Chapter icons from www.flaticon.com
Guernica Editions Inc.
1569 Heritage Way, Oakville, ON L6M 2Z7
2250 Military Road, Tonawanda, N.Y. 14150-6000 U.S.A.
www.guernicaeditions.com

Distributors:
University of Toronto Press Distribution,
5201 Dufferin Street, Toronto (ON), Canada M3H 5T8
Gazelle Book Services, White Cross Mills
High Town, Lancaster LA1 4XS U.K.

First edition.
Printed in Canada.

Legal Deposit—First Quarter
Library of Congress Catalog Card Number: 2016952736
Library and Archives Canada Cataloguing in Publication
Codispoti, Bruno, author
Food Fight Inc. : an entrepreneur's journey and subsequent
lessons on trying to make money in the grocery business / Bruno
Codispoti. -- First edition.

(MiroLand imprint ; 11)
Issued in print and electronic formats.
ISBN 978-1-77183-224-3 (paperback).--ISBN 978-1-77183-225-0
(epub).--ISBN 978-1-77183-226-7 (mobi)

1. Grocery trade--Canada. 2. Food--Canada--Marketing.
3. New business enterprises--Canada. 4. Entrepreneurship--Canada.
I. Title. II. Series: MiroLand imprint ; 11

HD9320.C32C63 2017   381'.4564130971   C2016-905972-3   C2016-905973-1

Contents

Preface

On a late afternoon in fall, escape from the office often leads to a quiet patio table at the closest Starbucks where the sight of people 'brown bagging it' is of no consequence. The surprise interruption of my solitude with one said brown bagger would demand my time and attention. The man sidling up to my table has obviously other intentions than to take delight in his homemade lunch and his introduction to me is a fully confident one: *"The lady in your office said I would find you out here. I understand you take popular restaurant recipes and food ideas and introduce them into grocery stores across the country."* The awkward pause that follows does not deter him. *"You have to try one of my wife's famous* dulce de leche *infused mini scones; she tops them with chunks of crunchy real Canadian bacon dunked in dark chocolate! Go on, try one."* He leans in closer and whispers in my ear: *"We'll make millions together."*

Now, aside from the fact that reaching my hand into a stranger's brown bag, however deliciously described, is beyond unappealing, I am now faced with the dilemma of the short or long answer as to how financially risky and utterly nervy his assumption really is. Where do I start? Do I tell him to take his head out of the bacon and chocolate covered clouds and send him and his brown bag on their way? Or, do I take the more responsible and onerous road, as I want to do, and begin to sketch out the fundamental blueprints for the epic, and frequently fruitless journey. I often begin by saying: *"You learn more about what not to do when you lose money doing the wrong thing. I can tell you how I've lost a boat-load of it over the past 20 years playing this game of delusional buffet-sized profits."*

This book is a hard-earned collection of stories that have to do with being fanatical about finding the next big food and drink thing, that next sliced-bread or Coca-Cola idea. It's about surprising, and sometimes unplanned, successes and carefully planned product launches ending in agonizing failure. Generously filled with themes of persistence and perseverance, and spiked with a pinch of humility, *Food Fight Inc.* is a spoonful of reality mixed with sugar to make the medicine go down. In the same breath, it's a testimony baked with fundamental lessons and practical guidance that can be applied to any aspiring entrepreneur's crusade, particularly those with only modest means, looking to unchain a product idea so that they can share it with the world. Regardless of the industry you're trying to break into, I hope that my adventures, particularly the brutal failures, the really sour lemons, will cause you to take a big step back to rethink your path.

From crafting tequila cocktails for former Van Halen front-man, Sammy Hagar, to popping too much popcorn for Pope Saint John Paul II, there's a little somethin' somethin' for even the pickiest of eaters. At times, the lessons and guidance may be a little difficult to taste because they'll be soaked in tales of booze and butter. But trust me, they're in there, sticking to the sides of the bowl. Learn, respect and practice the basics in this book, and you'll be able to make your product launch mission tastier and much more financially digestible should the soufflé sink when it's pulled from the oven.

As with any maiden journey, the first attempt is generally the hardest one. More often than not, it's also the most painful one. And like with most journeys, you'll begin to move faster and more freely with a knowledge of avoiding danger zones the more the road is travelled. It's nothing short of exhilarating and liberating to dream up your own product idea, sketch it out on a cocktail napkin and then gaze up at the outcome on a retail shelf a year or so later. When you get the launch formula right, it's a beautiful thing. When you get it wrong, and chances are that you will, more than once, chalk it up as a valuable lesson learned, wipe the counter clean and then start over again. Making mistakes is not only acceptable gameplay, it's a secret ingredient. Remember, it takes repetition to build muscle. To that end, if I can save one person from betting the farm on their Grandmother's secret Saskatoon Berry Jam, or help them in successfully selling a truckload of the silky organic sesame miso marinade they discovered in Osaka Japan—then my food fight will have been worth it.

Gathering Substance

It's Always Been About Food

My brother Dave and I have always had our own personal strengths, his being academia and mine, despite my body type being reminiscent of Shaggy from Scooby Doo, was being able to eat a lot. Perhaps not the typical strength to brag about, but it has served me well now in my pursuit of delicious food and has been a source of amusement for my family and friends for as long as I can remember. My Uncle Lou loved to watch me devour a thick stack of fried veal cutlets during Sunday lunch, and then jog the block to digest just enough to put down another plate. The staff at Chinese Food Buffets were warned that "all you can eat" was a dangerous proposition when I walked through the door. My friends cheered me on to tackle a third soft serve cone, or the Flintstone-sized steak.

It is only fitting then that my first job was as a stock boy at the local Red & White grocery store. There I was, a thirteen-year-old budding foodie making $3.81 an hour facing-up canned goods and carrying out paper grocery bags for nice old ladies for a 25-cent tip. Ten years, and many more veal cutlets later, I would find myself working for my Uncle El in his boutique design and print firm, Rockprint (now Creative Rock / creative rock.net). His main gig was, and still is, designing and printing food packaging for a large (and now monster large) food company called Johnvince Foods (johnvincefoods.com). This is an over-40-year-old family owned establishment that both repacks (other companies' bulk products) and manufactures a colourful multitude of both commodity-driven and unique food products, selling to nearly every retailer in Canada—and more recently in the US—that vends food.

Looking back to the mid '70s, Johnvince was fundamental in kick-starting and then shaping the concept of ditching expensive packaging to sell food in bulk to save consumers money. My Uncle introduced me to Joe Pulla, the company's owner and opportunity-finding savant, who instantly became a welcome mentor. Joe was, and remains, the most alarmingly clever and convincing entrepreneurial warrior with whom I've crossed paths. The words *impossible* and *surrender* are not in the man's dictionary. If he should ever decide to write his memoir, buy it. Trust me. Following him into his warren of food glory changed my life's trajectory for the better.

In the late '90s, J.P. (as Joe is affectionately called by his close peers; or the BrandFusion-staff exclusive nickname, 'Jeepers') scooped up both Planters Peanuts® and Lifesavers® from Nabisco, which immediately injected a level of admiration and notoriety into his already thriving food empire. The acquisition of the lovable, monocle sporting Mr. Peanut® gave him one of the most identifiable brand icons in the world. Lifesavers was enlisted into another of his growing subsidiary companies called Beta Brands.

In an effort to score myself a more permanent spot on JP's stacked bench of regular players, I took a long shot by offering up a very simple 5-page marketing plan detailing some ideas I had on rebuilding the dangerously out-of-date Lifesavers brand. If truth be told, it was my first attempt at penning a marketing plan, and although it was admittedly the absolute worst plan that I had ever produced, it proved to also be the most profoundly life-changing. The very next week I was given a job and a small desk located right outside JP's office door. I like to think that it was because he was able to see past my cryptic ideas and found a hungry and trustworthy student to mould. The position paid very little in salary, but paid off in spades in terms of providing a driver's seat vantage point, and to opening my sheltered eyes to a fun new world where anything seemed possible.

Beta Brands operated out of the timeworn, but very charming McCormicks Candy® manufacturing facility in London, Ontario. Eager to learn the food business, I packed my bags and moved into a small townhouse that the company had rented for management relocating from Toronto during the weekdays. Although unseasoned, I was an energetic player in a crowd of accomplished and driven food-athletes. The early mornings were launched with a couple of short espressos in order to reach the office by 6:30 a.m. and work straight through until 8 p.m. We grocery shopped, cooked and ate dinner together, caught up on the local evening news and would all then beat a hasty retreat to our rooms.

It should be noted that there weren't enough bedrooms so I was delegated to crash on a mattress placed on the floor in the living room with musty and ancient brown office dividers for a little privacy. For me, this unusual frat house served as a CPG (consumer packaged goods) Food Industry University, but instead of spending time with beer guzzling frat brothers, much of my precious waking time was spent with the CEO, COO, CFO, CIO and specialized consultants. Being in their proximity made it inevitable that I would pick up a few golden food-biz nuggets.

In the candy factory I spent the next few years happily tucked away on the vast and nearly abandoned top floor with a fellow recruited from the Willy Wonka candy company. Unlike the Oompa-Loompas in Charlie's Chocolate Factory, the sprightly Mr. Blair Neuss was a buttoned-down and veteran marketer with an infectious laugh that echoed down the lonely fifth floor halls like rolling thunder. The 432,000 sq.-ft factory was our candy-playground to experiment with. On shoe-string budgets we developed and helped launch over a hundred delightful and funky confectionary creations. Some were instant hits, like sour green apple alien head gummies, and others, like the Dr. Suess inspired green 'chocolate-y' eggs with multi-coloured marshmallow centres, were blockbuster sugar-bombs.

Unlike working in an overly structured, cubicle-freckled corporate environment, we had complete free rein to self-indulge in any crazy idea our hungry hearts desired. This was a fortunate opportunity and effective method to learn what worked and what didn't on someone else's dime. It also didn't hurt to have a 10kg shipping carton of peanut butter cups hidden under my desk at all times. Purely for inspiration, of course.

On an early morning bike ride during a weekend getaway at JP's cottage, he and I chatted openly and intensely about my next career move. I explained that it might be a suitable time for me to take leave of the cozy rabbit-hole in search of a more corporate company chapter with whom to continue my food journey, with the promise to return one day with more to offer both him and myself. With a charming and heavy grin, he gave me his official blessing. Three weeks later I received my first offer from The Quaker Oats Company in Peterborough, Ontario and I swiftly accepted it. Little did I know that, over the course of the next ten years, all of my major career decisions would be thoughtfully discussed and forged during early morning bike rides at JP's cottage. Always over a hot Tim's coffee and a freshly buttered 'everything' bagel while dangling my feet from the same public picnic table overlooking the lake.

Quaker was a barn-sized culture shock for me, as my vast fifth floor playground was replaced with a closet-sized cubicle. Where I once had the freedom to exercise my impulsive ideas and get involved with all things marketing, sales, operational, and legal, I was now boxed in by a very restricted set of marketing responsibilities and measured deliverables. Everyone spoke in a strange foreign tongue filled with acronyms and buzzwords I didn't understand. I felt like an Italian immigrant getting off the boat at Pier 21 into Halifax trying to settle into my strange new surroundings. As with all new adventures, there was an adjustment period and things did eventually click and I found a voice and my groove. The majority of my fellow Quakers proved to be fabulously sharp and highly motivated companions.

I learned how to dig deep into the countless dollars spent on consumer research to decode the food business at a different level. I learned how to structure, deliver and execute a proper product launch. I enjoyed exercising my multi-million marketing budget and I picked up a little corporate-poise along the way. Thank the food Gods for my brief stint at Quaker, as without it, the recipe that ended up becoming my career would have been dangerously void of salt and pepper. I like to think I made an impression on my new family at Quaker: the Marketing Director told me the prudent and well-respected then CEO blurted out a 'Fuck No' when he heard of my departure.

With my feet dangling once again from the lakeside picnic table, JP took a bite of his buttered 'everything' bagel, looked over the water and made me a casual and hefty offer. *'I have an opportunity. It won't pay anything for at least a year, but it could turn into something.'* I was still unmarried, with no brood of my own to watch over. The timing felt right in the pocket as the corporate life, although stable and promising, just didn't feel like me. With a few exchanges and high-fives, it was done. (Seriously, there were, and usually still are, solid old school high-fives to consummate such decisions.) JP and I were now business partners in a company that I would operate and he would watch over with a helpful hand and a keen eye.

Settling into my entrepreneurial life at the newly formed Brand-Fusion Ltd. (brandfusion.ca), I could faintly sense the value and strength that my experience up until this point had given me. I was able to meld together the youthful spirit and take-no-prisoners approach of working in a private and flat-structured organization with the discipline and methodology of working in a large public corporate setting—I've tried to uphold the right balance between these contrasting worlds ever since. Over the next 17 years, with a growing band of fanatical foodies, I would be devoted to trying to unearth the next food product sensation. And I'm still at it.

CHAPTER 2

Grocery Math

What to Expect

For those of you wanting to get into the grocery game, or into any product launch game for that matter, here are the Coles Notes; for a small start-up enterprise it's all in the cold math. How many store shelves can I squeeze my product onto? What will it cost me to get there? How many units per week, per year, can I conservatively move? Do I have the mandatory cash flow and the patience to wait until my return on investment clears the breakeven hurdle? If my product doesn't move can I finance the messy aftermath cleanup? Therein lies the rub. And unless you're cutting a deal in some quaint Farmer's Market where a transaction is consummated with a firm handshake, things can get costly and complicated quickly.

Let's start from the ground up. To get the ball rolling, you have to find a reputable and accessible contract packer (also known as co-packers or private label manufacturers) that will translate your small-batch kitchen recipe into one that can be commercialized and cost effectively mass-produced. Essentially, contract packers are manufacturing companies that you can commission to produce and pack your product. They can also be positioned to appear as if the product were manufactured directly by you. This is the stage where your virgin recipe usually ends up somewhat manhandled and transforms into a slightly adulterated version of its former self. It's important to stick to your guns. Do not compromise your recipe concept and vision in an act of desperation. A contract packer will always reach for the big red easy button and opt for what's economical and most closely aligned to his existing production capabilities. Unless you have a proven track record, or can demonstrate that your innovation will make big money in short order, or you are able to create an alliance with a rare and benevolent contract packer, you'll be charged a nominal lab fee—your first donation into your contract packer's notorious food bank, a bank that witnesses far more deposits than withdrawals. If your product calls for unique ingredients or components that the contract packer must procure and store exclusively for you, you'll be on the financial hook for their entire minimum commitment should your product eventually see daylight.

Before you get ahead of yourself and start spending money on whimsical packaging designs, understanding the contract packer's requirements, production limitations and flexibilities is vital. Granted, it is feasible to start fishing around for prospective retailers without investing upfront time with a contract packer. However, what's your end game if you miraculously convince a smaller mini-chain store to take a chance on you without knowing your true cost of goods (COGS), your minimum production run size commitment and lead times, packaging format capabilities, the product's shelf life or chemical reactions over time, etc.? Selling 100 cases of an authentic spicy Greek taramosalata when you have to pay your contract packer for a run of 500 cases will eventually leave you having to sell 400 cases to a shifty clear-out artist for the cost of a dinner at one of Mario Batali's New York City restaurants.

Armed with your mass-production recipe requirements and a reasonable grasp of how to navigate through the contract packer's requests and limitations, you would then move to honing your brand vision and crafting a packaging design. For a start-up mission this is a critical stage because the packaging design must perform the lion's share of heavy lifting with respect to drawing consumer attention. It's very possible to create a contagious brand buzz without having a consumer-marketing budget (i.e. print, television, radio, social media, PR, couponing, sampling, etc.) but it doesn't happen all too often. When it does, it is because someone has found the elusive and magical combination of introducing the right product with a design that speaks the perfect message, at just the right point in time, merchandised in a perfectly precise place in the store.

The design phase is also a liberating stage as your personal vision and aspirations become a more tangible reality. The process is very personal but also demands a fluid and open mind for constructive criticism. God knows that every friend, family member and the mailman will have a spirited opinion. Be sure to smile politely, nod acceptingly and process the suggestions and criticism internally. Only you can sort the treasure from the trash. The design phase is also the first potential financially hazardous stage because it's where the second and considerably larger contribution is made to fund your mission.

There are many echelons of design firms in both Canada and the US. A fresh and new-fangled design can run anywhere from $2,500 to $25,000 per sku. If you're taking a chance on your first food venture with a modest to medium tolerance for pain, I advise sticking to the former. The downside is that the risk is heavily weighted on your natural ability to recognize a brand design and narrative that will look suitable, will have both a memorable and proprietary feel to it, and will communicate the right message to your target audience in a meaningful way. The upside is that saving $20,000 in design suggests that you'll be 20,000 units closer to a breakeven scenario based on a food product that puts $1 per sale back into your pocket.

I imagine this will be a controversial point because someone (most likely, and rightfully so, a marketing agency or pricey design firm resident) will argue that an out-of-the-park design and brand message conjured up by a seasoned pro will help sell truckloads more product. I completely agree. Maybe. Sometimes. However, I've had the privilege to peruse the balance sheet of quite a few food start-up failures who were badly in need of a shot of capital to keep them alive. Spending beyond their financial means too quickly in the game for brand development, packaging design and website development is usually the first menacing number that jumps off the page like a signal fire. It's a tough call as I've had the pleasure of introducing both successful brands and products built using minimal outside aid, and the pain of unleashing stink bombs built with small fortunes and over countless pricey strategy dinner meetings; why do consultants always seem to choose the overpriced Brunellos? Once again, it depends on your risk tolerance against the size of the opportunity and how strongly you believe that your drilling for the ultimate packaging design will help tap into a sales-gusher.

I can stare at the first mocked-up product for hours on end. It feels so damn good. It's like staring at your baby wondering what it will grow up to be. Will she be strong and admired or awkward and reclusive? With a decent mock-up and reliable COGS in hand, it's finally show time. Do not spend another red cent until you have a decent sized fish hit the bait hard enough. You could, I suppose, invest in a small packaging run and convince your still somewhat sceptical contract packer to run the absolute minimum number of cases so that you have an actual finished product to flaunt. At that point, however, consider that you're now fully invested to make things fly. A little pressure and a sense of urgency is undoubtedly useful, but it also means that if you can't get a retailer interested you may also start to panic because of the skin you now have in the game. If your concept is in fact worthy, and the buyer knows and does his job properly, they'll be able to see past the scotch tape and fugitive glue dots. The leading advantage of clenching your purse strings tightly at this stage is that you'll safeguard the ability to tweak and improve your product by incorporating the buyer's requests and recommendations—that little dash of retailer ownership is usually worth its weight in gold. What's more, if the sales performance begins to falter, you might just get that indispensable helping and forgiving hand you wouldn't have otherwise experienced.

Boom baby! After a sack full of email requests and countless phone calls into a seemingly always-full voicemail box, you get a rare chance to deliver your sales pitch. And you pretty much nail it. That once unbelievably impossible to reach buyer has bought into your vision, and better yet, your precious creation. This is it; your chance in the big leagues to make an honest buck after probably a year of dispensing cash like a human ATM. Ah, wait a minute. How did we go from a snazzy scotch-tapped sample to a profitable product on the shelf, you ask? Well, it's quite simple. It's all about the 3 P's, baby—you'll need the persistence of Rocky Balboa coupled with the presentation skills and passion of Steve Jobs. Did I overkill my point? Of course I did, but this is the mother of all junctures in your napkin-sketch-inspired quest. If you do nail it, it's the one moment that you'll most likely take the time to truly celebrate because it's now legitimately game-on. Once you're in the pool using both your hands to tread water, there's no opportunity for high-fives. Your presentation handout must be succinct and compelling, and your delivery must be confident and convincing. The squinty-eyed and usually intense personality sitting on the other side of the negotiation table is waiting to jet back to their desk to respond to 500 new emails, most of them peppered with fires needing to be extinguished.

Let It Simmer ~

1. *Does your product concept adequately fill a meaningful consumer void and opportunity gap within the category it will be sold in?*
2. *Are the driving benefits of your concept truly valuable and unique, or have you simply created sexier packaging for a me-too product? Remember, you can put lipstick on a pig, but it's still a pig.*
3. *Have you personally scoured every store shelf to ensure that your product concept will help to enhance their existing assortment offering?*
4. *Have you cut (i.e. taste tested) your product against the competition's to ensure that it meets or exceeds your pledge to the consumer?*
5. *Is your product concept priced realistically and fairly when compared to similar offerings in the marketplace?*
6. *If shelf space is limited, what is your recommendation to the retailer for possible placement? Which competitive products should get the cold boot to clear space for your undertaking and why?*
7. *Try to snap a picture of your mocked-up product set up on a retailer's shelf to see how it looks in action (note—always ask the store manager for permission, or a smock-sporting bouncer may ask you to kindly leave).*
8. *How will you support and nurture your product concept once it's impatiently sitting on the shelf?*
9. *How much money can you stomach parting with to help mop up the aging inventory should the product not meet with the retailer's expectations?*

CHAPTER 3

Show Me The Cheddar

Rules of Engagement

how me the golden cheddar! That first cheque stub deserves to be proudly framed and displayed on the fireplace mantel beside your kid's first picture with creepy mall Santa. So be prepared, and avoid personal devastation when that cheque finally arrives in the mail with a figure that's only a mere fraction of what you expected to receive. Build your pricing model with great care. Retailers will want to keep you fed and alive, but do not want to fatten you up. How much they believe you take home versus how much you actually end up banking are two very different stories. Don't be greedy, or if you're lucky enough to get through the door and onto the shelf, your retails may end up hopelessly high. Don't price your product too low just to get through the door, or you won't have the necessary funds and fuel to travel far enough on your journey.

Striking the ultimate balance between achieving a realistic retail while giving the retailer the top end of their desired gross profit margin, and still managing to keep enough bread for your table, isn't always easy. Before you slide a piece of paper with a penciled price across the buyer's table, you have to know the retailer's pricing program expectations. Except for a select few, each retail chain has a custom mélange of financial contribution requirements; no doubt spurred on by crafty accountants. And unless you build in a reserve for a 5% Co-op fee, 2% Volume Rebate, 2% Damage Allowance, 1.5% Business Development Fee, 1% Cash Terms and a .025% Clean Underwear Fee, you'll squeeze yourself out of the financial picture.

Like most business ventures, planning for the worst-case scenario while secretly hoping for the best outcome is always a prudent approach. Crunch and munch the numbers to ensure that you can store enough acorns away should the retailer turn the tables and want restitution for poor performance.

In addition to the retailer's obligatory programs, build in some monies to protect your precious new real estate by supporting the marketing efforts needed to draw in attention to your tasty vittles so that they don't collect dust sitting on the shelf. When operating with a restricted budget, temporarily reducing your sell price to help fund in-store feature deal activity (e.g. 2 for $5.00 vs. a regular price point of $2.99 each) is a safe wager among the many more futile and fruitless retailer managed marketing options. Its effectiveness is highly measureable and, for the most part, it can still be profitable if your COGs (Cost of Goods) are intact and the retailer chips in on the deal. Unless you can piece together a consistently effective social media campaign, most other aggressive out-of-store consumer marketing activities are ordinarily beyond financial reach at the start line.

Confused? Don't be. I'll compare and contrast the paybacks and pitfalls of **out-of-store advertising** vs. **in-store promotional** marketing in *Chapter 31: Milk Money*. For now, let's make a note to play it safe by building in a set amount of money for marketing activity contribution into your pricing model. For example, for a product that retails for $3 up to $5, try to work in 50¢ per unit. Better yet, if you can afford to assign 75¢ to $1.00 per unit, you're groovin'. If not, allocate what you can comfortably afford until your volumes and production efficiencies eventually increase, thus causing your COGs to decrease, at which point you should be able to start setting aside more marketing monies. Take heed. In the early going you'll find that production and order fulfilment efficiencies are thrown out the window in an effort to stay afloat. Until you fall into a steady supply and demand rhythm, plan for your COGs to be a conservative fifteen percent north of your initial calculations.

Aside from the more conventional marketing expenses, there's a handful of supporting role services that will serve to raise your tab. For example, hiring a third-party merchandising team to visit high traffic stores to ensure that your product is in stock as well as properly placed and represented on shelf will become an eventual rule of engagement. However, at $20 to $30 per store for a one-hour call, you'll have to put this one on ice until you can build your empire a little. More often than not, we'll price out a product putting every minuscule drop of profit we pocket within the first two years straight back into the campaign to ensure that we have a fighting chance. As long as you can afford to wait it out, breaking even in the short term is not only customary, it's prudent if you know that you'll gain efficiencies and pick up more margin down the road.

Take into account that buying a truckload of butter, or sugar or black mission figs will be much cheaper than buying only a couple of pallets at the onset. Ordering 50,000 cartons or impressions of packaging film will be significantly cheaper than ordering the minimum amount—which is customarily plus or minus 10,000 units or so. Let's say that you save 20 cents per unit as a result—on a master shipping case of 12 units that's an additional $2.40 in your piggy bank. Having said this, it's tempting to bite the bullet and fork out the cash required for the larger run in order to start your race with lower COGs and a more comforting profit. Personally, unless the overall cash outlay is close, I'd rather order fewer materials and take the temporary margin hit upfront associated with ordering a more controlled 10%-15% over what's truly required. Otherwise you'll be gratuitously chewing up your bank account, increasing your cash burn rate, and may run the risk of indeterminately storing unused packaging and wasting warehouse space (or worse yet, valuable garage space). Don't fret. We'll delve deeper into the numbers and the corresponding success metrics a little later in the book.

Seeing the first Purchase Order (PO) appear in your otherwise empty inbox, or patiently resting in the fax tray, is a wonderfully euphoric, yet anxious moment. Feelings of jubilation and fist pumps are closely followed by pensive thoughts of: *'Can I pull this off in time? Have I covered all my bases with respect to the other players involved that will need to do their part in order for me to pull this off?'* The irony is usually that it will take a dog's age to squeeze the first order out of the retailer, yet they'll want you to deliver it yesterday. And, by the way, if you don't deliver the goods on time you'll be fined, tarred and feathered. This is when you need to exercise your basic management skills. Triple check absolutely everything. Walk through every step with everyone involved in the game—your team, the packaging company, the contract packer, the guy on the line attaching the doohickey to the whatchacallit, the freight company, etc.

Murphy's Law: the one single and seemingly inconsequential step or piece or person that you don't check will bring down your house of cards. It's remarkable how many folks in business, irrespective of the industry they work in, don't practice this attention to detail methodology. After my first year in business, the president and founder of Kernels Extraordinary Popcorn®, Scott Staiman, expressed this notion to me: *'It's surprising how many people don't have "it" when "it" is the most important quality to have.'* I never forgot that.

You park in the tic-tac-toe of cars and abandoned grocery carts. Walking through the sliding doors, you feel giddy and your stomach is in knots. Did my product make it into this store or is it helplessly trapped in the retailer's distribution centre, or lost here somewhere in their box-city of a backroom? Walking down aisle 5 you catch a glimpse of a red box on the shelf at the other end of the store. Is that my little red box? Tears of joy and pride christen your cheeks as you realize it is your glorious, most perfect crimson little red box of promise smiling back at you on the very top shelf. You wish it wasn't on the top shelf because you can't reach it and worry about who actually can. But, that's a problem for another day. For today is your first official day in business.

CHAPTER 4

Breaking Bread

Compatibility

Many of our business escapades have dealt with licensing and leveraging a well-known restaurant or an established food brand. In the beginning, we were super-green and super-eager, so we ended up saying '*Hell YEAH*' to 95% of the opportunities that crossed our vacant desks. Today, we have double the opportunities and say '*Hell NO*' to 95%. Most often it's because we don't get the right vibe from the prospective business partner. The business idea could feel rock solid. The strategic fit with our business, existing relationships and capabilities may make perfect sense, but something will just seem uncomfortably ... alien. At first, we fooled ourselves by thinking that the awkwardness would eventually wane the closer we worked and grew with a person or another company.

After a dozen or so such partnerships we eventually realized that there was a strong and undeniable correlation between people that we felt naturally comfortable with and a product's ultimate trajectory. Similarly, we noticed that the partners we couldn't relax with would eventually cost us the most time, money and aggravation. Perhaps it's a self-fulfilling prophecy to evaluate people and opportunities with this jaded lens? I don't think so. Having fun and gelling with those involved in your mission is an absolute must. These days, our standard issue acid test is what we call the breaking bread factor. Can we sit down at a table with a prospective partner and really enjoy a meal together? Does it feel forced or is there a natural spark (without the assistance of a bottle of

Brunello)? Do you wince when their call comes through or perk up in your chair with enthusiasm to pick up the phone?

For all intents and purposes, a healthy partnership isn't any different than a healthy marriage—if you can't sit across the dinner table and break bread with your potential spouse, would you want to get married? Dave and I have developed such trepidation for toxic relationships that we pull out the break-up card at the first sign of foreboding. Remember, the deeper you dive, and the more time you spend with one another, the tougher it is to pull the plug so you might as well be honest with yourself and them. As you read through the compilation of case studies that follow, many of which involve both fruitful and fruitless partnerships, you'll begin to see a pattern: the healthy relationships most often ended in making money. And the bad ones, well, save for the hard lessons learned, were bad ones all around.

CHAPTER 5

Eat Well, Sleep Well

Do What's Right

Nice guys finish last, do they? This may hold true in stories and myth, and occasionally in the real world, but we pride ourselves on running our business with integrity and respect. Perhaps we would be further ahead in the profit game if we played dirty, but empty victories won't sustain you. For every morally decent person out there, there are double the number of jerks without a conscience hacking away to get what they want despite any collateral damage they create. I'm not trying to sound self-righteous or ostentatious, it's just the mould in which I was cast. As a result, many of you might read a thing or two and disagree with how we ultimately handled a situation. '*You should've gone legal.*' Or: '*Come on, man, fight back!*' are a couple of choice phrases that you might want to mutter under your breath as you continue to read on. That's fine, I can respect that, but I need my sleep and can only get it when my head hits the pillow without preventable conflict or sobering regret. Lose money on a bad assessment or poor decision, so be it, you'll recover. Unethically torch an otherwise good relationship over anything other than an unrecoverable loss, particularly when a close friend or family members are involved, no thanks, I'll pass. I prefer to take in only what I know I can digest without heartburn.

CHAPTER 6

Eat In Moderation, Not Deprivation

Love What You Do

When the Toronto Blue Jays were battling it out in the 2015 MLB postseason, the fellas in the office and I took a minimum five-minute break to play catch in the parking lot at least once every 2 or 3 hours. Outside the postseason, we like to keep parking-lot-catch down to a more respectable once a day. Now, guitar playing in the office is a much more frequent and religious practice. My office-acoustic guitar (once owned by Glass Tiger's Alan Frew) is never more than ten feet away from my enthusiastic reach. Some people chain-smoke to calm their shot nerves. I enjoy bending and sliding out a few choice riffs to help regulate my blood pressure after either wrapping up a jittery customer call or to celebrate after intercepting a much anticipated purchase order.

Most of the time I sit on the cushy couch by the fireplace in my office and play softly so that I don't disturb the others. However, on Friday afternoons during our *'Gentlemen's weekly'* toast, I get a kick out of strumming a few fresh new licks for the fellas while we leisurely sip our single malt scotch and passionately chat about the upcoming week's ambitions. If Dave has cooked a little extra fare earlier that afternoon in our test kitchen, it's also a good opportunity to double back and clear out the fridge. If we've hosted a tailgate barbeque party in the parking lot earlier that week for our sales team, or as neighbourly thanks to our local Starbucks barista gang, chances are there's a giant foil-tray loaded with spicy Italian sausages. Which incidentally, goes perfect on a fresh bun with my Grandmother's homemade Sicilian caponata (chopped fried eggplant, olives, capers and sweet sautéed onions)—we always have a jar or two on hand.

During school holidays, a couple of jumbo ice cream sandwiches for dessert is also in the cards as my eleven-year-old son, Gabe, runs his beach-themed popsicle bar (*Gabo Wabo's*) from the sidewalk outside our office during lunch hour. On Thursdays during the late fall through to early spring (indoor pizza oven season) and sometimes during mid summer (outdoor pizza oven season), we try to schedule our meetings around making fresh batches of Neapolitan pizza dough, using a 'poolish' bread starter, before the long weekends. Before you judge me, let me explain, it's completely necessary because the *KicthenAid*® stand mixer at the office has a much larger bowl and is more capable than the ancient one I have at home. Plus, making pizza dough forty-eight hours before you actually need it, and then storing it in the fridge, allows it to gradually rise, giving your crust a bolder taste and airier texture—bada bing!

Throughout the day, it's customary for the gang to breakout into ridiculous wisecracker songs about Archie (our beloved veteran new product developer) and his interesting 80s-themed colourful fashion choices or his peculiar bird-like eating habits. Rest assured, it's only because we admire the ol' boy. Integrating silly humour and chanting foolish songs about coworkers and supply partners (i.e. contract packers and suppliers of raw material ingredients and packaging) plays an immense role in our work life. It lies deep at the core of our office culture. Without humour, and without lively song, the day somehow feels painfully long and the office vibe much too sombre—which also explains why everyone in the office loves to play Boom 97.3's *'Just a Sec'* daily name that tune challenge. (By the way, Arch is also our resident champion.)

I didn't realize how strange and outrageous our work philosophy was until we had our accountant spend a full day in the office with us. At first glance, I'm more than certain that we all seem shockingly childish and unfocused at best. Or at least, I hope we do. But listen up, don't assume that our light-hearted conduct means that we're unproductive or disinterested. Conversely, you'll find us problem solving until late in the evening and on the weekends long after the regular work folk have eagerly punched out. My best ideas, strongest inspiration and the courage to provoke big change, come to me when I step away from my desk.

The key, however, is knowing when it's time to hunker down. When the bough breaks, turning off the music and stepping up to quickly lick an impending issue should be automatic. Firmly taking hold of a slippery opportunity has to materialize instinctively and effortlessly. I do believe, and have experienced, that work cultures fabricated on enforced structure, management intimidation, and most notably, without simple amusement, are both stifling and downright depressing. It's a terrifying approach and scene that scares me to the point of constant paranoia of losing what we've built.

Over the years, success has become less about strictly financial reward, and more about being able to preserve the unique and quirky culture I've come to love. To boot, I know that our small seasoned and spicy team of loyal food warriors is more productive and determined than a room full of uninspired workers. When you have the right crew, they'll recognize when the line slips out of hand and needs to be reeled back in. If you have the best players on board, they'll be self-motivated and self-driven. Making sure that they're inspired, stimulated and unencumbered is where I focus my energy. (Speaking of comfortable, you can't beat the custom BrandFusion slippers we like to sport in the office during frosty Canadian winter days.)

I'm also too distracted being in constant awe over how quickly we can dream up, develop and bring a new food product to market compared to larger and more regulated companies. We may not always achieve the same level of case volume sales or consumer awareness that a larger and more financially equipped company can reach; however, our cost to operate the business, and the number of mouths we need to feed are both drastically fewer. If my memory serves me correctly, we've boldly pedalled through the entire launch process in 20 weeks. Granted, the path to market was considerably unorthodox and freckled with luck but we pulled it off just the same.

I don't sanction this loose approach or relaxed attitude on a regular basis by any means, but once in a blue moon it's healthy to throw caution to the wind. Don't try this at home without adult supervision, but the 20 weeks looked a little something like this:

- **week 1**—product concept ideation—*'Hey guys I have an interesting idea'*
- **week 2**—identified a popular brand licensor to partner with —*'I bet if we could market this product under that popular restaurant name, we'd sell truckloads more than any brand we develop ourselves'*
- **week 3**—designed preliminary packaging design and mocked-up a credible sales sample—*'Whoa! This actually looks credible! Well worth the $500 investment. Let's flaunt it around to a few choice retailers to see if we can get a decent bite before we're in too deep and spend too much time and money on fine-tuning things'*
- **week 6**—locked-up a retailer and an opening order commitment before we actually knew who would build the product for us, or if the brand licensor was even interested —*'Glad to hear you like the product. We'll fill out the new item forms and get back to you in a few weeks with a confirmed lead-time for shipment of the first order'*
- **week 9**—approached and locked-up the brand licensor partner based on the retailer's commitment to purchase
- **week 12**—sourced and secured a manufacturing contract
- **week 19**—completed recipe development, product testing, regulatory requirements, polished up packaging design, ordered raw materials and production; week 20—ran product and fulfilled opening order
- **week 21**—take an extra long weekend

In order to pull off this hocus-pocus of a product launch, you'll need a very fluid project management approach, a giant pot full of luck and a big love for what you do. Trust me, without a genuine affinity for the game, you'll want to tap-out long before the PO appears in your inbox. I'm constantly amazed at the sheer volume of projects we can comfortably balance efficiently at once and how each member of the team can easily slip in and out of wearing multiple hats-of-responsibility on any given day; from researcher, to data analyst, to designer, to lawyer, to sales person, to production manager. I'll spare you from citing the old cliché that says: *'Do what you love and you'll never work a day in your life.'* So let me just say this and be done with it: *'Do what you love and you'll never work a day in your life.'*

Let it Simmer ~

1. *Do you truly love your product concept, its ultimate purpose and the impact that it will have in the marketplace? Bear in mind that at some point, or more accurately, at multiple points in the process, your affinity for your product and the mission will be your solitary touchstone.*

2. *Are you building a team and company culture that will keep both you and them interested in the long run, and that will attract and preserve the calibre of players you need to succeed?*

3. *How quickly and competently can you launch your product when your back is against the wall with a do-or-die opportunity? What factors would be holding you back from racing through a hurried product launch? Can you deal with and improve those factors now so that you're ready if and when the opportunity presents itself?*

4. *Are there amusing rituals and activities related to your industry that you can incorporate into your day to help create an inspiring and creative environment? Making Neapolitan Pizza dough, playing guitar and scarfing down jumbo ice cream sandwiches are my vice, what's yours?*

CHAPTER 7

Pop Goes The World

First-Mover Advantage

I love hot, buttery popcorn—the childlike anticipation of waiting for the first kernel to reach 450°F, where moisture turns into steam and creates a transformational and magical 'pop'. Be that as it may, I never would have guessed I'd spend my first two years at BrandFusion convincing retail chains and Canadians alike that they ought to eat the beloved snack generously sprinkled with Kernels Extraordinary Popcorn® seasonings (kernelspopcorn.com / kernelsfun.ca). Long live *Mmmm ... White Cheddar* and *Dill-irous*! It took well over a year's time and the patience of Job, but soon Blockbuster Video and Walmart and then Loblaws jumped on board our flavour-train. Had I not started the company with this seemingly cute and impulse-driven snack food product, I might not have had the privilege to share the many adventures that follow this lucky one.

This product launch effort is chockful of fundamentals with respect to introducing the right product, at the right point in time and in all the right places. I also have to take this opportunity to offer a solid chunk of credit to the strategy and instinct of a lay-it-on-the-line food sales warrior named Don Lock. Before I strolled into the Kernels Popcorn picture, he was the guy who insisted that Kernels (a 30-plus-year-old Canadian franchise with over 70 kiosks popping perfect popcorn flavours) shouldn't make its entrance into the grocery game with yet another bag of popped popcorn. Why fight for a share of the consumer's stomach and the retailer's self-space with the brash titans of the potato chip world? Why not invent a new sub category by giving consumers a choice to dial up the flavour and customize their microwave popcorn—a potentially much smaller segment, but one wide open for innovation?

The timing was textbook for me as I had just spent the past two years at The Quaker Oats Company delving deep into the salty snack world with *Crispy Minis*® Rice Chips. The core idea was essentially the same as Kernels Popcorn Shakers. They both are rooted in offering consumers a healthier alternative to potato chips without sacrificing the crunchy texture and the funky and intense chip flavours.

So, what were the big lessons jammed into that little clear plastic jar? Unlike many of the other popcorn-related products that we developed in subsequent years, our seasoning shaker concept had enough profit seared in to allow us to finish the lengthy and exhausting race with a little gas left in the tank to spare. Remember, no margin, no ticket to ride. If you latch onto an opportunity that doesn't pay you back a useful amount of margin after all of the pipers are paid, and ugly messes are cleaned up, you won't travel too far down the road. We all know that it takes money to make money. In the case of the game of grocery, paying yourself back is a luxury if it should miraculously happen within the first year or so.

We were first to market in grocery stores with our popcorn shakers. Granted, there were a handful of lesser known and more regional popcorn shaker products in the market at the time of our incursion, but their presence and approach was small-scale in comparison. To boot, many Canadians already had a sweet love affair going on with Kernels Extraordinary Popcorn so our duty was more about accurately representing and respecting the consumer's great expectations of the brand rather than disappoint them. As an entrepreneur, if you're smart and fortunate enough to invent and then successfully introduce a truly new concept platform, respect that it's a rare opportunity and give it all you've bloody got. Always manoeuvre as if your competition is close behind nipping at your heels and trying to lift your idea—because they are.

If you can reach solid ground and penetrate the market quickly and then protect what's yours by doing right by your product and brand (i.e.

avoid cutting corners on quality, service and customer satisfaction), you'll have a chance to drive from the pole position for a while. When the big boys come knocking (and they eventually will if the prize is worth it), you'd better have pulled so far up in front of the race that they have to sweat hard to catch up with you. The paranoid survive. On the flip side, if you're trying to break into a category that has an established player driving in the pole position, irrespective of their size, you'd better have a meaningful and enduring product advantage— something much much sexier than merely a slight price or packaging design and/or format improvement.

One of the most undervalued advantages we had going into the game was that the ritual of shaking chip-inspired seasoning flavours onto popcorn was already well established with consumers. Folks were already conditioned to dress their hot and fresh popcorn with White Cheddar, Dill Pickle, Ketchup, BBQ, Salt & Vinegar and Sour Cream & Onion seasonings at movie theatres and concession stands in sporting areas, etc. We didn't appreciate how valuable this well-established ritual was until we tried to follow up our Kernels Popcorn Shakers success with similar seasoning concepts in various other food categories using various other quick service restaurant brands—among others, New York Fries® French fry seasonings, Teriyaki Experience® Pan Asian seasonings, Golden Griddle® egg seasonings, Schwartz's deli seasonings, Mr. Greek® Mediterranean seasoning and Sbarro® pizza seasoning.

While each of these follow-up seasoning products were supported and validated by well-known quick-service restaurant brands, they eventually flopped. Granted, the absence of a deep-rooted consumer eating ritual wasn't the sole missing ingredient in each of these failed attempts, but I believe it was the driving factor. Had we needed to invest adequate marketing funds and our time to educate consumers on why they must have the Kernels product, our journey would've been radically more expensive and a lot trickier. The usefulness of the product was already more or less proven so it also made for an easier sale with retailers. And because the product added new, impulsive and incremental sales to the microwave category, negotiating a more digestible cost of entry (i.e. listing / slotting fees) was often the case. Had we tried to push our way into the popcorn category with yet another copy-cat ready-to-eat or microwave popcorn product, I believe the reverse would've been true and we'd have to have paid a higher than average ticket to ride. Put differently, the more innovative your concept is, the more you'll be able to fly under the radar with respect to the retailer's arbitrary costs of entry and successive account maintenance charges.

Product placement within the store was a massive game changer. Would you buy as much salsa if it wasn't sitting next to the tortilla chips? Had we been relegated to the spice section alongside black pepper and cumin, Kernels Popcorn Shakers might've eventually gone stale. Grant-ed, being awarded prominent shelf space within the colourfully crowd-ed snack section was also a rare and real coup for an unassuming jar of seasoning. But then again, we were packing a well-established snack brand with plenty of popcorn prestige.

The physical size of our product also gave us an unexpected leg up on the economics of our mission. Despite the similar retail price points, our popcorn shaker jars are quite small in comparison to the cartons of microwave popcorn and pillowy bags of ready-to-eat popcorn that they sit beside. On the other hand, despite taking up a fraction of the shelf space, their profit contribution per unit of sale for the retailer is nearly equal to the other products in the category. As a result, we're able to oc-cupy much less real estate and still deliver a higher profit per square inch. Given that shelf space comes at a stiff premium, I guess size does matter. What's more, from a freight cost perspective, shipping a small and dense product from coast to coast is also much more cost-effective than shipping a larger and airy one. For example, there are 3,168 shak-ers on a pallet compared to 456 cartons of microwave popcorn. Consid-ering that it costs about $350 to ship one pallet of goods from Toronto to Vancouver, freight would eat up a digestible 11¢ per shaker vs. a more indigestible 77¢ per microwave popcorn carton. Remember, when it comes to shipping product, good things do come in small packages.

Admittedly, there were a few contributing factors to our success which were less about strategy, and perhaps more about good fortune. The core competency of Johnvince Foods, our distribution partner and a terrifically close ally, is the sale and distribution of snack foods into grocery stores. Their flagship brand is Planters® Peanuts which conveniently is sold through the same salty snacks category buyer, and sits right next to the popcorn section within the store. Ergo, building the Kernels brand with Johnvince at our side was mutually beneficial rather than a stretch and a strain on both their business and on the relationship with its owner and my business partner, JP.

The other Godsend was our rare relationship and the mutual respect that we shared with our licensor partners at Kernels Extraordinary Popcorn. Going back to *Chapter 4: Breaking Bread*, we naturally gelled with our popcorn partners and ended up forming an incredibly concrete and dynamic bond. They avoided smothering us with undue pressure and unrealistic expectations, and in return we were able to breath freely and build the business on solid ground. Conversely, we couldn't wait to part ways with the licensor partners that called daily to check up on our progress. Last but not least, I'm a glutton for intense cheese popcorn, and ended up becoming a heavy user of our product so having to travel the country to sell it was more of privilege than a chore.

Let It Simmer ~

1. *Does your product concept provide enough profit margin to fuel the entire race plus leave you with a decent amount money in the bank?*
2. *Can you partner with a likeminded brand that has established recognition, consumer loyalty, and realistic expectations?*
3. *Is being first to market in the cards? If so, are you doing what's necessary to protect your lead?*
4. *Can you tap into an established consumer usage ritual to reduce your time investment and avoid steep consumer product education costs?*
5. *Does your product concept add material value to the category you hope to play in? Will it add incremental sales or will you have to fight to source all of your sales volume from a competitor?*
6. *Is your product innovation clever enough to evade, or at least mitigate, some of the retailer's more arbitrary financial demands?*

7. *Standout! Can your product be placed in an area within the store that will serve to help generate complementary and impulse purchases?*

8. *If you're tapping into a connection with a close friend or family member in the industry that can help you get to market, try to ensure that it's mutually beneficial or you'll risk putting an undue strain on the relationship.*

9. *Do you enjoy breaking bread with the key players in your game? Recognize that if the battle breaches your own organization and inner circle, breathing easy and functioning freely will become increasingly difficult.*

CHAPTER 8

Pope Goes The World

Lessons From Failure

O ur grand goal was to sell 20,000 bags of freshly-popped Kernels Popcorn from July 23rd to July 28th, 2002 at the 17th World Youth Day in Toronto—a celebration of faith begun by Pope John Paul II held on an international level every two to three years. It was also Pope John Paul II's final World Youth day celebration. Although the event was designed for Catholics, it attracts sizable numbers of youth from other faiths and denominations and is presented as a multi-faith celebration of young people from all over the world.

'Come on! Are you sure we'll sell that much popcorn?' I asked the event organizer. *'20,000 bags will fill up an entire 48' tractor trailer container!'* It was then carefully explained to us that our forecast model should be built on how quickly we can reach out one hand to collect five bucks and then reach out our other hand to give out a bag of popcorn. So, we did the math on the event's anticipated attendance of a few hundred thousand against the percentage of attendees that we projected might want popcorn and somehow came up with a conservative guesstimate of 20,000 bags.

JP and Johnvince Foods were heavily involved in the event as it took place at Downsview Park, which sits only a few blocks down the street from their offices. Among other things, they were involved with providing storage and logistics for the event assets (i.e. think massive crosses), and co-packing knapsack kits chockfull of goodies that were distributed to each youth in attendance. It was hard for me not to get caught up in all of the boundless enthusiasm as the event promised to be nothing short of historic. At the time, our only sanctioned source for securing the crazy number of bags required was directly from the handful of Kernels' retail kiosks located in shopping malls within a 30-minute drive from the event. To boot, fresh popcorn packed in tent-top-folded theatre-style paper bags, especially in the humid summer weather, has a narrow shelf life of only few days so my cousin Chris and I had to orchestrate driving around the city cramming our cube van with what seemed like enough popcorn to fill an Olympic-sized swimming pool. Yes, I know what you may be thinking, but popping popcorn onsite, a la movie theatre mode, unfortunately wasn't a viable option if we wanted to sell the product under the popular Kernels Extraordinary Popcorn® brand name using their proprietary preparation techniques and recipes.

Before this, we spent a couple of weeks in the garage hand-painting gigantic Kernels signage, assembling uniforms, constructing the booth fixtures and laying out our detailed site plans. To pull off the event we knew we needed a team of dependable people (who'd slave for less than minimum wage) who could also follow a strict game plan—we'd need a few smiling cashiers, a couple of healthy runners to re-fill the popcorn display fixtures and someone tough enough to collect and guard all of that cash money. My brother Dave wasn't working for BrandFusion yet but we summoned him to build an MS Excel spreadsheet program to track our hourly sales, inventory, and staff breaks. Perhaps being slightly anal, we even recorded the bags of popcorn our staff ate so that the sales reporting wouldn't be tainted. As most of the staff was comprised of BrandFusion employees and their families (the less than minimum wage compensation should make more sense now), none of us had the compulsory food training the event required us to have by law. Man, what a weird and wonderful sight it was to see cousins, aunts, neighbours and friends sit attentively in a massive city auditorium classroom taking notes on cross contamination and how to properly wash your hands and food contact surfaces. Needless to say, they all answered our call to action and were ready to rock and roll.

Chris and I took our Kernels cube van to the site one afternoon a few days before the event—note, we had a serious Kernels cube van that we leased and decked-out with Kernels Popcorn shaker graphics for such events. After a few months into the lease, however, we ended up using the damn thing more for family moving requests so I got royally pissed off and had to break the lease and lost some serious money ... 'You need me to do what? *Oh No! Please, not another king-sized mattress or 8 drawer credenza.*' We drove up to one of many gates surrounding the 572-acre Downsview Park and noticed a giant '*Do Not Enter*' sign hanging from the swing-gate. Peeking through the chain-link fence, we could see that our assigned booth space was only a few hundred yards or so in the distance.

The truck was crammed with jumbo tarps, tents, signs, bungee cords and wooden folding-tables that we needed to unload to make more space, so we decided to ignore the warning sign. As we slowly rolled onto the field we noticed a horde of officers in military uniform standing beside a serious looking army helicopter far off in the distance. We reached about half way to our site when the van got stuck in a mud patch. I punched the gas so hard that both back wheels buried themselves deep into the wet ground. '*Come on. Damn it!*' I roared. '*Ok, Chris, I'll jump out and try to push and rock the van from the front and then you throw it in reverse, ok.*'

Just as I stepped out of the truck, the helicopter fired-up and took flight. Chris rolled down his window and screamed: '*Oh no, I think they're coming this way!*' My heart raced at a jackrabbit's pace as we were completely alone in a vastly open field and obviously trespassing—and from what I've seen on TV, the Pope packs some pretty heavy-duty security. 'Quick, *hit the gas!!*' I screamed in pure panic. Chris hit the pedal so hard that a slab of muddy turf the size of a fat beavertail flung out from under the van's back wheel, tore straight up into the air and then landed flat on my head like a soggy mud-toupee.

The military chopper now hovered 30 feet above my head. '*What is your business here?*' or something like that came thundering over the aircraft's external speaker system. The force of the wind ripping off the propeller generously splattered more mud over my clothes and face— '*Oh Man ... Sorry! We're very sorry. We'll turn around and leave now. Thank You.*' *And* that, my friends, should have been the first sign that this event was not going to go in the heavenly manner we had prayed for.

The day of the event, we set up a small but well organized tent-city behind our popcorn booth so that a group of us could sleep onsite to close and re-open early the following morning—note, sleeping over was key as the traffic accompanying the transport of 500,000 people was nothing short of nauseating. (Yes, the final attendance numbers had climbed far beyond expectation.) Things were looking decent before the gates opened. There were two or three large food zones that sat a couple of football fields apart. Along with a handful of other vendors —most notably and memorably a fresh red watermelon fruit stand run by some uncompromising fellow Sicilians, our food section was located a hundred feet or so from one of the main entrances on route to the massive centre stage.

Once the gates opened there would be wave upon wave of teens jubilantly marching and singing right in front of our well-stocked popcorn booth. On the way to the port-a-potty 'village' (there must've been hundreds of toilets), I ran into a guy selling bottled water with special World Youth Day labels from the back of his truck. 'Damn, *we should be selling water, too,*' I thought. '*I'd like to buy one pallet, Sir... no wait, what am I thinking ... I'll buy three pallets.*' What a beautiful last minute move, I proudly thought nodding my head in self-approval. Mere minutes before the gates officially opened, we were sitting on 20,003 bags of fresh popcorn and 3,500 bottles of water to unload.

The team was primed and super pumped and I was giddy with anticipation ... and then it happened. We saw the gates in the far off distance swing open. From where we stood, the people looked as small as ants, but we could still see that they were all making a beeline for the main stage in order to get a proper seat and view of the Pope. Twenty-five minutes passed and the gate closest to us remained closed. We then realized the crowd behind 'our' gate had begun to dissolve as people made their way to the open entrances in the far distance. '*Um, okay guys,*' I addressed our troops with confidence. '*I'm sure they'll get hungry and will start exploring the grounds.*'

A few hours passed and we sold maybe 5 bags of popcorn. All I could think of was that we had twenty-friggin-thousand bags and about what had happened to the mound of five-dollar bills we were promised. For the first few hours, Dave and I respected and stuck closely to our detailed spread-sheet protocol ... 'Hey man, listen, if you take a bag please remember to record it. Okay!' As the day wore on and we acknowledged that it wasn't exactly going our way, it became more like 'Bruno, how do I record this bag of popcorn I'm taking for my snack break?' —'Bahh! I really don't care what you do or how many bags you eat!' The watermelon mafia were more ostensibly and vocally distraught and disgusted. Their war cry, that we still laugh about and use as a catch phrase today was: 'I'm gonna drop the Sicilian hammer when I catch the guys that screwed us over'—an instant classic line.

As the sun set on our first day, we were deeply wounded but still a little optimistic that the next day would somehow be better. To make matters worse, JP came to visit that night, driving up in the dark on an official World Youth Day golf cart with one of the event's organizers. We desperately tried to share our discontent and to pull him into our fight but he could only focus on how we could and should be merchandising the product better. Later that night as our troops retreated to their tents, I tried to grab some sleep in our booth as it was the only available space to lay down. As I stretched out on a spare foldout table and looked up at the curious earwigs starting to crawl around the tent ceiling, my Blackberry Bold rang. 'Hey Bud, it's Joe—you awake?' whispered JP. 'Don't worry, tomorrow will be a better day'—in his own way, he had called to apologize for not acknowledging my distress call.

Well, the next day came and so did the clouds and rain. I sent home half of the staff as soon as they woke up and unzipped their tents. I also decided to make my own pilgrimage to the far side of the park to see what the scene was like. I bit my lower lip hard enough to make it bleed when I got there. 'Oh Shit! What's this all about?' I muttered as I witnessed the long snaking lines of hungry and happy youth standing in front of Pizza Pizza's booth as well as the other lucky food stations. The other food zones were living our dream and had experienced the waves of hungry people we had patiently expected would visit us. I remember thinking to myself: 'I bet they'll sell 20,003 frickin slices of pizza.' I sprinted back to our camp like an angry panther and shared the news in complete disbelief. I think I remember the red watermelon crew overhearing my conversation and then officially proclaiming that *'the Sicilian hammer was going to drop!'*

In a last ditch effort, we loaded up industrial-sized black garbage bags with our popcorn and travelled deep into the crowds like tired and wet candy stripers. At the end of day 2, we sold something like 75 bags of popcorn and a case or two of warm bottled water—yup, a whopping .3% of our inventory. Based on the dismal sales tally, the persistent rain, our crushed spirits and the fear of curious earwigs, we called it a day and completely packed up shop. The icing on the cake was the desire to be home so very badly but having to sit in 6 hours of brutal blockbuster traffic. At one point, I parked the cube van in the middle of an intersection and slipped out to grab a slice of pizza. When I returned the same car was still idling six inches from the van's front bumper.

Needless to say, despite some half-decent efforts in the days following the event to sell the popcorn before it expired, we took quite a financial and emotional bath on the event. Actually, we could've literally taken a bath as we still had enough warm bottled water to last us two years. To this day, I don't fully enjoy walking through a large event or trade show and seeing all the eager and ambitious small business start-ups in their crowd-less booths. I can literally taste and feel their risk and fragile sense of hope—almost like hearing a distant dog whistle.

Lessons learned. We should have planned to have much more control and flexibility over our production flow—more influence over the basic demand and supply. If we had had the wherewithal to meet the actual volume requirement as it unfolded, and not a delusional forecast, we wouldn't have started the race with so much crippling and distracting weight on our shoulders. Choking on too much inventory, with a ticking shelf-life clock, usually leads to irrational and ill-planned decisions that will weaken margins and compromise brand integrity out of desperation to move product. Would we really have sold that much less if we had popped product onsite as it was needed, offered it in a generic package and then marketed it as 'seasoned with' or 'made with' Kernels' flavours? After all, we were in the popcorn seasoning business. Granted, renting a generator to power up a theatre-style popcorn machine might have also been a risk and limitation if the crowds ended up being too large to properly service, but the cash outlay would have been less than buying 20,000 bags up front—moreover, our breakeven would have been far, far less.

During the introduction stage of a product launch, we'll always gamble with producing lighter inventory quantities even if it means that we short a few retailers in the short-term. Yes, the COGs (cost of goods) will be slightly higher, but it's safer to pull the ripcord if you need to abort the mission and the damage on impact isn't as messy. We've been through situations with contract packers that want to buy the packaging or ingredients unique to our product (instead of having us buy it) and then secretly purchase three years' worth to hold down the cost. Then, of course, they end up sticking you with a hefty five-figure invoice for the remaining components when sales come in weaker than anticipated.

If you can make the economics work based on a temporarily inflated cost and with smaller production runs, you'll be pocketing all the sweet upside when your volumes allow you to start buying and holding more raw material, packaging and finished goods inventory. Do not stock up unless you have legitimate volume commitments (not soft promises) from a retailer. Play it smart and safe until the time is right. Better to break even in phase one of your launch then lose your pants and have to run home to Mommy.

We probably would have and should have enjoyed the rare experience of witnessing Pope John Paul II enlighten half million teens from around the world. Nope, not us. Instead, we ran around aimlessly in circles like circus monkeys while the mighty Sicilian hammer dropped.

Let it Simmer ~

1. *Do you have concrete retailer commitments against your first production run? If not, can you run a more digestible, and albeit less efficient and costlier, amount and still be able to pocket some profit margin?*

2. *Would you be better off to run a more digestible case quantity but lose a palatable amount of money per transaction, or to run a higher*

quantity to lower your COGs and make more per transaction despite risking an expensive chunk of inventory going stale?

3. *If you do decide to start with a larger-sized packaging and production run in order to achieve better efficiencies and to lower costs, be sure to understand the financial threat if you only sell 25%, 50% or 75% of your inventory. Will it only hurt and cripple or completely slaughter your ability to keep the business afloat?*

4. *Do you really need to run full scale production in order to begin selling? Or, can you invest in a set of slick mock-ups (and credible tasting samples) to lock in a sale before you pull your wallet out and start the ROI clock? Note, the other benefit to this approach is that you'll be able to react by incorporating your customers' and critics' suggestions (if they're in fact valuable).*

CHAPTER 9

Lost In New York

Product Placement

L ike most entrepreneurs, I'm cursed with an eternally restless mind. When the good ship finally breaks free from choppy waters and begins to sail smoothly, life somehow becomes a tad too still and quiet. Ergo, once we had Kernels Extraordinary Popcorn® Shakers up and running efficiently, we felt a burning need to use our newfound ability, goodwill and infrastructure to drop another powerhouse QSR (Quick Service Restaurant) brand into our hungry grocery basket. Wanting to keep the expansion blueprint simple, and to better leverage both our existing in-market positioning and manufacturing capabilities, we thought to approach New York Fries® (newyorkfries.com) about doing a French fry seasoning. On the face of it, the idea of smattering potato-inspired flavours on freshly cut and fried French fries seemed as relevant and meaningful as offering chip-inspired flavours for fresh popcorn. Both concepts were anchored to popular and intensely flavoured seasonings for common comfort foods that consumers were accustomed to enjoying at our brand partner's restaurant, but that weren't available for sale in grocery stores.

Given that Kernels, in particular the fiery and very loveable founder, Scott Staiman, gave us our first shot in the big leagues, I felt it was prudent that we had his certified blessing to start popping our business beyond popcorn. Of course, it didn't hurt that Scotty also personally knew the President of New York Fries, Jay Gould. Gratefully, not only did he support our aspirations to grow, he picked up the phone in his office with me standing in front of him to make the introductory call. *'Listen Jay, I'd like to introduce you to Bruno Codispoti from BrandFusion. He's a good guy who's done some very good things for our brand'*—or some supportive commendation, more or less, similar to that.

Jay and his loyal crew were a slight bit more austere and governing than the perhaps easier to work with and congenial family at Kernels. Their longtime VP, Warren Price, was an outwardly astute and somewhat charmingly pensive man that was as acutely attuned to his iconic brand and its consumer as ketchup or malt vinegar is to French fries. At the outset, I found it challenging to completely relax in front of him as one might find it awkward to spend one-on-one time with their high school math teacher. In time, however, I grew to admire his deep comprehension of the business and all, well most, awkwardness eventually melted away like Quebec cheese curds doused in hot Poutine gravy.

Following a few months of collective deliberation, we agreed to launch two of the most popular fry seasonings offered at their counter, *California* (a Sweet BBQ profile) and *Cajun*, and also crafted two more original flavours from scratch, *3 Cheese (Cheddar, Parmesan and Romano)* and *Smokey Bacon*. The packaging design was modest and straightforward, but also extremely recognizable as we relied heavily on the brand's classic and omnipresent yellow, black and white taxi cab inspired checkerboard pattern. Droves of faithful fans generously doused their premium russet potato New York Fries in the very same savoury seasoning each day at one of their nearly 200 tasty locations. The seasonings were so well-liked, they actually had a persistent problem with customers five-finger discounting the seasoning shakers from their condiment counters to enjoy at home. At $2.99 to $3.49, our suggested retail in grocery was right in line with our Kernels retail program.

So, why did the product helplessly struggle for a couple years and then eventually burn up and perish in deep fryer? In hindsight, the leading contributing factor with our failure was somewhat obvious and simple, but also difficult to pre-calculate and fully control: a fundamental variable we luckily got in the pocket with Kernels Shakers, but failed to understand the importance of until we started to nosedive with New York Fries—in-store product placement and the consequences of in-store product placement inconsistency. We just couldn't pinpoint, build from and protect the right retail shelf-space location.

New product concepts, particularly unique and unproven concepts, require more logical and consistent homes within a store—a cozy little spot where consumers will, at first intuitively, expect to stumble on it, and then demand to find it there each and every time. Shoppers shouldn't be expected to dig too deep for their treasures. When it comes to in-store placement, a big and clear 'X' should clearly mark the spot.

Out of the gate, we fought hard with retailers to be lined-in along-side the ketchup or malt vinegars. Why not? So we thought. Aside from salt, these are two of the most prevalent North American French fry condiments. It turned out, however, that most retailers weren't altogether thrilled with merchandising small seasoning jars next to ketchup, plus the stipulated listing fees (cost of entry) were rather punishing from a workable ROI perspective. Going back to the listing fee economics we discussed in *Chapter 2: Grocery Math*, how many months of conservative sales will it take to make your investment back. In this case, the time-line was nearly two years. I suppose it should've been more foreseeable that we'd score very little ground against this first placement strategy.

Licking our wounds, we then came up with a superior and more relevant in-store placement location. We'd try to hang the product on the glass freezer doors directly in front of the walls of frozen French fry bags. No brainer, right? The correlation should've been just as natural and fertile as our popcorn shakers living next to microwave popcorn. We invested heavily in designing, manufacturing, and placing custom-ized gravity-fed wire racks that hung securely from the freezer doors.

After a month or so, we noticed the change in course started to click with consumers as our product reorders began to steadily strengthen. Folks were noticing, buying, trying and then coming back for more. And it could've slowly flowered into another success if the company that owned and leased the freezer units to grocery stores hadn't flexed their frozen muscles. It turned out that suspending wire racks from the large glass doors created a slight opening that allowed cold air to es-cape. Game over. Both the retailers and the freezer company had zero degrees of interest in hearing about possible racking remedies.

Our last stop on this trip was to spud-town, adjacent to the fresh potato bins in the produce section. Looking back, this was a starchy stretch as we were counting on the consumers who bought potatoes to make homemade fries—which we now realize is a much smaller, and simple butter-and-salt, kind of crowd. To boot, we already had two messy strikes on the board so retailers were now dubious of our ability to bring this one home. We went so far as to try to forge a cross-promotional driven partnership with the Province of Ontario's potato growers' co-op association, but our pitch fell flat.

More than five years after we discontinued the line, I received a call from Warren Price: *'Are you still selling the French fry seasoning? I was told an independent grocery store still has product on their shelf!?'* Turns out that there was still exceedingly old product hiding in dark corners in the marketplace and it was now rock solid. I imagine that Warren was just reaching out to make sure that we didn't fire up the business again under the radar. Needless to say, I was more surprised to hear about the surviving French fry seasoning than he was. I guess neither of us should've been surprised as potatoes tend to grow best when you bury and forget about them. All kidding aside, take note of the lingering damage and brand denigration that a botched concept can bring you should you not take full control of the clean-up process.

During our short-lived fling with the gang at New York Fries, we developed and launched a handful of other food concepts, and even had a few promising ideas die in the R&D hopper. Jay Gould was very keen on introducing a best-in-class potato chip under his brand. We resisted the temptation for a couple of years as succeeding in the chip-world takes deep both ultra deep pockets and an aggressive infantry platoon outfitted with direct-to-store-delivery trucks. We eventually surrendered, gave it a shot, fell short and in the process burnt yet another decent savings account over nine months of squandered work.

The one tasty concept that never did graduate from the scribble-filled pages of our big idea journal, that I'd still like to see come to life, was a deluxe poutine kit complete with premium Quebec cheese curds and New York Fries kickass gravy. Oddly, and quite contrary to our modus operandi, one of our most successful and profitable New York Fries' branded initiatives was a premium hot dog. Yep, go figure, a friggin' wiener. How seemingly unoriginal and uninspired is that? It was a fresh eye-opener, however, as the product's success was perhaps solely predicated by the fact that we offered it exclusively to A&P / Dominion in Ontario (acquired by Metro Inc. in 2005)—i.e. the product could only be purchased at their stores.

That summer BBQ season, they pleasantly pushed our fabulous frankfurter of their own volition by offering aggressive special feature pricing in their weekly flyer ads that they completely self-funded. The valuable takeaway was our fortunate glimpse into the very good things that come when you provide exclusivity to a retail chain—a strategy that has the potential to trump our belief in needing to focus on innovation or catching trends ahead of the curve in order to earn our place in the store. I'll save this tasty topic for the next chapter.

Let It Simmer ~

1. *Can you work with retailers to carve out a productive home within the store that's both consistent and instinctual with the consumer's expectations?*
2. *If you achieve success by securing a new, virgin in-store placement location, will you be able to continually protect your newfound home or will you eventually become vulnerable to external forces?*
3. *Before making the mistake of following-up a successful product launch with a seemingly similar concept, appreciate that it only takes one fickle ingredient in the recipe to spoil your entire dish.*
4. *If preserving the credibility and value of your brand after you exit from the market is important, take care in thoroughly mopping up your mess.*
5. *If your concept is somewhat of an uninspired me-too product, what can you anchor its success to? Can you offer it exclusively to a retailer with an ability to move enough volume to make it worth your while?*

CHAPTER 10

Opa!

Retailer Exclusivity Programs

Ah yeah, the blistering sound of Eddie Van Halen's thick and monster crunchy guitar riffs shaking my car stereo to the brink of explosion. It's a much-needed confidence building ritual I rely on when driving to a make-it or break-it meeting—ever try to watch a super hero movie on mute? On this particular cold and rainy morning, we were in talks to bring Ontario's most popular Greek restaurant chain, Mr. Greek Mediterranean Grill® into A&P / Dominion grocery stores. Securing the business would dramatically open up BrandFusion's product portfolio allowing us to reach deep into multiple food categories—e.g. protein products via pork shoulder and chicken breast souvlaki, deli products via tzatziki and imported feta cheese, fresh produce via ready-to-eat Greek salad kits, and into frozen foods via moussaka (layers of ground lamb and roasted eggplant topped with a cheese sauce) and stuffed phyllo appetizers.

We had lined up a meeting to pitch our big-picture-plan, alongside Mr. George Raios (President of Mr. Greek), to a handful of executives and category managers. The meeting went exceptionally well (thanks EVH), and I exited the building knowing we had locked ourselves into something special and meaningful with the retail chain. Unlike many other stories in this book that end in mild discontent and prolonged frustration, the Mr. Greek at A&P saga was an immensely gratifying and profitable toga ride that equipped us with an exceptional and powerful go-to launch recipe.

Loblaws is Canada's leading innovation powerhouse in the sport of grocery, especially when it comes to introducing and then wooing the market with untapped premium and avant-garde food trends. In 2005, grilling up juicy souvlaki (skewered meat) and serving it on authentic Mediterranean pita bread with fresh tzatziki was all the rage. As usual, Loblaws met the consumer demand early in the game with its line of *President's Choice* branded products. At the time A&P / Dominion had its own esteemed private label brand called '*Master Choice*' (yes, Master not Master's). At any rate, with respect to the group of products that we aimed to launch, we believed that their brand didn't carry as much punch and allure as the President's Choice program so our pitch was simple and super straightforward—provide A&P with a well-known, authentic and respected culinary Greek brand so that they could compete more aggressively with Loblaw Companies. The Mr. Greek brand would become their customized instrument to play with in grocery, and theirs alone.

Disclaimer: offering a retail chain brand exclusivity, and to an equal extent, offering exclusivity on a particular product (if the brand it's under is also sold to other retailers) is more of a clean slate strategy that's better served for newfangled launches with no baggage. Most retailers, especially the larger national chains, will frown heavily upon you generously handing their competitors an advantage that they cannot have access to. Before letting things fly, make certain that you can avoid falling into this inopportune hot seat, and that you can make a financially solid go of things based on the sales volume with a single retailer.

A brand and/or product exclusivity program may seem like a basic notion on the surface, but it can be a very persuasive and powerful device if you can encourage all the players in the game to embrace the arrangement at a level where they wholeheartedly believe that the program is their own to both aggressively flaunt and to protect. Try to frame your role and relationship with the retailer as being more of a mutual partner and brand ambassador than a traditional vendor. Angle to work shoulder to shoulder with them, as opposed to the sometimes more usual and uncomfortable foot to ass connection.

Actually, to be honest with you, most buyers working for larger retail chains tend to operate and negotiate cordially and collaboratively. We have many productive and longstanding relationships with prestigious individuals over at Longos, Loblaw Companies, Walmart Canada, Sobeys, Safeway and Costco. However, I'll also make no bones about the dying minority of ball-breaking buyers who unfortunately exist with what seems like a quiet thirst to keep you feeling dejected. Thankfully, we no longer have any such sour grinches in our circle of influence. Ok, I feel better now. Enough with the ranting.

In exchange for agreeing not to offer your program to another would-be buyer, try to frame your opening dialog by speaking in tones that affirm your unique role and increased impartiality in the deal. If you can set the table properly, the retailer will quickly adopt a pride of ownership in the mission that will pay you back in spades. When your buyer walks into their store and proudly gazes upon your product in the aisle, they should experience the same sensation as admiring a new car parked in their driveway. Sorry, I admit that was a little overkill, just wanted to drive my point home.

Ultimately, that pride of ownership will hopefully translate into much better than average in-store product placement and visibility, an increased frequency of pro bono flyer advertisements, and a genuine willingness to help keep looming product copycats at bay. Put simply, what often eventually develops is that the retailer will apply a greater than average amount of control in ensuring that your product flourishes. Conversely, when you're slugging away to sell that exact same product to every retailer in the marketplace, it becomes increasingly more expensive and challenging as you fight for your fair share of voice with each one.

With an exclusivity program arrangement in tow, you and the retailer are working more with a collective pocket of money to invest in the product's evolution. You're singing from the same song sheet. For example, where getting the buyer to financially chip into supporting an aggressive TPR (temporary price reduction) can typically be futile, exclusivity arrangements can help to relax their purse strings. There's also the case of conjoint accountability and a shared fear of failure. Should the product(s) bomb, it's a reflection of the buyer's capabilities and strategy judgment as much as it is yours. As things go, the pressure for the product and program to thrive becomes a somewhat unofficial, mutually binding pressure. And when your product does make its mark, getting the buyer tightly aligned with a follow-up launch of another product within the program may not only be in the cards, they'll be the ones shouting for an encore.

Granting all this upside, exclusivity deals should be firmly governed by a contractual time limit. After a year, or more likely two or sometimes even three, use the privilege of having achieved a better than average scorecard and impressive product awareness to approach other spectating retailers to open up distribution and kick sales up to the next level.

Let It Simmer ~

1. *Can a retailer exclusivity program work for your upcoming launch? If so, can you frame your role as being more of an equal partner vs. a common vendor?*
2. *Can you get a certain retail chain to share in a pride of ownership with your product?*
3. *If you do offer an exclusivity program, can you convince the retailer to share more in the costs required to promote your product? Can you use an exclusivity deal to improve your product's in-store placement, ad support, and to hold your competition at bay?*
4. *How many years can you afford to offer an exclusivity arrangement for? How will you explain your unique preferential arrangement to other curious retailers?*

CHAPTER 11

Damn Turmeric

Are You Solving a Worthwhile Problem?

I f you're from Toronto, Canada chances are you'll remember the beloved 80s TV personality, Chef Pasquale Carpino (1936-December 30, 2005). Before the Food Network craze, during a time when most non-Italians had never heard of espresso, there was *Pasquale's Kitchen*. The Chef was an exceedingly passionate and charismatic man, always dutifully sporting a blue smock, a white necktie and a red chef's toque. He also happened to have studied opera at the Royal Conservatory of Music and was able to creatively combine his talent for bombastic operatic singing with his love and knowledge for cooking all things Italiano. During Sunday red-sauce lunches at my Grandparents, we would all gather round the wood-paneled television to watch Chef Pasquale as he masterfully julienned red bell peppers while belting out *O Sole Mio* at the top of his lungs—very impressive and very 80s in a good way. (Check it out: http://www.youtube.com/watch?v=uTOTb8FVrlk.)

Despite our successful foray into grocery stores with Kernels Extraordinary Popcorn, New York Fries and Mr. Greek Mediterranean Grill, I still had too much valuable time on my hands and too much bottled energy to burn. It was only natural, then, that, when JP asked me to take the reins on a new gastronomic venture with Chef Pasquale, I jumped perhaps a little too quickly and enthusiastically at the chance. My Italian heritage upbringing was a big bonus, if not an unspoken prerequisite, with this one. The product was a line of Italian sauce-base enhancers (i.e. add a heaping tablespoon of Chef Pasquale's magic into your pasta sauce to make it sing sort of thing).

Pasquale was very Italian in a way that reminded me of my own Uncles. The speciality food distributor, Molisana Imports, was also exceptionally Italian in a way that made me feel I was visiting Southern Italy each time I had to pay them a visit to talk shop or to collect a cheque for product payment. I'd wait patiently in an eerily quiet and dimly lit warehouse at the bottom rung of a barn-style wooden staircase leading up to the offices. The owner's son, Frank, who I believe still runs the show, is my age and a very convincing guy, smart beyond his years—we hit it off like two good Italian boys sharing their greasy brown-bag lunch in the school cafeteria.

Keeping Chef Pasquale content, God rest his big beautiful soul, was an equal task with trying to build the business. Part of the business plan was to have the Chef suit up in his trademark ensemble to put on in-aisle cooking demonstrations in the numerous grocery stores that supported the product launch. It was sometimes a strange and awkward scene to digest as I felt Pasquale, and rightly so, found this obligation slightly humbling. Of course the shoppers and passers-by wouldn't have picked up on this vibe, especially the older big-haired ladies who swooned over the culinary icon. It was the behind-the-scenes spectacle. To me, watching Pasquale lug pots and pans back to his car in a congested parking lot was a bit like witnessing the department store Santa removing his beard and hat.

The business venture itself was an uphill battle. The volume of product sold wasn't nearly enough for Chef Pasquale, the distributor or myself to start singing opera over. Suiting up to serve pasta out of a grocery aisle on a cold and rainy Saturday afternoon is sobering when you're making some decent coin, but when the commission cheques are a little light, it's just irritating. After a few months, I started to get fairly comfortable with being exceedingly open and honest, as sugarcoating projections and results to keep everyone content catches up with you—I like to sleep peacefully at night, remember.

One of the main snags with the product concept, I believe, was that Pasquale's central audience was Italian-Canadian. While his legion of fans certainly loved meeting and chatting with him while grocery shopping, I'm not entirely sure that they were the best candidates for buying and using the product. To explain, when it comes to cooking, among other things, Italians are colossally patriotic to their own family's recipes and preparation techniques. They are stubborn to a fault. Visit Italy and drive from town to town and you'll notice that everyone has a different recipe and preparation style that they'll protect aggressively and very publically until death. You'll see old men assertively squinting their faces and wagging their wrinkled fingers proclaiming: '*No, the sauce has to be made with freshly picked, not dried, oregano or it doesn't taste right. Bah, I refuse to try it!*' Do yourself a favour, avoid debating religion, politics and the proper preparation of tomato sauce with Italians at all costs.

So it's only logical that a proud (and overtly stubborn) Italian-Canadian woman or man wouldn't want to modify or embarrassingly experiment with their perfect and sacred family recipe. '*Hey, don't you know you can't improve on perfection!*' Sure, they'll politely smile and nod approvingly in front of the Chef as they chew his dialled-up rigatoni, but they're still walking out of the supermarket with crushed San Marzano tomatoes, fresh garlic and basil, black pepper and a really good olive oil—real Italians don't do quick and easy.

Ultimately, it was Chef Pasquale's own patriotic protection of his recipes, and perhaps one too many glasses of red wine for us both, which ultimately caused us to part ways. While in Montreal, I received an untimely phone call from the Chef at 10 p.m. while resting in my hotel room bed. '*Bruno,*' he began in a quiet and unsettled voice. '*Who put the turmeric in my sauce? My recipe does not have turmeric!*' I replied calmly: '*Pasquale, which sauce are you referring to?*' '*On the jar, it says turmeric in the ingredients.*' (He's sounding increasingly more irritated now.)

I understood that he was referring to the ingredient deck published on our retail product. I imagine he'd just detected that our contract packer ended up including turmeric in the commercialized version of the recipe without his blessing. The product and packaging were already developed, produced and in the warehouse when I was brought on board so this was also news to me. Be that as it may, maybe it was because it was late and I had been travelling all day. Or, maybe because this felt like a deleted scene out of the *Godfather*, it was enough to unhinge me and give into the writing on the wall. I saw red. '*Listen Pasquale,*' I said in my best Michael Corleone voice, '*I've had enough of this! Please. Relax!!*

Do not take this out on me. I respect you immensely and have been trying my very best to help sell the sauce! It's not my fault that it's not selling.'

We eventually simmered down and calmly apologized to one another. I genuinely adore the man and still hold him in high regard. After all, if I was hoping to play a young Pacino in our relationship that night, he would've been playing the esteemed king Brando. But, perhaps the old axiom holds true: beware should you meet your heroes.

Let It Simmer ~

1. *Are you gauging the true size of the potential market that you'll be going after, or are your assumptions dangerously overstated?*
2. *Does your product concept look to solve a consumer problem that may not want to be solved? If so, should you be tweaking your product or changing your sights to a different target?*
3. *How relevant and useful is your product concept to consumers outside of the core target group? Is there a strategy to widen your net without watering down your concept?*
4. *Take heed before you peek behind the curtain.*

CHAPTER 12

A Slice Of Pizza Pie

Getting it Right

JP and I sat in Michael Overs' boardroom like anxious school kids waiting in an 8th grade classroom for the seasoned and stalwart principal to make an appearance. After all, this was the same brilliant Michael Arthur Overs that founded the Ontario-omnipresent Pizza Pizza® restaurant chain and helped to pioneer the ingenious centralized single-number ordering system now used by oodles of restaurant chains throughout North America ... sing it out loud, you know the jingle ... *'967-11-11'*. After six months of courting one another, we were down to the short strokes with signing on Pizza Pizza to have BrandFusion introduce their illustrious pizza dipping sauces into grocery stores—a product, especially the creamy garlic, with a strong cult-like following in Ontario, Canada.

Michael and his gang were among the first on the block to offer dipping sauces for pizza versus today where every pizza restaurant chain offers their own riff on the popular concept. A few months beforehand, we had almost signed a contract with their restaurant rival, Pizza Nova, but decided to cut bait and roll out the dough with Pizza Pizza when they showed real interest because of their stouter market presence. Making the letdown call to Michael Primucci at Pizza Nova was one of the most agonizing calls I've had to make to date. He was a solid guy, a real gentleman, and had been open to a brand licensing deal with us. When he found out what our plans were, and especially with whom, the conversation and our rapport melted like mozzarella really, really fast. Sorry Michael, no hard feelings, I hope.

Sitting at the boardroom table with JP, my only real worry was getting through the product sampling as he has a disdain for most cheeses —especially the melty, drippy and dippy ones. As Mr. Overs squeezed a walnut-sized cheese blob onto JP's paper plate and handed him a plastic tasting-spork to sample it with, I cringed and quietly giggled simultaneously. We looked at each other like juvenile brothers at the dinner table wondering how we'd ever eat our pile of boiled broccoli. I love cheese and was happy to clean my plate, and thankfully, like always, JP pulled through. After much discussion we left the meeting with a firm handshake and agreed to the basic economics and terms of our deal.

To this day, we consider our Pizza Pizza Dips program one of our most successful retail endeavours and continue to delve deep into why and how the product and program worked in hopes that we can help creamy-garlic-lightning strike twice. The only unfortunate account in the Pizza Pizza chapter was the loss of Michael Overs (1939-March 31, 2010). Being in the same room with the man was always nothing short of edifying and entertaining as he was somewhat of a J. Peterman storyteller in food and restaurant circles ... and I'm a sucker for life lessons through storytelling.

So what made our Pizza Pizza Dips successful? Why have we enjoyed consistent sales growth year over year for the past ten plus years since the launch? Why has preserving the growth and our shelf space been somewhat easier and less inexpensive to achieve relative to most of our other product launches? It turns out, there are a host of good explanations—some intentional and others purely accidental. Arguably, the most important contributor was leveraging the deep-rooted ritual that Pizza Pizza engrained into its legion of loyal fans. With our humble consumer budgets, and without the brand, it would have been near impossible to educate and cultivate pizza eaters to dip and dunk their lonely pizza crust into a non-tomato-based sauce.

Even if the concept, packaging and flavour experience was a direct hit, creating a population of loyal dippers and dunkers doesn't happen overnight—it takes repetition, significant time and big money. How would we have reached enough pizza eaters to make a decent business out of it? Without Pizza Pizza's expansive customer base, frequency and reach, we wouldn't have been able to influence enough consumers at the grocery level to accomplish a worthwhile volume impact. Believe you me, over the years we've launched plenty of aspirational concepts using brilliant packaging designs and recipes that we loved and believed completely in that ultimately nose-dived because they had no established consumer ritual to spawn and grow from.

As illustrated in the previous chapters, carving out a relevant and consistent home within the store that's intuitive to consumers is nothing less than compulsory. For the pizza dips, we sliced out a zip code right next to the take n' bake fresh pizzas in the open-bunker refrigerators positioned in the home meal replacement (HMR) department —grab a fresh pizza and you're likely to toss the dips into your cart along with it. Part of the magic was that the dips needed to be refrigerated and are packaged in a convenient single-serve deli-style cup format. This helped us to generate a fresh and better ingredient underlying narrative. More importantly, Pizza Pizza packed and served the same dips to their consumer in the same deli-style cups, giving our retail format an instant familiarity and credibility. Put another way, if the dips were shelf stable, packed in a salad-dressing bottle and sat in an aisle far away from the fresh pizzas in another part of the store, they'd be collecting dust.

If you plan and tackle the first six months of sales wisely, being first to market, especially when you're operating with a limited budget, can give you the head start you need to dig your feet in firmly. After six months or a year's time, you can bet that either the larger corporate CPG vultures or scrappy start-ups working from their garage will be fervently circling your lunch. At the time, there were already similar cream-based dips sold in the deli department, but they were positioned as more all-purpose and not expressly made or promoted for pizza. Planting the first flag allowed us to more or less define the product and space that we wanted to own and play within (i.e. pack size, packaging format, retail price point, etc.)

Conversely, if you're attempting to enter a category with other brands vying for, or protecting, the same space and message, the product concept focus is usually placed more heavily on trying to match or improve on costs, retails, serving size, packaging design or on pretty much any distinctive product or program benefit that you can push —e.g. ingredient and/or recipe quality, health benefits, merchandising vehicles, or superior consumer and trade spending, etc. It's not easy to create a truly new platform every time you go to market, but it sure as hell helps make the long climb easier when there's nothing but sky above you. With our Kernels Popcorn Shakers, and now our Pizza Pizza Dips, we had managed to achieve a worthwhile first to market advantage once again.

Depending on the size of the retailer we're planning on selling to and where we want the product to end up in the store, we often use specialty direct-to-store (DSD) distributors to get to market. Selling and shipping product directly to retailers versus using a distributor to sell and ship your product is a sales topic worth tackling separately—see *Chapter 26: Planting Seeds*. For now, let me say that there are decent arguments to make for both cases; however, your situation and view on this decision will certainly change and morph dramatically over the life cycle of your product.

In the beginning, it's usually easier to give 15 percent up to a more common 30 percent of your beloved profit margin so that a distributor with a large, well-established retailer customer base and a well-oiled delivery infrastructure can purchase and warehouse an attractive quantity of your product. It's also less onerous, stressful and cash-flow-friendly to sell pallets of product to a single distributor and carry one large receivable instead of chasing multiple accounts who will ultimately and inconsiderately hold your money for way too long and then pay you far less than they agreed to. As your volume and ability to stage and ship orders grows and the economics start to suggest that you can eliminate a distributor's margin, you'll inescapably toil over the decision of making more money at the expense of taking on a lot more work and responsibility.

At any rate, in the case of Pizza Pizza Dips, we found the perfect distribution partner in Western Creamery (eventually acquired by Liberté in 2006). At the time, they were the right sized partner who valued what we brought to the table. Note: coercing a distributor, or a retailer for that matter, to take on a product almost always ends undesirably (and expensively). When a distributor wants your product and can see the finish line, the communication and your relationship have a better chance of being open and mutually constructive. Unless you're desperate, which I respect can be the case, you never want favours; you want a partner that shares your vision and appetite for the mission.

We sold the Pizza Pizza Dips concept into Wal-Mart, Loblaws and Sobeys head office while Western Creamy hit the ground running at the store level and drove the stake in nice and deep. Going back to the 6-month timeline rule, they helped initiate enough success in the onset to create the momentum required to endure the retailer's unofficial probation period—thanks Louise McIlravey and Angelo Eleusiniotis.

At any rate, looking back, I now clearly see that the most pivotal moment and telling crossroads in this story was when JP, despite his disdain for cheese, managed to gulp down the blob of Jalapeno Cheddar Dip that Mr. Overs served up.

Let it Simmer ~

1. *Does your product concept tap into an established consumer ritual? If not, can it survive on the shelf until you build one? Are your pockets deep enough and your persistence strong enough to hold on until a ritual catches on?*
2. *Can you build a case for having your product displayed in a consistent and relevant home where it will benefit from an impulse purchase with another established anchor-product? Think ice cream and sprinkles, salsa and tortilla chips.*
3. *What's the subtle and unspoken messaging to the consumer as a result of your packaging format and where you'll be merchandised? Think fresh versus processed.*
4. *Is your product an original idea? If not, are there enough unique and meaningful points of difference that you can lean on to stand out against your competition?*
5. *Do your distribution partners believe in your product and vision? Are they interested and engaged or do they seem bothered and unenthusiastic? Will they continue to support you if the mission takes longer than six months or a year?*

CHAPTER 13

Cocktail Dreams

Reality Checks

It's bright and early on a sunny Friday morning in June. Van Halen's soul-lifting song *'Dreams'* (my favourite tune since age 14) is dutifully waking me up on route to the office. While flying down Highway 400 South, it hits me square in the chest like one of Eddie's wailing guitar solos: *I should get into business with Sammy Hagar. Seriously!* To explain, the day earlier, while nosing around on the website for his Mexican cantina resto in Southern Baja California called *Cabo Wabo* (*cabowabocantina.com*), I noticed they offered a few trademark items on the menu (e.g. Sammy's Tequila Shrimp). A month earlier I had just completed reading Sammy's autobiography (*Red: My Uncensored Life in Rock*) and had been pleasantly surprised to learn that, aside from his role as the former Van Halen front-man, he was quite the consummate businessman. For complete disclosure, I'm a Van Halen diehard and now I'm thinking: '*Who wouldn't buy a delectable Cabo Wabo frozen shrimp entrée at Loblaws or Sobeys? Of course it'll fly, it's a rockin' foolproof concept. Right?*' Anyhow, I sold myself enough to speed to the office, squeal into my parking spot, bolt through the front door and dive for the phone.

After a month or so of depositing overzealous and persuasive voice-mail messages, the then President & CEO of *Cabo Wabo* Enterprises, named Barry Augus, called me back. I'd like to think I at least sounded cool and composed on the other end of the line. Truth be told, I was standing in my chair sporting a Cheshire grin. I explained to Barry that

I felt introducing a line of *Cabo Wabo* frozen entrées into Canadian grocery stores would both shoot a little extra royalty cash into Sammy's rock n' roll empire and also serve to create consumer interest in visiting the Cabo Wabo cantina.

Barry quickly and politely shot down the frozen entrée idea, but then offered up a super cool consolation prize for my consideration. At the time, the cantina's namesake tequila was making its mark in the alcohol industry selling nearly 40,000 cases in its inaugural year. As such, Sammy was contemplating expanding his *Cabo Wabo* brand via offering a high-end margarita mix. *'No problem,'* I said assuredly. *'Leave it with us for a few weeks, and we'll come to the table with something worthy of the challenge.'*

Despite BrandFusion's hopper being congested with other much more laudable projects and our resources being spread way too thin, I called in the boys for a download session. *'This is it, fellas. This is the big ship and it absolutely has to sail.'* Archie proceeded to brief our flavour house and beverage supply partners and within two short weeks we had a few stubby glass bottles filled with a unique, albeit kind of murky and mysterious, natural lime margarita mix in our impatient little hands. *'There's some weird stuff collecting at the bottom of the bottle. Is it okay to drink?'* Barry asked. I answered instantly: *'No worries. It's natural fruit juice pulp, give it good shake and give it a go.'* (Side note: as you'll read in *Chapter 28: Fruit Pulp Clouds & Chocolate Bloom*, pasteurizing a natural fruit juice containing any traces of pulp typically results in what's called flocculation, which in fact can be off-putting to consumers.)

We waited a couple days or weeks for some constructive feedback. And then, we got the call (to paraphrase): *'Sammy tried your margarita mix. He said let Bruno know it's way too sweet and tastes more like Limeade than the more refined taste profile that we're looking for. But, you know, please remember the tastes buds of a seasoned rock n' roll star have been exposed to more wear and tear than most of us. Can you make it less sweet?'* I customarily would've responded with something like: *'No problem, we'll bring down the sweetness and have a new tasting sample to you within a week or so.'* I, however, stopped biting down on my knuckle and probed further: *'Did Sammy actually say let* <u>Bruno</u> *know?'* *'Yes, yes, I believe he addressed you by your name,'* he said. *'Just checking,'* I confirmed, beaming back at my subtle reflection in the laptop screen.

I leaned way back in my big, cushy leather chair after the phone call and rested my feet up on the desk. Staring out the window for what seemed like a good half hour, I knew exactly what the next step had to be. Disengage immediately. Carefully bow out as quickly as possible. Sorry, did I lose and confuse you? Why, you ask. This story could've perhaps ended with Sammy and me holding the same bottle of margarita mix high over our heads on stage with *'Dreams'* blaring in the background during the official product release PR event.

Here's what I asked myself and realized in that pivotal half hour staring out the window: Was I doing this because it was good for the company and for our bottom line, or was it a mission straight into Vanity-Ville? Was I using our limited resources wisely or wastefully? Had we really combed through the opportunity to understand the market size, cost of entry, our point of difference, the brand's strength outside of Sammy's core audience, etc.? Or, had I overlooked every single touchstone to fight for that moment to be up on stage at the release party? Perhaps, most importantly, if the deal went south or tanked miserably, would I be able to listen to Sammy's music and experience that same jubilant take-no-prisoners feeling? Or, would the songs just completely piss me off every time I heard them? Hubris baby, it's a dangerous little sucker.

Who knew that years later, Dave and I would craft *Crazy Uncle®* culinary cocktails (see *Chapter 19: Catching A Buzz*), as it would have been a much more natural cobranding effort. Sammy, if you're listening, we're still interested. It should be noted that in 2007 Sammy sold 80% of *Cabo Wabo* tequila to an Italian beverage company called Gruppo Compari for a reported $91 million.

Let It Simmer ~

1. *Have you carefully scanned the impetus for pursuing your product concept, or is your mission driven by self-indulgence?*

2. *If your mission is driven by self-indulgence, can it still be supported with a sound business strategy and a worthwhile financial reward? If not, should you consider disengaging before the damage becomes irreparable?*

CHAPTER 14

Not So Easy Peasy

Lessons From Failure

A good year or two before the passionate and spirited superstar chef Jamie Oliver became super-popular in North America, our people reached out to his people in the UK in an effort to strike a licensing deal. After a few calls, we managed to generate some curiosity with a woman named Tessa Graham, one of Jamie's business administrators at the time. Although she was based out of the UK, Tessa was originally from Western Canada so I thought we'd have a little homeland advantage. We booked a meeting a month out which would take place in the Jamie Oliver headquarters located above his philanthropic restaurant project 'Fifteen' in London, England. It would be an expensive meeting to attend and execute properly, but the mission felt promising and, to say the least, different and exciting as I had never been to the UK.

I rushed to the closest Chapters bookstore to acquire his cookbooks and immersed myself in his colourful TV shows to understand what made him tick and to determine what leading product concepts would connect him with Canadians. We ended up with three starting concepts. Artisanal, yet approachable—alternative cooking oils made from nuts and fruits with high mono-unsaturated fats, and a line of funky spice rubs packed in metal shoe polish-like containers, both of which have since become prevalent in the marketplace. The main thrust was a Home Meal Replacement (HMR) program where Jamie would provide trendy and healthy recipes for supermarkets to prepare on site and sell fresh as part of their hot-table counters. Information leaflets would be offered gratis alongside funky Jamie Oliver counter displays. Admittedly, both concepts seemed either marginally niche or slightly ahead of their time. Nonetheless, they were crafted to showcase our understanding of Jamie's growing brand and that we weren't about to milk or diminish his name on the typical tropical salad dressings and pork marinades.

I purchased my $2,650 plane ticket, an affordable hotel room and a slick new navy blue single-breasted suit and headed for the UK. By now, after delving into so much of his work, I had become somewhat of a fan and was looking forward to breaking bread with the man. I hadn't been to London before, so the day before the meeting my travel mates and I painted the town red and took in the usual tourist sites. My cousin Chris had secured a meeting with one of the larger movie theatre chains in an effort to sell the Brits on our popcorn seasoning program.

Side note: The top salty snack flavours of the day in England were markedly more complex and ultra savoury than what we're used to in North America—roasted lamb with mint yogurt, and spicy curried chicken were a couple of interesting flavours that come to mind. These were unheard of and unsalable recipes in Canada and US ten years back, and a far cry from the much more one-dimensional flavoured salty snacks back home. I imagine that today, these funkier flavours would bode well. Not surprising, given that the UK seems to be perpetually ahead of us by a number of years with respect to grocery food trends.

The next day, I slowly peeled open my eyes to check the clock on the night stand and realized my meeting started in less than an hour somewhere across the other end of town. *'Oh Shit. Oh No! ... Oh Boy.'* I cursed out loud. I had prepared extensively, flown 5,728 kilometres and bought a new suit for this meeting; being late wasn't an option. Despite crafting my tie knot and combing my hair in the cab, I made it to *'Fifteen'* with a couple of minutes to spare. I announced my presence to the maître d' and waited in the restaurant lounge for someone to come and escort me upstairs into Jamie's office. I was thankful for the twenty-minute wait as it allowed me to calm my jet-lagged nerves and to forget the stressful blur of the past hour. After all, I was about to jam on some culinary ideas with the *Naked Chef.*

As someone marched me up the narrow staircase, I took in a super deep breath and smiled hard. *'Who would've thought BrandFusion would flourish to a point where Jamie Oliver would want to sit and chat about having us build his brand in Canada?'* I'll never forget the next proud moment. As the boardroom pocket-doors quickly parted open, I felt the climax of the journey burning in my belly. It's show time, baby! Surprisingly, however, Jamie wasn't in the room yet. Tessa was sitting there, poised, ready and waiting to hear me out. Dispensing with the pleasantries, I grinned politely and inquired: *'Where's Jamie?'* *'You just missed him,'* she responded. *'Oh. Huh.'* I swallowed hard and paused for what seemed like too long of an awkward moment. I felt my body temperature uncomfortably rising and in my head I'm grunting: *'She does realize I flew in from Canada for this, right?'*

Anyhow, wrong or right, it threw my mojo way off centre. I'm sure my presentation had all the flare and charm of a guy discovering his blind date is still married. Removing the heart and passion from your pitch is like yanking the engine from your car. Your chances of failing are now better than average. I truthfully can't recall how the meeting actually went. I only recollect shaking her hand and reading her facial expression and body language. To me, it said: *'Kinda interesting, but fat chance my fellow Canuck.'*

Feeling majorly snubbed, I also found it slightly challenging to enjoy Jamie Oliver's shows or to watch his guest appearances on talk shows. However, once his mini-series on the Food Network called *Jamie's Great Italian Escape* aired, I began to admire the guy again. I'm a sucker for both food travel shows and for unadulterated, simple Italian food, so it was only a matter of time. Soon after that, Jamie launched his very successful global *Food Revolution* campaign (jamiesfoodrevolution.org) which aims to educate children about healthy food choices, as well as protect them by lobbying government and industry to do the right things.

By this point, I've gradually converted back into a full-fledged fan. Perhaps more vindicating, I noticed that in the years that followed my less-than-fruitful meeting in the UK, Jamie ended up launching an avocado oil and a line of funky spice rubs. More impressively, at least to me, in the summer of 2013, Jamie announced a partnership with Sobeys Inc. 'designed to educate, inspire and empower Canadians to eat better.' This was the very core and essence of our presentation pitch nearly ten years earlier! We were either ahead of our time, didn't package the concept with enough clarity and credibility, or simply didn't make that much needed special and unspoken connection with Tessa. Live and learn, I suppose. Although if I do score another shot to sit down with Jamie, I hope the meeting is no further than in London, Ontario.

Let It Simmer ~

3. *Tactfully selling yourself before selling your product will always help to produce a more optimistic outcome for your pitch.*
4. *If making a solid personal connection with a prospective partner or buyer isn't achievable, try not to get rattled and screw up your pitch. Keep moving forward with a smile!*
5. *Timing is everything. Are consumers ready for your product concept or is it perhaps ahead of its time? Unless you have the muscle and clout of a sizeable company or that of an established retailer, it's hard to properly convince and educate consumers about something truly new and pioneering.*

CHAPTER 15

Chicken Wings & Other Things

Too Many Cooks Spoil The Broth

When Hooters® Canada unexpectedly reached out to chat about bringing their signature namesake butter-based chicken wing sauce into grocery stores, I said: *'What the ...? Listen, I'm sorry, buddy, but we don't want to meet with you because we find your brand innuendos much too offensive and downright chauvinist!'* ... Yeah, right, that's exactly what I said. It was more like: *'Yep. I'm free in five minutes, can you come over.'* During the intro meeting, the most memorable part was when the chief Hooter stopped speaking in midsentence, paused, and declared: *'We all know Hooters can also mean big boobs, right? We have to be very careful about that.'* I bit my lower lip and nodded my head in what felt like a very Chevy Chase manner. *'Yes, of course. Please proceed.'*

The wing sauce was good, really good—loads of fatty real butter resulting in a satisfying richness compared to the very overly tart and vinegary options in the market at the time. The brand, despite your initial dirty thoughts, is meant to be fun, cheesy and cheeky. It was also hard to overlook that the exact same retail line of sauces and wing breading was already well-established in US grocery stores and was pulling in millions. We liked the play. We liked the guys. And heck, who doesn't love a good chicken wing? To help vet out and validate the concept's viability, we packed up a few big baskets of piping hot wings, fresh made from a local Hooters restaurant, and fed them to Sobeys' Deli manager. If I remember correctly, she totally dug the product and saw past the big boobs thing. So why did we waste nearly a year and not sell a single drumstick's worth? Well, there were a couple of double-D sized problems.

Our main contact at Hooters, and would-be business partner in the venture, was well-versed and highly effective at running his handful of licensed Hooters restaurants and had what seemed like a concrete relationship and respect from all, or at least some, of the original six brand founders in Clearwater, Florida. He was both super quick and super gracious to share the retail opportunity with us, along with two of his local food supplier friends. More impressively, he offered us a decent number of shares in the business they formed to eventually house the monies coming from grocery store sales.

That said, I'm always apprehensive and on high guard when offered a piece of the proverbial pie when it's divided into too many slices—especially before scrubbing the true economics of the opportunity, and knowing everything about all the players at the table who will receive a slice. Contrarily, I find it agonizing to dish out a slice of my unbaked pie unless it's the absolute last option left on the table required to secure a player for our team that promises to have an invaluable talent or contacts. No way, there's a million other much less-committal solutions to adequately move and motivate a candidate to action. Otherwise, I'll protect each and every share point like the last few drops of fresh water in a canteen.

At any rate, each time we met as a team to discuss our game plan, I'd ask to see a formal agreement and the comprehensive COGs to ensure that we were getting a thick enough slice for our role in the chicken wing parade. We weren't virgins when it came to getting worked over as a direct consequence of choosing to operate without a signed contract. Getting our hands on an agreement sanctioned by all the players who were promised company shares, most notably a shadowy figure in the US that we hadn't met, proved to be over a year-long hunt. Perhaps more conspicuous and telling, the US figure also happened to be the master licensor of the Hooters brand for retail with exclusive access to the manufacturing co-packer(s) that produced the wing sauce in question.

The retail product COGs, basic ordering parameters and requirements remained undefined. How much would the product cost us to buy and would we be left with enough margin to pocket for ourselves?

What was our minimum production order quantity commitment and who would be responsible for buying the Canadian-tailored packaging design? Would the co-packer award us with workable payment terms or would we need to prepare to fund the orders upfront? Despite the camaraderie with the fellas involved, and the plentiful free baskets of deep fried buttery drummies and flatties, the gravity and probability of the mission began to vanish with each wing-pull. Definition: one of my only publically celebrated talents is called the *'wing-pull'*; it involves shoving a flatty chicken wing into my mouth and then quickly hauling it back out with absolutely zero meat left on the bones. Don't laugh, I'm very proud of this party trick.

It seems obvious now, but the more the Hooters team was unable to present us with a proper agreement and the basic operational mechanics of our involvement, the less engaged we became. At the time, I suppose that the attraction of being associated with an internationally celebrated brand, and potential size of the jackpot, kept us hanging around for a lot longer than usual. In retrospect, however, I can also appreciate that the group's inability to consummate the deal allowed us to peer deeper into the crystal ball to get a clearer understanding of how our future dealings with the new company and our would-be partners might operate.

Considering that actions speak louder than words, I'm relieved for having had the accidental opportunity to conduct a proper, albeit too lengthy, due diligence if the alternative might have been to try and build the business without a firm hand resting on the steering wheel. It was all for the best, as once the COGs were finally nailed down, there wasn't nearly enough meat on the bones to keep us from eventually going hungry. The Hooters crew were a real hoot to hang with. A solid bunch of guys that I'm certain we would've had many good times with—but when it comes to business, I'm not a fan of wingin' it.

Let It Simmer ~

1. *Before you dive into a new venture, insist that you meet and get to know every player in the game that will have a stake in the business.*

2. *Be suspicious should a prospective partner offer you ownership in their company too quickly and easily, particularly if the fundamental costs and metrics are not yet understood.*

3. *No margin, no deal. It's amazing how far and deep into a business courtship people will go without knowing if there's enough meat on the bones.*

4. *If you're thinking of offering someone ownership in your new company to secure their commitment, slow down to consider if an alternative motivation is possible; at least until a generous period of examination has passed.*

5. *Beware of lip service. Before locking yourself into a long-term commitment, carefully take stock of what a person does and doesn't do vs. what they repeatedly promise you. In the words of Ralph Waldo Emerson:* 'What you do speaks so loud that I cannot hear what you say.'

6. *Put a strict timeline in place, particularly once the rope starts slipping from your grip—if it ends up being missed by a mile, it might be a blessing in disguise and provide you with the time required to flush out the facts.*

CHAPTER 16

Rotten Fruit

Even the Smartest People
Make Big Mistakes

One bad apple can spoil the whole damn bunch. Hastily surren-
dering ownership in your start-up mission in an effort to recruit
business partners and to secure their resources is somewhat of an
exposed nerve for me. Ok, relax. I realize that we've just covered this
subject in the previous chapter, but at the risk of overdramatizing, I'd
like to spend a little more time on this to nail down my point. Don't be
short-sighted; think long and hard before offering a precious piece of
ownership in your newfangled firm. Too many start-ups give away a
slice of their company, and then eventually their ability to operate freely, much too easily and early in the game in an effort to help them climb
that first monster step. Whether it be for a lack of financing, sales relationships or industry experience, I've seen capable food entrepreneurs
with super strong and promising personalities and product platforms
hand over a set of spare master keys to their front door like it was no
big deal.

The decision on handing out an ownership offer to someone that
might be able to help you advance in the game shouldn't be taken any
less seriously than deciding to slip an engagement ring on your date's
finger. Okay, well maybe it's not that serious, but it can be damn near
close in some instances, especially when you factor in the divorce repercussions. Consider that once you clear that first seemingly giant
step, you may not need a partner as much or even want them at all. I
can also tell you that once you finally clear the first few steps that there

are an infinite number more, shifting and winding up an endless stairway to financial-heaven. And with each new set of obstacles, a partner
with an entirely different skill set and familiarities may be needed to
help to advance. Keep in mind that, once the honeymoon is over, you
have to learn to live and compromise with that person for the long haul
while they continue to share your burgeoning bank account.

I've had the fortunate opportunity to have either accepted or have
been offered ownership and a voice in dozens of considerable food company start-up undertakings. Other than those with my brother and JP,
each chapter has ended in a prickly and costly separation. I know what
you may be thinking, but it wasn't always me that was the problem.
Hold on to each and every percentage point of your company's ownership until you're absolutely certain that it's time to pull the golden ring
from your breast pocket. Hold on to your ownership and operating control like a kid clutching his pillowcase full of Halloween candy. Offer an
overinflated commission incentive, tie in a handsome performance
based bonus, or put them on a plane with their spouse to Cabo San
Lucas, but try to keep your company undivided until the long-term picture reveals itself. Remember, even the smartest, most experienced and
well-funded partners will make great mistakes and drive you to drink.

We've had our share of prematurely getting down on one knee to
make an offer. Here's a story of someone else impulsively asking for our
hand in partnership. When Nick Antonopoulos called to ask if we'd be
interested in having him fly us out to Montreal to hear a business pitch
on a packaged premium frozen fruit concept for retail I said: *'Sure, why
the hell not.'* Having worked with Nick on another food related mission,
I knew first hand that he was an exceptionally successful and prudent
businessman in the Quebec restaurant and food service scene, plus I
love visiting Montreal anytime I can—especially Old Montreal; if you're
ever in town, make a point of having your morning cappuccino and
croissant at Olive & Gourmando.

When he picked Dave and me up from Pierre Elliott Trudeau International Airport, looking very spruce in his crisp, mauve Lacoste pull-
over and designer jeans, Nick was noticeably keen to fill us in and set
the stage for the meeting he had organized with Hans Schmid. Hans

was a veteran in the fruit importing business. Having held a senior procurement position at Danone, he was well-connected and exceedingly well-versed in the game of sourcing produce from the four corners of the world.

As we pulled up to Hans' stunning lake front-home, situated in a picturesque and charming community, Nick pointed out the lakehouse-turned-office at the back of the property which sat a mere stone's throw from the water. *'Man oh man, I could get used to having our meetings out here,'* I whispered to Dave as Nick finished taking a phone call in his car. It was even more spectacular inside. Custom carved wooden boardroom chairs and grand cathedral ceilings overlooked sprawling views of the lake. As we sat on the weathered leather couch in his dimly lit and most godfather-esque office, we were introduced to another two seasoned and well-established venture capitalists that were to be part of the mission.

Nick and Hans proceeded to paint a fruitful picture of the opportunity at hand. A company named Europe's Best® had taken the freezer section in Canadian grocery stores by storm with its introduction of premium frozen fruit assortments packed in attractive re-sealable stand-up bags. Big and luscious medleys of strawberries, blueberries and mangos were selling like Eskimo Pies® back in 1922 and the fellas wanted a crack at shaking the money tree. With Hans' knowhow and international contacts, Nick and Co.'s financial resources and counsel, and our sales and retailer relationships, it was tabled as a no-brainer.

Our point of difference would be to offer retailers a like-product, if not a superior one, at a better value for their private label (store brand) program. It was a difficult offer to refuse—and not only because we were sitting in an office worthy of Don Corleone. We were being offered ownership and equal control in a new company without having to invest our own money and it was backed by established, motivated and sincere partners with proven track records. *'What's the risk?'* we asked ourselves. The following week, we formally accepted their invitation to join forces.

We would start drawing a decent salary once the first billable sale was secured and collected. Despite advising the group to register the company name as *Nature's Fruit* (singular), the company was officially registered as *Nature's Fruits* (plural)—which, to us, sounded a tad peculiar and comical, but then again I just re-read *Chapter 6: Eat in Moderation, Not Deprivation* and do realize that I shouldn't be so quick to call the kettle black when it comes to peculiarity.

Within a month or so Nick & Co. each deposited a nice chunk of cash into a Toronto-based bank account that Dave and I would be responsible for managing. As our first order of business, we all gambled on ordering a container of assorted frozen fruit samples from overseas, designed and printed a few thousand colourfully branded stand-up re-sealable bags to house the sales samples, and strung together a rather technically impressive sales pitch that spoke to Hans' global procurement procedures and plans. By this time, Dave and I had become suspicious of Nature's Fruits' ability to match, let alone beat, the incumbent brand's pricing. We had spent the month tapping our industry relationships to better understand margin requirements, volume expectations and the likelihood of penetrating the category—which, by the way, we would've been wise to do before choosing to sign on as official partners willing to work pro bono until the profits were ripe for the picking.

Our discoveries suggested that our sell prices might actually end up erring on the side of being more expensive. We attempted to counsel the group, and proposed to cancel the ten-thousand-dollar investment required to secure the container of fruit samples we had ordered until our position of strength became clearer. It was decided, nonetheless, that we should move forward with the investment in order to build momentum and to be properly prepared. Worst case, we'd have to unload the product at a discount. Nevertheless, from our perspective, the honeymoon had ended and we were left feeling anxious about marriage.

Looking back, I feel more for Nick & Co. as they had put their trust in our contacts and capabilities. Sometimes I wish I wasn't so good at selling myself upfront because it typically leads to having to live up to an expectation that I haven't the time or impetus for. Fearful of failure, I circumvented the usual chain of command, and called for a sit-down with Mr. Al Cussen, one of our most senior vice president contacts at Wal-Mart Canada, to present our program. Note: Going above your buyer's head is a risky card that you can't play too often, and is one that should be reserved only for certain tactical situations—it's sort of like floating aimlessly in a dingy at sea and knowing when to fire off your only flare in the emergency gun.

On any other day, I would've tried to lock in a meeting with the appropriate private label buyer, but this situation was somehow different. I felt the pressure of the group weighing heavily on my integrity and wanted to both prove my worth and to flush out our new company's potential. Could 'we,' and perhaps more important to me, could 'I' pull this off? I wanted to fast track the usual drawn-out vendor-buyer tango to flush out the truth about our chances for success. That afternoon, however, we left the meeting knowing that Walmart didn't consider our big opportunity as much of a no-brainer as we had sitting in Hans' lake-house office. A couple of weeks later, we left Sobeys' National head-office knowing that they too were on Walmart's *'sorry fellas, it's no-go'* page.

On top of everything, as we had predicted, our pricing was in fact higher than our would-be competition. Wasn't our *raison d'être* better pricing and value? Isn't that why we all wanted to climb this fruit tree? We tried to be as open and candid with the group as we could by explaining that, in light of the preliminary feedback from retailers, the mission wasn't as promising as we all had imagined it to be. Looking back, I wonder if the drawback was us? Would the results have been the same had Nick & Co. recruited someone with a deeper understanding of selling in the fruit business? Given our sense of accountability and ability to see a few steps ahead, we stressed that we should give consideration to taking our ten-thousand-dollar loss in samples and time versus taking a hundred thousand dollar hit in the foreseeable future. Again, looking back, would the right partner with a stronger know-how and drive for the mission have begun to pull the plug at this point in the game?

I recollect Nick responding to our admission of defeat with something along the lines of: *'Really guys? Let me tell you of a little frozen fruit company called Europe's Best that started from nothing and that is now worth tens of millions of dollars.'* I remember firmly palming the phone receiver to mute the call and looking over to Dave and saying some-thing along the lines of: '*How is that any different than saying, let me tell you about a little computer company called Apple Computers that is now worth tens of billions? Okay, so now what?*'

By that point, we just wanted out. I'm always amazed at how quick-ly relationships can spoil despite everyone's absolute best efforts and interests to get along and to build something great. I suppose it's how and why wars can start. At the time, I remember thinking that, if Nick and Co. had focused on flushing out the accurate product costs and uncovering realistic selling prices before unleashing their expectations and offering Dave and me a share in the business, the story may have unfolded a little differently. And then again, in hindsight, I can also now appreciate that's why they brought us on board and now realize that a more motivated and determined partner could have perhaps used the company's resources at his disposal a little better to devise a revised game plan. Nonetheless, we quickly found ourselves at odds and, within a week or two later, had totally separated from the company. The group was left with a container loaded with frozen fruit, a slightly bruised bank account and the deflated hope of trying to shake any fat fruits from the tree.

It's years later now and I continue to wonder how such a well-es-tablished and experienced group of entrepreneurs, myself included, could make such poor business decisions and be so blind to the facts. Our pricing was just too high to take a big bite out of the competition. Why didn't they appreciate this fundamental flaw in the plan? The ori-ginal working title for this chapter was actually 'Even the Smartest People Make Mistakes.' But, as I started to reminisce and write down the nuances of this story, I began to appreciate that we may have just been the wrong partners, with weaker than required relationships and talents for this particular mission. Maybe I was the smarty-pants who had made the greater mistake. Maybe I was the rotten apple. Having said this, I'd still much rather be on the receiving end of an ownership offer. If you can't already tell, I'm that kid clutching his pillowcase full of Halloween candy—well, apparently, except for the one or two apples that folks sometimes give out.

I know it's tempting to offer someone seemingly better suited for the mission a piece of your company pie in exchange for a better chance of real progress. But if and when your hopes are dashed and your pockets are lightened, consider that you may regret inking a formal partnership agreement and signing over even a few points of ownership in your company. There are many other less committal ways to secure and compensate a valuable member of your team and to ensure that they feel both the benefits and pressures of having some skin in your game. Be careful what you wish for. I'd rather call off an arrangement with someone over the phone or in a coffee shop rather than after a honeymoon in paradise with the first joint-mortgage payment waiting in the mail.

Let It Simmer ~

1. *Can you offer a creative incentive, other than sharing ownership in your start-up company, and still get what you want out of the relationship?*
2. *Will your partner be as good of a match down the road, or are you tempted to offer them ownership simply because they are what you need at this very moment?*
3. *Hold off on offering, or at least on officially signing over, ownership until a few key pieces of the puzzle are revealed—e.g. accurate costings, retailer interest, volume assumptions, minimum product guarantees, etc.*
4. *When the story changes and the climb becomes trickier, will your candidate still be up for the mission? Or, has their vibe and approach quickly dampened?*
5. *As the factors and gameplay become clearer, ask your candidate questions that expose their evolving mindset instead of instinctively pushing them towards your goal? Does their analysis and drive align with your own, or are they trying to convince you otherwise because they've lost interest?*

CHAPTER 17

Milkin' It

Pushing Too Far With
Product Line Extensions

Any veteran storm observer will explain that lightning can, in fact, strike in the same place more than once. It may take only a few months or up to multiple lifetimes, but it is possible if you wait it out long enough. When it comes to trying to repeat the booming thunder of a successful product launch, you may not have to wait a lifetime for another solid hit, but chances are that it won't occur as quickly or as naturally as you want or need it to. Following up a big win with a product line extension (*a product under the same brand name within the same category*) and/or a brand extension (*a product with the same brand name in a different category*), or a seemingly comparable brand or product strategy (*a product with a different brand name in the same category*) is a common strategic reaction. But storm chasers beware, unless you're in Venezuela where the Catatumbo River meets Lake Maracaibore, relocating the strike zone is a rather elusive game.

A few years into building our Kernels Popcorn shaker business, we tried relentlessly, and fruitlessly, to create another successful seasoning product line. The sales volume, profit margin and our growing production capability and supply partner network (i.e. contract packers and suppliers of raw material ingredients and packaging) for all things shakers was just too appealing and obvious to ignore. In under three years, we struck brand licensing deals with QSR (Quick Service Restaurant) giants New York Fries® to create a French fry seasoning, with Golden Griddle® for an unlikely breakfast egg seasoning, with Teriyaki

Experience® for an exotic Pan Asian rice and protein seasoning, and with Sbarro® for an authentic Italian seasoning.

With the exception of the Teriyaki Experience and Sbarro seasoning shakers, the other products collected a thick layer of dust on the grocery shelf. Despite using the same distinctive shaker container as our Kernels line, our best-in-class flavour recipe approach and our let's-make-boring-seasonings-look-funkier-than-the-norm strategy, we couldn't generate another positive electrical charge. As discussed in *Chapter 7: Pop Goes the World*, our success with Kernels Shakers was built on much more than solid brand awareness, patented recipes and good-looking packaging. We enjoyed first to market status for a product concept that stood on the shoulders of a well-established consumer ritual, and in the process succeeded in filling a meaningful category void.

The market was not only ready to add intense flavours to their naked popcorn, they were avidly seeking a solution. Kernels had been selling flavoured popcorn for nearly twenty years before our foray into grocery; movie theatres had also been offering moviegoers complimentary popcorn seasonings for years before we decided to shake things up. Consequently, consumers had acquired a taste for popcorn seasoning but had no option to purchase it outside these two arenas. And whereas sprinkling established chip-like flavours onto hot and fresh microwave popcorn wasn't much of a stretch for consumers, it seemed too foreign to shake exotic and unestablished flavours onto their French fries, scrambled eggs, fried rice or pasta. Instead of leaning on other well-established eating rituals to help satisfy a genuine consumer demand and to fill a category void, we aimed to invent a new demand but ended up missing the mark each time.

When our Mr. Greek® frozen souvlaki line started to fly out of A&P / Dominion's freezer bunkers (see *Chapter 10: Opa!*), we assumed that consumers would naturally take to all things Greek and would readily support brand extensions marketed under the popular Ontario restaurant name. Store managers seemed to openly rally behind the notion that we had given the Mr. Greek line exclusively to their company. As a result, we enjoyed better-than-average product in-store placement and aggressive flyer ad support. At the time, there were no qualms over

whether or not we should invest more time and money into a few additional tasty baklavas. After completing the first season, it also became clear that we had earned the trust of our buyers and of the coveted senior management (a hat tip to Tom Williams, Tony Morello, Paul Del Duca and the late and great Paul Fortin). The door was held wide open and we knew it could close unexpectedly at a moment's notice.

Thus, we proudly threw on our togas and laurel leaf crowns and dove straight into the Parthenon of brand extension development. In just over a year or so, we worked intensely with Mr. Greek's congenial founder and President, George Raios, to develop the following ostentatious list of Greek delicacies under his restaurant's brand name—moussaka, spanakopita, breaded shrimp, breaded kalamari, tzatziki, feta cheese, souvlaki burgers, Greek-style potatoes, Greek-salad kits and Greek-inspired seasoning. A&P green-lighted each and every one. To boot, this list doesn't include the product concepts that we worked on that didn't end up on the shelf because of either sourcing or manufacturing snags—whole wheat pita bread, taramosalata, baklava, kefalotyri cheese, and bottled Greek salad dressing to name a few. Needless to say, we jumped the Greek shark.

To this day, thinking about all the convoluted contract packer agreements and the list of unique ingredients and packaging guarantees makes my laurel leaf crown spin. Now, we did have a couple of valuable, Olympic runs with the Mr. Greek Tzatziki, Feta Cheese and fresh salad kits because I believe our timing, quality, pricing and packaging held its own against the competition in the respective categories. Despite receiving a decent level of product launch awareness from the retailer, the volume of the other misfit products paled in comparison to our inaugural brand launch with the frozen souvlaki line. In most cases, we had to discount the introductory shipment to help stores clear their inventory. This also meant that our collective return on investment for these products wasn't too attractive. We had spent more money to cultivate recipes, procure ingredients, design and build packaging, and to guarantee minimum production runs than we were able to pocket in profits.

More damagingly, we overloaded and eventually soured both the

consumer and the retailer with the brand's new product blitz. Had we focused on protecting our core souvlaki line and recognized the budding success of the three new brand extensions earlier, our energy and money would have been invested elsewhere. Luckily, in the end, after a stellar three or four year outing with the Mr. Greek brand at A&P / Dominion, we did end up hauling in a Herculean profit despite the unexpected dead weight associated with the failed concepts.

It took me over ten years to learn how to firmly say *NO* to a seemingly interesting offer from a willing brand licensor or an eager retailer and still feel at peace with my decision. It's in my nature to say *YES* when my gut says otherwise as I'm the type of guy who wants to desperately please people, or at least I used to be. Nowadays, it's exceedingly difficult for me to accept most offers—admittedly, it's now to a fault. As I revealed on the first page on this book: '*You learn more about what not to do when you lose money doing the wrong thing. I can tell you how I've lost a boat-load of it over the past 20 years playing this game of delusional buffet-sized profits.*'

The usual hitch with those who table us offers to shepherd them into grocery stores—whether it be a prospective restaurant brand partner, a critically acclaimed chef, or a humble home chef—is they find it impossible to comprehend the flagrant distinction between what's possible in their kitchens and dining rooms versus what's probable in a crowded grocery store aisle. I regard Pizza Pizza® Dips to be one of our most celebrated and long-standing accomplishments. The Pizza Pizza brand is an extremely well known restaurant chain in Ontario that moves copious amounts of dough, tomato sauce and mozzarella through their busy commissary. Their dominant share of the crowded restaurant pizza market is remarkable to say the least. Perhaps not as commonly acknowledged, Pizza Pizza also procures and sells a staggering quantity of chicken wings.

Nonetheless, when the veteran crew at Pizza Pizza suggested that we follow up the successful launch of our creamy garlic dipping sauce with a frozen chicken wing program, we instantly sensed that it would be a dubious and over costly undertaking. Their opportunity paradigm was based and built on the fact that they sell more chicken wings than probably any restaurant in Ontario. The potential consumer interest in a grocery program was supported by the droves of repeat orders and high consumer praise that the restaurant enjoyed on a daily basis. I imagine that they may have also been stoked by their strong poultry supplier relationships and buying power that we'd be able to tap into and leverage.

We, on the other hand, instantly sized up the mission a little differently. The frozen chicken wing category in grocery was already chockful of both competitive and competent national and private label brand offerings. The cost of entry into the frozen protein aisle was much costlier than it was to play in the dairy category where we had established the brand in grocery—upwards of $50,000 per sku compared with a more digestible $5,000 per sku, respectively. Yes, Pizza Pizza's chicken wings are of high quality, a nice size and are damn tasty, but what would our key point of difference be against the established incumbent brands?

Most importantly, when assessing whether or not we should take a recipe into grocery, we ask ourselves this question—would a consumer react the same way about a product if they had to buy it outside of the restaurant's busy four walls or off their high traffic website? When consumers are standing at a restaurant's order counter, or chatting with an order-taking operator on the phone, or clicking through their online-menu order system, they're making an uninterrupted purchase decision within a brand vacuum. Walk out of the restaurant, hang-up the phone or power down the smart phone and stroll into a retail store and the rules of engagement dramatically change. Your captive audience is now overstimulated and confused by too many choices and, unless you give them a compelling reason, they'll default to what they know; to what feels most comfortable.

It's about quality, price, packaging, in-store placement, share of shelf space, and established purchase rituals. It's about competing with, and trying to disrupt, an emotional connection a consumer might enjoy with another brand. In our case, licensing the Pizza Pizza powerhouse might have scored us some initial product trial because of the brand's ubiquitous consumer awareness. However, if the product should fall short on realizing the other equally significant purchase metrics, scoring repeat orders would have been challenging.

It's for this reason that we wince when a popular restaurant or chef, or more painfully, an overzealous home cook presents an opportunity by starting the conversation with: *'Everybody that's tried this recipe goes absolutely crazy for it and insists that I should try selling it in grocery stores!'* In my head, I'm saying: *'Well, listen here, my wife can crank out an impressive homemade arrabiata tomato sauce that's hands down the best I've had the joy of shovelling into my mouth—but ... the only way I'd invest in bringing it to market is if Chef Boyardee was my only competition.'*

Let it Simmer ~

1. *Have you peeled away enough layers and looked deeply enough to understand why your product was a hit before trying to clone its success? Get to the very bottom of it because 'only the spoon knows what is stirring in the pot.'*
2. *Are you in jeopardy of taking your product extensions / brand extensions too far and to the point of souring and tiring retailers and consumers?*
3. *Will your recipe perform as well in a retail store environment jam-packed with comparable products as it does in your restaurant or at home with friends and family?*
4. *Can your product extension / brand extension maintain the same key points of difference from your competition as your original product introduction?*

CHAPTER 18

Boiling Over

Quality Over Quantity

The path to profits and prosperity isn't always about launching as many new product concepts as your budding company can bear to handle. While fostering innovative new product development is the engine for big growth for many established companies, try to go for meaningful depth over significant breadth until you have both the necessary resources, financing and time in your corner. Don't get too brave or cocky when you start to see and taste a little palpable success. Avoid letting the new product pot boil over because you have too much cooking on the stove. Assign a serious chunk of your newfound revenue stream wisely to help strengthen the roots of your core product; otherwise, you'll risk burning up your cash and ability to stay afloat.

Of the more than one hundred foodstuff skus that we've managed to squeeze out into retail, we have cupboards more stuffed with half-baked concepts that somehow siphoned our bank account and clogged our calendars with make-work—all at the expense of stealing that extra oomph from building and protecting our core lines. We have a row of abandoned cupboards in our test kitchen filled with mock-ups and franken-samples of products that either died suddenly after the first order, or that have never seen the light of day. We call this culinary gravesite '*The Lost Pantry.*'

Crack open the cupboard doors without letting any boxes, bags or cans come tumbling out, and you'll find Booster Juice® Smoothies, Hooters® Chicken Wing Sauce, Jack Astor's® Spinach and Artichoke Dip,

Eating in Japan Stir Fry Meal Kits, Golden Griddle® Sausages and Planters® microwaveable glazed almonds. Heck, we even have an entire corner cabinet dedicated to our Kernels Extraordinary Popcorn® mishaps. Praise our loyal and understanding partners at Kernels, especially Eli and Scott Staiman, for having supported the majority of our big bright ideas. Scan those lost shelves and you'll unearth Tornados® puffed corn snacks, Swizzle chocolate drizzled caramel corn, packs of paper popcorn bags for kids' parties, Spring Fling fruit glazed popcorn, Kernels Karamel popcorn topping, and my all-time favourite, Kernels chocolate covered caramel popcorn packed inside a jumbo foil-wrapped Easter egg—all duds.

Granted, I'd be remiss not to mention that for every few misfires, we've managed to hit the bulls-eye. And by the way, launching a dud takes no less time, money and effort than unleashing a grand slam selling product onto shelves. We've also had to redistribute hard earned profits from our successful core lines to feed these ill-fated escapades.

Ironically, most of our meaningful financial growth has come after we've misfired by concentrating on way too many new initiatives at once, causing us to recoil, re-energize and refocus. To be clear, however, innovation can and should equal big growth, so always keep at least one strong and hopeful product innovation in the hopper, and work to foster and protect it. As your resources and ability to pick out fighters from the litter strengthens, cultivating more than one or two new concepts becomes less risky. Hush-hush, I'm actually munching away on a new Kernels inspired killer concept as I'm writing this chapter. If all goes as planned, we'll be unchaining it, alongside Staiman & Co., around the same time that this book is set to be released.

During the mid 2000s, at any given moment, we had a minimum of twenty new and ambitious product concepts on our development list —or as we chose to dutifully refer to it at BrandFusion, our *'FusePath.'* I respect that an NPD (new product development) list of this magnitude isn't anything extraordinary or ambitious to most medium or large sized companies. We, on the other hand, had a team of one or two somewhat inexperienced staff tackling the list (who, by the way, were also accountable for sales, manufacturing, and accounting responsibilities).

As the face behind our growing company, courting and negotiating with illustrious restaurant chains for the licensing and use of their brand mark became my thing. Over the course of two very prolific years, we must've tried to woo every popular restaurant chain in the country to join our food fight in grocery stores, as well as a few chains south of the Canadian border. Although I shouldn't whine as in most cases we typically scheduled our meetings in their restaurants, allowing me to happily sample everything off the menu. Putting on a passionate pony show while scarfing down a cornucopia of appetizers and mains became a most welcomed weekly ceremony.

Holding meetings in Hawaii with Cilantro Mexican Grill and in Fort Lauderdale, Florida with Muvico Theatres also had its advantages. I knew that the wheels had started to come loose from our caboose when I began to screw up the basics and thoroughly embarrass myself in the process (and, of course, when my Levi's began to tighten around the waist from all the Friar-Tuck-style gorging). One of my colleagues at Johnvince Foods had secured a meeting for JP and me with two senior VPs from Allied Domeqc, who at the time owned Baskin Robbins®—the world's largest chain of ice cream specialty shops. Our game plan was to license the Baskin Robbins brand for a line of premium retail ice cream toppings.

Normally, I would have made it a key point to prepare for the inaugural meeting by visiting one of Baskin's busy locations to study the menus, sample ice cream flavours, and to snap pics of marketing signage for future use and reference. For this particular get-together, however, I did not prepare whatsoever. I had dined and chatted with a handful of other prospective restaurant partners in the weeks leading up to the Baskin Robbins meeting so I hadn't the time or energy and arrogantly felt that my wheels were good and greased enough for another spin around the discussion table.

As I slid into the room a la Cosmo Kramer from Seinfeld, JP had already begun to chat with the folks from Allied Domeqc. In well under the first five minutes, I would single-handedly kibosh our chances for inking a contract with the ice cream moguls. The first words out of my mouth were: '*I have to tell you; my family and I are huge fans of your ice cream. I just love that new Caramel Apple product that you recently introduced!*' There was an awkward pause, and then one of the two ladies politely retorted: *'Um, that's not ours. I believe you're thinking of Dairy Queen's new product.'*

JP shifted his eyes in my direction and shot me the same clenched teeth stare that my Father used to give me as a kid when I asked for ketchup on my eggs (a big no-no at a Calabrese breakfast table). *'My apologies, what was I thinking. Actually, I was referring to your new Grasshopper Mousse Pie!'* I said trying to put the cool-train back on the tracks. *'Nope. Sorry. That's also one of Dairy Queen's flavours!'* replied the other lady. By this point, JP is stepping on my toe under the table. As you can imagine, we didn't end up launching the ice cream toppings. We just had too much on our plate for me to give the opportunity the appropriate attention. I should've played it safe and opened with giving props to the Peanut Butter 'n Chocolate ice cream shake, as that's always been my bag at Baskin Robbins.

I also find that, when we're involved with too many new concepts, it's tough to completely stay madly in love with them all. And if I don't completely love and believe deeply in a product and its purposefulness, sitting in front of a squint-eyed and sceptical buyer to sell it becomes next to hopeless. I'll say it again: until you have the resources required, it's about the depth, not the breadth. When you've toiled over every minute detail and it literally feels like you've finally given birth to a perfect and beautiful product, you're not out there selling it per se. It's more like you're sharing your infectious enthusiasm with the customer —which always makes for both an easier and triumphant presentation.

After years of taking a good beating at the hands of wanting to do too much, we've tightened the development sieve to a point where we'll only support the advancement of two new food concepts at the very most. Based on our available resources, our NPD garden has become less about growing as many varieties as possible, and more about cultivating a couple of blue ribbon contenders. We also appreciate that growing conditions will change overnight and either prolong, or even end up killing the harvest.

Whether it's because of a sudden change of players in the game, a fading expectation in your contract packer's capabilities, or an interminable launch timetable, the path to market will constantly elude you.

When the boutique burger joint Lick's® decided to launch a retail version of their Home burgers in A&P / Dominion, consumers couldn't get enough of the meaty stuff. The over-the-top ten-dollar restaurant hamburger craze we're seeing today was still years from hitting the dining scene, and Licks was cashing in on the unexploited category in grocery.

It was hard to overlook their accomplishments in crossing over to grocery so we decided to follow suit by approaching Webers burgers with a plan to develop a retail version of their iconic burgers for sale in Loblaws grocery stores to give A&P / Dominion a run for their money. The landmark hamburger restaurant was established in 1963 and sits on a highway just north of Orillia, Ontario. Webers was so popular that in 1983 it installed the first and only privately owned pedestrian bridge built over a public highway in Ontario so that it could accommodate more folks jonesing for a good burger.

Paul Weber—son of the restaurant's creator Paul Weber Sr.—and I hit it off instantly. It didn't come quick or easy, but on a Canadian-cold January night, as we strolled through the International Car Show with our wives, I eventually convinced Paul to accept the food fight mission. Just a few weeks later, however, we regrettably learned that Paul had decided to sell his longtime family burger business. By this point, we were already in discussions with his meat processing plant contract packer to duplicate the family's famous recipe for retail. We met the new owner of Webers during a product cutting at the plant. Where Paul had been charming and collaborative, I could instantly see that the new mayor of burger-town wasn't digging our tune much. He spent most of the hour-long meeting using his pencil eraser to tap on his calculator to assess our significance in the deal. By the time we reached our car in the parking lot, I had decided that we would cut bait and move on.

I hate leaving money on the table, but I hate working through unrest far more. In my experience, the conditions for a healthy launch have to look and feel just right during the courting and initial collaboration stages. Don't get me wrong; I realize that choosing to stay in the ring to fight for your prize can pan out too. It's just that I'd rather save my energy to fight an opponent that's not on my own team. Later that year in early summer, while shopping in Loblaws with my wife Lisa, I stopped dead in my tracks as I caught sight of the Webers® burgers display in the freezer bunker. This wasn't the first unmerited case of someone else taking a food product concept that we started to the finish line without us, and it would be far from the last. Don't get me started on East Side Mario's! Based on the level of exposure and merchandising support, the burgers seemed to sell modestly for a couple of years and then slowly faded away.

The path to market is very rarely a straight and measurable line. The more complex and ambitious your product concept, the more you'll end up chasing the launch date. Unless you're launching a relatively simple and straightforward concept, or a simple line extension (i.e. new flavour for an existing product line), the finish line will continue to keep moving further way. But then again, does the world really want another boring citrus vinaigrette, bran muffin mix or spicy pasta sauce? Well, I'm sure they might but will it be a five-hundred case opportunity or can it be the fifty-thousand case monster you want it to be?

Whether the magic lies in your distinctive recipe and preparation style, or the packaging format and design, it's important to remember not to let deadlines completely steer the ship or dictate the ultimate quality of your product when you're on the verge of launching something truly original. Be patient. Get it right the first time. Consumers and retailers will be unforgiving and quick to remember your failures. When Dave and I teamed up with BeaverTails® to create a unique retail item for grocery stores, we operated with the weight and awareness that we'd be judged unforgivingly if the concept didn't properly capture the iconic brand's deep fried dough addiction and Canadiana narrative. After well over a year of dragging a couple of willing manufactures through countless recipe iterations we refrained from giving into our restlessness to punch the big red launch button despite seeing a formidable interest in some of the product submissions that came out of our test kitchen. Our goal was to keep on digging deep until we unearthed exactly what we were looking for.

A few years back, the pressure of cycling through our prodigious list of twenty-something concepts would have clouded our judgment. This time around, the conditions for patient cultivation were bang on —our relationship with the good folks at BeaverTails was exceptional, our new product hopper wasn't choking with caramel and apple pie ice cream and the brand's relevance and originality remained relevant and inspiring to us throughout our development journey. So we continue to tweak, tinker, polish and taste until we get it just right.

If all goes well, I'm hoping there's a BeaverTails baked grocery goodie in your local supermarket by the time you're reading this. If not, it's either because we couldn't nail the results we wanted, or because we missed the mark again and it's already come and gone without you even noticing. Listen, when I launched Kernels Popcorn Shakers back in 2000, I loved the brand, the concept and the people involved in the mission. It turned out to be a painstaking obsession for nearly two unpaid years. It was also the only product that I fixated on in the that time. I dug super deep, past the heavy layers of supply partner and retailer scepticism, past the concern that others seemed to have for my crusade. If you're a one-person-army, focus on building your food empire one single crop at a time.

Let It Simmer ~

1. *Have you gradually bitten off more than you can chew at the expense of neglecting the evolution of your core product(s)?*
2. *Go for depth over breadth until you have the adequate resources to spare. Prioritize your new product development list by profit and volume potential. Investing in new product development is a critical piece to increasing your business, but realistically weigh out your reserves and finances against what you'll also need to cultivate and protect your core product(s).*
3. *Prepare or be aware! Are you offering each food product in your incubator the devotion and energy they need to evolve, or are you in danger of heading towards your own 'Baskin Robbins blooper?'*

CHAPTER 19

Catching A Buzz

Staying the Course & Rolling with the Punches

After more than 10 years of raising someone else's prized brand high up on our sore shoulders, Dave and I began to hear the same inner-voice urging us to whip up something magnificent from scratch. A food brainchild, with a cool brand name and image that we believed in and obsessed over so deeply that we wouldn't, or physically couldn't, compromise our vision for—one that had the potential to eventually garner a legion of loyal foodie-fanatics. The end result would be different in a grander and more meaningful way compared to the other, tamer in-house creations we had introduced along the way—i.e. *Eating in Japan* stir fry kits, *Nature's Fruits* frozen premium fruits, *361°* *Magic Miso* and *Flavour Station* salty snack toppings to name but a forgotten few. It's a colourful story built on a foundation of classic axioms that speak to embracing constant change, stubborn persistence and the difference in outcome when you choose to drive instead of navigate from the backseat. This is a significant and career defining story that we continue to write today.

We sat down for a much-needed espresso break in the busy tradeshow hall to reboot and discuss all the new and funky food products we just sampled at the SIAL show in Montreal 2011. Despite eating close to my body weight in free Belgian chocolate and Italian charcuterie samples (yet again—sigh), we came up empty on potential new ideas and inspiration. It's always more of the same, just packaged in a slightly new way. On the plane ride home, however, Dave and I came across an article in *Saveur Magazine* (a subscription must for any respectable foodie). It was on 'Paletas' which are basically fancy Ice Pops sold roadside in Mexico. The flavours, however, are made from wonderfully sweet and savoury recipes and, unlike most of our frozen-fructose-crap in North America, are made from purely natural and often local ingredients—for example, there's a popular flavour called *'Chamoy'* which is a sweet-spicy mixture of mango and red chilies.

By the time we touched down in T Dot, we penciled a game plan on the back of a cocktail napkin (which is, by the way, the best place to pencil a plan). Our idea was to create a line of funky Paleta flavours; the added twist was that we'd infuse the pops with premium alcohol —fancy-schmancy adult ice pops if you will. The idea was far out enough from the norm to make a meaningful innovation statement, yet not so far that consumers wouldn't understand the concept—which is really that desirable sweet-spot you want to play in. Either way, it was one of those neat ideas that still felt mission-worthy a few sleeps later.

Time passed and our excitement was tempered only because we couldn't find a small batch juice contract packer that also had the capabilities and the alcohol license required to produce the frozen beast we were chasing. Until, Bartly James Murphy, one of my closest child-hood friends, swung by our office with an interesting juice pouch package. It looked and kinda-sorta functioned like an upside intravenous bag. No straw required, just rip, invert n' sip. What's more, the pouch was freezable so the juice could be served as an ice-slushie treat. Bart had just begun to work for the company that packaged the pouch and was instrumental in setting up a meeting with its affable owner, Darryl McDaniel.

We eventually pitched Darryl our alcohol-laced Paletas concept and he graciously agreed to help us flush out the concept and to commer-cialize it. It turned out that the pouch was being used for a vodka-based frozen beverage so his company was also in the process of securing their alcohol license. And to that end, all of our ducks seemed to be lining up. Following our initial get-together, however, many months passed with zero progress as the company was too busy with more pressing and worthwhile business, and to boot, still hadn't secured their alcohol license. If an idea is strong enough, set-backs can also allow you and the idea to breathe and to change course on to a more accessible and down-hill road. A vital lesson we've learned on a number of occasions is that if it's meant to be, the simplest milestones with your supply partners shouldn't be impossible or painful to achieve. When you've locked into the right person or company, the easy steps feel somewhat easy and the hard ones eventually get sorted out.

At the crux of our fascination with the Paleta concept was the idea of mixing common, yet sexy, ingredients in surprisingly uncommon ways. It was also about mixing seasonal and natural ingredients with booze in a crafty and artisanal fashion that appealed to foodies (of a legal drinking age, of course). Perhaps it was only natural then, that our concept eventually morphed into a culinary mission to create and pion-eer best-in-class, all natural, mixologist-inspired cocktails into retail. A mixologist, or a bar-chef, is the bar equivalent of a culinary chef. They extend the creativity and quality of cocktails by utilizing culinary con-cepts and exotic, often premium, ingredients with chef-like skill.

We jumped from alcohol-laced Mexican popsicle bars to chef-in-spired crazy cocktails—go figure; but the point here is that this type of unplanned progression shouldn't be an unwelcome surprise. It is, in-stead, to paraphrase the great David Lee Roth, what happens when you '*jump and roll with the punches to get to what's real.*' A couple of weeks later, Dave stumbled upon a glowing article about a much lauded To-ronto drinking establishment called BarChef, located in the city's eclec-tic and electric Queen Street West. Frankie Solarik, the bar's co-owner and resident mixologist, was being heralded as one of Canada's bright-est stars in the industry—a master flavour-wizard concocting magical elixirs in his hipster lair. '*Let's try and score a licensing deal with Frankie,*' Dave suggested.

Up until that point, we had paid well-known restaurants a royalty rebate based on our net sales for the use of their brand-mark, propri-etary recipes and category expertise; why not use the same licensing model to pay Frankie a royalty for his cocktail recipes and our product's endorsement? At first, I was indisposed to having someone else join our booze-cruise given that I knew we had to sail the seven seas before seeing a profit and would have to do all of the navigating and bankroll the excursion. In the end, we realized that the alcohol sector was uncharted waters for us so we decided to invite Frankie aboard. Dave made the call to Frankie and he accepted the invitation to hear us out. Knowing that we'd be consuming multiple weeknight-cocktails, I bribed my wife's younger cousins to chaperone Dave and me to the bar and picked up their dinner tab while they dined nearby.

We also invited Leigh Bailey, a seasoned specialist from one of our preferred flavour development suppliers (a company that takes a chef's recipe and helps bring it to commercialization in an efficient and economical way; and, if they're good, in a way that doesn't lessen the impact of the chef's original recipe). Frankie also invited his agent to sit in. Yep, that's right. Total Rock Star. The man had an 'agent.' We sat at the back of his dimly lit and posh bar and sampled four or five of his most popular and potent libations. If I look back at my meeting notes, I can tell that by the fifth drink I was feeling slightly buzzed as I can hardly read my tiny scribble. We all left the meeting inspired to work together. It was settled, we'd develop three flavours, a 'Basil, Honey & Lime Daiquiri' a 'Spiced Cola & Mint Julep' and a 'Vanilla, Lavender Tequila Sour'—each bevvy complete with its own artisanal rimmer made of citrus rinds, cane sugar, sea salt and various floral aromatics.

Aside from spending the following couple of months trying to replicate Frankie's recipes en masse, seeking out unique bottles, alcohol-licensed bottlers, sales agents, distributors and industry consultants, we tried to figure out how to connect with the LCBO. To my friends living outside of Canada, the government in Ontario not only governs all sales and distribution of alcohol (including to restaurants, which are referred to as on-premise customers), they retail it themselves; aside from licensed wineries, select grocery stores that sell beer and wine, and a handful of other ambiguities, consumers buy their spirits from a, albeit exceedingly attractive and well-merchandised, government-run store. This is also the case with many other Canadian markets, but not all of them.

The deeper we delved into what was required of us in order to conduct business with the LCBO, the more alien and overwhelming the project became. Most folks in the industry we looked to for counsel looked at us the same way you smile at your six-year-old kid when he insists on taking over the stove to make Saturday morning breakfast: '*So cute and ambitious but you're gonna get burned badly pal!*' As a side note, all three of my kids, especially my son, Gabe, cook like mini-molto-Marios despite having to stand on a chair when making proper gently folded scrambled eggs and crispy Canadian bacon.

After we navigated through and completed the never-ending government forms and mandatory requirements, and successfully acquired our official agent's license, we were ready to face the alcohol's industry's oligopoly giant in Ontario—the LCBO, the single largest purchaser of alcohol in the world. They also represent nearly half of the country's sales for many alcohol companies. We filled out what we could of their on-line product submission process but knew that an old fashioned face-to-face was needed if we were to stand a chance. As a side-note, over the past ten or so years, selling food and alcohol has become more of a clerical-sport in filling out ever-changing Excel spreadsheets and on-line forms—what ever happened to cutting a deal in the dimly lit stockroom over a makeshift upside down milk-carton-table? Get ready to fill out forms—seemingly useless short forms and appallingly long multi-page, multi-tab and multi-painful forms; for the most part, being a key account sales manager means you'll regularly be bashing in your computer screen with your mouse trying to figure out if the sale is actually worth the aggravation.

Our growing army of sceptics insisted that, without an established relationship, being awarded a coveted face-to-face meeting was a pipe dream. Nonetheless, I kept calling the buyer, carefully depositing eager voice messages. '*I realize you must receive a ton of requests,*' I started with in one such attempt, '*but this lil' sucker is right in the pocket with where you want to take the one-pour cocktail business. Give us a shot, we'll make it short, sweet and worth your while.*' At the time, we knew the LCBO was both ready and hungry for RTD (ready-to-drink) craft cocktails because they had started to feature more ambitious recipes in their widely read and highly regarded, *Food & Drink* Magazine. In the end, the buyer graciously granted us a meeting. Deep breath. '*Ok. We're on, Dave ... two weeks from today,*' I hollered from my desk over to his.

Now, this is where you separate the men and women from the little boys and girls. This is the big juncture on the road to launch-town that gets me all fired up like a soft taco loaded with ghost pepper salsa. In the beginning, cold-call sales pitch meetings gave me instant nervous pangs. However, after years of practice and acclimatization I've grown to love and respect the dance. In a more corporate setting, agreeing to a meeting with the world's largest purchaser of alcohol despite having no industry background, no legitimate product samples, no packaging designs, no pricing or no plan just isn't done. Period.

It's all nonsense, I say. The only things you need neatly packed in your attaché case is genuine passion, credible knowledge, an infectious vision and ... big brass balls. Our flavour development supplier was months away from presenting us with a workable tasting sample, we had no idea what style of packaging, let alone a brand or design vision, we wanted. Here's how we strung it together *tout de suite*. That weekend, Dave and I were in San Francisco at the Fancy Food Trade Show. Thirty minutes before we had to leave for the airport, we came across an alcohol contract packer, stationed in Canton, Georgia, that was at the show unveiling their new, unique shaped aluminum can. We liked the look of it. They agreed to bottle a beverage for us under our own brand name. We swindled three can samples from their booth display and jammed them into our carry-ons, already bursting with food-samples (most of them plane-ride snacks of course).

We also come across a contract packer with the capability to pack liquids into small squarish pouches with a re-sealable spigot. '*Hmmm, perfecto,*' we thought, for the bitter herbal extracts we thought we wanted to include with our original beverage concept. For the brand name, we went with '*Bar361°*'—named after 361 Degrees Inc., the company we had incorporated to sell alcohol products. Time was short, but more importantly, we didn't want to invest serious cash until we knew there was concrete interest to fall back on, so I asked my neighbour's boyfriend to whip up a couple of design concepts. He had come to see me for career advice a few weeks earlier as he'd just graduated from graphic design school.

It was a win-win as he got the chance to design something meaningful for a start-up brand to add to his portfolio, and we scored a fabulous freebie design within a few days—when you're starting out this type of experience should be considered valuable 'career-currency'—JP drilled this notion into my head at an early age. He'd often declare with fervour: *'Listen, you're not getting financially compensated for being involved with this project. In fact, I should be asking you to pay me for the ride!'* I bought some matte black spray paint from The Home Depot, went out to the office parking lot, gave the aluminum cans we scored at the food show a few coats of paint and spray-glued the label design on —voila! For the tasting samples, we asked Frankie to mix-up a large batch of the cocktails and then poured them into some fancy apothecary bottles adorned with '361° LAB SAMPLE' labels.

Piecing together the actual pitch wasn't an issue. I love building a compelling case for a product concept that I believe in. Ask me to pitch something I don't dig and you'll see right through me like my wife does when I sneak a few tablespoons of Nutella after the kids have gone to bed. If I believe in it, and know the retailer and consumer will benefit, I'll stand on the buyer's desk and tap dance like Danny Kaye—controlling and properly channelling my energy and enthusiasm is my daily challenge.

As we slowly trailed the buyer from the quiet lobby waiting area to his office, we walked past a myriad of classic neutral coloured cubicles happily occupied by conservatively dressed and astute looking LCBO personnel. I remember being five minutes into the pitch, gently kicking Dave under the table and throwing him a very subtle smirk as if to say: *'We're actually flowing pretty nicely here.'* The clincher happened when we moved our pony show from the buyer's office into a special room the LCBO uses for bevvy tastings.

As we were about to crack open our tasting samples, the buyer said: *'Hold on a sec, fellas. Let me grab my boss and a couple of other colleagues.'* Boom baby! This is the moment. The one that comes along every few lunar eclipses or so. Do or die. Always be prepared with a two-minute tune of your sales pitch—a 'best of' track. With our adrenaline kicked into monster high gear, Dave and I continued to riff back and forth. And then, the tasting itself—I can only remember the group raising the glasses to their lips in super slow motion. That first swirl and sip, followed by an eventual revealing facial expression that immediately follows. Yes. Yes! YES! They loved it. Well, at least two of the three as the 'Vanilla Lavender Tequila Sour' had too much of a perfume-y potpourri thing going on.

Despite loving our other two craft cocktails, they explained that it was regrettably too late in their buying season to accept any new spring and summer themed products and that it would make more sense to introduce a winter themed flavour as our inaugural one; retail chains evaluate and work to build their seasonal product assortments six to nine months ahead of time, so you'll be pitching a Christmas concept over the phone with your feet dangling in the pool. Remember now: 'You've got to roll with the punches ...' We left the building with a handshake agreement that, if we could properly polish the product concept with relevant and attractive packaging and pricing (AND now come up with a completely new holiday themed flavour), that we'd be awarded a shot on the big booze stage.

The LCBO meeting was on a Friday. Leaving the house for work the following Monday somehow felt strangely different, in a rare and special way. By this time, we weren't strangers to being given the coveted green light by a retail chain giant, but man-o-man this was the LCBO, the world's largest purchaser of alcoholic beverages. We needed a kickass brand with a strong voice and a brand narrative that people actually cared about. We needed to create a lifestyle brand, not just another message in a bottle lost in the sea of competition we were about to face. I needed to place a call I'd been reserving to make for a lunar eclipse spotting like this one. My childhood mate was, at the time, the president of one of Canada's most celebrated advertising agencies called TAXI.

I'd never dared called Jeremy Gayton in the past, as I knew his agency's fees would be hopelessly out of reach and we never had an opportunity that I felt was worthy. 'Jer, I need a favour buddy.' As he always does, he listened carefully before speaking and then, when I was done explaining our position, he asked all the right questions. 'Let me digest it, see if we can spare the resources and get back to you' were his closing remarks. Needless to say, he called back a few days later, laid down the rules of engagement and came to our rescue—and then some. *'What about the fees?'* I asked hesitantly. *'Let's not worry about that for now,'* he replied. *'This is also a rare and relevant opportunity for TAXI to create a meaningful brand from scratch. One that we can use to canvass our company's talents.'*

He then proceeded to assign a Creative Director (Dave Watson), a designer, a copywriter and an account manager to our project. Together, under Watson's über inspired guidance, we drilled deep into who we would target, why they would or should care about our brand, and how we could stand out and make a difference on a shoestring budget. In the end, we shortlisted the brand name to be either *Batch No1* or *Crazy Uncle*—the latter, a name someone had half-jokingly blurted out in a previous creative meeting that we all had snickered over. *Batch No1* felt right, and categorically much safer than the riskier and mischievous *Crazy Uncle*. Nonetheless, we toiled over the decision for a solid week. *'How the hell are we going to call up the LCBO to tell them we decided to change our brand name from Bar361° to, um ... Crazy Uncle?'*

We called Watson to half-heartedly declare that our choice was Batch No1. Later that evening Jer called me on the drive home. *'I rarely interfere at this point with the client's decision, but the team and I are feeling like we're on to something bigger with Crazy Uncle.'* Long-car-ride-story made short, he convinced us to roll the dice and take a chance on the Uncle and we agreed—thankfully.

Once we locked into the brand name and messaging, the design and personality started to take shape. The team's desire to create something that Watson affectionately called 'shabby-chic' led us to an elegant, yet fun design inspired by dandyism—the *'shabby'* part was our old-world moonshine jug: the kind your European grandfather uses to bottle his homemade gasoline-wine. (Note: somewhere along the line, we dropped the unique shaped aluminum can, among other options, and opted for the jug.) The *'chic'* part was the handsome custom-calligraphy logo drawn by world renown lettering design artist Ian Brignell, and the crisp men's pocket-square influenced patterns. Here is the copywriter's summation of Crazy Uncle® that ultimately sealed the deal for us:

We all know the eccentric uncle. He wears a captain's hat but doesn't own a boat. He boasts about his impressive Russian Jazz record collection. He marches to the beat of his own drum. It's that same unpredictability and uniqueness that inspires this drink. Our Crazy Uncle one-pour cocktails have deep complex flavours and a bitter undertow. With an appreciation of detail, and an artistic expression in liquid form. Why be like everyone else, when you can be something completely different?

In between the brand building exercises, glass bottle hunting, bottler negotiations, production challenges and sales meetings with our new distributor, we spent months, and a few sleepless nights, trying to commercialize our cocktails. Frankie had come up with a little holiday number that both we and the LCBO thought was seasonally splendid —Blood Orange, Rosemary & Maple Punch:

Perfect for the punch bowl at a suave cocktail party, or a cozy winter night by the fireside, this sophisticated punch has the tart acidity of blood orange infused with deep wintery spices like clove, cinnamon and cardamom, and finds its balance in the rich, natural sweetness of Canadian maple syrup.

We sat on the cozy couch in our family-room-style strategy room (complete with a fireplace, acoustic guitar and a wet bar) to taste the third hopeful iteration of the beverage prepared by our flavour development supplier. It was still far from perfection. Much too heady-sweet and watery, without nearly enough flavour depth—where were the subtle back notes of clove and cardamom? Why couldn't we taste the pure maple syrup? We were aiming to push the quality of ready to drink cocktails to a previously unreachable level where they tasted as if they were mixed with care and love in a bar by a pro. The flavour lab was in Kentucky a mere hour and a half flight away. I looked over at Dave and then at Leigh. *'It's clear that we have to visit the lab, sit down at the table with all those involved, and then tweak and taste until we nail it. There's just no time to go about it any other way at this point in the game.'*

I had been in this very same hot seat many times before and knew the benefits of a well-planned and intentioned plant visit would far outweigh the costs associated with carving out a few days of travel. Even if we provided meticulous tasting notes and direction to the flavour experts and chefs in Kentucky, the risk of waiting another three weeks only to be thwarted once again was one we couldn't afford to take. When it's crunch time, insist on a full-day tasting and tweaking session. Leigh pulled some strings and we were off to Erlanger, Kentucky. It's also highly constructive and recommended to take the time to explain your vision and expectations to the team. Let them jump on your carpet ride so they can better see and believe in the magic. It was worth the trip. We left the session satisfied that we had captured the quality, versatility and the true essence of Frankie's cocktail recipe—we also left the meeting with a fierce buzz after having sampled over ten different attempts.

After a few more heartaches and handfuls of uncomfortable production related ups and downs—namely the stubborn metal cap removal caper, the cockeyed bottle-label fiasco, the not-so-sticky adhesive on the custom elastics that fastened the rimmer sachet to the bottle, the too-thin-for-LCBO corrugated cases, and the surprise presence of unwanted flocculation (i.e. floating sediment clouds caused by exposing the juice pulp to high heat in the pasteurization tunnel), we were ready to ship our first order. LCBO had positioned our entry into their stores as a test that they'd be following closely.

In order to secure a listing in their Spring 2013 program, they mandated us with a sell-through target of forty-five percent of the order by December 17th (nearly 4,000 bottles). If we were able to achieve a sixty-five percent sell-through by the same date, we would be awarded two new listings. Based on Crazy Uncle's uniqueness and originality of the product, memorable brand name and packaging, LCBO chose to showcase us in their high profile 'What's New' section in the Holiday edition of its Food & Drink publication. Our brand name and package design played a pivotal role in securing a decent amount of prominent print and television media appearances. With TAXI at our side, we also ended up being recognized in the design world scoring a few nods such as one of '*2013 coolest packaging deigns*' and '*Top 10 Inspiring Packaging Designs.*'

Dave and I spent a few weeks visiting four or five key LCBO stores per day with our sales reps to chat up the store staff and ensure we pushed, what the industry refers to as, liquid to lips. Many key locations chose to showcase Crazy Uncle as a '*Staff Pick*' resulting in prime merchandising locations (i.e. next to the check-out counters); taking the time to visit and meet the staff in these stores was time well invested —something we still insist on with each new launch.

For a few weeks in December, I started each day by jumping out of bed with my heart in my throat while making a beeline for my laptop to check the previous day's sales. By the target date, despite a paltry, yet logical, forced push by the LCBO into only a couple of hundred of their nearly 700 locations, we exceeded the requirement and reached a seventy-five percent sell-through. By New Year's Eve we hit 97%. As such, the two flavours we'd originally presented to the LCBO (*Basil, Honey & Lime Daiquiri* and the *Cola Bitters and Mint Julep*) were green-lighted for the following Spring.

We ended up selling the Blood Orange, Rosemary & Maple punch over the next four consecutive winter seasons with nearly the same results. It was a prodigious win for us as the road had been dark and long —we had started the journey from nowhere without a map. In the years that followed, we pushed hard to defend and nurture our new baby brand by continuing to introduce whimsical and unexpected flavour combinations made using best-in-class ingredients. It's years later and I still smile at the faded black spray paint splat tattooed to the parking lot asphalt as I walk into the office each morning.

Let it Simmer ~

1. *Should you be changing course in light of new facts or are you stubbornly holding steady because of your ego and the inconvenience associated with changing direction midstream?*
2. *Are you in bed with the right supply partner? Do the easy steps feel easy?*

3. Before you open your wallet too far for costly prototypes and the like, think 'clever arts & crafts' and make it work with super-snazzy mock-ups backed by a proper and compelling story and plan.

4. When your supply partner is in a development-rut, can you jump on a plane, train or automobile and visit them to help things move along and stay put until the job gets done?

5. Ignorance is bliss and can sometimes work in your favour. Are you backing down or changing your approach or slowing your speed because you should, or only because someone's told you 'that's not the way it works around here?'

6. Even if you're ready to launch your product, is it the right time of year? Will waiting another few months or more increase the degree of your success? Take a breath and rethink before you pull the trigger.

7. There is no task beneath you on the road to launch—visit stores one-by-one if you must to get the job done.

8. Believe in your mission and its purpose deeply and it will go light-years further.

CHAPTER 20

Worst Thing Since Sliced Bread

Proper Due Diligence

A smoky, salty, meaty and gooey cheese revelation—this was my first impression of my first heaping mouthful of the Reuben sandwich from The Bread Vault Bakery. Let me explain. This was no ordinary lunchtime sandwich; the fat-ass cut sourdough bread was baked in-house in a wood oven using an ancient recipe that incorporated a two-week-old pre-fermented 'poolish' dough starter. The primo smoked corned beef brisket and tangy Russian dressing were also made in small batches with love. Their finishing move, however, was the culinary clincher—whipped butter generously slathered on the outside bread slices to sear the entire sandwich on a flat top grill and seal in the goodness with molten Gruyère cheese.

The result was a crusty and chewy golden food-porn masterpiece. To boot, it was served on an attractive reclaimed-wood plank. Despite our initial trepidation with investing in the business, Dave and I stared at each other confidently after downing the first bite with nostrils fully flared as if to say: '*Hot damn, this is too good! Way better than we expected.*' If it weren't for that corned beef narcotic, we wouldn't have lost $80,000 in less than three months.

Jimmy was beyond intense, he was a borderline madman—but we liked him instantly. We quickly got the feeling that he was grossly misunderstood (by literally everyone) and took on the demanding role of becoming both his protector and his interpreter to the outside world. After a meeting, we used to say: '*Okay, let's try to decode what Jimmy actually meant.'* Or: *'Did you run that one through the Jimbo-filter?'* In the beginning, we blindly trusted his capabilities; after all, he'd once been the President for a number of years at a successful and well-known power tool company. Now, he was a skittish entrepreneur desperately looking for guidance and a quick capital injection to take his budding, but bleeding, upscale quick service bakery / restaurant concept into the black and on to the next level.

It was something fresh and different, but as always, still all about great food. We are forever searching for that extra degree of passion that causes a true foodie to dig deep to find those culinary gems. To find the too good to be true and to make discovery of the rare and great and then to share it with like-minded consumers. Our interest, however, wasn't in taking over the restaurant's operations—instead, it was in polishing the concept so that it was marketable on a much larger stage as a franchise restaurant opportunity.

With its fresh baked artisanal breads made from ancient recipes, extravagant sandwiches and sinfully decadent desserts, we had the feeling there could be a lot more neighbourhood street corners inhabited by The Bread Vault. As we sat across the white-and-red-checkered table in the local diner down the street from our future investment to close the deal, I should have paid closer attention to the fidgety guy sitting next to Jimmy. He was a key staff member at The Bread Vault that had tagged along with Jimmy for moral support—or so we thought. Thinking back, we also should have paid more attention to the Head Chef's odd behaviour.

A week or so before offering our agreement terms, we walked through the restaurant to get a sense of the assets, the processes, the people and the problems. Chef Ted pulled me aside in secret to explain that the restaurant's concept, the wonderful recipes and the staff were all his doing, not Jimbo's. Although I recognized his actions and angle to be peculiar at the time, I thought he was just trying to impress me or lobby for early support and respect—boy, was I wrong with this one too. In the end, the condition we used to structure our agreement would prove to be a life (and bank balance) saver; namely, complete strategic control in exchange for general guidance, business planning and capital investment via a line of credit that could be converted into fifty percent ownership in the business at our option within a certain period of time.

The key was that we didn't sign on as legal partners out of the gate. We were lenders with a set of house keys and a significant voice—this type of deal structure is called a convertible debenture—I suggest googling it before you sign on as an official partner to an existing business in need of capital and guidance. Just think of it as living with your potential spouse before officially tying the knot. If they turn out to be nutso, you can pack up your things and bolt. You may have to leave behind a high-priced cappuccino machine and fancy Dyson vacuum, plus a few months' rent—but it's cheaper, quicker and less painful than hiring a divorce lawyer and getting dragged through the mud.

Before we officially visited the restaurant to address the staff and key suppliers, we took it upon ourselves to call up every person on Jimmy's list who was owed money. The list of irritated suppliers and lenders holding out their hands for money was plentiful. I was honest in my approach: *'Listen, I'm not the new owner. Our company is lending money and guidance to help The Bread Vault from going belly up. If you wait this thing out, you get a big fat zero. Good luck taking legal action as there's not even enough value in the business to pay the secured creditors (i.e. the banks, the equipment leasing company, etc.). Agree to take half (or less) today, and we'll cut you a cheque tomorrow.'* Aside from an uncompromising Calabrese-Italian food supplier (surprise, surprise), the lion's share of supplier grievances was mopped up—or so we thought based on what was formally shared with us during the due diligence period.

A few days before signing the agreement, it became all too clear that Chef Ted and Jimmy were at great odds. Daily disputes and a power struggle between the two were taking a toll on the staff, and ultimately, on the business. Jimmy felt that he had had no control over the business he had bled for to build. What's more, the Chef found that ensuring Jimmy stayed out of the building on deliveries and menial chores was mandatory to keeping the peace.

The genuine problem, as it is with most restaurant start-ups, was the financials. Each week, it was costing twice as much as the sales they generated to keep the doors open. A deeper exploration revealed that the Chef's salary was a huge encumbrance. Jimmy felt confident that he could strap on a Chef's apron without having the restaurant lose a beat. *'I know how to make most of the menu, and we can learn the rest,'* he assured us. Parting ways with the Chef, although risky, was inevitable. The Chef called me shortly after he was asked to leave. It was difficult, but we were able to reach a place of mutual respect and I agreed to help him transition elsewhere with regards to money he was owed, among other things. By this point, Dave and I contemplated cutting bait as we hadn't invested any serious funds and began to smell something funky, but then decided that the risk was still tolerable and held off on releasing our catch.

As we pulled up to the restaurant on a crisp and early Monday morning in September, we were genuinely excited to meet and address the team. We had flown to New York the week prior to scout out a few popular bakery concepts and returned inspired. We had innovative ideas, unique designs, clever promotions and fresh recipes in tow—all crafted to make The Bread Vault sexier and more marketable as a franchise opportunity. We knew a good year or two was needed to let the new direction settle in and take shape, but we were game.

As I stepped out of the car, I noticed Chef Ted nervously pacing back and forth in front of the restaurant. *'That's interesting and unfortunate,'* I thought, as I knew Jimmy had let him go the week before. How did the staff feel about his sudden departure? How would they feel seeing their ship-less captain bobbing around the restaurant window? Not good, it turns out. Not good at all. As I addressed the young men and women wearing their baker's whites, Jimmy's uncle and that fidgety guy who sat beside Jimmy during our contract signing watched awkwardly from the sidelines. The more I explained that Jimmy would be assuming the reins as the rightful heir to his bread throne, the more his subjects seemed in pain and discomfort. And then ... bada bing, bada boom —the brown bagels hit the fan.

Some staff decided to quit and storm out while making a dramatic exit, while the others seemed distantly interested, yet very much guarded. From that point forward, it was a downhill ride to mouldy bread town. Every day, beneath every small and large stone we unearthed complications and silliness. Solving them should have been easier than it was, but we also had to operate within the mental quicksand that the 'Jimbo-filter' added to the equation.

Weekly sales routinely fell short by about fifty to sixty percent of covering the restaurant's basic overheads. Our first order of business was to understand the production processes with a fundamental goal of restructuring labour, challenging food costs and the menu itself. The amount of spoiled and unsold goods, and the labour it took to prepare them, was ugly. The thing about baking artisanal fresh bread the way The Bread Vault was preparing it is that you require an experienced baker or two to work throughout the night. To boot, without Chef Ted, Jimmy and his adorable uncle had to try and figure out how to prep and bake, in addition to running the bakery during its hours of operation.

As you can imagine, trying to run a struggling business on next to zero sleep, few breaks or sign of daylight is like leaving your buns in the wood oven until they burn black and dry up. Instead of focusing on what made the bakery unique and popular, Jimmy panicked and tried to find solutions by concentrating on new ideas and investments. Instead of worrying about why we were losing $1 for every beautiful homemade butter croissant that we sold for $2.50, we spent exhausting hours convincing him that we shouldn't renovate the second floor into a private dining / event space; or, despite their apparent popularity, taking his uncle's famous cheese and wiener windups off the menu so that he could hone his skills on executing the menu we wanted to eventually franchise.

What should have been an undertaking that cost us the equivalent of investing a full day or so per week, quickly mutated into a full-time responsibility that, above all else, was hugely physically and mentally exhausting. Dave and I would leave the restaurant feeling like we'd just stepped out of a boxing ring—dazed and confused. On the days we didn't visit The Bread Vault, we'd both spend our car rides to work and back home, and everything in between, on the phone trying to get Jimmy aligned with our thinking. Near the end of our short journey, we were spending more time trying to correct wrongs and dodge perilous bullets from a handful of parties owed money that weren't 'captured' on our original clean-up list.

By this point, we had been sufficiently warned about Jimmy's peculiar modus operandi by staff, suppliers and even store customers. Buying the business outright didn't make sense either as aside from the warped baggage and inconvenient travel time, Jimmy's compensation expectations were out to lunch compared with what the business was actually worth.

Of course, the circus eventually had a destructive, time sucking effect on our core business at BrandFusion. Once we realized this, we pulled the ripcord hard and fast. Yes, it hurt, but after a few days or so, we felt our energy return and decided our financial loss should be viewed as an investment to further our food education—four years' tuition and residence fees squeezed into a quarter of a year. Most importantly, and the reason for our relatively easygoing departure, was the structure of our deal. The convertible debenture allowed us to disengage and move on without the fear of further penalties or exposure with the host of new conflicts bubbling and brewing. Although, in all fairness to Jimbo, that damn Reuben sandwich and those bedevilled beautiful butter croissants were off the chart delicious.

Let it Simmer ~

1. *If you are investing in an existing business, can you structure the deal so that you can walk away relatively easily and inexpensively if it's not what you thought it would be?*
2. *Do you trust your inner voice or are you ignoring it and your gut instincts because it's too difficult or uncomfortable to cut bait and disappoint others involved?*
3. *Have you worked to expose all the rotten layers before taking the reins, or should you listen and observe more before taking the stage?*
4. *New opportunities take time and patience before they can stand on their own. Can you be there and be fully engaged and involved until the business can survive with less of your time?*
5. *Is your core business suffering as a result of newer and perhaps more 'seemingly' exciting prospects? If so, can you divide your time wisely and competently?*

6. *Will your prospective new business partner bring value and save you time or create additional work and avoidable anxiety?*

7. *If the business owes unsecured creditors money, have you tried to settle or simply assume the liabilities at face value as part of the deal?*

CHAPTER 1 | Gathering Substance. **TOP LEFT:** Standing on the front steps of the Beta Brands candy factory in London, Ont. — aka my CPG Food Industry University (June 1998, photo credit: Derek Ruttan); **TOP RIGHT:** *Strategy Magazine* photo shoot with JP (Aug 1998, photo credit: Stephen Uhraney); **BOTTOM:** Good times (Summer 1999). My Beta Brands farewell bash: Unbeknownst to me, coworkers had the local radio station (FM96) broadcast that the woman to eat the most Lifesavers candy off my body wins tickets to a Matthew Good Band concert. After feeding me a few too many barley pops and decking me out in a hand-sewn ensemble, a pack of she-wolves was unleashed. Check out the hungry lady snacking on a candy chunk from my armpit!

CHAPTER 6 | Eat in Moderation, Not Deprivation. **TOP:** An open window with a colourful view, taken from my office at BrandFusion. **BOTTOM:** Grand opening of Gabo Wabo's Popsicle Bar. My Son, the little bugger, must've raked in more profit than BrandFusion that day—and that's even after factoring in the rent we charged him to set up shop.

2000

2004

2008

2014

CHAPTER 7 | Pop Goes the World. Keepin' it fresh. Packaging evolution of Kernels Popcorn Shakers.

CHAPTER 8 | Pope Goes the World. **TOP:** Popcorn pop-up shop at World Youth Day (Toronto 2002). **MIDDLE:** Popcorn purgatory: Over 500,000 hungry mouths and we end up selling a whopping 75 of the 20,000 bags of popcorn procured for the event. **RIGHT:** Events van—aka dreaded family moving van.

CHAPTER 9 | Lost in New York. **LEFT:** Gravity-fed wire racks created a slight opening that allowed cold air to escape from freezer—game over. **RIGHT:** The *New York Times* Headline ... Potato Chips Chase Goes Stale. Underdog Wiener Wins!

Grilling ... Mediterranean Style.

Available exclusively at these fine stores:

We're fresh obsessed.

CHAPTER 10 | Opa! **TOP:** Retailer exclusivity programs may seem like a basic notion on the surface, but can prove to be a very persuasive and powerful device. **BOTTOM:** The guys and I serve up souvlaki to A&P / Dominion head office staff in their office parking lot. Yep, that's me, 3rd from the right, standing beside Mr. Raios (President of Mr. Greek). And yes, I'm well aware that I look a tad, um, George-Costanza-stocky? Blame it on the ultra-strict diet of barbequed jumbo pork souvlaki and Kefalotyri cheese! Listen, I take my work seriously ;)

CHAPTER 11 | Damn Turmeric. The original television celebrity chef and our family's first food hero, the much-loved Chef Pasquale Carpino (1936-December 30, 2005).

CHAPTER 12 | A Slice Of Pizza Pie. Creamy garlic gladiator: Thanks to tapping into an untapped consumer eating ritual and to finding the perfect space in the grocery store, our Pizza Pizza Dips have endured many years in the deli refrigerator.

CHAPTER 13 | Cocktail Dreams.
TOP: A decade after I pulled the plug on my chance to collaborate with Sammy Hagar, I was able to share our Crazy Uncle Über Caesar with him.
LEFT: Full circle—although we never did launch a Cabo Wabo lime margarita cocktail mix, we ended up creating a Basil, Honey & Lime Daiquiri under our Crazy Uncle culinary cocktail line.

CHAPTER 17 | Milkin' It. Ease up on the gas pedal. Avoid embracing too much, too quickly: *'Fast is fine, but accuracy is everything'* — Xenophon, Greek Historian of the 4th century BC.

CHAPTER 18 | Boiling Over. Luckless patrons of The *Lost Pantry*: Kernels chocolate covered caramel popcorn packed inside a jumbo foil-wrapped Easter egg, Golden Griddle Breakfast Sausages, Booster Juice Alphonso Mango Smoothies, and Eating in Japan Stir Fry Meal Kits.

CHAPTER 19 | Catching a Buzz.
TOP ROW: The birth of Crazy Uncle—from quick n' dirty retailer presentation mock-ups to an award-winning packaging design.
MIDDLE LEFT: Strength in numbers—Dave and I visit our flavour team in Kentucky to put a final spin and approval on the recipe. **MIDDLE RIGHT:** Our Blood Orange, Rosemary & Maple Punch finally hits the shelf in the LCBO.
BOTTOM RIGHT: *The Globe and Mail* newspaper photo shoot with Dave (Oct 2013, photo credit: Jennifer Roberts).

CHAPTER 21 | Stinky Cheese & Anchovies. **CLOCKWISE FROM TOP LEFT:**
(1) Magic Miso marinade packaging design dilemma; (2) Kernels Blue Cheese
challenge; (3) 'Do you like my green eggs? No, we do not. We would not, could
not eat them anywhere!'. **BOTTOM RIGHT:** Crazy Uncle All Natural Über Caesar.
BOTTOM LEFT: Dave and I (left) chat with Michael and Guy Rubino about our
newfound partnership in advance of the launch of the latest Crazy Uncle
product (*Vaughan Citizen*, May 2014, photo credit: Adam Martin-Robbins).

CHAPTER 22 | Tomato Potato.
TOP: Rimmer seasoning sachet fiasco.
RIGHT: Butter oil packaging and
product positioning debacle.
BOTTOM: jack-o'-lantern candles
NOT included.

Brothers Bruno, left, and Davide Codispoti launched Crazy Uncle Hard Root Beer in Toronto this spring as "craft soda for grown-ups."

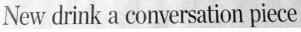

New drink a conversation piece

CHAPTER 24 | Feeding the Beast. **TOP LEFT:** *The Toronto Star* photo shoot with Dave (June 2016, photo credit: Melissa Renwick). **TOP RIGHT:** all natural Hard Root Beer. **BOTTOM LEFT:** waterbed-sized floor retail display. **BOTTOM RIGHT:** Following our serendipitous one-minute-sidewalk-pitch, *The Thirsty Traveler* snaps and posts a pic of our chance encounter. Photo credit: Kevin Brauch.

CHAPTER 28 | **Fruit Pulp Clouds & Chocolate Bloom**. Despite best-in-class ingredients and packaging, our Hail Mary pass, ***Crème de la Crème***, quickly spirals into ***Crème de la Crap*** because of humidity issues.

CHAPTER 30 | The Candy Man (Almost) Can. LifeSavers *NSYNC Sweet Sounds of Summer promo results were far more prosperous than my one night as a music mogul.

CHAPTER 31 | Milk Money. **ABOVE:** $120,000 for YTV's Marty the Mad Flavour Scientist provided zero sales lift. **RIGHT:** Limited Edition movie themed promotional shakers proved to be a win-win campaign, year after year, for both us and the movie studios.

CHAPTER 32 | Family Table. **TOP:** Family Circus: Cousin Chris, Enza Pulla and I participate in the Maple, Ontario Santa Claus Parade (Nov 2002). **BOTTOM LEFT:** Dave fires up the office grill to barbeque Korean short ribs for yet another bloody magnificent, yet typical, office lunch. **BOTTOM RIGHT:** A familiar face: My wife Lisa, lending Johnvince Foods her smile for a Sam Mills gluten free pasta TV commercial.

CHAPTER 33 | Putter or Butter. **TOP:** Choosing the butter over a putter: hanging with the boys around a smoking cauldron of Brother Milan's 'Beans Plus' soup simmering over an open fire. **BOTTOM:** Dave teaches a class on Neapolitan pizza making using Brother Milan's hand-forged-iron stone pizza oven at Waupoos Estates Winery in Price Edward County.

CHAPTER 21

Stinky Cheese & Anchovies

Cast a Larger Net

P ersonal taste can be awfully subjective—just because you love and crave a certain food or dish, it doesn't automatically mean that others will, or should, too. Archie, our long time BrandFusion associate, once told me his former boss at one of the leading Canadian grocery chains aimed to launch products under the premise of '*feed the masses if you want to eat with the classes.*' In other words, you'll need to move as many cases as you humanly can if you want to uncork that bottle of Bruno Giacosa Collina Rionda, Barolo DOCG. Yep, I know. I completely realize that this sounds super shallow and uncomfortably pretentious. That said, it's an accurate and brutally honest rule to remember if your endgame is to move volume. Incidentally, I've yet to uncork a Bruno Giacosa.

Speaking of wine, for example, I typically serve my homemade reserve when family and friends, less concerned with an appreciation of oenology, come over to dine. Once again, it's not that I'm shallow or pretentious, it's just that it truly pains me to watch a freezer burned ice cube bobbing up and down in decent glass of red. Once in a while when I do uncork a real beauty with the same crowd, and refuse to offer ice, the glasses remain nearly full. '*What's wrong with your wine?*' I'll inquire. '*It's too bold and barnyardy,*' they'll reply to which I'll then apologetically shrug my shoulders and retort: '*But, but ... that's a good thing!*'

Having said this, I'm the only one bothered at the table while my guests cheerfully sip their refreshing wine-coolers. The point being that they are in fact my guests (my customers) to please, so why should I force them to like or want or appreciate what I do. Conversely, when I was in high school and university, I made it a very premeditated point to order party-sized pizza, half with extra anchovies, as I knew it would guarantee me half the pizza, plus a couple of slices from the other side of the pie. When I worked at Quaker, one of our most popular *Crispy Minis®* Rice Chips flavours was Salt & Vinegar. The acidity level in the vinegar was so robust that it could make the roof of your mouth momentarily raw. After receiving a few consumer complaints, we decided to lower the acidity bite only to find that our most dedicated Salt & Vinegar fans stopped buying the product as frequently because they craved for and missed the burn.

In this particular case, our most dedicated fans drove enough of the overall sales volume that we decided to reinstate the vinegar-punch; go figure. It's difficult to assess how consumers will respond. Our experience suggests that, if you have the slightest inkling that consumers will nag about something, they eventually will; and let me tell you, there are some pretty aggressive and vocal people out there who spring at the chance to let you know how they feel. The good news is that most of the time, a speedy and favourable reply can ease the most boorish of critics. Who are you hoping to serve your dish to?

The story that leads up to Archie's '*feed the masses*' lesson is a good one to start with. He was part of a product development team that set out to re-engineer the Oreo® cookie by making it out of superior ingredients. The cream filling was made from pure Madagascar vanilla bean paste and the biscuits out of real cocoa and cane sugar. Amazingly, the consumer taste panel results were less than unacceptable. '*It just doesn't taste like my Oreo!*' consumers protested.

Scott Staiman (Kernels Popcorn Founder) refers to this situation as '*the burnt chocolate cake*' syndrome. He grew up eating and loving his Mother's chocolate cake, which always had a faintly burnt outer crust. No other chocolate cake could give him the same euphoric food-buzz. For Scott, his ultimately satiating recipe was much more about fond and comforting memories than about using good quality cocoa. Now, that's obviously not to say recipes and concepts that aim to elevate the status quo can't work. Today's taste buds have become dramatically more experienced, adventurous and selective.

A good friend of mine, Sal Consiglio, runs an established and popular namesake family business called Consiglio's Kitchen wear on St. Clair Avenue West in Toronto. He's been prominently displaying and selling quality imported espresso machines for well over a decade. It wasn't too long ago that he remembers non-Italian customers fearfully opting out of investing in a machine because espresso just didn't taste like their coveted Tim Horton's blend; it was too strong, too dark and too foreign. Nowadays, Sal is peppered with questions like: '*Are your espresso beans single origin? Is the machine's grinder ceramic or metal? How do I achieve a denser crema?*' Mama mia, are we in Toronto or Milan!?

Come to think of it, this also feels like a good time to quickly touch on the weightiness of product consistency, and how it can even trump product quality at times. Sticking to the topic of espresso, I was once bewitched by a hauntingly perfect cappuccino. The café's owner-barista was a veritable maestro on the *Faema*®.

On an otherwise very routine morning, I stopped in to visit the maestro and to order my roasty-toasty narcotic. Alas, he wasn't there. When the nameless barista handed me my drink, I could immediately tell that the magic was missing just by how the bubbly foam stared back at me in the cup. One tiny sip and ... Yup, I was right, it tasted average at best.

A few mornings later, the maestro was back at the wheel. '*Just so you know, the past few days my cappuccinos haven't come close to your beautiful babies*' I declared with a slight smirk. He glared back at me with a step-off-buddy look. '*What a backhanded compliment!*' he started, '*you don't know how much I hate hearing that! I haven't been able to teach any of my employees to make their coffees look and taste line mine. It's killing my business whenever I'm not here. I can't bloody leave. I've actually decided to lower the quality of my own cappuccinos a bit so that they're at least more consistent with how the other baristas make 'em. That way, eventually, no one will complain, and I can call in sick every once in a while.*'

Unreal. The maestro actually chose to operate below his capabilities and personal standards in an effort to *not* disappoint customers and to keep them coming back. Consistency is king. File and bank that frothless wonder before signing off on your final masterpiece.

I've had my fair share of food creations that have soared high over everyone's head—my first and most memorable was early in my consumer packaged goods (CPG) career at the McCormick's candy factory in London, Ontario. *'I have a feeling this one will be the runaway confection hit of the Easter season!'* I remembered promising Blair. *'I know we can't technically license Dr. Seuss' Green Eggs & Ham property, but ... if we make the egg's chocolate-y coating green and then colour the marshmallow-yolk fillings with a vivid red, purple or blue, folks will surely make the connection.'* Blair looked at me funny. *'Trust me!'* I reassured him further. *'We can even design our packaging in a very familiar, but not exact, Seuss-ian style.'*

I respect Blair for granting me the freedom to try such a stupid idea, and then backing me up with the sales department when they looked at him funny. I remember having such a strong emotional tie to the book and to the idea. I also remember not showing my green eggs around enough when Pam Watson from our R&D lab furnished me with tasting samples. I must've eaten the box and saved one or two for Blair and the sales team. The packaging didn't end up having that *Seuss-ian* vibe I envisioned as apparently no one else made the connection to the popular children's story. Nearly twenty years later, Blair and I still laugh about this fiasco. *'Do you like my green eggs? No, we do not. I would not, could not eat them anywhere!'*

A few years back, Dave and I rallied to launch a blue cheese Kernels Popcorn seasoning. We had become bored of introducing straightforward chip-inspired flavours like cheddar, dill pickle, bbq, ketchup, etc. Outside of the office, our love of good food and food exploration had matured so we wanted to introduce a flavour we thought was more culinary-worthy. *'Who doesn't like a strong and stinky blue cheese?'* We chose to ignore the fact that most of our consumers were kids and families. We gave little thought to better understanding and to respect our existing sales rankings—dill pickle and white cheddar had been our workhorse flavours since the beginning.

Nonetheless, during the flavour development phase, we scarfed down bowl after bowl of blue cheese popcorn in the office and at home.

It was indisputably our new favourite flavour. It ended up being our worst selling flavour ... ever. In a desperate attempt to bolster sales, we changed the packaging design and product name to *Blue Cheese RANCH*, thinking and hoping that the addition of the more chip-familiar 'RANCH' reference would connect with more folks. It actually did, but not nearly enough as it's all about repeat sales and not deceiving someone in order that they pick up another bottle, bag or box.

Similarly, the ready-to-eat popcorn category (popped popcorn in a bag) has been on the rise as of late. Walking the Fancy Food Show in San Francisco a couple of years ago, we couldn't help but notice the number of start-up companies trying to squeeze their way into the clogged category with similar off-centre flavours such as Curry & Cool Yogurt, or Sundried Tomato & Parmesan to name a couple. The flavours sounded and tasted great, the packaging looked fresh and attractive. And yet, aside from a select few brands (namely the ones with either established distribution or deep pockets or both), the majority of product introductions failed when we checked back a year or so later. Show me the volume!

Funnily enough, a number of popcorn companies, both established and start-ups, have recently found success, and the ability to co-exist in a clogged category, with the simplest of flavour approaches—premium popping corn, small-batch popped using a good salt and healthier oil (i.e. avocado oil, expeller pressed coconut oil, etc.). It was frustrating to witness the market entry and triumph of so many new popcorn players with such a simple concept, while we self-indulged in our stinky blue cheese.

The paradox then becomes: When does improving on certain food products fail (i.e. using Madagascar vanilla cream for Oreo cookies), and when does it work (i.e. popcorn made with sea salt and expeller pressed coconut oil)? Consider that the impetus for eating an Oreo cookie (or in my case, an entire row or two) might be reward or stress determined so comfort and gratification in familiarity is key. For eating popcorn, choosing a healthier snack alternative might be the goal, in which case changing the status quo by offering better ingredients is both acceptable and desirable.

These days, we try to hit the sweet spot between satisfying our maturing culinary palates while staying relevant and engaging to a market segment that's large enough to reach the necessarily volume targets. It's about having to be willing to massage and to compromise your recipe and packaging. It's also knowing when to stand your ground and take a chance on pushing something fresh and new. It should go without saying that, if you don't fully and completely believe in your product and its narrative, it'll be a short-lived love affair. When you compromise too much, it'll surface in the form of uninspiring sales pitches, an unwillingness to invest enough money, etc.

One of our fan favourites and proudest culinary accomplishments is with our Crazy Uncle® cocktail brand, aptly named the *Über Caesar.* (Note: the Caesar is Canada's self-proclaimed official cocktail; it's similar to its US cousin, the Bloody Mary, but is made using a tomato-clam-based juice vs. a straightforward tomato base.) At first, we toyed around with dialling up the standard recipe with a clever culinary twist by adding in subtle notes of aged balsamic vinegar from Modena, Italy, and smoky Canadian bacon (a recipe trend that we noticed was becoming common in high-end restaurant prepared Caesars). In the end, we decided to stay true to the classic recipe by leaning on premium and all natural ingredients.

All other brands playing in the Caesar cocktail space were manufactured using MSG (monosodium glutamate), high fructose corn syrup and artificial colours and flavours. Our blend was inspired by the original all natural recipe (invented in Calgary, Alberta 1969), made using vine-ripened tomatoes, clam broth, grated horseradish, Lea & Perrins® Worcestershire and Tabasco®—by the way, I probably put Tabasco on twenty percent of everything I eat. The final result, which we enlisted the help of celebrity Chef Guy Rubino to assist us with, was a veritable culinary accomplishment in the field of pre-mixed cocktails. The experienced taste-panel at the LCBO were blown away. Sampling the cocktail at trade shows, parties and other events was a pure joy as people showered us with compliments and high-fives. Consumers were even willing to accept the slight settling of natural ingredients in the bottle despite being used to the competitor's more artificially homogenized and electric red appearance.

Our main obstacle was the higher retail driven by our small-batch process and expensive ingredients. Depending on how you define success, the launch was both a moderate triumph and a moderate letdown. Had we indulged our personal taste by adding in the aged balsamic and bacon notes, I don't think we would have sold a quarter of the bottles that we did. We were right in thinking that people would rather consume a straight forward, clean and honest Caesar that they in turn could personalize at home by adding other interesting ingredients. However, despite the accolades and glowing reviews from both consumers and media critics (feel free to google *Über Caesar reviews*), we only sold a quarter of what we forecasted in our first season.

The market segment that found purpose in our mission to provide an artisanal product without artificial ingredients just wasn't large enough. The majority of Caesar fans opted for the safer, more familiar and more affordable beverage—they went for the side of the party-sized pizza without the anchovies. Nonetheless, we still push and proudly sell the *Über Caesar* each spring and summer season. It hasn't made us rich, but it's worth the fight, both financially and strategically. For now, I'll have to hold off on buying that $1,031 bottle of Barolo and be happy with drinking my homemade red (without ice cubes).

At times, the fight isn't worth a long and drawn out battle so you'll have to find a clear path and pull the ripcord early enough to cushion the financial blow. There are a few food product categories that I wouldn't touch with a ten-foot zucchini; shelf-stable salad dressings and imported olive oil, to name a couple. Everybody and their brother has 'the best one ever' to sell and there's just too many players in the category vying for the same precious real estate. I was surprised then, when we found ourselves agreeing to take Chef Guy (and big brother Michael) Rubino's (star of the Food Network's '*Made to Order*' television show) miso-based marinade to market. Guy handed Dave, Archie and I a tasting-spoon each of the magic marinade in the kitchen of his (then) restaurant Ame. It tasted more like a wonderfully silky smooth savoury vanilla pudding than a marinade. What's more, miso paste is packed with enzymes that can efficiently tenderize protein in record time (which comes in handy in the restaurant business).

We ended up developing three skus using three different and unique miso pastes, all blended with sake (Japanese wine), mirin, tahini and cane sugar: a saikyo (golden) miso for fish, an aka (red) miso for chicken, and a hatcho (black) miso for beef. To help make our product stand out from the saturated sea of dressing and marinade bottles, we hired a marketing agency and charged them with the unlikely task of designing a brand and a package that was unorthodox and noticeably different than the norm. Like with most marketing agencies, we first spent a few good months delving deep into who we were both as individuals and as a company, what the narrative of the brand message should be, where we hoped the brand would be in 10 years, yada yada.

It's easy to get swept away in such self-indulgent rhetoric, so much so that you don't end up challenging the basics perhaps as much as you should. I remember reassuring ourselves with their design concept proposal saying: '*Hey, if the head designer and copywriter think we can be more distinctive by not showcasing the product name or flavour description as much as we usually do, let's roll the dice! After all, we did ask for something different, right?*' The agency believed that a simple and bold wallpaper-type pattern and the absence or diminished treatment of common design elements, such as emphasizing the product's purpose or description, would engage consumers and get them to pick up the product.

Well, it was a bad gamble. Consumers didn't know what the heck we were selling. Which, in hindsight, was unwise because we were trying to sell something slightly unknown and ethnic to begin with. Conversely, when we sampled the product at higher end grocers, such as Pusateri's, we couldn't keep the product from flying off the shelf. To be fair, I think it was also a case of falling in love with a niche product that could only cater to a select demographic. We had, yet again, fallen in love with the more adventurous side of the pizza stacked with anchovies and blue cheese.

Faced with the decision of sinking more money into a packaging redesign and increasing our marketing communication efforts, we decided to take a less onerous road. Instead of investing more money and then waiting for a year or two to see if the financial tide would turn, we approached one of Canada's largest food retail chains and offered our magic miso marinade to them exclusively for their more artisanal and selective private label product line. Sure we only made twenty percent of the profit we'd make selling the line under our own brand, but over the next couple of years we recouped the total cost of our investment—around $20,000. Had we continued down the original path, we would have had to dump three times as much in redesigns, listing fees, trade and consumer marketing, and most importantly, our time.

If you don't have the funds to invest in proper third party qualitative tests (a deep dive into what people think and feel) or quantitative tests (a measurement of how many people think or behave in a particular way), take matters into your own hands. Have friends, family, neighbours, your kid's classroom, etc. sample your product and provide structured feedback; just make sure you're getting feedback from the target audience you hope to eventually sell to—my Grandmother loved the Green Marshmallow Eggs but then again, she loves everything that I do. Most importantly, develop a thick skin. Listen, don't speak and defend. When people tell you to change everything that you've done, take a breath and find that one worthwhile nugget to use. When you push the go button and finally move forward, keep your high-five hand in your pocket.

I never get overly excited when the first purchase order finally comes in, no matter how large it may be—it's only the pipeline fill required to stock the shelves. If it doesn't sell, I'm eventually getting the cleanup invoice. I don't even care about the second order—it's only the back-up refill for the retailer's warehouse so they have product 'if' your product should sell. If it doesn't sell, now you're getting an even larger cleanup invoice. Now, the third order, that's something worth grinning about and giving your teammates a quiet low-five over. It suggests your product isn't collecting dust. And remember, in the food business, we make our fortune one dollar at a time. If you're looking to generate volume, consider that it's sometimes best to stick with an affordable and basic good quality cheese pizza and lay off the anchovies if you want everyone to enjoy a slice.

Let it Simmer ~

1. *What does success look like to you? How many cases will you need to conservatively move in order to keep your head above water?*
2. *Is your connection to your product concept mainly emotional or is it a logical and pragmatic one? Remember it's hard to hear and process reality, but it's crucial (and less expensive).*
3. *Is your mission fuelled by a self-indulgent passion play, or do you want to make serious money? Passion plays are okay too, but is there enough volume potential to provide the return required to keep things going and growing?*
4. *Does your product idea strike the balance between something you're passionate about but that many others will love and crave too?*
5. *Where do you expect to sell your product—at a weekend farmer's market or at 11,000 Walmart stores in 27 countries?*
6. *Have you tested your product to a point where you understand how consumers might respond? Have you tweaked and incorporated the results into your final masterpiece? Note: checkout surveymonkey.com.*

CHAPTER 22

Tomato Potato

What's in a Name?

Assigning a clear and clever product name and product description to your packaging design is considerably more important than you may think. Deciding on a perfect vessel to house your brainchild is equally as vital. It can be the difference between selling four hundred or four thousand cases. Consumers always seem to end up being both smarter and more capricious than you might presume. Each time we underestimate the finer points and nuances of what or how we communicate what we're selling on our packaging design, or what we pack it into, it comes back to haunt us. If the key messaging on your package design, or how it physically feels in the hand, overpromises what's in the box, bag or bottle you'll be reprimanded by consumers with softer than anticipated sales. If you offer your product in a jar or bottle when consumers subconsciously expect to buy it in a carton or a box, don't be surprised when it gets delisted six months after it hits the shelf.

Don't stretch the truth about what's actually in the package. Be clear and tell people what you're offering and why they might consider buying your product instead of the one sitting next to it. Taste, and in most cases smell, don't come in to play until the product makes it home, so shoppers will scrutinize your product on at least two basic and instinctive levels before tossing it into their cart—sight and touch. Now, you might fool folks the first time with a mixed matte and metallic printed carton, complete with holographic logos and high-definition images, but building your empire ultimately relies on creating sustainable purchase habits that lead to healthy repeat orders.

Does your product deliver on what it promises? Before making a decision on what to order in a restaurant, don't you study every option on the menu and carefully examine each ingredient and preparation technique associated with each dish? I sure do, and when my plate arrives at the table, it had better deliver on each seemingly little promise —my *carrot, ginger, coconut and lime soup* had better not taste like watered down *carrot and lime soup*. Every published detail becomes an impending consumer expectation by which you will be measured. If you're going to sell the sizzle, make sure your steak is worth the money.

One of the most challenging and chancy missions for a start-up enterprise working on a Slim Jim budget is to introduce products that are perhaps too original and ambitious. It usually takes a meaningful marketing budget and/or ingenious product awareness strategy to educate consumers on the efficacy and superior benefits of a completely original concept creation. Throwing down ten or twenty thousand dollars at a top marketing agency is like shopping at Harry Rosen with fifty bucks in your pocket—the most you're walking out with is a pair of dress socks or a pocket square. There's an army of smaller and more willing boutique agencies out there that are much more affordable— i.e. ten or twenty thousand dollars will get you the full wash and hot wax. In our experience, they seem to be most proficient at deep diving to better understand the relationship consumers have, or should have, with your product and brand. However, the execution and impact of their plan usually falls flat.

After six months, you'll realize that the same program and results could have been engineered in-house for a fraction of the budget. You'll also realize that your money would be better spent investing with retailers on in-store activities—e.g. aggressive temporary price reductions (TPRs), flyer ads, air mile contributions, off-shelf point-of-purchase (POP) displays, sweepstakes and contests, rebates, product sampling, etc. If you do have a truly innovative product concept and a worthwhile story to tell, consider ringing up a PR agency specializing in consumer packaged goods to help you spread the good word. Note: Despite your Mother's incredible excitement for your adventure, most products and stories aren't as newsworthy and interesting to the public as you might think. Be honest with yourself before putting too many eggs in this basket.

Until you build your business to a level where empowering the right marketing agency match is within financial reach, your package and design has to do the majority of the heavy lifting. Before you start piecing together your packaging art brief for the designer, run out to a handful of grocery stores, drug stores and club stores to buy both the products that you'll be competing against as well as any products that have a look and feel that you'd like to integrate into your efforts. What can you learn from their design, messaging and overall approach and how can you improve on it? What mistakes have they made and how can you avoid making the same ones?

In 2001 we developed a naturally flavoured butter oil for both popping and topping popping corn. We marketed the product under our Kernels brand as a no trans fat, shelf stable, easier alternative to using real butter. To make the launch both less risky and more affordable, we decided to use our contract packer's stock plastic bottle to avoid having to invest in a custom shaped bottle. Unfortunately, the stock bottle looked much too conventional and felt more evocative of a cheaper cooking oil so it confused consumers and completely missed the mark: *'Why would I pay $3.99 for a 400ml bottle of cooking oil when I can buy a 1L bottle for the same price?'*

The 'real butter flavour' messaging and the product's 'popping and topping' purpose was also difficult to decipher for the consumer. As a result, in 2004 we decided to source and invest in a more playful bottle and adjusted the focus and balance of the package design. At nearly twelve thousand dollars, the new bottle mould wasn't cheap, but we felt that, with another new and fresh design and clearer messaging, it was worth the risk.

We ultimately failed with this product concept after less than a year in the marketplace. Was it because we launched with an ill-suited and undesirable bottle format? Yes, I think so, in part. But my gut says the main contributor was because we also over promised and under delivered on what was inside the bottle. We over-packaged and over-designed what we were selling. In retrospect, I don't believe the product concept solved a meaningful consumer problem. Popcorn is, more or less, considered a healthy snack alternative, so dousing it in a *'butter flavoured'* oil might not have been a popular choice. If a consumer is looking to occasionally cheat and indulge, they'll reach for the real McCoy and a pot to melt it in.

We've run and tripped through the same motions with our Kernels Popping Corn product. The product was originally launched in a clear and humble looking plastic jar with a simple and straightforward label design. The sales volume was more than worthwhile. Actually, it was our best seller from a per store, per week, per unit perspective. Somewhere down the line we decided to kick the packaging up a notch and called it *'Premium' Popping Corn* and packed the corn into a fully printed and re-sealable stand-up pouch. The new design relied less on showing the actual product, and more on flair. It cost us slightly more, so we charged slightly more for it. Consumers responded loud and clear by cutting our sales in half. Once again, we over-packaged the product.

I've always found it challenging to balance personal tastes with what will actually work with, and engage, consumers. I respect that many have succeeded by never compromising their vision. I've read the Steve Job biographies and get the whole *'consumers don't know what they want'* mantra. In the consumer packaged goods business, however, I believe it's more of a careful balance between tapping into existing consumer expectancies and behaviours while sticking to a unique vision. Sure, you want and need to be in love with what you ultimately end up with in order to actually believe in it and then sell it. But, at the same time, you have to be relevant and connect with a large enough pool of shoppers to float your boat.

Remember the *'feed the masses and eat with the classes'* adage. Let's delve deeper into the misstep on the packaging design for our Magic Miso Marinade that I touched on in the previous chapter. We desperately wanted to avoid looking like every other marinade on the shelf because we wanted to stand out from the competition—the salad dressing and marinade category is inundated with similar looking bottles and jars. Perhaps slightly less obvious, but equally important, we also needed to be different in order to be emotionally attracted to the mission. Contrary to our proven packaging design modus operandi, we reluctantly agreed not to underscore the product's name or even its usage intent—that is, we didn't come out and scream 'Miso Sauce' or 'Miso

Marinade' in big bold letters smack dab on the front of the package. This design relied heavily on being more interesting and eye-catching than obvious and informative.

I remember being at the printers for the press approval thinking that our gamble to be different than the norm would either payoff handsomely or cut us off at the knees before the race began. As I admitted to you earlier, it was the latter. We had sacrificed clarity for trying to be distinctive and paid for it. Had we possessed the consumer marketing budget to spread the good word, we might have stayed in the race for a while longer. More importantly, had we invested in balancing a more utilitarian design approach with a few unique elements, we could've finished the race unbroken.

In Canada, try not to fall deeply in love with a packaging design until you see how it looks and reads with the proper CFIA bilingual labelling requirements. I love Quebec. I love the French language, it's beautiful. To be sure, all three of my kids attend a French Immersion school in Ontario. It's unfortunate then that the implications of having to incorporate this second language onto your packaging design usually ends up upsetting the visual balance and appeal—the smaller the area you have to convey your messaging (i.e. spice jars vs. a cereal box) the more complicated the task.

Make sure your designer doubles up on the English copy before presenting you with any concepts for review. Doubling up on English copy defers having to pay for French translations before you're certain of what you want to say on your packaging design. Once you do commit to your copy and source the French translations, have a French speaking person examine the copy to ensure that it properly captures the nuances of what you're trying to communicate. I'll never forget getting a call one November from a confused consumer who had just bought a carton of our Kernels Halloween microwave popcorn—it actually popped up orange. They had called to let us know the orange candles weren't included in the box? 'Sorry Sir, orange candles?' I shrugged my shoulders. 'Yes, on your box it says Chandelles orange!' he explained.

I looked at a box in my office: 'No, sorry. Chandelles orange means that the popcorn pops up orange!' Are you crazy, he scoffed, 'then your *translation should read Éclatement orange? Chandelles means candles! My wife thought that you included candles in your box for lighting up jack-o'-lanterns.'* Needless to say, triple check your translations if you want to accurately connect with the twenty plus percent of Canadians that speak French as a first language. Unless, of course, you can afford to squeeze a couple of candles into your carton.

There's a real finesse in choosing the right shade of a certain colour, or deciding how to express the inclusion of a key ingredient on your packaging design. It can make the difference between the product feeling fresh versus fake, or the recipe coming off as relevant versus tired and boring. I can't tell you how many swatches of orange I've stressed over in an effort to accurately depict the quality and taste of cheese enhanced products. Softer and warmer oranges typically feel more natural than what we facetiously refer to as *'pylon orange'*, which marks a more electric and artificial cheese. Or better still, our number one orange-enemy, 'Brady Brunch orange' which we use to describe oranges that fall into more of a seventies–shag-carpet kind of space—who wants to eat cheddar cheese pizza dip from a 70s coloured container? I'm also constantly amazed at how slightly tweaking a package by changing a colour's shade and a word or two can give a struggling product its second life.

During my brief stint at Quaker Oats Canada, we couldn't understand why our *'Original'* flavoured Crispy Minis® was our worst seller, despite *'Original or Regular'* potato chips representing the lion's share of all potato chip sales. We decided to keep the recipe exactly the same, but tweaked the packaging design by changing its primarily navy blue bag to a more pleasing aqua blue colour. We also changed the product name from *'Original'* to *'Sea Salt.'* And boom, there's your double digit growth. The *'Original'* flavour description and navy blue bag was much too dull against the other, more alive, flavours in the line-up. Our changes were successful in making the product more interesting without over promising what was in the bag.

One of our best Crazy Uncle® cocktail inventions was our *Cola Bitters and Mint Julep.* Up until a few weeks leading up to the maiden production run, the colour of the liquid was a refreshing bright caramel brown. The colour of the foil-stamped copy on the bottle label was set to be a refreshing Caribbean-ocean blue. During production, we made two last minute changes that ultimately killed the consumer's first impressions of what we were offering them. Feeling uncertain that consumers might not connect a cola-themed cocktail with a lighter and brighter brown, we darkened the liquid colour significantly so that it resembled a traditional dark brown cola soft drink. During the press approval of the bottle label, the pressman apologized at the last minute for not having enough ocean blue foil and offered us the option of using a silver foil instead. We agreed. We were wrong.

The cocktail was developed for summertime. It was meant to come across as fresh, fun and refreshing. Instead, the darker liquid colour set against a more serious silver foil gave the product a more refined and mature appearance—instead of screaming pool party, we screamed old guy drinking alone in his living room—we missed the mark. Consumers that actually sampled and purchased the product repeatedly commented on how the cocktail surprisingly tasted so much more bright and refreshing than they had expected it to taste. When in doubt, hit the pause button—even if you have to temporarily upset your supply partners and retailers. Ship your product the way you know it should look and taste, as everyone involved will eventually move on to putting out the next fire. If you push things through because you're not up to rocking the boat, it's over before it's even begun.

It's amazing how one tiny little packaging element can become the single thread that unravels your chances for success. To boot, it always seems to be the most unexpected and seemingly frivolous detail, that one stupid thing that you never bother to have your eye on. It can take years to line up all the various pieces of your puzzle—i.e. recipes, formulas, supply partners (i.e. contract packers and suppliers of raw material ingredients and packaging), designs, retailers, a sales team, marketing campaigns, etc. It seems unfair then, that it only takes a seemingly petty product or packaging calamity to destructively change how your story unfolds.

Picture this: Days before your opening order is set to ship, your manufacturer notifies you that they can't, and in fact won't, pack your order as they can't seem to fit the declared weight into the package.

What will you do when you receive a phone call from your custom's broker informing you that your fully-loaded trailer of goods isn't being permitted into the US as your packaging design should've included a 'Made in Canada' declaration? What's your plan when a large retail chain commands you to take back your forty pallets of fresh product because it has become apparent that the majority of the bags appear to have broken seals?

Been there, done that. Our most germane story is a painful tale of not-so-sticky elastic bands. When we launched our Crazy Uncle Cola Bitters and Mint Julep craft cocktail, we sold it with a free sachet of artisanal rimmer seasoning attached to the bottle. It should be noted that not many, if any, alcohol brands include a free add-on with their bottle as part of their everyday product offering. Finding a dependable solution for attaching the rimmer sachet to the bottle was challenging. We spent a great deal of time and too much money to get it right. Searching online, we stumbled across a manufacturer of custom elastic attachments out of Worthington, Minnesota.

We worked closely with them to develop a horseshoe-shaped elastic with adhesive applied to each end. We then manually threaded the elastic through the handle-ring on the bottle's neck and attached the sachet to the sticky ends. The system, and sachet of rimmer seasoning, cost us way too much and ate into our margins more than we felt comfortable with—a difficult decision given that the sachet was a free add-on.

Otherwise, everything else seemed to line up in our favour during the inaugural production run. Our carefully crafted small batches of booze tasted fantastically delicious. You could imagine our disbelief and instant heartache when we walked into a store the very day after the product was shipped only to learn that each rimmer sachet was either missing, or worse, was crumpled up and sitting on the shelf or floor. Turns out that, when we tested the adhesive's effectiveness, we used an unvarnished material instead of using the varnished substrate we ended up using for our sachets. The adhesive wasn't sticking to the varnished material.

Nearly two years of jumping through hundreds of mini hoops to get the launch just right, and within three days of hitting the shelf we were fielding irate calls from our sales team, shoppers and (gulp) retailers asking us what the deal was. In the end, we lost a great deal of sales because consumers assumed the bottles were picked over. Once again, it was a classic case of the tail wagging the dog as our free add-on had cost us dearly in both margin and the consumer's first impressions. It's years later and we're still apologizing to store managers for the not-so-sticky elastic debacle.

Please, don't underestimate any detail. The price of being labelled as *'annoyingly repetitive'* is much smaller than a not-so-sticky elastic band that wards off consumers. Funny story: I remember trying to explain to one of my first reports at Quaker that holding someone's hand can be a pain in the ass, but it's necessary to minimize unwelcome surprises. Instead, it mistakenly came out something like this: *'You know, Kelly, holding someone's ass can be a pain in your hand, but it's very necessary if you want things done right.'* Luckily she had a decent sense of humour.

Let it Simmer ~

1. *Is your product name and its description perhaps too cute and clever, at the expense of being clear enough for consumers to quickly recognize what you're offering? Does everyone get 'it', or is it just you? Mock-up a package or two, and show it around to friends and family. Visit a store and ask the manager if you can put your mock-up on the shelf next to your competition (and quietly snap a picture or two)—which package stands out more? Which one looks more enticing and appetizing?*

2. *Who is your main target audience? Is your product 'dressed' to their tastes, or more towards your own?*

3. *Have you conducted a decent cross section of store checks to better understand what consumers are habituated to seeing and buying (e.g. large chain stores, smaller independents, department stores, drug stores, club stores and convenience stores)? What do you think a shopper's initial instincts and expectations might be? Is your packaging design and vessel in line, or does it miss the mark because it's either too plain, too novel or just too much?*

4. *Have you stretched the truth in an effort to build a superior packaging message or have you accurately described what's in the box? Have you over designed and over complicated your packaging, or does it reflect the standard and aim of your offer?*

5. *Is your product creation actually solving a consumer problem or filling a category void? If so, is your targeted retail premium worth the solution?*

6. *Before you run to invest all of your consumer budget with a marketing agency, have you sufficiently budgeted for in-store trade marketing efforts? One way to avoid this misstep is to assign a set dollar amount per case towards both trade and consumer marketing budgets—skip ahead to* Chapter 31: Milk Money *for more info on this topic.*

7. *Have you judiciously combed over each seemingly trivial detail with an OCD-worthy filter, or are you blindly trusting your supplier partners a little too much?*

CHAPTER 23

Chew With Your Mouth Closed

When to Debut Your Idea

'Work hard in silence, let success be your noise'
—Frank Ocean

D ave and I have had more than our fair share of bright ideas blatantly ripped off and plagiarized. With each ugly pilfering, we become slightly more jaded and protective. However, most of the time, we're only pissed off for half a day and then let it slip and slide off. It's not in our character to harbour destructive feelings and allow them to cultivate. Our sacred golden rule has always been to operate in a mode that holds the conscience clear and free. Or, as mentioned throughout this book, to operate in a way that allows us to sleep well at night. By this very nature, despite sometimes sacrificing investments and prospective profits, we usually let things slide and then try to unearth and preserve the lessons learned. We have our Dad to thank for us being built that way.

I could ramble on about certain episodes where we opened our mouth a little too early with the wrong guy or gal—like the time we were too hyped and perhaps too indiscreet about opening a walk-up window artisanal fast food concept in the charming ski village at Blue Mountain in Collingwood, Ontario. In search of feedback and advice, we shared our plans with someone who was already operating an eatery in the village.

While we waited patiently for the right piece of real estate to free up, *'BAM'* along comes the very same funky walk-up window food concept a mere few months later. Most likely, no one is interested in hearing us whimper about such immaterial events, as they're all too common. I can hear you screaming into the book: *'Your fault, buddy! You opened your big mouth and were too slow to the mark. Speed up, or get off the track.'* Okay, I'll give you this one. Reserve your final judgment, however, until I tell you this next little curious affair.

During the final celebratory confetti-filled scenes of the season finale for *American Idol* (Season 8, 2009), I turned to my lovely wife Lisa and whispered: *'I have an idea, Hun.'* I then began to wildly scribble down ideas and contacts for a reality food show that would centre on the grocery sector instead of restaurants, traditional cooking shows or food travel. Note: There were a hell of a lot fewer reality concepts on the food and travel focused networks in 2009. I remember looking over at the digital clock on my nightstand, noticing that the time was now 2 a.m. I had been in a trance, madly jotting down ideas and possible contact names for hours. I'm now thinking: *'I can't wait to share this beauty with the boys tomorrow morning.'*

Gripping my Thursday morning cappuccino too tightly, I proceeded to paint the big picture for the guys. We would conduct a cross Canada contest in search of the next big food idea to introduce into grocery stores from coast to coast. Home chefs would converge in various cities presenting judges with their culinary masterworks. The finalists would be given a set budget to enlist supply partners, built product prototypes, create packaging designs and shape marketing campaigns, etc. Dave and I would sit on the judges' panel. I appreciated—and was well aware—that we would be complete nonentities from a TV personality perspective, but I was banking on a likable and relatable brothers in business, investing their own skin in the game angle. The show would also serve as a stage to expose how challenging it is to introduce a food product into the retail market space.

The day after the final episode, we would have grocery shelves stocked with the winning item that Canadians had chosen themselves. We would most likely approach Loblaws, Walmart or Sobeys as an exclusive partner, but not until we had our ducks lined up in a perfect row. After all, we didn't want the idea to be snatched from our hands before we could properly anchor ourselves to it.

In order to preserve the concept, I strung together a Keynote presentation demonstrating the basic structure of the show, which relationships we could tap into, etc. My childhood mate, Jeremy Gayton, was a shoo-in to play the role of marketing mentor for the episode centred on building a marketing campaign. As mentioned earlier, Jer was the President of TAXI advertising. At the time, we also began a working relationship with Toronto celebrity chefs, restaurateurs and television personalities, Mike and Guy Rubino, and thought they'd be textbook mentors for the recipe-refinement episode.

For a while, the Keynote presentation rested unmoved on my MacBook desktop. Then one day, Dave recalled he had met a television producer earlier that year. We decided to ring him up and asked if he'd be interested to have us pitch him our idea. Sure, it was an extra-long shot, but like everyone, we appreciate and crave the elation that comes along with stepping out of your comfort zone and sometimes colourless daily routine. We met Rich Goodman (whose production company shall remain unnamed) at a charming little Greek restaurant in Bloor West village for lunch. As far as producers go, he was exceedingly approachable and immediately easy to like.

Rich was super interested and wanted to go for the ride with us ten seconds after staring at the concept-telling cover page imagery of the presentation. The big vision clicked for him instantly. We spoke of our industry and what the logical next steps towards developing a perfected pitch for the network station (which shall also remain unnamed) would look like. I vividly remember politely excusing myself from the table to visit the restroom and gaping into the mirror thinking: '*OK, now this could be a refreshingly different ride in a very cool and desirable way. There's a real, albeit very minute, chance Dave and I will be hosting our own TV show.*'

The next few months with Rich were nothing short of entertaining and, yes, refreshingly different. Each week we would convene at Brand-Fusion in our samurai-themed boardroom (or 'bushido war room' as we like to call it) to build and polish our television show pitch. Rich is something of a seasoned script-doctor so he'd challenge us to keep milling and reworking the ideas and episodes until a super clean and pure version was finally extracted. We even compiled a list of celebrities we'd approach for the show's host—Kevin Brauch from *The Thirsty Traveler* and *Iron Chef America*, and George Stroumboulopoulos from *George Stroumboulopoulos Tonight*, were our top choices.

When we felt the pitch document was worthy of our vision, a meeting with the network was scheduled. Although we intrinsically knew how vital being present at the inaugural meeting was, we half-heartedly agreed to have Rich break the membrane alone to get the ball rolling. In hindsight, it may have been a much larger issue than we anticipated. Operating in the dark is always scary, messy and much slower than it actually needs to be. With bated breath we waited for a status report, the final results and an outlook on our future as TV personalities. When Rich finally called with the network's official response, we were told something to the sombre tune of: *'Boys, they really loved your idea, but the issue is that the network's available budget for supporting new content is significantly underfunded by its parent media company. It's strictly a money thing.'*

Despite the holdup, we remained carefully optimistic as we knew that our concept for the show was fresh, very relevant and right in the pocket for the network at that time. We agreed to chill and sit back, collect our wandering thoughts and think of another approach to woo the network with. A few months after receiving the initial verdict, Lisa and I were up north with the kids visiting a close friend of ours at his cottage. He happened to work in the television business. Very early one morning, while our kids and wives were still asleep, we tiptoed out the back porch and made our way down to the dock for a little bass fishing.

As we drank coffee and watched our red and white bobbers sit motionless in the still waters, we traded stories of what we were both up to in our work lives: *'Hey, you're in TV. Tell me what you think of this idea that Dave and I are working on. Let me know if you think it has any legs.'* As I proceeded to tell my friend (who shall remain unnamed), his eyes and mouth began to widen like a largemouth bass. By the end of my fish-tale, he honestly looked as if he'd witnessed me reel in a 10-pounder. (FYI, the Ontario smallmouth bass record is 9.84 pounds.)

'WHAT?' I gasped. *'Um, Bru,'* he began, with his eyes still stretched wide open, *'just last week, I read through a new pilot series for the same network that you just mentioned. The concept and episode details are verbatim*

to what you've just described to me. As far as I know, it's been green-lighted [pause]. Uh ... what is the name of your TV show concept.' With my eyes and mouth now strained wide open, I told him the working name for our show. Slowly nodding his head in agreement, he responded in a very low and slow voice: *'Yep, I believe that was the working name ... but they're working on changing it to something else.'*

After that, we sat quietly for a long moment and both looked out onto the still lake. I'm now thinking: How surreal is this? One night I'm scribbling down an idea for a television show and today I'm fishing off a dock, four hours from the city in the middle of nowhere, being informed that it's been 'green-lighted' without me. I called Dave on my way back up to the cottage: 'Morning, lil' Bro! *Are you sitting down?'*

That Monday, I began to angrily compile all my notes, research and the like, that I had accumulated on the project. I had been super enthusiastic over the prospect of getting our own show, and had made it a point, if not an obsession, to accurately document the ride. Despite the gravity of the situation, Rich was reluctant to press the network on the matter. Unlike Dave and I, he had a valuable reputation and a steady pay cheque to safeguard in TV town. We respected that. Period.

As if the situation wasn't weird enough, a few weeks later, I get a call from my childhood buddy, Jer. *'Hey Bud. Thought you should know that I received a call from the TV show you either are, or aren't, a part of. They asked me to be a judge and sit on the panel to help mentor and evaluate the contestants from a marketer's viewpoint.'* A long and awkward silence ensued. *'Whaa? Did you accept?'* I asked, feeling stupefied, but also pleased for my friend. *'No!'* he asserted. *'I just can't spare the time. Plus, if you're not involved it doesn't feel right.'*

Ok, I thought, this thing is moving beyond TV town and into bizzaro-world. All the while, Dave and I remained conflicted about picking up the phone to call our lawyer. Was it all just a grand coincidence, or did the network unconsciously build off our idea with a more credible and established line-up of players?

Whether or not the actions were above board, however, was extraneous to us. It was our big idea and we wanted, at the very least, some credit. That said, just when we thought it couldn't get any more unnerving, during a lunch with the Rubino brothers, the topic came up. We had asked for their opinion and input on the pitch to the network before Rich had fired it off for evaluation. Guy and Mike were television show veterans with their long running food show, 'Made to Order.' Mike acknowledged: *'We were asked by a producer buddy of ours to be part of a new show on that network. After he explained the concept, we figured that it was the thing that you were working on. I asked him if he was working with you. He wasn't. What happened?'*

By this point in the ordeal, all we could do is snicker and think about how much more interesting the story was becoming for posterity and dinner conversation purposes. By this point, the network had begun their marketing campaign for the new show. With the frequency of promotional ads that they were airing to push the show, it certainly seemed that it was one of the properties the network was banking heavily on for the new season. We ended up calling a lawyer that specialized in the entertainment industry. Upon laying out my chronologized collection of notes, research and the like, it was clear that she was wetting her chops. After the one meeting with the lawyer, however, we agreed to release the 10lb smallmouth bass back into the lake.

Could it have all been just a giant star-crossed coincidence? Maybe. Be that as it may, there were enough fish to fry back at the office so we decided to focus our energy on the positive rather than get sucked into a long-drawn-out, expensive and epic David-and-Goliath battle. It was our miscalculation in deciding not to push harder to be present during the pitch—rookie mistake. Had we scored some face time with the network, I'm confident that our chances of being involved, even remotely, would have been measurably better.

When the show finally aired, I couldn't get myself to watch it. When I finally did, I realized that our original concept had been watered down to a point where the show's vibe felt much more contrived vs. the more relatable and likable entrepreneur attitude we had cooking in the pot. When I came across the first winner's product concept staring back at me in the grocery store, I picked up, bit my lip and then put it back on the shelf.

The very next morning, in the locker room at my gym, a colleague that worked for the grocery chain that supported the winner's new product was addressing someone's question about the TV show. No one in the room knew my history with the show. *'Oh ya, it's a great show.'* Then he said something like: *'The product isn't setting the world on fire, but the show has been a surprising success.'* Unbelievable, I thought to myself, standing there in the buff. I guess it's best to leave the rest up to karma, pull up my socks and move on.

Let it Simmer ~

1. *Keep your big mouth tightly zipped until you are absolutely and positively certain that it's safe to debut your big idea.*

2. *You are the best person to represent yourself, your ideas and your capabilities. You are your own brand. Go to the pitch and don't take no for an answer.*

3. *Protect your ideas and position until they are ripe for harvesting. When in doubt, insist that a non-compete agreement is signed, especially if you're on unfamiliar ground and in the company of unfamiliar players.*

4. *Before you pull the legal-trigger, aside from the financial repercussions, time investment and slim odds of winning, consider how the negative energy may wreak havoc on your ability to perform in other areas of your business.*

CHAPTER 24

Feeding The Beast

Maximizing Rare Opportunities

A riddle for you: What do you get when you combine impeccable timing and nearly flawless product execution with sassafras and vanilla beans in a frosty mug and then top it with a big creamy dollop of luck? Well, in our case, you get one final and fortuitous chance in the booze biz that ends up being the rainmaking difference maker that you were praying for. Despite what you may be thinking, 'feeding the beast' thankfully isn't about how to cook for your ungrateful father-in-law. Nope, it's a story about what it feels like when you've been floating aimlessly at sea for what feels like forever, and then finally catch that mythical *Humunga Kowabunga from Down Unda* wave off guard.

In *Chapter 2: Grocery Math*, I made mention of rare and extraordinary circumstances where the absolute perfect product is unveiled to a ripe and ready marketplace at precisely the right point in time and space. It's a wonderfully magical combination that defies conventional wisdom and strategy. Like a solar eclipse, the spectacle may only last for a brief period of time so being prepared, avoiding the blinding bright lights and knowing how to react becomes the game. This little ditty is also a hefty reminder to keep swinging hard for the fences regardless of how many times you strike out—don't give up after the 20th embarrassing disaster, because your 21st shot could turn out to be your moment in the hot sun.

We had just received an inopportune notice from the LCBO stating that, after four successful holiday selling seasons, our Crazy Uncle®

Blood Orange & Rosemary Maple Punch would not be supported in their 2016 winter program. On top of everything, in spite of a loyal and steadily growing fan base, sales for our Über Caesar cocktail weren't nearly on pace with what we, or the retailers, had expected. Our future in the alcohol business wasn't looking too bubbly.

Meanwhile, back at the ranch, Dave and I had been messing around in the kitchen with a female-focused cocktail concept that we christened 'Spritz-ology' which was, more or less, lightly and naturally flavoured vodka-based seltzer water with spa-inspired flavours such as fresh mint, basil and lime. At the same time, we were also toying around with hard (i.e. alcohol-laced) craft sodas made using natural bitter extracts and stumbled on a pleasantly familiar flavour profile that tasted very much like creamy root beer.

A few months later, while visiting a supply partner in Chicago, we also stumbled upon a hard root beer brand that was catching fire south of the Canadian border. We asked a seemingly too-young store clerk in a nearby liquor store how it was selling. 'Man, we can't keep this stuff in stock, it's totally flying off the self!' was his enthusiastic Bill & Ted's Excellent Adventure sounding reply. Weeks later we inevitably found ourselves sitting in the LCBO's big boardroom pitching the idea of introducing both cocktail concepts under our Crazy Uncle brand mark. After proving to the LCBO, repeatedly, that we were capable of properly and quickly executing on our ideas, the alcohol retail giant quickly developed into a tremendously supportive and proactive partner for us—especially our direct contacts, Lisa Chapman, Jeryca Dillas, Stacee Roth and Alanna Bailey. When it was all said and done, our Crazy Uncle Hard Root Beer: Craft Soda for Grown-ups was green-lighted, but the 'Spritz-ology' spa-inspired cocktail line prospect eventually fizzled out.

For the record, though we didn't end up scoring an approval on the latter concept, it seemed that we were tightly aligned with what the marketplace was looking for. Later that same year, another brand, backed by Arlene Dickinson (of CBC's Dragon's Den) launched a cocktail line concept with pretty much the same flavour inspirations and positioning targeted specifically to women.

In this particular case, however, being granted a chance to bring a hard root beer to market in the summer of 2016 was the luckier of the two choices and a genuine godsend. We put our game-faces on and obsessed over perfecting our product, specifically the flavour profile. As Dave put it plainly in one newspaper interview: *'If we're doing a hard root beer, we want it to be the best root beer out there. We're not just trying to put a product out there in time to ride the trend.'*

At first, we blindly thought that Crazy Uncle would have the category cornered with a first-mover advantage for at least the lion's share of the inaugural selling season. As usual, fat chance. As our launch date loomed, we learned that not only would we not have a first-mover head start, we'd be one of three local Canadian brands launching that summer, along with a handful of other US hard root beer brand entries. Surf's up! Everybody and their uncle (pun intended) into the sudsy water!

No worries though. Rest easy my friends. It turned out that the benefits and fanfare associated with multiple hard root beer product entries generated way, way more noise, outweighing the voice and volume that we would've brought to a table set for one—think Marty McFly in *Back to the Future* when he slowly turns the overdrive knob to 100 on Doc Brown's gigantic guitar amp.

Within our first few weeks of shipping product out to stores, we immediately recognized that the ride would somehow be different than our other crusades. For starters, our opening order case quantity was forecasted to have lasted well over a month or so to comfortably meet the volume demand which was to be driven by a marketing promotion that we invested in with the LCBO—i.e. prominent in-store product placement supported with summer-themed signage, backed by an out-of-store consumer advertising campaign. Without any communication to consumers of our product's debut, and even before the big LCBO promo had begun, store inventory was immediately sucked up by thirsty consumers.

We had launched the second or third week of April, and by the middle of May we had been awarded with a handful unsolicited write-ups in various national and local newspapers. The *Toronto Star* newspaper ran a fun editorial piece on upcoming summer cocktails worth opening your wallet for. Among other product group evaluations, it compared the taste and overall drinking experience of the three Canadian hard root beer brands and declared us the winner. In years past, we had grudgingly thrown our brand's savings account at promising PR agencies in an effort to drum up such activity, and now there we were basking in the limelight for free.

Needless to say, Dave and I weren't prepared for the *Kowabunga wave*. We had been gearing up for the better part of a year, working with our supply partners to order and build, what we had thought, was plenty of stock to pacify the demand for the summer. Lordy lordy, were we ever off our mark. Imagine having only one or two cheese burgers to satisfy a famished Shaggy and Scooby Doo. Our social media platforms started to light up with hard root beer enthusiasts who had either purchased and loved our product, or with folks who just couldn't get their hands on an ice cold can. In retrospect, this was a very fortuitous thing —well, at least at first. The inventory hiccups served to create both concrete store and consumer demand for the product.

The exceedingly nerve-racking and imminent reality, however, was that it took way too much time to receive the required raw materials and packaging orders that we needed in order to stay in the game. What good is a 10-week lead time when the peak summer selling season is only 15 weeks long? To boot, although our contract packer was giving us more than our fair share of production line time, it wasn't nearly enough to manufacture what was actually required to douse the quickly spreading fire. It was our big shot, and probably the biggest one we'd have for a very, very long time. Talk about feeling helpless. Too much drama for hard root beer, you say? Hmm, maybe for most, but try to appreciate that before the hard soda storm, we were nearly five years and countless dollars and hours invested into the brand without a prayer of making the steep climb into the black.

With the pressure and tally of lost sales continuing to mount, we proceeded to work closely with our sales agents across the country to plug the slowly growing holes in our fragile boat. In an effort to pacify hot pockets of sales activity in and around certain urban areas in Toronto, we attempted to re-allocate inventory from a handful of liquor stores that had succeeded in hogging crazy amounts of inventory for themselves. I recall one such store in Ottawa having 1,000 cans on display despite a handful of stores within driving distance having next to zero product. It was late one Friday afternoon, so I asked a sales rep to collect a decent number of cans from the Ottawa store in question and then to redistribute them into a few nearby stores that following Monday.

It was the week leading up to Victoria Day. Pending the weather, this is one of the biggest weekends for alcohol sales in Canada. To my surprise, that following Monday, the store had sold nearly the entire 1,000 cans. Turns out that weekend, before the Victoria Day weekend, we had pushed through 10,000 cans in 400 or so liquor stores. Talk about an impressive early fireworks display. Dave and I were nothing short of stupefied. The weekend following Victoria Day, I was visiting London, Ontario with Lisa and the kids for my son's baseball tournament—Go Vaughan Vikings!

In between the ball games, under the sweltering summer sun, the team would retreat back to the hotel to recharge with their exhausted families in tow. With a rambunctious gaggle of eleven-year-old boys tearing up and down the hallways riding on luggage carts, I decided to quickly and quietly slip out to conduct a few liquor store checks in the area. Lo and behold, each and every store I popped into was completely out of stock. Not a single can anywhere to be found.

By this point in the summer, the grand, and grandly expensive, promotion that we had invested in with the LCBO was just starting. Our Crazy Uncle Hard Root Beer price tags were in fact prominently displayed in the front of each store I visited, but behind each lonely, white $2.95 ticket was a big, deep empty slot. We had invested some serious coin for in-store promotional artillery to make a loud statement, but ended up firing all our rounds straight up into the air, miles away from the target. Of special interest, the store staff in each of the stores immediately knew of the product and made mention of its popularity.

The next morning, after the tournament, Lisa and I decided to visit the beautiful lakeside village of Port Stanley, located on the north shore of Lake Erie, before heading home. We enjoyed a chicken wing and pizza patio lunch with the kids at a fun little beachside bar and grill called GT's On The Beach. *'Hey now!'* I thought to myself, *'This place would be perfect for selling our Crazy Uncle Hard Root Beer float program.'* Hard root beer ice cream floats also happened to be the creative thrust of our marketing and brand awareness program for restaurant accounts. The majority of our competitors made their hard root beers using a malt-base, where ours was fashioned with craft soda—a much more logical vehicle for preparing a proper ice cream float. So much so, that we brought JP's son, Vinny, on board that summer in an effort to forge as many partnerships as possible with willing ice cream, BBQ and burger joints.

I singled out the manager working the floor at GT's and confidently strolled over to him. Immediately, I sensed and could see the expected *'what in the hell does this guy want to sell me'* facial expression. The moment I mentioned hard root beer, however, his demeanour immediately lightened. *'Hard root beer, Eh! Which one do you sell?'* To which I proudly replied: *'Crazy Uncle!'* After a very short pause he smiled and said: 'That's *funny, I just bought your product last week and I actually really liked it. It's too bad that I printed my menus for this summer as I would've included your product. Come see me next year, ok.'* Seeing as it was only a few weeks since we had shipped the first orders out, had literally just begun the awareness campaign, and every nearest liquor store was sold out, the fact that he was already presold on our mission was a strangely foreign, yet emancipating, chance encounter for me.

On a more serendipitous note, one crisp and sunny afternoon, Dave, Vinny and I fought the usual disgusting gridlock traffic from our uptown office into the downtown Toronto core to deliver a pitch to Claudio Aprile (celebrity chef and judge on *MasterChef Canada*) on serving our Crazy Uncle Hard Root Beer float in his critically acclaimed restaurant called *Origin*. Alas, he was caught up elsewhere and was a no-show. What's that? You're having Jamie Oliver no-show déjà vu moment, you say? You and me both.

Leaving *Origin*, on the way back to the parking lot, and feeling somewhat deflated, we end up passing celebrity bartender Kevin Brauch on the sidewalk. You may recognize Kevin from such TV shows as *The Thirsty Traveler* and *Iron Chef America*. *'Hey! Wait up, Kevin!'* Long story short, we handed Kevin the last can in our bag and gave him our best one-minute-sidewalk-pitch (aka elevator pitch). He was extremely gracious, a true gentleman, and seemed very interested in what we were up to. 'Listen boys,' he professed, and then said something like: 'I don't usually do this, but let's snap a pic right here so that I can post our encounter and your product on my social media feed.' 'If that don't beat all!' we laughed to ourselves as he walked away. 'Talk about a great Food TV celeb consolation prize.'

At any rate, the stories continued to pour in like sweet, frothy root beer. Our Calgary, Alberta agent, Mark Kuspira, was also experiencing the same zealous reaction with our product in his marketplace. Here's a quote from a retail chain in Edmonton that was sourced for a newspaper interview:

> Our customers cannot get enough of the Crazy Uncle Root Beer! We tell them that it's all natural and made in Canada and the response has been overwhelming! Every time we taste people on it, they get hooked and we literally can't keep it on the shelves. We love root beer, and we love the Crazy Uncle Hard Root Beer!—Ryan Tycholas, BASE-LINE Wine & Spirit Co.

Jeryca Dillas, our supportive and reliably upbeat buyer at the LCBO, also provided an official quote for the media:

> The Crazy Uncle producers pride themselves on their foodie, all-natural approach to beverage alcohol and with one sip of their hard root beer, this is very clear. During Crazy Uncle Hard Root Beer's brief time in market, this product has already made quite a name for itself!

In accordance with the title of this chapter, 'feeding the beast' speaks to corralling, controlling and pacifying product demand when consumers are behaving like a hungry pack of wolves. In some ways, if you're managing the flow of inventory and order fulfillment properly, it kind of feels like a back and forth choreographed dance between you, the retailer and consumers. Bear with me here. Give them too much product at once and you might step all over their feet and smother 'em. Give them too little too late, and they might lose interest, become annoyed and look for another partner. And just like the magnificent Mikhail Baryshnikov, you'll need to know how to skilfully lead, tempt and playfully flirt with your partner.

In our case, the unpredictable out of stock episodes and teasing stores with hardly enough inventory seemed to help build serious interest, intrigue and genuine cachet for the product. By the way, teasing retailers with 'hardly enough inventory' wasn't all completely by design. It was, in truth, all that we could manage to have produced despite begging our raw material and packaging supply partners for better lead times and our contract packers for more line-time. Nevertheless, and hallelujah, the dance also succeeded in provoking substantial, and very unplanned, pantry-loading among both stores and consumers.

In fear of constant and looming out of stocks, many stores began ordering unprecedented quantities of product to ensure that supply was secured. By way of illustration, some locations built towering, massive 3,500-can displays. Despite selling our cans individually for $2.95 each, as opposed to selling them in the more traditional four or six packs, many consumers stocked up and bought full twenty-four count cases—that's over $70 of hard soda! Despite all the craziness, and of course, our family and friends calling to congratulate us on our big win, Dave and I remained cautiously optimistic and more guarded than usual. After all we had been habitually and badly burned so, so many times before in somewhat hauntingly familiar situations.

We knew all too well that there still could very well be an ugly outcome that had to do with us sitting on a warehouse of deserted, unspoken for inventory. Meanwhile, retailers were imploring us to hurry up and build more product: *'What? Can't you just build more and ship it in next week? Don't you want to take hold of this rare opportunity?'* Our largest account actually told us that if we couldn't ship a truckload a day that they would either put the product on hold, or delist it altogether. With each such fair warning, we accepted, acted and achieved what we needed to. Chris Churchill, our agent in Ontario, called us up one frantic afternoon to recognize our determination and commitment to the mission.

'Thanks boys. Most other companies your size would've turtled up in the face of such chaos.'

Quite honestly, I was on the other end of the phone, sitting in the office parking lot scratching my head and thinking: go figure, it took us nearly twenty years to score a beauty of a hit and now we're in danger of being punished for not being able to make enough product instead of not being able to sell enough. After the first six weeks of sale, we had concluded that despite having shipped a conga-line of transport trucks, we had actually lost more sales volume than we had cashed in on because of an incapacity to produce enough product.

Ironically, we had spent so much energy and money on our Über Caesar cocktail as we knew that it was a far superior product to any other Bloody Caesar offered on the market, yet we couldn't muster up a fraction of the numbers we had projected. Now, with our hard craft soda platform, we had succeeded in casting a much wider consumer-net. As evidence, nearly three times the number of stores decided to carry the hard root beer within the inaugural three weeks, compared to the total number of stores supporting our Caesar after nearly three years of sale. Looking back, it's clear that, where our Caesar may have been slightly too niche, the hard root beer in some way hit that ultra-sweet spot in-between niche and mainstream.

More importantly, when would the soda tap shut off? When would the music end and the dancing stop? Would we only be given another week or two to bust our moves out on the floor, or could the party last the entire summer, or even longer? Would one of the other looming competing hard root beer companies begin to gain the high ground amidst our period of product shortage? We were dealing with a fast moving target. We appreciated the fact that the potential for us to mismanage the opportunity was still very much at large. The competition seemed to be nipping at our heels three times as fast as they usual did. If our out of stocks continued on for too much longer, we'd have royally pissed of everyone eating at our table. A few more slip-ups and we would've spent the entire summer setting the dinner table beautifully for another hard root beer company to sit down and eat our supper.

Understand that it takes a 10-week lead time for printed cans, with big upfront—pay before delivery—money. And when it's not your manufacturing facility and you're producing with a contract packer, it also usually takes a ton of massaging and sweet talkin' to squeeze in more valuable line time. I'll never forget how Dave and I felt that summer in June: each day was a test of our character and mental stamina. We seemed to be trapped in one of those haunting stuck in slow motion nightmares: we saw the promised land, but just couldn't reach it as fast as we wanted to. I felt like a starving hound, chained to a brick wall with a huge bowl of primo chow, unreachable, just inches from my nose. It also takes deep pockets, or more sensibly, clever cash flow management manoeuvres, to string together the finances needed to tango.

On top of everything, one bad move and we'd lose the ability to pay ourselves and our lenders back. Heaven forbid, we'd need an emergency exit plan, should the fun abruptly end. All this to say, regardless of our financial and supply partner resource vulnerabilities, it was high time to grow a pair and just flat out go for it. In spite of the risk of having the proverbial plug pulled before we could successfully convert our investment into saleable finished goods, we dropped the Sicilian hammer and invested in serious, serious raw material ingredients, packaging and in finished goods inventory.

Our sights were now on the bigger, long-term picture. We weren't interested in trying to recuperate the small fortunes we had sunk into our brand. We were more concerned with digging our heels in even further. It was time to go long on our position. We had grown tired of the feast or famine sales pattern that the Crazy Uncle brand had been mocking us with. We needed a more predictable, stable and strong cash flow rhythm to help secure our future in the business. So what did we decide to do next? Well, in response to the risks and pressures, we actually decided to up the ante by betting on a number of new follow-up Crazy Uncle product line extensions.

In other words, instead of leaving the blackjack table, we decided to double down. Despite the constant urge to cash in, and to pay ourselves for the years of investing in the brand, we believed it would pay us back in spades if we continued to invest every penny into the business. I wish I could tell you how this story ends, but we're still smack dab in the middle of the sarsaparilla storm. If all goes well, you should be able to still walk into a liquor store in, and possibly outside of, Canada to buy a can at least a few years after this book hits the shelf. If you can't find it anymore, it's hopefully because the product has naturally run its course and we've used the momentum to *funnel gunnel* (that's Crazy Uncle lingo for 'parlay') the business into another connected opportunity. If you remember only one message from this story, it's to keep dancing, even when the music stops, the lights turn off and they launch you out the back alley door.

Let it Simmer ~

1. *Are you feeding the beast properly, or do the wolves have you cornered?*
2. *Can you leverage your temporary inability to supply enough product to help create more demand, interest, intrigue and cachet with retailers and consumers?*
3. *Have you planned for a possible high volume success scenario with your supply partners that takes their lead times, payment terms and other order requirements in account? i.e. consider asking for a floor stock agreement (for more info, see* Chapter 25: Only Salmon Swim Upstream).
4. *How can you parlay the awareness and momentum of a successful product launch into another connected opportunity before the music stops?*
5. *When the rainmaking difference maker that you've been praying for finally arrives, will you turtle up or go all ninja turtle on it? Will you fold and cash out or will you try to maximize the opportunity and go long to build a deeper foundation to allow for future growth?*
6. *Keep swinging hard for the fences regardless of how many times you strike out.*

CHAPTER 25

Only Salmon Swim Upstream

Choosing Supply Partners

Whenever I sit down with an aspiring entrepreneur, I can be certain that one burning question will be about where they can go to transform their homemade prototype sample into a proper commercialized product fit for retail. Securing supply partners (i.e. a contract packer and suppliers of raw material ingredients and packaging) is a critical stage that should not be hurried. Mind you, most of the time, it'll take you next to forever to find the right one so rushing isn't always an available option.

For new start-up companies without experience or industry credibility, think back to *Chapter 4: Breaking Bread*: Do your negotiations feel forced or is there a comfortable and natural spark between you and your prospect? When you ask for something basic do they make it seem like you're asking for the world, or for something that's within their wheelhouse? The easy things should come easy when choosing a supply partner: Can they reproduce your food invention relatively effortlessly or will they have to risk investing capital in special equipment or new manufacturing processes and more people or exotic ingredients? If they can produce it, do they really want to, or is your volume or margin, or both, viewed as too insignificant to fire up their machines? If they can and will run product for you, will it come at an unnecessary cost premium and with back of the bus status when it comes to scheduling pressing and important production runs?

Whenever we've had to push unnecessarily hard for a supply partner to accept our business, it eventually ends poorly (and expensively). Experience has taught us that, when basic negotiations feel unnatural or drag on for much too long, we should pack up camp and hunt elsewhere. The good news is that, if you search hard enough, there always seems to be another company out there who is more than willing to go to bat and run your modest start-up requirement with a handshake and a smile. Don't force it, your gut will tell you when you've found your match; so don't get overly excited and climb into bed with your first date—there are plenty of good fish (contract packers) in the (supply partner) sea.

When convincing a supply partner to accept your business becomes trickier, more time consuming and more stressful than selling to a chain store buyer, think about moving your business elsewhere. Typically, larger contract packers will command larger minimum production runs compared with smaller run size requirements from smaller to mid-size contract packers—e.g. approx. 750 to 1,000 cases of product versus a more eatable 200 to 400 cases, respectively. It is for this reason, despite sometimes having to pay a premium price, that building your business with a smaller to mid-size contract packer is advisable in the early going. If the economics of your business can work despite paying a premium, the chances of choking on too much idle inventory decreases, plus you'll pocket the extra margin down the road when your volume starts to build.

There are, of course, trade-offs in trusting your baby with a smaller operator. Firstly, smaller companies often operate super-lean, stretching themselves and their staff too thin. As such, the completeness and value of their responses during your courtship may not always be as structured and accommodating or as clear as that of a more staffed and organized company. However, having a bit more patience is worth the initial aggravation if your gut tells you that you've found your match.

Secondly, a smaller supply partner may not hold all the current Good Manufacturing Practice certifications (GMPs) that Canadian and US retail chains have come not only to appreciate, but to cogently demand. GMPs guarantee that the integrity of food manufacturing processes, and the traceability of ingredients and materials, complies with a strict global food safety regulation and standard. Google GS1, *HACCP, ISO 22000, ISO 9001, SQF or Kosher Certification* and you'll get a sense of how extraordinarily deep and comprehensive these certifications run. To be clear, I'm not suggesting that you hire a supply partner that works out of their garage. The company must possess the fundamental GMP practices at a level that promises both you and the retailer a product that meets or exceeds the industry standards.

If they don't hold any official GMPs, do they have a plan and time-line in place to secure one? Ask them if they have any certifications and you'll quickly see if they skirt the topic or begin to brag about their hard-earned achievements. If you're dealing with proteins (e.g. beef, pork, chicken, etc.), the plant will need to be federally licensed, regis-tered and inspected by the Canadian Food Inspection Agency (CFIA) in Canada, or the U.S. Department of Agriculture (USDA) in the US, in order for you to sell your products to most grocery store chains. There are quite a few non-federally registered meat processing contract pack-ers with adequate production capabilities, but they primarily exist as suppliers to either the restaurant sector or sell to the public directly.

It's been my experience that smaller to mid-size contract packers are also usually run by spirited and colourful entrepreneurs willing to engage with you directly. Larger companies will have you work with an area sales rep, most often without the authority or jurisdiction to make a call without putting your request through their company's elaborate hierarchical systems. If you can make a solid connection directly with the owner, your initial journey will usually be smoother and much more agreeable—at the very least, you'll instantly know where you stand. However, you're bound to encounter a few less accommodating, blunt and brash characters along the way.

In the end, you do have to sell your contract packer, and your supply partners on the whole, on your business plan, and of course, yourself. As I've said before, you are your own brand so you'll need to collect and carry as much goodwill as possible from one project to the next. At some point, you can bet each contract packer has been badly burned by an overly ambitious entrepreneur overpromising and radically under delivering on a forecast estimate and on their knowledge of the industry.

Years ago, I was working with a popular Chef from Hawaii. He wanted to make his unique honey pomegranate vinaigrette available to grocery retailers in the US and Canada. He made the long and costly voyage all the way from sunny Maui to visit us in Toronto on a cold December day to meet the owner of the dressing contract packer that we had sourced. As the Chef took everyone through his background credentials, recipe concept and our grocery goals, I couldn't help but notice that the manufacturing company's owner seemed displeased and irritated.

'*Let me ask you this before we continue,*' he said, stopping the Chef in mid-sentence. '*Are you doing this to pacify your ego? Producing thousands of bottles and then endeavouring to sell them to grocery stores isn't all fun and games. It's a very tough go, you know. And, quite frankly, I'm tired of superstar chefs assuring me that their loyal fans will run down the salad dressing aisle to buy their product. I've lost way too much money and time going down this road!*'

Yikes, let's get the hell out of here, I remember thinking to myself. It's important to clearly show your supply partner that you're not green behind the ears. Bring a notepad filled with well thought out questions to create an air of credibility and comfort in the room. Here are a few questions we might have considered asking during our uncomfortable honey pomegranate vinaigrette meeting:

1. What is your typical minimum batch size and approximately how many cases is it equivalent to if expressed in the standard 250ml x 12 bottles per case? *To which he would have answered 1,600 liters per minimum run giving you approximately 500 cases. It's up to you to know how digestible this number is—can you comfortably sell 500 cases at full price well within the product's optimal shelf life? If you're charged for the full amount of cases up front, can you finance the inventory until it sells?*

2. Do you have a minimum annual case commitment? *In this case, the contract packer requested an annual volume commitment of 2,000 cases per year (one run per quarter) to ensure we weren't wasting their time; although annual commitments are much more negotiable and avoidable than minimum run sizes.*

3. Do you provide the glass bottles or do we have to source and supply them? If so, do you stock any bottle profiles that we could choose from to make it easier on us both? *They'll appreciate this approach, as bringing in custom glass means they'll have to inventory and monitor its supply—and nobody likes adding in more cost and work than is normally required. To boot, you'll have to contend with the glass bottle supplier and their outrageous minimum orders, lead times and unpredictable supply hiccups—try dealing with an Italian glass supplier during Italy's month long holiday in August, 'Ferragosto'—that being said, sometimes, a standard stock bottle just doesn't cut the mustard.*

4. What are your standard delivery lead times and will it help if we provide a preliminary monthly forecast build? *By offering this info you're indirectly telling the contract packer that you understand that they have processes in place, and a host of quickly moving parts that you'll never appreciate. Most importantly, it tells them that you hopefully won't be nagging them to pick up your order every couple of days. As frightening as it seems to expose yourself with a forecast, you won't be crucified if your numbers change ... because they always change with a new business. Forecasts are best built using relevant historical data.*

5. Can we structure our arrangement so that we buy and manage the packaging requirements instead of you buying, storing and building the cost into our price? *There's a lot to consider with this option. You don't want mortgage-sized packaging invoices coming back to haunt you if your product collects dust on the shelf. Be prepared and have an exit strategy. Conventional wisdom suggests that handing over your packaging design art files to the contract packer is easier and seemingly cheaper—i.e. they have your boxes, cartons and film, etc. printed on their account and only charge you for what's used in the production, or better still, the draw of your finished goods. But (and it's a big but), consider that they'll likely over order to get a price break and will possibly add a couple of cents per impression to what their printer has charged them. Also consider that if your product bombs, you'll be quarrelling over the invoice they mail you for the pallets of wasted packaging sitting on their (always seemingly jam-packed) warehouse floor. Incidentally, this is why you'll want to*

*have a decent co-pack agreement drawn up and signed that protects you
from packaging liabilities beyond a reasonable amount—e.g. if your
contract packer is purchasing and providing the packaging, agree to
pay for up to no more than six months of packaging equivalent to the
previous six months of sale. Take it from someone that's battled over
an invoice for over two million futile cartons of microwave popcorn
which, at the time, represented seven years of sales. Be conservative,
e.g. a decent minimum bottle label run is 20,000 to 25,000 labels—
which represents one full year's 2,000 case commitment noted above.*

Here are some additional questions and considerations when sourcing
and negotiating with a supply partner:

1. Do they have the in-house capability to accurately commercialize
   your kitchen recipe by translating it for mass production and
   ensuring shelf-stability? Or, will you need to also source a third party
   to assist with the recipe translation? Note: If the contract packer
   can provide you with this service it is usually free of charge as long
   as your agreement terms have been negotiated and are in place.
2. Can the contract packer provide you with the mandatory
   packaging declaration (i.e. ingredient panel, Nutrition Facts Table,
   allergen statements and the optional on-pack claims (no/low/
   reduced fat and calorie claims, gluten-free, No MSG added, etc.)?
   Visit inspection.gc.ca for industry guidelines and requirements. If
   you require a third party to conduct food science and safety tests
   on your recipe to determine its ingredient itemization, allergen
   exposure, nutritional analytics and shelf-stability visit Maxxam
   (maxxam.ca). It's money well spent.
3. Once your contract packer nails the commercialized recipe target,
   request that a detailed product spec sheet be created, mutually
   agreed upon and frequently referenced. This will help the quality
   from eventually dropping, your taste profile from changing, etc. It
   not only gives the operator a bull's-eye to hit each time they fire
   up the machine, it gives you a measurement instrument to wave if
   consistency drops; some slight variance in size, flavour and

appearance is to be expected—however, in many cases, a variance could wreak havoc on your brand with consumers. Remember to ask me about both over-salted and under-salted microwave popcorn, or about not enough fat in our Mr. Greek pork souvlaki.

4. What is your supply partner's declared wastage or permissible scrap factor? What are their compensation terms in the event it's exceeded? The amount can vary depending on the type of product or service provided. Certain printed film substrate or label suppliers will run up to 10 percent over or under (although, it's usually over) your order request and it's considered to be fair game in the industry—anything over 10 percent should at least be questioned. A contract packer will discard a certain amount of packaging and ingredients during the set-up of their machines—usually plus or minus 3 percent. Make it clear that you want to be compensated for any wastage above the declared and agreed to levels; at the very least, it'll keep the machine operator more honest as they'll know you're counting the pennies.

5. Does your contract packer have a manual inventory system or do they use a software tracking system? *'Mind your own business,'* keep a watchful eye on the packaging and raw materials that you buy directly and have your supply partner warehouse for you. Misplaced or miscounted boxes and bags of inventory add up in cost and will throw your ordering requirements off. Request a monthly report of any and all components that you've purchased and are recorded in your books.

6. Will the contract packer warehouse your packaging and unique raw materials in their warehouse or at third party warehouse? If it's at a third party warehouse, ask to see the rate card so that you under-stand the 'pallet in, pallet out and monthly storage charges'. Can you have them stored for less? They can add up and throw your cost of goods off by a significant margin. Having things stored in the supply partner's warehouse is best from a control, cost and visibility standpoint. However, smaller operators don't always have the space, especially for larger and more cumbersome items—storing flat cartons is less onerous than storing one litre glass bottles.

7. How often do you require a production forecast? Be honest with your numbers and just stretch the truth slightly, or be prepared to encounter issues down the road.

8. Once sales become more frequent and consistent, can you put a floor stock agreement in place to ensure both an uninterrupted supply and a shorter lead-time? Asking your supply partner to keep a minimum and maximum number of finished good cases on their floor, and on their dollar, can help to ensure that out-of-stocks are minimized. For example, you may decide that you only need floor stock of your bestselling skus; ask your contract packer to keep 250 cases minimum and up to 500 maximum cases at all times. It should go without saying that if your sales movement isn't predictable, don't risk putting a floor stock agreement in place as you'll eventually get the invoice and have to find an exit strategy for unused inventory.

9. What are your standard terms of payment? Can you stretch your supply partners out from their standard 30-day payment terms in order to be more creative with managing your cash flow—i.e. try to receive payment from your distributor, or in some cases, the retailer, before paying your supply partners? Albeit, many retailers will always take your cash discount terms off their payment despite making the payment weeks past the required date, so don't rely exclusively on them for creative cash flow strategies. Naturally, if you do have the cash sitting in your bank account, be sure to take advantage of cash payment terms to help improve your profit margins.

10. Are you certain that you've built in enough margin to feed from? Try to find out the gross margin percent range (**formula: sell price—cost of goods / sell price**) that the retailer and distributors command—i.e. for retailers, a decent dry-grocery product gross margin is 35%; for a produce or deli item it can climb closer to 50% because of high spoilage. A turnkey distributor that will buy, store and sell your product might ask for 15% to 30% depending on the channel(s) of service. Don't fool yourself by massaging the numbers to work in your favour. Will you be left with enough

margin per case to fund the mission, and to eventually put some money in your pocket? Is your contract packer located out of the country, or do they import certain components or key ingredients? Padding your sell price to cushion the margin blow from foreign currency exposure, and increases traced to commodities, freight or labour is also key.

There's a sweet spot when it comes to creating a truly innovative food product that has volume potential and then finding the right supply partner(s) to launch it with. It's about finding a meaningful, and hope-fully breakthrough, point of difference from your competition—and then about motivating, and most often pushing, a supply partner out-side their comfort zone to help you get there. In many cases, if you're not challenging your supply partner, chances are that you're perhaps comfortable with being only slightly unique on the shelf—i.e. the thrust of your point of difference is a new flavour or packaging design.

When Dave and I worked with a contract packer to commercialize our *Crazy Uncle*® culinary cocktail line, getting our bottler to agree to use real clover honey instead of high fructose corn syrup wasn't easy. It's an expensive ingredient to carry, challenging to work with and significantly slowed down production target throughputs. Despite the whining, we pushed hard to roll with pure pain in the ass honey because it met with our ultimate product vision, but only did so because we sensed it was more of an initial and palatable irritation than a longer term, and per-haps eventual, deal breaker. We were willing to pay for the honey because we had built the added cost into our pricing model and felt we could get the retail premium for it. Our vision for the brand was National, if not International, so a high fructose compromise wasn't in the cards.

We've also pushed too hard at times. When we found a supply part-ner to produce Mr. Greek's Moussaka exclusively for A&P / Dominion (a much smaller and limited time opportunity), we hastily gambled on having the contract packer invest in a minimum supply of fire-roasted eggplant cubes to ensure the recipe's authenticity. The contract packer had every other ingredient that we needed to produce the item; their ingredient assembly and cooking systems yielded a perfect retail product

—we just needed the eggplant. Two months after the launch and it was clear that consumers didn't take to the Moussaka as we had hoped. Six months later and we were still battling over the contract packer's seventeen-thousand-dollar tab of unused fire-roasted eggplant cubes, and dealing with the retailer's fierce deductions and mark-down invoices. We had pushed too far based on the contract packer's comfort zone and the scope of the opportunity.

When your product does take off, making certain that you have an uninterrupted supply becomes both increasingly critical and more complicated. Inevitably, Murphy's Law always seems to kick in when sales finally start flowing and you gain some consistent traction. Consumers start to repeat their purchases, retailers finally start to believe and support you ... and then boom, supply issues quickly become your central focus and you find yourself eating a thread of spaghetti from both ends. When our Kernels Popcorn Shakers started to sell at Blockbuster Video and Wal-Mart back in 2000, I spent at least three quarters of my day, and 110% of my energy, solving supply issues and assuring buyers their shelves wouldn't stay empty for too long.

How quickly will you outgrow your supply partner? Our first co-packer, *Loretta Foods*, was great for the first year or so. Our volumes were manageable and our lead times less than demanding. As our volume grew, they began to drop the ball frequently, leaving us without enough inventory as their filling-machines weren't fast enough to both satisfy our needs and also keep their own products in stock. Our next co-packer, *Newly Weds Foods*, had superior equipment, systems and capacity but we still kept getting bumped off the production schedule for better and more lucrative customers.

By this point, we had listings with most of the larger Canadian grocers so finding the right supply partner solution became paramount to our survival. This time around, we teamed up with a company called WG Pro Manufacturing who actually acquired a state of the art filling line just for our business; the thing was a veritable beast, filled an entire warehouse bay and cost them handsomely. After about a year, the pressure for us to meet and beat our forecast promises became too challenging as WG depended on our volume to make the economics of their equipment investment work. Despite being content with our growth rate and performance, our supply partner was choking on their equipment lease payments. It turns out they invested in a Ferrari when all we both needed was an entry model Honda.

After having painfully survived three failed supply partner attempts—and feeling a little like *Goldilocks* cycling through her '*much too small, much too large*' options—we found a co-packer with the help of our trusted co-packer source extraordinaire, Mr. Glen Millichamp (or as we affectionately call him, *Glenzo* ... which kind of sounds like Gonzo, my favourite Muppet). Run by the über trustworthy and industrious Ravi Thambiah, *CPI* bought the Honda and we've been doing business together ever since. Remember, you should be focusing more on creating sales and demand for your food product, not spinning out on supply challenges. As the saying goes in our office: '*Bring in the sale and the back of the house will eventually figure out how to ship it.*'

Let it Simmer ~

1. *Have you found the right supply partner match or is it time to grab the cheque and move on to the next courtship?*
2. *Have you made an effort to engage with the owner, or are you stuck in an email and voicemail match with a useless regional sales rep?*
3. *Are your simple requests being met with quick and simple answers or are you left scratching your head?*
4. *Is the sales volume opportunity size worth the clean-up risk?*
5. *Do you have a realistic exit plan if you can't move the inventory? Can you survive the financial hit if you can't move it?*
6. *Are the supply partner's minimum runs digestible? How long will depleting the inventory take based on your opportunity size and conservative volume build expectations?*
7. *Can you make enough money to keep your head above water if you decide to pay a higher cost premium to support a lower volume commitment? Do you know what the retailer's and distributor's gross margin targets are?*

8. *Does the contract packer have the necessary Good Manufacturing Practices (GMPs) in place? If not, are they at least working towards securing them?*

9. *Are you challenging and pushing the supply partners out of their manageable comfort zone to achieve a worthwhile and innovative point of difference?*

CHAPTER 26

Planting Seeds

Establishing brokers & Distributors

Debuting your newly minted masterpiece to the world can be quite the bewildering and emotional experience. It can take many months, if not years, of working in near solitude to get your invention and operating blueprint ready for business. So when it's time to emerge from the cave to share your accomplishments with the world, make sure that you fully understand and properly leverage the right sales approach and solution. With that said, the absolute best preparatory solution, hands down, is not to rely on anyone but yourself when it comes to venturing out to secure the first purchase order. You can arm the best sales person with all the fancy selling tools, slick samples and brand swag you can muster up, but it's only you, and your explosive passion, that will prevent buyers from brusquely deciding to shut their notebook long before the pitch has ended.

You are your own brand. Send in someone else to do your work and, despite their self-proclaimed exceptional relationship with the buyer, they'll ring you up from the chain store's head office parking lot after the meeting to solemnly declare that *'sorry, it was a NO this time.'* When it's you that's enthusiastically sitting on the other side of the negotiation table, the story always seems to advance and unfold beyond the definitive and ugly little word *'NO'*. Maybe it'll be because of your uncanny knack to paint the opportunity in a certain attractive bright light, or an ability to deflect the buyer's bullets of doubt from your chest, but I bet you hear the word *'NO'* far less than anyone else would.

And, heaven forbid that you do receive a flying 'NO' straight to the fore-head. At least you know that no means no and it's not because your sales representative was more focused on selling someone else's merchandise loaded in his briefcase that morning. Listen up. Tomorrow morning, have a sip of good freshly ground coffee, take deep breath and then ride the bullet—pick up the phone and call the retailer yourself.

Once you've personally laid some decent track and have made concrete progress to share, enlisting a sales broker or a distributor will help you travel faster and further. A sales broker will be either a self-employed one-person operation, or it can be a much larger firm housing multiple sales account managers, each one overseeing either a specific set of retailers or a particular product category. A broker will only request 5% of the net sales that they rustle in for you; however, the order fulfillment requirements and costs remain with you. In which case you may also need to eventually appoint an outside warehousing company to store and ship out your goods (i.e. when your contract packer is unable or unwilling to store and stage orders out of their facility).

Plan on spending $5 to $6 per each pallet that you ship into the warehouse (in-charge), a monthly storage fee of in and around $7 per pallet, and another $5 to $6 for shipping full pallets back out, or a 25 cent per case picking fee on less than full pallet orders (out-charge). Depending on the channel(s) of sale, for 15% and up to a 30% gross margin return on your goods, a distributor will buy, warehouse and facilitate the order fulfillment. In addition to representing you and your product to the retailer, they'll also handle the multitude of individual store level sales, and via a tactical sales team, provide valuable merchandising and account maintenance services.

To be clear, contracting sales support without having first made progress on your own is actually more common. It's just my opinion that the probability of the sales company agreeing to accept your food fight, and their interest in your game, will dramatically increase if you've proven its worth. More importantly, it also helps to balance the tables and places you in a healthier negotiation position. Beware, if this is your first rodeo and you haven't any credibility, goodwill or accomplishments sitting in a store to point to, a sales company may prod you for a monthly retainer. More explicitly, they may mandate from $1,000 up to $2,500 per month for pioneering the mission up until the first billable sale comes rolling in.

By choosing to lay down a sales foundation before approaching a third party sales solution you'll cut down the requisite retainer, and if you're a decent negotiator, you might even be successful in reducing their fee against the portion of the business that you've secured and handed over. For example, ninety-five percent of the time, a sales broker in the food industry will want 5% of your invoiced sales to the retailer for their services rendered. However, if you've closed the sale yourself and have already begun to fulfill orders, one of the most challenging and time-consuming phases has already been accomplished. So in this case, you may want to offer 3% or 4%, for a specific mutually agreed to time period, and with an opportunity for the sales party to earn the full 5% based on a mutually agreed to sales growth target.

After you've appointed a sales company to help with your food fight, it's paramount to ride shotgun to every inaugural sales presentation to a key retailer account. Not only will the probability of emerging from the pitch meeting victorious increase, your sales person will witness what and how to communicate directly from watching you in action. Your presence will ensure that they know what you expect from them when you're not tagging along for the next call. It should go without saying, but it'll also aid in building a solid rapport with each sales representative responsible for the future of your company.

Before you throw down your John Hancock on a formal sales broker or distributor contract, which by the way, should be mutually cancellable in no more than 90 days, be sure that you're teaming up with a partner that's right for you personally. Going back once again to *Chapter 4: Breaking Bread*, are you getting the right vibe from the guy or does something seem uncomfortably alien? Are you fooling yourself by thinking that the awkwardness will eventually wane the closer you work and grow with the person? Do you wince when their call comes through or jump with enthusiasm to pick up the phone?

By the way, hiding behind your email is never a prudent option. The quest for space on the shelf will take time and the patience of Job, so you'll want to be über comfortable and click with whoever joins you on your culinary crusade. It has been my personal experience that there will be a heavy-duty direct correlation between the strength and ease of a relationship with a sales person and the level of effort, ultimately leading to success, that they place in selling you and your products.

Despite what you believe your sales potential is, not all product concepts are greeted with open arms and optimism by sales folk, and especially, by buyers. Where hiring someone with plenty of knowledge and skill in your product's category is perhaps more obvious, finding someone with a genuine desire to sell your product sometimes takes a backseat with respect to decision criteria. Finding someone qualified who fully wants to sell your product, however, is fortunately a key variable that you can have a hand in nurturing. The more that I can easily and freely relate with a sales person, the deeper our relationship will eventually become and, as a result, the stronger that sales person's sincere desire to see you win will be.

Looking back over the past nearly twenty years, it's extremely clear that the sales people who have contributed the most to our bottom line are also the ones that I worked to connect with the most on both a personal and professional level. They are the individuals that I enjoyed sitting down to a big glass of juicy red with, long before they dutifully faxed or emailed in their first big fat purchase order—I'm looking at you Ursini, Ciambrelli, Glusak and Lock. I knew about their families and ambitions as they knew all about mine, and I'm more than convinced that it counted when they were up to bat for me and our company.

I'm not proposing that it takes a certain degree of wining, dining and greasing to motivate someone to perform. I'm saying that investing in talented sales people you also happen to enjoy spending time with will help you to reach the finish line in a much more effective and gratifying fashion. I realize that conveniently being matched and attuned with your entire sales force is impracticable, but do make sure that there are a handful of prospective compadres in the mix who also happen to represent your largest prospective buyers.

Once you have managed to consummate a representation contract, keeping your newly adopted sales squad engaged and focused will become a weekly dance between you and them. Brokers in the food business are notorious for always wanting to sell a modified version of your product that you don't offer: if you make it with Dutch chocolate, they'll ask for French vanilla in order to secure that elusive big order. It's your duty to recognize when facilitating such requests can actually help to close a deal, and when it'll just end up wasting your time and money. But be careful, keeping a sales broker or distributor adequately interested and engaged is also critical so you'll want to bend as much as you can comfortably handle so that they don't lose interest.

Pushing hard while knowing when to step back is a balancing act that you'll learn to master over time—and no doubt, after making a few awkward mistakes. That said, the squeaky wheel gets the grease so don't expect to sit back and wait for an e-order to pop up in your starving inbox. When your sales broker or distributor does eventually forward you a buyer's offer for your review, brace yourself because they may start the negotiations by asking you for the world plus your first born. Your sales person may also be skittish and eager for you to accept the deal because they've been working for you without pay for way longer than you both had predicted.

Either way, remember that it's your business and your lint-filled pockets so do what you can to earn a space on the grocery shelf without compromising your company's wellbeing. For a start-up food enterprise, I can tell you that it's exceptionally atypical to make a return on your investment within the first eighteen to twenty-four months. It took nearly two years to make our investment back on our first few product launches. Between product development related expenses, ongoing packaging and raw material costs, listing fees, inside programs, unpredictable deductions, markdowns and freight charges, don't be startled when you're chasing your break-even target down the deli aisle.

So, where do you start searching for your army of mighty food fight warriors? It can be as simple as probing online or at one of the many industry food shows (see *Chapter 29: Poking The Yolk* for show resources) for food brokers or food distributors that are aligned with your mission. Aside from larger brokerage firms, such as well-known Acosta (acosta.ca), that cover key retail accounts from coast to coast, most smaller broker outfits operate regionally. And whereas the US marketplace can be more fragmented with respect to distributor coverage, there are a handful of very capable Canadian distributors that can represent your product on a National front—assuming that they are interested and don't carry any competitive products.

Aside from my brothers at Johnvince Foods (johnvince.com), we often use UNFI (unfi.ca) and Tree of Life Canada (treeoflife.ca) to get to market. Both these distributors also have their head office in the US, making it easier for you to travel south of the border once you have your game figured out in Canada—and take my word for it, it's better to play, win and learn the game in your own backyard before paying a visit to our American neighbours. Yes, it's a much greater and more attractive arena, but the rules of engagement are different and the consequences following failure are tougher to survive.

If your distributor does not have enough capable feet on the street to ensure that your product is both sitting in the right store location and is selling to the retailer's expectations, you'll need to consider augmenting your sales plan with a third party merchandising team. At around $20 to $30 per half hour store visit, it can get expensive quickly, but in most cases the increase in sales as a result of a properly merchandised product will help to offset a majority of the expenditure. Brand-Momentum is one of our preferred merchandising partners in this field (brandmomentum.ca).

There are also more creative means to hunt for a sales solution outside of the more traditional broker, distributor and merchandiser routes. Scan the grocery store for an established product line that can complement both your crusade and theirs. For example, a company introducing a new bruschetta seasoning might consider striking an agreement with a nationally distributed tomato company for the sale, distribution and joint-placement of their product in the produce section; or, a company launching a fish marinade might approach a fresh seafood company, and so on. In these two examples, the products also benefit from being creatively co-merchandised in a location with a higher impulse purchase intent instead of flying solo and ending up lost on the shelf in their respective overcrowded categories.

In any case, once you have your funky little food product in hand, working like mad to get an order should become your prime fixation. All too often I notice start-up businesses spending an inordinate amount of money and time on building and polishing their websites, company brochures and logo wear all at the expense of focusing on that first life-altering order. Remember, it's a waste of time to stay home heating the skillet before you're able to bring home the bacon.

Let it Simmer ~

1. *Have you tried to present your product directly to the retailer or have you been anxiously sitting back for months waiting for someone else to bring you good news?*
2. *If you have heard the word 'NO' from a retailer, has it been from your sale person's mouth or directly from the buyer?*
3. *Do you need to appoint a sales broker or a full service distributor?*
4. *Does the personal connection with your broker or distributor feel natural and productive or unnatural and strained? Does the potential exist to build a strong and long-term relationship?*
5. *Will your broker or distributor let you ride shotgun to retailer presentations so that you can help set the tone and your expectations?*
6. *In the early going, for each hour that you spend on tasks that aren't connected to securing an order, spend three hours on trying to sell your product.*

CHAPTER 27

Feeding Your Kids

Step Up, or Step Off

This next riff may come off as sounding self-indulgent—but, it may be my one and only genuine chance to tell it like it is to both those who have approached us with a *'million-dollar idea'* expecting to reap a handsome reward without investing their meaningful time and/or money; and to future partners that may play an important, albeit supporting cast role, in our production who also expect serious remuneration. Listen up, damn it! Bringing an unbelievable idea or contribution to the table and then stepping back to let others make the deadly and expensive climb [sometimes] deserves nothing more than a sincere thank you and maybe a $100 iTunes gift card. Relatedly, asking to be part of a company and to share heavily in its profits in exchange for a short-lived cameo appearance is as bizarre as getting to have a few nights of remarkable sex, getting pregnant and then handing the child off to someone else to raise.

Quickie sex is the fun and exhilarating part. Raising the child and devoting your life to its healthy upbringing and its protection is nothing short of colossally life altering—I know, I have three kids. The sleepless nights, the complete devotion, the emotional and financial investment, these are all part of the journey. I get to pay for 4 years of University education and you casually show up uninvited at their graduation to share in the credit and enjoy a piece of chocolate cake? In the words of my all-time favourite comedian, John Candy, in the classic 1985 movie *Summer Rental*, as he's smashing his crutch against the refrigerator door in pure rage after coming home to find an uninvited party of beach patrons abusing his summer home (44:28): *'Get out! Party's over! Get OUT, Get OUT, GET OUT OF MY HOUSE!!'*

I had the idea for this chapter long before I wrote it. What stirred me to start writing it was a bizarre phone call. Over fifteen years before I received this demented and irritating call, a chap by the name of Arnold initiated and facilitated the inaugural meeting between one of our more popular licensed brand partners and my partner JP at Johnvince Foods. The outcome of the meeting eventually gave rise to launching one of our most celebrated product introductions. To my knowledge, Arnold's contribution concluded after making the introductions and perhaps championing the initial follow-up period. Years later I inadvertently discovered that, for his participation, our fabulous (and generous) brand partners rewarded Arnold with a most healthy chunk of the brand license proceeds that they received from BrandFusion—considerably more than one might expect is fair for the introductions and the duties performed.

Fast forward to 2015: *"Hi Arnold, how have you been, we haven't spoken in over ten years—what's up?'* I asked. After dispensing with the pleasantries, he replies with something like: *'I'd like to pass by your office to chat about some new opportunities ... and about the product line sold under the brand I introduced you to.'* I immediately felt something awkward and curious lurking in the air. *'What about it? I'd like to understand what you're thinking about with this one right now,'* I said.

It turned out that he felt he was owed more money and was hoping that BrandFusion would consider, despite never having discussed the arrangement with us, paying him something over a decade after we had taken the reins. *'It wouldn't be that much, really,'* he promised. I felt the fucking hair on the back of my neck stand up as my temperature rose to a *'snapping'* level. Am I dreaming or is this guy actually calling me out of the blue fifteen years after our business was built asking for a goodhearted handout of our hard-earned money? Maybe I should swing by the walk-up window fast food resto at Blue Mountain, or ring up the *TV network* that borrowed our food show idea to ask for some lunch money. Um ... *'Get out! Party's over! Get OUT, Get OUT, GET OUT OF MY HOUSE!!'*

Setting your party's role and expectations early on in the game, and then working to hold them in check throughout your mission will greatly help to keep unnecessary external pressures and distractions at bay. Proceed with extreme restraint when providing an important player in your game (e.g. brand owners, new business partners, supply partners, brokers, the bank) an estimate (e.g. revenue, profits, case volumes). Learn to skilfully squeeze out their expectations early on in the game to make sure you're on the same page, and then get it in writing. Newcomers will always lock into the first number you slide across the table—even if they don't admit it, they'll measure success by your initial guesstimate. Don't blurt out an aggressive number unless you're willing to repeatedly waste time and patience to defend yourself down the road. It's tempting to embellish the story to keep the group interested and engaged, but if you must provide a number, think about a super conservative outcome and then divide it in half!

When Dave and I sat down with Crazy Uncle's first recipe contributing master mixologist (Frankie Solarik) and the agency that represents him, we were new to the alcohol business. At some point in the conversation, after understandably being probed for volume estimates a few times, we carelessly mentioned that sales could be upwards of 20,000 cases in the first year. It was the only number offered during our lengthy conversation which was meant to be centred more around how connecting with our project would serve to build both our brand and his own; not to say that financial reward wasn't part of the offer's allure, but we were open and honest about the chances of failure and the less than desirable volumes.

By the time we put Crazy Uncle® on the map, well over a year had passed. We had spent the better part of each week, invested well over six figures, and overcame many setbacks getting there. Based on how the opportunity ended up coming together (i.e. our first sku was positioned as a one-time seasonal buy, sold in stores over a 10-week period), we sold less than 2,000 cases into the LCBO—less than 10% of what we had told the guys in our inaugural meeting. Despite the lacklustre sales, we were content with our accomplishment given that the odds were stacked heavily against us. We had successfully broken into the difficult alcohol market, had achieved nearly a 100% sell through at retail of the inventory we sold in and, via a fruitful PR campaign, had begun to develop a devoted and growing fan base.

It takes time and a load of patience to properly raise a child, and for the first year of its life, our precious little boy had grown into a crawling toddler trying to find its way out of the crib. Nonetheless, our relationship and the good vibes with Frankie's agency became mutually awkward at best. While we celebrated our accomplishment and readied ourselves, both mentally and financially, to navigate the next section of the steep climb, Frankie's camp seemed faintly deflated and disillusioned with the mission. Aside from providing the, albeit beautifully brilliant, recipes and initially posting some props on social media, the love seemed to grow dim on both sides of the bar. Maybe it was our fault?

Looking back, we should never have offered such an aggressive case volume estimate. I understand that now. I also believe that, despite the positive Crazy Uncle PR Frankie received from a handful of major newspapers, online blogs and even local television interviews, the gap between the size of our royalty cheques versus the number we speculated about in our first meeting contributed to preventing our relationship from progressing. I imagine both sides were left thinking the same thing: *'They don't appreciate what we've contributed and accomplished here?'* I'm convinced that, just as with Arnold's point of view, Frankie's agency felt eligible for a much greater reward. Perhaps, in someone else's hands, with a more established partner in the alcohol sector, more money could've been made. Sure, maybe. Then again, perhaps a more empathic understanding on everyone's part of what it took to achieve the final results could've taken the business to a healthier level. Or maybe it was our distorted paradigm and overly exposed nerve that served to sober up our relationship buzz. That said, in the case of Frankie Solarik himself, setting our likely differences in financial suppositions aside, I deeply respect his contributions to our cocktail crusade and still think he's *the* grandmaster flavour-wizard.

Either way, it'll be your money, your titanic time investment and exposed neck. Make sure you're at ease with everyone's expectations and motives. If you know that you'll only need someone's participation for a limited time, or only for a particular phase to make progress, choose your words (and numbers) very wisely—if it feels awkward and unnatural, despite getting what you want in the short-term, chances are you'll have to field an unwanted call ten years down the road from a forgotten someone looking for a sizeable charitable handout?

Let it Simmer ~

1. *At what level, financially or otherwise, should you involve a third party based on what they might provide to your mission over the long run?*
2. *Have you clearly set the roles and expectations, or have you unnecessarily embellished the storyline to keep the party engaged and involved? If so, can you weather and stomach the possible repercussions down the road?*
3. *What does an acceptable outcome look like to you? Is it also acceptable to your third party or will only the very best outcome be good enough for them?*
4. *Are the numbers you've provided reflective of half of the conservative outcome, or did you stretch the truth to a point where you'll be constantly backpedalling?*
5. *Do you really need the third party, or should you save the money and risk and go it alone despite the trickier road?*

CHAPTER 28

Fruit Pulp Clouds & Chocolate Bloom

The Mysteries of Food Science

Whether it's pesky flocculating fruit pulp clouds or unexpected chalky-white chocolate bloom, the science of food, the biochemistry of intermingling ingredients, can show up uninvited to your grocery get-together just when things are starting to move and groove. If comprehensive shelf-life testing isn't a possibility because of pressing launch deadlines, or simply because of limited funds and resources, keep a sharp lookout for this irritating and destructive party-crasher.

It wasn't easy, but we were able to team up with a first-class contract packer to replicate Great Canadian Bagel's® gourmet cream cheeses. It took us eight months or so to nail down the recipes to our liking, but we managed to pull it off. In the process, we dutifully scarfed down more than our fair share of double toasted multigrain bagels generously smeared with the famously yummy Zesty Cheddar, Vegetable, and Feta & Spinach cream cheeses. The product was good, very good.

You could imagine my frustration then, when I slid into my local Food Basics store to check on our newly christened product line a few weeks after we had shipped the first order only to discover that the Vegetable cream cheese sku had transformed from an appetizing creamy white colour into an unsightly and unappetizing blush red. It turns out that the pieces of fresh radish had slowly seeped into the product. I ended up buying all twenty units on the shelf to help clean the slate in that particular store. Unfortunately, I couldn't visit and attend to the other 116 Food Basics locations so a costlier and unfortunate recall was in order.

The bright red cream escapade was bad, but not as befuddling as the cloudy white and milky mass that grew in the centre of our Crazy Uncle® Blood Orange and Rosemary Maple Punch. Admittedly, during our many smaller lab test runs, as well as the inaugural production run, we did notice a very faint cloud floating in the bottle, but it looked more than reasonably natural and normal. After a couple of weeks of sitting on the shelf, however, we noticed that the cloud increased in size, density and colour. We knew the product was safe for consumption as our lab tests and continuous weekly pH checks were all in order. We purchased, cracked open and drank a few bottles and found the flavour profile also to be in accordance with our taste targets—(at 14% alc. vol., we also found that catching a warm buzz was a little too easy).

It turns out that the unsightly flocculation was triggered by our natural red colouring (made from purple carrot, beet and elderberry juices), unpredictably mingling with the fleshy pulp from the unfiltered lime juice. Our competitor's cocktails used inexpensive artificial gums and stabilizers to create a more homogeneous product and to avoid product settling. We had intentionally spent more money to source and incorporate all natural and premium ingredients and it nearly ended up backfiring on us—go figure that one out. Needless to say, we drove around the city for a couple of weeks visiting more stores to shake more bottles than I care to remember.

There's no doubt that the funky flocculation in our craft cocktail kept us awake at night for a few weeks, but at least in the end the product sold through at retail—97.7% of it to be exact. We made our money. I wish I could say the same for our dollar-store-focused popcorn seasoning gamble. It was 2005 and our Kernels Extraordinary Popcorn® Shakers had gained decent national distribution and popularity amongst consumers and retailers alike. But when Canada's largest dollar store chain came knocking and asked us for a smaller and more affordable version of our product, we were reluctant to offer one in fear of damaging our premium brand by making it available in a discount retail environment.

Not wanting to let the opportunity go, we developed a similar product offering and created a new brand called Flavour Station® Popcorn

Shakers. The savoury chip-inspired seasonings were packed in cylindrical shaped composite (cardboard) containers that were less than half the size and fill weight of our flagship Kernels Shakers, sold in a more attractively shaped polypropylene (plastic) container. They would retail for an even $1.00 compared with $2.99 for the Kernels product line sold in grocery stores.

In order to seal the new composite containers, we gambled and purchased a special machine for slightly north of $50,000 called the Angelus 10P Seamer. It wasn't necessarily a cheap or easy capital investment decision, but the projected conservative sales estimates more than justified our return on investment. Within a year or so, the machine should have paid for itself. With the 10P and the mini canisters on order, we hit the streets and began to peddle our new product to not only dollar stores, but to any bargain-hunting retailer that we had initially passed over for our Kernels line.

By the time the mighty Angelus 10P Seamer was installed, we had a couple of truckloads of purchase orders to fill and ship out. Following a few fits and starts with the new equipment, we managed to build the orders. As we were loading the maiden order onto the truck, a few canisters tumbled out of the retail-ready floor-stand we had packed them in, and made an unexpected solid '*ka-thunk*' sound as they hit the concrete warehouse floor. '*That sounds peculiar,*' I thought. I picked the product up off the floor and gave the little container a firm shake. '*Oh. My. God!*' I murmured through my clenched teeth. '*It's rock solid!*' I was stunned. We had tested the product earlier and didn't experience any sticking or hardening. I recall having a sample for the initial 10P trial sitting on my desk for a couple of months, and it was still fine. What the hell happened?

I'll tell you. It turned out the composite material that the canisters were made from didn't prevent humidity from creeping in as well as our Kernels polypropylene containers. Although the same composite canisters were used universally for other types of seasoning, such as salt or pepper, our product was designed to be more susceptible to retaining moisture so that it could adhere to hot popcorn. The damp warehouse environment was just enough to trigger a hydroscopic reaction that caused the seasoning to absorb moisture from the air. Despite a futile attempt to rework the product, the entire smorgasbord was deemed pure garbage. The real kick in the composite container was trying to return the Angelus 10P Seamer. By the way, if you're getting sick of hearing this name, then welcome to the party. We eventually got rid of the 10P all right, but it sat idle for nearly two long years and only sold for a meagre $6,453.08! Talk about rubbing a little seasoning salt into an open wound.

The rock solid seasoning shakers damaged our pocketbook and pride, but it's not the only time pesky hydroscopic ingredient problems have wreaked havoc on our little business. Before we decided to close down our Snack Brands popcorn plant in Ottawa, Ontario (see *Chapter 32: Family Table*), we created an over-the-top indulgent popcorn-based masterpiece called Crème de la Crème. We had four crazy innovative flavours—Black Forest Cake, Ultimate Chocolate Chip Cookie Dough, Banana Cream Pie, and Maple Pralines with Toasted Oatmeal.

The stuff was diabolically off the snack-charts compared with the status quo popcorn concepts on the grocery shelf. For example, our Black Forest Cake recipe was made using decadent caramel popcorn prepared in three different ways (coated in chocolate, coated in yogurt and flavoured with dark cherry essence), then mixed together with plump real dried cherries and buttery chocolate cookie buttons.

Given the product's indulgent positioning, and premium SRP, we decided to sell it in a Häagen-Dazs style pint-sized container. To pull this off, we had to invest in yet another unique sealing machine so that consumers would have to peel off a protective film to get to the product in the same fashion as a container of ice cream. Needless to say, this popcorn snack wasn't on the Weight Watchers® approved list. We're talking heavy-duty delicious here. What made this mission heavier than the cream cheese escapade, the funky cocktail flocculation and the rock hard seasoning blowout was that we had everything riding on the line with this sucker. We had recently purchased part ownership in the struggling popcorn Ottawa plant in hopes that we could turn it around. A year later it was still hurting badly and we were about ready to call it a day. We were up to bat in the bottom of the ninth, with two out, two strikes, no one on base and trailing by one run. An epic World Series homerun was needed to tie things up and to stay alive in the game. Instead of gunning for a base hit with another boring bag of butter or cheese popcorn, we decided to swing for the fences with something the likes of which consumers had never seen. It was an easy sale.

Our first pitch was to Shoppers Drug Mart—who is also one of the leading Canadian retail pharmacy chains when it comes to offering unique seasonal confections. The buyer took one look and one taste and it was a done deal.

Before the product left our facility, it looked and tasted tremendous —the popcorn and the cookies were fresh and snappy, the cherries were chewy and the chocolate was creamy. Although we shipped the orders on time, Shoppers Drug Mart ran into a few floor space logistical issues, which is common for all retailers during key seasonal periods, and wasn't able to display our product until a few weeks after they had received it.

When Crème de la Crème eventually emerged from the crowded stock rooms and made its way on to the busy store floor, it was rock-hard déjà vu. We started to receive the typical unfiltered phone calls and emails from irate consumers. *'Who do I speak with to complain about being ripped off! I just bought my son's teacher one of your $8 popcorn tubs and it's inedible! I'm embarrassed. You should be embarrassed!'* As a side note, the consumer is always right, no matter how much you'll want to reach through the phone to honk their nose a la Mr. Miyagi style. That's not to say that you can't scream in frustration into the rear-view mirror at your reflection on the drive home.

We ran across the street to the nearest Shoppers Drug Mart to buy a few popcorn pints. The popcorn and the cookies were soggy, the dried cherries were stiff, but at least the chocolate was still creamy! Fluctuations in temperature and humidity had, yet again, triggered moisture in the dried cherries. The contents in the package had morphed into one hydroscopic sweet and sticky ... lump. *'Perfecto,'* I lamented as I muttered *'Crème de la Crap'* under my breath. Batter swings; strike three. Game over. Plant closes. Baah!

After nearly two historic decades of ingredient related misfires, we've honed our ability to recognize early warning signs of any bleaching, cracking, burning, hardening, softening or blooming. Having said this, as the old proverb goes, only the spoon knows what's stirring in the pot. For each failure on the public stage, we've had twice as many food science related saves behind the office-curtain. One of the more recent averted incidents was with our newest brand partner, Beaver-Tails®. A Canadian-based chain of pastry stands, its namesake product is a fried dough pastry that resembles a beaver's tail; for my American friends, it's more or less like the fried 'elephant ears' you'll find at carnivals (mmm, carnie treats).

The company, run by the super sharp and stylish Di Ioia bros, had been toying around with creating a CPG retail product concept for grocery using the brand's unique proprietary cracked wheat base-mix and distinct oval shape. They had come up short in partnering with a handful of other interested grocery concept developers because of either an inability to create a product that translated the brand's essence successfully for retail, or simply because they just didn't feel like the right fit. Pino Di Ioia and I hit it off immediately like Italian second cousins chatting at the Sunday lunch table over a plate of fresh pasta. We seemed to instinctively land on precisely the same page each time we chatted about his brand, our business or our opinions of the industry at large. We respected one another to the point where I didn't push to have a contract commitment in place before we began the quest together—which is rare for us and for good reason.

We began to court donut manufacturers with the capability to hand stretch and fry the trademark cracked wheat dough. By way of our COO at Johnvince Foods, the resourceful Luis Deviveiros, we were introduced to Tony Lam, a veteran in the donut business—a master deep fryer if you will. Standing at the end of his massive industrial fryer to catch fresh and hot donuts off the line and then pop them directly into my mouth was one of the many fat guy highlights of my career —and hopefully not the last one. Tony was super patient and super helpful when we commissioned him to provide sample after sample of various recipe tweaks and shape iterations of the product.

At one point, our office fridge and backup freezer chest were both crammed full of nearly eight months' worth of fried and failed attempts. We like to retain samples from each trial run to measure our progress and to gauge changes that occur to the product over set periods of time. As a side note, it's very common for the recipe fine-tuning stage to drag on for so long that your contract packer begins to lose interest and faith in both you and your mission. Be aware and be prepared. Try to keep your finger on their pulse and do what you must to keep them engaged in the project by sharing your progress, package design concepts, etc.

Just days before I bit the bullet investing in a second back-up freezer chest to house the ever-growing number of fried dough rejects, Tony showed up at reception with a smile and a carton of fresh samples still warm from the fryer. This time, their shape, texture and taste were in the pocket. So much so that Dave and I jumped in the car a few days later and drove five and half hours to Montreal to hand deliver the samples to the BeaverTails gang. As we quietly sat around the boardroom table in their ultra-funky Canadiana-themed office, marvellously munching on the latest submission, everyone grinned at one another with a similar *you know what, I think that this is the one* look.

Fast forward a few weeks after our meeting in Montreal and we had already designed a slick pastry box and pieced together a launch strategy worthy of the brand's potential. Just a month or so after that, we presented our program to a key grocery retail chain who was not only immediately on board, they wanted an exclusivity on our product for nothing less than a three-year term. The stage was set. We were given an aggressive launch date expectation and hit the ground running to prepare.

Upon completion of the packaging design, we couriered a mock-up of our pastry box filled with samples to our buyer for review by her peers. A few days later, we received a disparaging email asking us why the product was now so dry compared with the moist samples we had tried together in her office a couple of months back. We ran to our freezer chest and slacked-off a few of the samples we had sent her. Note: As with many goods sold in the bakery department, the product was designed to be shipped frozen into grocery stores, and would be stored frozen until it was time to thaw and display in the bakery section with a four-day window best before date.

'Doh!'—literally. The buyer was right; the texture had changed dramatically in under two months. The expectation was that the product would last for at least six months when frozen. It was much too dry and had lost its just-fried texture and allure. Upon closer investigation and inquiry, we were told that incorporating a common bakery industry preservative called calcium propionate would extend the product's shelf life, but we decided that the ingredient didn't jive with the brand's mission to use ingredients that consumers could relate with—it wasn't a guaranteed fix either.

Despite both the retailer and our brand partner encouraging us to work on a solution, we decided to deep-fry the idea. Had we not survived the Flavour Station seasoning and the Crème de la Crème product texture fiasco we might have given into the temptation to press on. After all, we had been developing and chasing the product concept for nearly a year and now had a willing contract packer, slick packaging, launch plans and a serious retail chain lined up. The drawback is that you only get one good first shot when bringing a well-loved brand into grocery with established consumer expectations. Not to mention, it's our money that's at stake.

Thanks to our coloured past, it was actually surprising how very easy it was to let go and to shift gears. Within a few weeks of deciding not to pursue the concept we had worked so hard to sell everyone on, Dave established a relationship with yet another contract packer specializing in a completely different type of bakery product capability. He's deep into developing a completely new pastry concept. If we end up keeping this one on the tracks, it'll make the previous concept look less than mediocre. Everything happens for a reason. As long as they don't ask us to buy an Angelus 10P Seamer, I think we'll be game. But then again, let's see what happens.

I've always considered cooking and baking to be two very distinct culinary activities. Most notably, where cooking doesn't always require a calculated hand, only loose interpretation and inspiration of a recipe, baking is much more about precise steps, science and measurements. Metaphorically speaking, you'll need to bring both your cooking and your baking game to the table when designing your label, bag, box or bottle. It's about making your product look original, creative and innovative, but it's also about ensuring that you carefully comply with the necessary government regulations tied to your ingredient declarations, allergen statements and any product claims. The minutiae in which you declare your ingredients on the back of your package, and showcase certain choice ingredients front and centre, deserves nothing less than a well-measured quadruple cross-check.

If it's your first kick at the can, consider searching on-line for a *nutrition labelling* or *food label consultant* in your area. For a palatable $100 or so per sku, a food label consultant will review your design to guarantee that it's in full compliance with either the CFIA or FDA legal requirements. In today's world of food allergen hyper-paranoia, miscommunicate or leave out just one word, and your company risks becoming more vulnerable than Mr. Peanut® making a surprise appearance in a school cafeteria bursting with EpiPen® armed Moms.

A few years back, a single unnamed consumer called into the CFIA to advise them that her child experienced an allergic reaction after having eaten our Kernels Salt & Vinegar popcorn seasoning. The severity of the reaction was never shared with us so I can't tell you how minor or major it actually was. I do hope that is was nothing serious. I have kids, so I obviously can understand and sympathize with how this Mom reacted. We declared *lactose* on our product's ingredient statement that, at the time, we had considered was sufficient to forewarn consumers with a dairy allergen. It turns out that we were dead wrong.

Despite having sold millions of bottles of this particular seasoning flavour well over a ten-year span and having never encountered a consumer dairy allergen inquiry on the product, let alone an actual allergen related incident, the CFIA rang us up to let us know that they were sounding the red alarm and commencing with the highest level of product recall communication to the general public that also ensured all product was immediately removed from grocery shelves from coast to coast, and was quarantined in our warehouses.

The only decision we were given was to either go public with the news ourselves or to have the CFIA make the announcement of their own accord. We quickly appointed a public relations specialist to help craft an appropriate response, and within less than twenty-four hours of circulating the news we were drowned with calls from worried retailers, distributors, brokers, consumers, CFIA plant auditors and, to a slightly lesser extent, my concerned Father. Within forty-eight hours, we were brought to our knees and gasping for air as the hammer continued to fall and the associated recall costs continued to mount.

When the dust settled (or should I say when the seasoning settled), the episode had cleared our bank account of nearly $250,000 in related penalties and charges. You know how much blood, sweat and tears it took to save that much money in this game of nickels and dimes! You see, it's much more than the cost of your product being pitched in the trash that comes into play here—setting aside the fact that you're charged back for product at the retailer's purchase price, it's also the cost that they incur to have the product physically pulled from the shelves and then thrown into the trash. To boot, many larger retail chains tack on a sizable five-digit fine. This isn't to mention the cost of lost sales, PR agency assistance, discarded packaging, re-worked product and brand humiliation.

For our size and stature of company, the recall was a mighty and massive blow to the head and chest that we barely survived. In some cases, we asked for the opportunity to reclaim and re-label the product since there was technically nothing wrong with the seasoning inside the bottle, but the majority of retailers discarded the product immediately upon receiving CFIA's broadcast. In one case, our largest retail chain account erroneously deducted the recall-related fine twice from their outstanding payments and then it took us four months to get the money back into our account. In another case, a retailer wanted to play it safe and made the aggressive call to throw out inventory of all the Kernels flavours they carried. Before the recall, Salt & Vinegar was the third best seller out of eight flavours. It was a real workhorse product for us. It's been years since the catastrophe and we're still being punished with weaker than normal sales on this particular sku. Lesson well learned. Never estimate! Calculate by using a measuring cup when it comes to nutritional labelling nitty gritty. Dot those tiny little 'i's' and cross those godforsaken 't's'.

Let It Simmer ~

1. *Collecting and understanding data on the chemical and physical fluctuations of your new product over time are required before you launch. How extensively have you tested your product to understand both how it will behave over time, and what you can safely declare on your packaging as the official shelf-life or best-before date?*

2. *Can your contract packer and/or ingredient supplier provide you with the necessary test results and formal shelf-life validation? If not, can they help connect you with the right company. For example, we often use a third party company called **Maxxam** (maxxam.ca) which provides analytical services when our contract packers cannot. It may cost us a couple of thousand dollars, but it's well worth the investment.*

3. *If time isn't on your side, ask your contract packer to conduct an accelerated shelf-life test (ASLT)—a cost effective method used to determine a new product's shelf life in a fraction of the time that it would normally take. It's not as dependable as leaving the product on your desk for six months or a year and watching to see what unfolds, but it's better than nothing.*

4. *Have a look at the ingredient deck of other similar products in the grocery store. Do they have preservatives that you do not? Why haven't they attempted to sell their products without these preservatives? Is it because of the risk?*

5. *If you're at a crossroads between either holding up a new launch or pushing things through without getting your hands on shelf-life data, consider delaying the launch until you have peace of mind. That is, unless you can use a fridge full of bright red cream cheese.*

6. *Hire a nutrition labelling or food label consultant to ensure that your packaging design is thoroughly compliant with government regulation standards so that you're not at risk with misleading or confusing the consumer.*

CHAPTER 29

Poking The Yolk

Moving to Action
With Calculated Risk

I t's time to gently poke the fragile membrane to let all that trapped goodness come oozing out. Onward! That's what I'd say to all of the hopeful food entrepreneurs deliberating over whether it's time to make their move into the wonderful world of grocery retail. I'm picturing the conga line of foodies and wannabe CPG (consumer packaged goods) moguls that I've had the pleasure of sitting across from, armed with their tasting sample in one hand and a skeletal business plan in the other. From the muesli-multigrain pancake mix maiden to the navy bean-based-butter-tart baron, I can still clearly see their expressions of determination mixed with a crumb of trepidation.

After dispensing with pleasantries, the barrage of routine and foundational industry questions begins to roll in. Questions like: Where and how do I begin? Do you think that my product has what it takes? How much money can I make? How much money will I need to bankroll the launch, and how long will it typically take to make my investment back? What should I expect to be on the hook for if it doesn't work? With whom can I speak to commercialize my recipe and have it mass-produced?

These questions, steeped in both enthusiasm and suspicion, are about the path and probability of transforming a leisurely cooking pursuit into a moneymaking food enterprise. Despite the unlikely probability of a positive from-play-to-profit transformation, I make it a personal goal to never smother or douse someone's craving for wanting something more. I'm sure that, before they've come in to chat, they have had to endure their fair share of killjoys.

The logical solution to quenching a thirst is to drink something, and take it all in. So, in my view, moving to action is always the best prescription. Move wisely and move slowly with a calculated risk and an acknowledgement that the likelihood of failure is lurking around the corner. Remember, scalability is vital. Start small, start local and move to poke the yolk and break the membrane to get the process rolling.

One of two scenarios will ensue: Either you'll find that the mission is going to take much more time, investment and nerve than you have to offer; or, you'll eventually trip and stumble into a manageable rhythm and make it to the finish line. Regrettably, the former scenario is the more prevalent outcome. However, even if the launch is disastrous, I'll bet the person who moves to exercise the following steps will be more satisfied, and will have achieved proper closure with how they arrived at the outcome compared with the person who places their concept on the back burner and ends up living with *"what if?"* regrets.

Okay, let's run through a few useful and inexpensive tricks of the trade to get you out of the kitchen and into The Hunger Games. But first things first. It should go without saying: Have you recently conducted a comprehensive store audit within each of your targeted retailers? Have you searched deep online to see if any similar products have recently popped up? If it has been more than two months since you've strolled down the grocery aisles to check out your competition, get into your car and double back to ensure that the coast is still clear. I can't tell you how many times Murphy's Law will spoil the broth when you turn your back for a split second. If I had a cucumber for each time we had a cool food concept, took too long to launch it, only to discover that another company marginally beat us in the race to the shelf, I'd have a full barrel of pickles by now.

Assuming that the cluttered grocery landscape still appears fertile and hospitable after conducting your store audits and extensive web-searching, there are a number of relatively inexpensive steps that you can take to start preheating the oven:

Food Shows

Visit Agriculture and Agri-Food Canada's website (agr.gc.ca/eng/industry-markets-and-trade/agriculture-and-food-trade-show-service/canada), or Food Reference's website (foodreference.com/html/us-food-festivals.html) in the US, for a comprehensive list of both consumer and trade events in your local area and abroad. Most of the shows are open to the general public for a nominal on-site entry fee. Aside from aisle after red-carpeted aisle packed with a wealth of free tasting samples, it's hands down *the* best venue to get a quick and conveniently itemized snap shot of new players, new product trends, enthusiastic supply partners and likeminded food entrepreneurs. You'll be able to rub elbows with more food industry folk in a chatty mood that can help you with your business in one afternoon, than you could travelling the country for months.

On any other day, it would be next to impossible to get a return phone call from that artisan contract packer in New Orleans that produces the killer Andouille sausage you want for your frozen gumbo entrée line. But at the show, you get to chat up the company's President and exchange stories, pork recipes and business cards so that when you ring him up a few weeks later, he'll probably call you back. You also get to toss a couple of fresh sausage links into your free tote bag so that you can try them in your recipe over the weekend.

Trade shows can also serve as a sobering eye-opener. You'll quickly notice how many new and remarkably interesting and attractive products are introduced; products that sadly won't graduate into grocery stores, or at least, won't stay there long enough for you to see and taste again. Perhaps more discouragingly, you'll also smell an air of desperation wafting out from behind the rows of vendor booths that haven't been able to draw interest from the hungry crowds.

Midway through a trade show walk, I'll take a rest across from a struggling booth to sip a free espresso sample while I try to appreciate the long road that's led them there. After having invested, and put faith in similar food events from Halifax to Vancouver, and from Florida to California, I can empathize with their situation. I'll ask myself questions like: Has their journey thus far been relatively stress-free? Or did they have to borrow start-up money from a relative or mortgage their home to finance the first production run?

Taking a closer look at their product, I'm asking myself why the heck they decided to go with a clear pressure sensitive label over a shrink-sleeve collar that could've helped to hide the offensive liquid separation in the bottle? I'm wondering if they've seen the uncannily similar beverage that's on display in the crowded booth a few aisles over. I'm hoping they sell enough cases and bank enough margin to be able to continue to fund the never ending battle that lies ahead.

Having said all this, please don't feel dejected. Instead, soak it all in because it might be you on the other side of the black-skirted foldable table next year. One of the most valuable items that you can grab at a food show, aside from the free prosciutto di Parma, is a show guide, which will have a complete list of exhibitor company profiles and their detailed contact information. It's typically crammed with contract packers and packaging suppliers.

Looking for something cheese related? From international artisanal cheese makers to extruded cheesie snack contract packers to spray-cheese-in-can companies, you'll find them in the book. If you decide to only hit one event, The Fancy Food Show (specialtyfood.com) is a safe, fun and tasty bet. There's one in San Francisco during the winter, and another in New York City during the summer. For the mother of all food events, jump on a plane to Cologne, Germany in October of every second year to visit the Anuga Food Fair (anuga.com). With over 280,000 square meters of exhibition area, you're bound to fly back home with a luggage full of promise.

Packaging Design

Unless you're an Adobe Illustrator design pro, investing in a praise-worthy package design is an investment I suggest that you may want to consider. Take my word for it. It'll be challenging for most folks to see, understand and believe in your vision unless you show them, more or less, precisely what the product will look and feel like when it's perched up on the shelf. An impressive napkin sketch, or a poor attempt at using Keynote or PowerPoint can end up creating more confusion, questions and doubt than interest and praise. What's more, unless your packaging design complies with the necessary CFIA (Canadian Food Inspection Agency) or US FDA (Food and Drug Administration) labelling guidelines, a retailer cannot legally retail your product—e.g. ingredients, allergens, nutrition facts, weight declaration and domicile statements all with a very specific font size, orientation and placement requirement.

Find a young and aspiring freelance graphic artist who's looking to add relevant CPG projects to their up-and-coming design portfolio and you might be able to dodge a very costly design bullet and spend practically nothing up to only a few hundred dollars. If not, budget around sixty to seventy-five dollars per hour, or a couple of thousand dollars per sku for a proper design. Search on-line or visit the local graphic design colleges in your area to begin your quest for a packaging Picasso. If you do opt for a more established and reputable design firm, consider appointing a smaller, boutique-sized company as opposed to enlisting a larger and potentially overly-structured one. You'll most likely find their services to be markedly cheaper, faster, flexible and less fastidious.

Once you find a willing and capable candidate, be sure to arm them with a clear, well-written and succinct packaging design brief. A packaging design brief document will aid both you and your designer, or marketing agency, in arriving at the target without wasting more time and money than is needed. If your direction is unclear, unfinished and uncertain, there will inevitably be frustration between you and the designer brought about by multiple design attempts that miss the mark and unnecessarily rack up the bill. A poorly thought out design brief and strategy will also eventually suck the fun out of the process. Try to operate under the mantra *'garbage in, garbage out'* instead of hoping that the designer can read your mind.

I suggest sharing the relevant project background info (who, what, why, when, where, how, how much), a snapshot of the current grocery landscape and the hierarchy of messaging you'd like to incorporate. It's not necessary, but I find it both fun and useful to name a well-known person or character who best embodies the essence of your brand. For example, Bill Murray is a great specimen for our Crazy Uncle® brand as he represents the loveable quirkiness and straight-up delivery that we shoot for. When I was at Quaker Oats, we wanted our Crispy Minis® rice chips to personify Meg Ryan (although, it was the late nineties, and was probably because I had a thing for her). It's also a good barometer for the designer to measure their work against.

Be sure to bring along packaging examples and tasting samples of other brands that capture the look, feel and vibe of what you're hoping to create. Always include a UPC (universal product code) in your design to ensure that you can officially sell your product should it graduate to the big leagues. Visit GS1 Canada (gs1ca.org) to register and secure a 6-digit company prefix license. It's well worth the initiation set-up charge and annual license fee. Once you have a kick-ass design, roll up your sleeves and mock up a sample, using glue guns, Avery labels or the like so that your prototype looks as legitimate and genuine as possible. Perfecto. Now you're more suitably armed and one full-size step closer to going live. It's also a prudent point in time to begin (cautiously) showing your product concept around. Share it with would-be consumers and visit prospective supplier partners (contract packers and suppliers of raw material ingredients and packaging) to gauge unbiased interest and to collect value feedback.

Genuine, Unfiltered Input.

It's time to develop a monster-thick and bulletproof skin. Presenting your masterpiece to friends and family at first, and then deliberately moving to show supplier partners, and yes, even prospective retailers, is an indispensable piece of the process. But beware, most comments, especially in the early goings before you've had a chance to tinker and tweak, will be painful pinches more than congratulatory pats on the back. Everyone's a seasoned critic and an industry expert when it comes to providing feedback. It'll be mondo uncomfortable, but keep the wincing down to a bare minimum and work to develop an aptitude for sifting the gold nuggets out from the wet sand. Consider the alternative of shutting out worthwhile feedback only to learn that you should've listened and made an adjustment to the recipe or packaging after the product hits the shelf. It's free to listen to and filter feedback, but it can cost you dearly to ignore it.

Gathering opinions can be as simple as staging a basic qualitative taste test among a handful of family and friends who best fit your targeted demographic profile. Your objective is to better understand the obvious and the underlying purchase intents of both your product and of the food category you'll be selling it in. If you want to structure a larger, more quantitative test, to help quantify preferences using numerical data, there are a number of turnkey online survey tools to help you out (e.g. visit surveymonkey.com). Either way, don't become too proud or fearful to open yourself up to criticism.

Connecting with Supply Partners

Even if you're not prepared to make a binding commitment to launching your product concept, simply knowing that you have a willing and capable supply partner network (contract packers and suppliers of raw material ingredients and packaging) waiting in the wings is advisable. More importantly, you'll be able to zero in on the associated start-up costs, nail down a realistic COGS (cost of goods) range, understand minimum production run requirements and plan ahead using their lead times.

This type of information is indispensable if you're to appreciate and accurately gauge your mission's financials and the feasibility of having your product manufactured as you continue to probe the market for interest and opportunities. Consider that, if you begin to see encouraging results, or receive interest from a retailer, making important decisions with unsubstantiated financial estimates will most likely backfire. What if it costs you double than what you expected to have your product made? What if the minimum run is more than you can comfortably sell within nine months and you end up sitting on a mountain of expired inventory? What if your recipe or packaging format has to change dramatically in order for the contract packer to produce it on a large scale?

A clear understanding of what you're working towards will also allow you to plan for a smoother evolution on the road to market. It will also minimize the amount of backpedalling if what you've been hoping to bring to market isn't possible to recreate from a contract packer's capability standpoint. To boot, it's free to speak with supply partners, source samples and secure quotes; just be sure to get any third parties to sign a basic NDA (Non-Disclosure Agreement) so that you protect your concept from being copied should your discussions end abruptly. Search the web for local manufacturing associations who might be able to pair you with the right sized outfit. For example, the City of Toronto has a food and beverage program that focuses on assisting local contract packers to build and promote their businesses. Our contact at the city, Michael Wolfson (a.k.a. 'The Fonz' in our office) is always ready and willing to hear about our newest product mission so that he can introduce us to the appropriate local manufacturing partner.

Full disclosure: It can be a delicate and awkward dance to court and carry conversations with a supply partner, particularly a contract packer, too far in advance of your launch for fear of being copycatted. It is, however, well worth the fancy footwork and stomaching the slight feelings of uncertainty as it'll help push to authenticate your mission and to radically improve your aim once it's time to pull the trigger.

Kitchen Co-ops

There's a deep and scary chasm between having to carefully whip up small batches of goodness in your home or office kitchen versus commissioning someone else to having your product mass-produced. Setting aside the risks and demanding obligations that come along with hiring a company to run your product, building orders out of a non-sanctioned kitchen comes with a serious accountability for food safety—not to mention that most big retail chains will require a facility audit before giving you a ticket to ride. In order to preserve foods using acidity, regulation requires the pH to be 4.6 or below. Sell just one improperly pasteurized mason jar of your wicked chimichurri marinade or use too little citric acid or potassium sorbate, and the Canadian Food Inspection Agency can shut you down like a culinary outlaw on the most wanted list.

Do yourself a big flavour, Google '**communal kitchens**' or '**kitchen incubators**' or '**kitchen co-ops**' in your area. There's a fantastic, fully decked out facility in Toronto, operated by a non-for-profit board, called Food Starter (foodstarter.ca). A relatively new, but quickly growing service, these useful establishments provide a proper food-regulated manufacturing space, complete with professional equipment, ingredient and finished goods warehousing, experienced production staff and savvy industry pros to help your budding business connect the necessary dots until you can become self-sufficient.

Producing your product out of a food-licensed communal kitchen may be prohibitive to making decent profit margins, but consider that your cash outlay and overall financial accountability will be dramatically more digestible. And, if your mission goes sideways, there's very little aftermath clean-up to concern yourself with. More crucially, if you can build a workable financial model using temporarily inflated COGs, you'll be laughing all the way to the bank once you graduate to using a more traditional, permanent and cost effective manufacturing set-up.

Before establishing your SRP (suggested retail price) range, visit the retailers on your target list to determine what the realistic SRP ceiling is. Also try to find out what the retailer's targeted profit margin range is by asking a willing department manager, or more conveniently, by asking the contract packer you have standing by. **Gross profit** is calculated by subtracting the COGs from the selling price. To calculate **profit margin**, divide the gross profit number by the selling price (e.g. a product with a $3.99 SRP and a COGs of $2.79 will have a gross profit of $1.20; divide the $1.20 by the selling price of $3.99 to get your profit margin, which in this scenario would be 30% for the retailer).

Tattoo this formula on your forearm, as this will be your equation to calculate both the retailer's financial objectives as well as your distributor's (and / or wholesaler's) and of course your own. For example, if the SRP ceiling for your product is $3.99 and the retailer requires a thirty percent profit margin, you'll need to charge them $2.79 if they are buying from you directly. If you're going to market using a traditional turnkey distributor with DSD (direct-to-store) shipment capabilities—who will purchase, warehouse, re-sell and ship your product for the $2.79 in the above example directly to retailers, they'll want anywhere from 17% up to a more likely 30% profit margin which suggests that you'll now be required to sell your product for as low as $1.95 to the distributor versus selling it directly to the retailer for $2.79. Note, for certain retailers (i.e. food service, convenience and gas stations), more often than not, you'll sell your product via wholesalers, who will require a more affordable 12% to 15% profit margin.

Can you make money selling your product for $1.95 based on the COGs associated with producing product out of a communal kitchen, or do the numbers only jive when you plug in the reduced COGs scenario associated with running product out of a more traditional manufacturing facility? Don't fret, remember that we're moving to poke the yolk and to move wisely and slowly until we're ready to take on more.

For your first legitimate selling adventure, consider selling directly to the consumer and cut out the retailer's, distributor's and/or wholesaler's profit margin. To start, consider selling your product in smaller, more flexible venues that will allow you to squeeze a dollar or two more out of the SRP to temporarily buff up your gross profit. Look for an intermediary selling-step that will allow you to watch, learn and to stay afloat financially until you can graduate to the big leagues. Use this phase to get a manageable and firm grasp on consumer interest and challenges, potential volume and profit, product issues, and most importantly, your comfort level. Use the opportunity to tweak, tinker and modify your product and your sales pitch.

Having already courted a contract packer prospect, you're now ready to advance out of the communal kitchen incubator and to start fulfilling the growing customer orders with your longer-term supply partners. Remember, with each step up, you'll need to generate and bank more profit margin to feed the growing number of hungry mouths at the supply chain table. Although, as your operations, capabilities and the economies of scale improve over time (we're talking a few years here), you'll likely tire of feeding too many mouths, double back and restructure to sell retailers directly in order to maximize your profits. But until such time, plan on setting and serving a crowded dinner table.

Preparing for the Big Leagues

There are quite a few meaningful and more manageable food venues to begin selling your product in than with a traditional grocery retailer. To test the waters and validate your concept's potential, before breaking the bank and your back on investments linked to gearing up for larger production runs, consider offering a single, medium-sized, regional retail chain a short-term exclusivity. For a start-up food enterprise, aside from the perhaps more common B-to-C on-line store opportunities, consider cutting your teeth at local farmers' markets and food fairs. My personal favourite is the Evergreen Brick Works in Toronto (evergreen. ca). To boot, the larger the retailer, the longer it will take to get a return phone call or email, let alone a meeting to pitch your product. Without a buyer relationship to lean on, you might end up watching the snow fall in December and then melt away in April before you get an ambiguous, one sentence voicemail or email reply.

A few years ago I had the privilege to work with Covenant House Toronto—an incredible organization that provides much needed 24/7 crisis care to homeless youth, aged 16 to 24—on a food-driven social enterprise concept. The catalyst for the program was The Covenant House's successful and well established 'Cooking for Life' program which teaches their kids the necessary culinary skills required to build a career in the food service industry. The program operated out of an onsite training kitchen armed with essential restaurant equipment. The social enterprise initiative was centred on utilizing the kitchen facility to support a food business that would manufacture a few choice homemade hot sauces that the kids had created. TAXI, the well-respected Toronto marketing agency that also happened to have fashioned our Crazy Uncle® cocktail brand, had created an exciting brand for the project that conveyed the mission's powerful message and unique point of difference.

As the project evolved, and particularly because I was the only participant with grocery industry experience, I felt a mounting sense of obligation to ensure that a foray into grocery wasn't viewed through rose-coloured glasses. Deep down I knew that, despite our product's admirable and influential social cause, we'd be primarily measured by the product's quality and efficacy, our ability to fill a category need, our packaging design impact, and ultimately, our ability to fulfill orders and generate a profit.

As much as I love a wickedly good hot sauce, there isn't a shortage of mind and mouth blowing options in the market. And, despite instantly falling in love with TAXI's clever brand name, narrative and design approach, I felt that grocers would be quick to accept a first order because of the charitable intent, but then hang us out to dry once the sales fell short. What type of destructive message would that send to the kids?

Instead, we decided to set up shop at local farmers' markets and food fairs. The scaled-down approach would allow the team the opportunity to engage with consumers first hand. It would allow them to learn and to tweak their recipes, packaging format, packaging design, and pricing before investing to print large minimum runs of labels and running too much inventory—you tend to think and operate differently with the pressure of having to stare at a warehouse full of impatient product. I was also banking on the farmer's market experience to temper the team's lofty sales volume ambitions.

Given that we hadn't performed proper shelf-life tests, these smaller venues would also allow us to understand how our recipe aged and reacted over time: Would the colour and flavour hold up, or would it brown and the flavour impact fade after only a couple of months? In the end, if your mission proves to be too complicated and costly to bring to grocery, or if consumers just don't respond as you had hoped, you'll know before you've bet the farm.

Walking food shows, investing in a proper packaging design, listening to consumer feedback, investigating supply partners, and setting up shop in a local market will not only help you cultivate your business safely and organically, it'll aid you in writing a compelling story and in mastering your one-minute-sales-pitch. You'll build a convincing case for the larger retail chains who will then be more apt to hold your hand and to collaborate when you bring them concrete in-market results. This scalable approach isn't only for newbie start-up companies. It's how we've carefully approached many of our more questionable product launches in the effort to learn before leaping, to avoid wasting money, and to keep the fire stoked when we're just not entirely sure how things will go on the big stage. Go on now, grab that fork and poke the yolk.

Let it Simmer ~

1. *Have you recently conducted a detailed store audit to ensure that another company hasn't begun to eat your lunch?*
2. *Have you visited a food trade show? If so, were you able to connect with any contract packers, distributors or brokers relevant to your mission? Did you find any product concepts similar to your own? If so, what's your takeaway on their brand, packaging, messaging, ingredients and retail price point? How does your product compare?*
3. *Have you taken the time to write a proper, clear and concise packaging design brief before collaborating with a designer?*
4. *Are you opening your mind to the feedback of others, or are you too proud and anxious to actively listen to what they have to say?*
5. *Do you have suitable supply partners waiting in the wings? Do you know how much they'll charge you per unit, what their minimum run is and what the overall start-up charges will be? Are they willing to amortize the start-up costs into the unit price over a period of time to make the leap more financially digestible for you?*
6. *Where can you start selling your product to gain momentum, to learn more and to iron out any kinks before you step up to the big leagues?*
7. *Is your business model scalable? How fast can you go from zero to a hundred if a large retail chain throws a purchase order in your lap?*

CHAPTER 30

The Candy Man (Almost) Can

Brand Promotion & Awareness

I n the summer of 1998 I was a brand manager for a confections company called Beta Brands (you remember, when I slept in the makeshift bedroom made of office dividers in the living room of our company frat house). Blair Neuss and I were searching for a persuasive and
affordable marketing strategy to make LifeSavers® hard rolled candy
relevant to tweens and teens again. The candy, originally invented in
1912 as a 'summer candy' that could withstand heat better than chocolate, had become more of a grandma's candy-bowl treat amidst the competitive sea of much hipper chewy, ultra sour and funky confections of
the day.

Around the same time, I received an invite from a marketing firm
named Big Bang which was promoting and licensing a DreamWorks'
theatrical release called *Small Soldiers*. The media event looked interesting enough, and it was a Friday afternoon out of the office, so I went.
Although we didn't end up buying into the Small Soldiers property, I
did click with the firm's magnificently energetic owner, Scotty Stevenson.
I loved spending time with Scotty as he had full access to the music and
film industry, was an exceedingly creative and ambitious thinker and,
above all, we got along instantly. Aside from working on some pretty cool
campaigns together, I spent some great time with him and his lovely
wife Lucy. It was long before I was married to Lisa so they tried to set me
up more than a few times. (Thanks guys.)

*NSYNC was an upcoming boy band in the era of boy bands. They had not yet reached superstar status, but Scotty and Co. felt they were destined for great fame. He also believed that he could get the band to put on a private LifeSavers concert, complete with a meet-and-greet for 500 contest winners at Toronto's The Guvernment bar. He was right. The campaign was aptly named 'LifeSaver's Sweet Sounds of Summer.' The connection between the candy to the band and to music was simple but on point—colourful, pleasurable, five flavours for five diverse band members, etc.

At the time, I was in my mid 20s (and as I just pointed out, still single) so the whole thing was right in my wheelhouse and I loved it. The secondary prize was a giant groovy LifeSavers jukebox. We had an extra one made for the office, and we still use it at BrandFusion. A few weeks after we signed on the band, their career started to blast off ... crazy fast. Throngs of young and painfully-screechy teenage girl groupies started to obsess over Justin Timberlake, Joey Fatone and the boys.

A few of the diehard groupies somehow found out about the private LifeSavers concert and that I was helping to organize it. They would ring me up and literally cry with intense excitement and raging hormones begging me to dish out a couple of free tickets. Two girls actually built and devoted an entire website to asking me for tickets. It shouldn't go without mentioning that this was 1998, so homespun teenager-developed websites weren't a normal occurrence. In the end, we did have two extra tickets so I called everyone into my office to witness the congratulations call to the two web-o-gram gals. My coffee mug nearly shattered into pieces with all the high-pitched screams and jubilant wailing blasting through the speakerphone.

The day of the concert arrived after what seemed like an eternity of build up and calls from everyone and their sister looking for tickets and backstage passes. I stood next to the band's beefy bodyguard a few feet from the stage to watch the warm-up set— 'It's tearin' up my heart when I'm with you, but when we are apart, I feel it too'—catchy stuff. The magnitude of the event hit home when I stepped out of The Guvernment's back door to assess the line-up. I was stupefied. It was huge and ... they were all female. The two girls I had awarded the free tickets to actually made a large picket sign that said something like 'Thank You,

Bruno! We Love You' ... or at least that's the way I remember it and tell the story.

As the people crammed in, the energy peaked uncontrollably. A funny side note was that, unbeknownst to me, my future wife Lisa was in attendance as a chaperone for her younger cousins who scored tickets. And then it all went very wrong—not the event, but my time in the glorious sun as the ultra cool guy with direct access to the band. Turns out that JT and the boys couldn't get through all 500 meet-and-greets because of tight timing. It also turned out that the girls to whom I promised the meet-and-greet—the ones that probably didn't sleep for weeks because of their bottled excitement—were the ones that got stiffed. They slowly sauntered towards me like angry teenage zombies forming a tight mob-like circle. The words 'Why? You promised' were mournfully barked at me, over and over. At one point (and this is the truth) one of the girls started madly pounding on my chest while wistfully sobbing. 'My God,' I thought. 'It wasn't supposed to be like this.' Needless to say, I watched the entire concert from the very back of the room peeking out from behind a pole.

The final results of the campaign were far more prosperous than my one night as a music mogul. LifeSavers sales rocketed up by triple digits for a few months and retailers were once again interested in what the brand had to say. Tethering the tired and unconnected brand to a fresh and new anchor in a meaningful and relevant way gave it the relevance it desperately needed. If the plan was for the forgotten candy to find its way into the back pocket of a few ripped and torn Levi's instead of buried under a change-purse in Grandma's handbag, well then mission accomplished.

To be clear, there was a host of sales tools (i.e. displays, posters, entry pads, concert tickets for store managers' kids, etc.) and volume targets that built up to the private concert finale. It wasn't just a case of let's throw a rock concert to get people liking the candy again. Of course, I realize this was really just basic marketing tactics. (I can just hear brand managers out there reading this last paragraph and saying: 'Tell me something I don't know.')

For an aspiring company looking to rapidly build brand value, the real morsel to pull out of the *NSYNC story is about gaining meaning-ful credibility through a creative and relevant association with an es-tablished and desirable third party brand. It's about tapping into some-one or something that will elevate your launch and street cred. In the case of *NSYNC, the timing was somewhat of a fluke as Big Bang was able to sign on the band right before they became literally untouchable.

When launching a product, we always ask ourselves, would it be better to build credibility from the ground up or is it worth it to pay a fee to an established and respected third party entity (via a license fee or a one-time amount) to help carry our heavy cart up the hill? [Cau-tion: Hitching your trailer to another brand's goodwill to help build your own brand doesn't suggest that you should be willing to sacrifice control or ownership in your mission—for me, that's a big no-no.] 'Might sound crazy, but it ain't no lie. Baby, bye, bye, bye.'

Let it Simmer ~

1. *Can you think of another brand, company or entity to associate with that will elevate your product launch, strengthen and validate your brand's narrative, and improve the chances of success? If so, can you enter into the agreement without giving up any ownership or strategic control?*

2. *If you choose not to associate or promote your product with another well-known and accepted entity, how much longer will it take to achieve the same level of awareness and success (i.e. product trial, media coverage, consumer / retailer / distributor interest, etc.)?*

3. *How long do you need to associate your product with another entity? Is it just for the initial launch period or for the entire life of the product? If so, have you clearly set expectations via a written contract before going too far down the road?*

CHAPTER 31

Milk Money

Spend Your Marketing Money Wisely

Back in 1983, like most rebellious ten-year-old kids, I rarely used my milk money allowance to purchase a plain old boring carton of 2% milk from the school cafeteria. Instead, on the way home from Mill Valley Public school, I'd duck into this small gem of a tuck shop inconveniently located at the back of a residential apartment building. My hot handful of quarters were often used to purchase a Mr. Freeze® banana freeze-pop, a sack of Gold Rush® bubble gum and the occasional lucky rabbit's foot keychain. (Remember those fuzzy things?) Sure, the milk was a considerably healthier choice and would've prevented many lingering stomach aches, but I just didn't have enough coin to afford both luxuries. I had to choose between making a sensible purchase or a much more entertaining and colourful one.

When I landed my first job at the local Red & White grocery store, I was so elated to pocket a whopping $3.81 per hour that each shift I spent the entire day's earnings on a hefty meal during my breaks and lunch, complete with a 650g container of Astro® Cappuccino yogurt and, of course, a small carton of milk. On the long walk home I'd hit the neighbouring tuck shop to grab a banana freeze-pop or a couple of jumbo ice cream sandwiches. I finally had enough coin to blow, but somehow always managed to arrive home with empty pockets.

Fast forward thirty or so years, and I'm still toiling over making the same sorts of decisions in the quest to have something left in my hot little hands when the day is done. This time around, however, it's all about whether to spend our modest marketing budgets on colourful and flashy agency-inspired out-of-store consumer advertising temptations, or on the safer and perhaps more staple in-store trade promotional tactics. Note: In-store promotions are generally account management activities arranged between you and the retailer, whereas out-of-store advertising deals with activities and communication directly between you and the consumer. In the ad agency world, they also refer to the distinction between advertising to consumers at the point of sale as **below the line** (BTL) and advertising to consumers via mass media as **above the line** (ATL).

In an effort to simplify things from here on in, with an omission of the eCommerce sector, let's categorize and compare these two disciplines as **in-store** vs. **out-of-store** marketing. And if in-store marketing is your milk, then out-of-store marketing is your banana freeze-pop and Gold Rush bubble gum. Either way, you're going to have to reach into your pocket further than you might think if you want a buy a ticket to properly play the game. Consider that, while a sexy and mind-blowing packaging design can be your greatest and most inexpensive asset in stimulating consumers to toss one of your products into their cart, you can't expect it to do all the heavy lifting. With only a few seconds on the clock to convince passing shoppers, you'll need to cover off all of your bases to get the job done.

For smaller start-up companies, I believe that until you earn more cash to play with (hopefully it works out to more than $3.81 per hour), it should be more about investing in uncomplicated in-store promotional marketing tools that will elicit more measureable and immediate trial, separate your product from the competition, and help to strengthen your relationship with the retailer; for example: aggressive temporary price reductions (TPRs), flyer ads, air mile contributions, off-shelf point-of-purchase (POP) displays, sweepstakes and contests, rebates, product sampling, etc.

While it will eventually become increasingly vital to invest in building product awareness and in shaping your brand's narrative via engaging out-of-store advertising campaigns that live beyond the retailer's four walls, be on guard with how much of your money you initially allocate; for example: television, newspapers, magazines, radio, outdoor ads, direct mail and (to some extent) online efforts.

The results of pure out-of-store advertising efforts, and their positive financial impact on your bottom line, are just too difficult to measure compared with the more traditional in-store promotional marketing efforts that can drive measureable sales volume; and unfortunately, a difficulty to quantify results often leads to growing disappointment, doubt and a resentment to reinvest in marketing programs. To clarify, allocating less of your budget on advertising doesn't also imply that you should spend less energy and time on out-of-store communication. Inversely, we probably spend much more effort and time managing our consumer advertising efforts because we have to be more creative and resourceful when operating with an insignificant budget.

As your pockets become heavier with earnings, shifting more of your budget to imaginative out-of-store advertising efforts will become possible, but it shouldn't be at the expense of the in-store promotional marketing side. Albeit, the dawn of social media and the proliferation of its available platforms, save for your time, has created the ability to balance and, better still, tie both disciplines together with integrated closed-loop marketing programs without adding much more cost.

Yet, if this is your first time around the block, know that before it becomes about making money, it will be more about keeping your company afloat and alive—and hopefully without having to endure a constant stomach ache brought about by misspending what few funds you have on the wrong marketing persuasions. Remember, your business will have an undying and insatiable appetite for rapidly chewing up all the cash you can feed it. Knowing how and when to feed your little growing monster, without having to take on more debt and paralyzing stress, can be the big difference between making it home with or without a few crumpled bills in your back pocket.

So, what's on the marketing menu? Where can you afford to dine? Which goodies can you afford to open your wallet for? Will they meet with your strict expectations and keep you from feeding your hungry business more than it actually needs to scoff down? In the early going, from an out-of-store advertising spend perspective, we typically try to find or create affordable brand building opportunities that we can mount and manage in-house ourselves. Sure, it's much easier and even more fun to hand the creative reins over to a hip boutique marketing agency to dream up an imaginative concept, but unless you have a worthwhile budget, and can still sleep soundly should their execution fall short, you're better off sticking with a home-grown plan.

The magic is coming up with an advertising campaign that will make your already-stretched-too-far $10,000 investment look more like a cool $100,000 to both retailers and the consumer. Squeeze as much blood from the stone as you can. When our Kernels Popcorn Shakers started to become more omnipresent on the grocery scene, we managed to store a few big nuts in the tree and then decided that it was time to up the ante in our food fight by investing more into our advertising efforts.

We ended up working with the tween television station YTV to invent a silly, Emmett Lathrop "Doc" Brown, Ph.D. inspired cartoon character we called *Marty the Mad Flavour Scientist* that YTV starred in a series of animated short promotional commercials. Marty's *'mix it up'* message was designed to inspire kids to come up with, and then share, their very own wacky recipes by mixing together our popcorn seasonings. The idea was playful and relevant. The production values of the cartoon were impressive and ended up looking very credible when aired alongside commercials for other more established brands.

It was the first, and regrettably, the last time that we dished out $120,000 big clams at one time on an advertising campaign. Like many of our other out-of-store marketing attempts, our sales didn't seem to spike whatsoever as a result of the significant expense. And, of course, we lost sleep because it was a lot of bread for our company to dish out.

Look, I've worked in the marketing department at larger CPG companies and was charged with the responsibility of allocating significant multimillion dollar budgets. I've sat and collaborated with the agency gurus on numerous occasions so I can appreciate and still subscribe to the importance of building product and brand awareness sustainably over time via integrated campaigns that weave both marketing disciplines together. The gravity of misfiring when it's your budding company and half-inch deep pockets however, is nothing short of life-altering and somewhat vomit inducing.

If you're able to raise the generous capital required to fund a properly weighted and integrated marketing campaign, then God bless you. But know that you represent the minority of crusading entrepreneurs. I can't tell you how many companies and hopeful brands that we've been offered up for pennies on the dollar because the owners ended up broke by overfeeding their cause with half-baked out-of-store marketing spend. There's no room for big and costly mistakes when you're feeding the monster from hand-to-mouth.

Consider investing in a marketing plan that focuses on leveraging an affordable out-of-store advertising effort to drive a more tangible, and most importantly, measureable sales impact. For the last few years, for example, we've teamed up with Sony Pictures to help them promote their theatrical movie releases by selling a limited edition Kernels Popcorn shaker which incorporates both a main character from the movie as well as a sweepstakes offering on the packaging.

Aside from the obvious and natural partnering of movies and popcorn, the program is remarkably affordable and also serves to leave our retailers with the impression that we've invested far more than we actually have. Think special edition packaging designs with Optimus Prime, Gru from *Despicable Me*, etc. In this particular example, we're also indirectly leveraging Sony's out-of-store advertising campaign to bolster our in-store promotional program.

Unlike our YTV media ad spend remorse, we also know that this program consistently yields a 10% to 12% direct lift on our sales because we can measure the lift by controlling the printing and distributing of the specially marked product. The affordability has also allowed us to comfortably repeat the program for a number of consecutive years, so over time, we've also been able to nail the forecasting requirement down to a science to ensure maximum sell through and minimal unsold product wastage.

If we're feeling ambitious, we'll use the movie partnership campaign as an instrument to venture out to try and secure new distribution by preselling point-of-purchase in-store displays filled with the limited edition product to new, untapped retailer prospects. If we're successful, we'll have generated additional incremental volume (i.e. beyond the 12% lift), and because we've presold the inventory before pulling the expensive trigger on building more production, there's little risk as we only need to build against the order commitments in hand. The real beauty is that, if you can sell enough incremental volume, you may not only completely cover the entire marketing costs associated with the program, you're actually in a position where you've made money—a marketing investment strategy I like to call reversed-cost-marketing.

As discussed in the previous chapter, synergizing with a complementary product or brand partner, that lives either in or out of your product category, can also be a resourceful technique to aid you in providing a major concrete value offering to retailers and consumers. For example, part of our strategy when licensing a well-known restaurant brand for a grocery retail product is to include a hefty on-pack bounce back offer from the restaurant partner—for instance, with a $3.79 purchase of our Pizza Pizza® Dips in grocery stores, consumers receive an on-pack coupon for a free small box of potato wedges at Pizza Pizza restaurants.

Our restaurant partners love the ability and the unconventional access to be able to provide an offer and an awareness for their brand in grocery stores. Considering that consumers are traditionally used to receiving 50¢ to $1 off deals that will only last for a week or so, we love that our partners can provide us with deals valued up to $5 that will last considerably longer because they are printed directly on our packaging. Oh, and by the way, given that we're providing both the canvass and the unique distribution for their offer, there's usually no charge to us! But then again, maybe it's just my lucky rabbit's foot finally starting to do its thing.

As your volume grows from a struggling few hundred cases per year to a more desirable few thousand, it's prudent to start assigning a fixed dollar amount per case towards your out-of-store advertising marketing efforts. Depending on how poor or rich your net margin is—the percentage of revenue left in your hands after subtracting all operating expenses, interest, and taxes from your total revenue, consider delegating from $5 up to $10 per case to play with.

Be forewarned. Periodic margin dilution is written in the stars irrespective of the game that you decide to play. If you're not making enough profit to contribute at least a few dollars per case, you should probably be very concerned. Consider raising your prices or find a way to chop away at your COGS. To quote Stephen R. Covey from his ubiquitous self-help book, *The 7 Habits of Highly Effective People*: 'No margin, no mission!' I'd also suggest baking the in-store promotional marketing funds directly into the sell price from the get go so that you're not tempted to zip your pockets shut when it really should be time to support the retailer by investing with them more aggressively. By the way, funding in-store promotions isn't cheap either so be sure that you're baking enough quality dough into your sell price.

When you build the muscle to financially step up and start playing with marketing agencies to create and execute your out-of-store advertising campaigns, don't rest on your laurels by expecting that whatever ultra-imaginative idea they formulate will result in pushing you further up the climb. It can take a few failed attempts for both you and them to discover what the best direction and narrative for your product and brand should be. Keep some poker chips up your sleeve and avoid doubling down until you see some success and can measure the results.

Despite the sometimes awkward breakup aftermath, don't be afraid to cut bait and hook into another agency should the understanding of your mission and their position begin to dramatically differ from your own. If you can invest more manageable chunks of money at a time, and both parties can continue to agree with and lean on the postgame learnings, staying the course together is more probable. Conversely, overspending and an inability to agree on the takeaway lessons from a botched campaign will end with an *'it's not you, it's me'* heart-to-heart chat.

The danger, however, in expecting an agency to work miracles with a starving budget is that you're tying their hands on being able to integrate and deploy the mechanisms required to win. Remember, they too must make money and live under their own *'no margin, no mission'* rule of law. So, that big investment that you're so proud to finally be able to offer up as your entire budget might end up being burned up solely by agency fees and in turn leave very little for a proper execution of the plan.

The other caution is that it can take a few months and numerous brand-questing exercises with the agency to better understand what your product's narrative should sound like and what direction your company should travel in. It's never an overnight process. Lately, I'm finding that presenting an agency with a limited budget recurrently leads to a plan that relies too heavily on social media tools. And, more often than not, I can tell you that you'll feel cozy and satisfied at first simply because you've at least made a concerted effort to work with a third party to understand your business and have taken a step towards promoting your product at a deeper level.

The trouble is, after weighing the results against the economics generated by your in-store promotional marketing efforts, especially if the out-of-store ad campaign hasn't been able to drive quantifiable sales, you begin to better appreciate where your delicate investments will work harder for you. There are always exceptions to the rule, for example if your product is truly newsworthy there's always the chance that your message and mission will go viral and drive consumers into the store, but such luck is not easy to come by.

Despite my marketing training and experience, it's unfortunately difficult for me not to sound pessimistic about serious out-of-store advertising expenditures in the early goings of building sales for your product simply because I've been thwarted by our return on investment more times than I can count. With that said, this book was inspired by and written for the starting entrepreneur with restricted funds at their disposal. The lessons were meant more for the would-be company and brand that has to continue hitting the mark in order to keep their product from ending up in the clear-out bin. I'm thinking more about your sustainability and your ability to responsibly scale up marketing spend over time.

Spending beyond your means with aggressive out-of-store advertising too early in the game could cause you to fall into a deeper financial and emotional hole. Spend your milk money wisely by focusing the lion's share of your marketing budget in-store so that you can stick and move before your banana freeze-pop completely melts and you have nothing left to show for your hard work.

Let it Simmer ~

1. *Are you relying too heavily on your packaging design to do all of the heavy lifting with respect to creating interest and awareness for your product?*

2. *What's on the marketing menu? Are you ordering the Wagyu beef when all you can afford is a burger and fries? Can you make every $10 of marketing budget work for you like it was $100 or more?*

3. *How much money can you comfortably afford to risk investing in an out-of-store advertising campaign without causing irreparable damage to your mission?*

4. *Are you applying more of your already-inadequate budget to lofty agency driven out-of-store advertising efforts than to more functional and measureable in-store promotional marketing programs? If so, make sure that it's for the right reasons and that the strategy will work before your well runs dry.*

5. *Can you synergize with a complementary product or brand partner to create cross promotions, joint sampling efforts, alternate distribution opportunities and valuable bounce back offers?*

6. *Are there opportunities for reversed-cost marketing campaigns that serve to cover your costs by creating incremental selling opportunities?*

7. *Are you ready to afford the luxuries that come along with hiring a marketing agency, or should you continue to mount and manage your out-of-store campaigns in-house? If you are ready to appoint an agency, how much money can you comfortably afford? Is it enough money for the agency to work their magic?*

CHAPTER 32

Family Table

Blood Before Money

Aside from eating out with clients or supplier partners, I haven't paid for my lunch in over fifteen years. Much more importantly, I eat like a bloody King. Here's a snapshot of this past week's menu:

- **Monday:** Niçoise salad (with each ingredient carefully prepared and served in separate glass containers to ensure a fresh assembly)
- **Tuesday:** cherry wood smoked Tilapia tacos with fresh Pico de Gallo and pickled red cabbage
- Wednesday: red wine-braised short ribs and sweet potato wedges with homemade hot antipasto spread—washed down with an icy glass of Crazy Uncle® Whisky, Cider & Chai Tea Cocktail
- **Thursday:** lightly charred Calabrese bread topped with ricotta from the corner bakery, juicy tomatoes and basil from my wife's vegetable garden, and my barber Kam's hometown olive oil from Lebanon.

It's currently Friday morning and I can't wait to see what's waiting for me in the office refrigerator—forget about it! Ready for this, my brother and Dad prepared everything from scratch—everything. To boot, if my brother can't bring lunch to the office for us because he's away, Pop makes it a point to drop off lunch so that I won't starve. (Yes, I'm 43 years old, but don't hate me.) Both are tremendous home chefs.

My Mum passed away at the tender and tragic age of twenty-eight when I was only eight years old. Consequently, my Dad completely amped up his game in the kitchen and found that he had both a love and talent for good cooking. Growing up, Dave and I would sock-slide into the kitchen before school to see what was waiting for us in the oven—seafood crêpes with a side of oven roasted paprika and rosemary potatoes (the man is crazy for potatoes) were but one of his typical 7 a.m. breakfast specialties.

Today, Dad loves to visit the BrandFusion office two or three times a week for a decent cappuccino and one of Dave's homemade chickpea-based biscotti. Note: We respect and handle the preparation of our morning cappuccino very religiously—whole milk at 140° to 160° degrees only, please and thanks. The staff and surrounding companies, courier delivery guys, etc. all affectionately refer to him as 'Papa Joe.'

For the record, I'll add in that my wife Lisa is also an inspired and fabulous home cook with a set of magic green thumbs. The woman will cheerfully pop into the kitchen at 6 a.m. to bake homemade focaccia bread with freshly picked herbs for the kid's school lunches. During the first year of our marriage, Lisa would make it a point to whip up more than she figured we could both eat for dinner so that I could bring the leftovers to work for lunch. After eventually realizing that I was pro-grammed to inhale every last morsel placed on the table, regardless of the stupid amount, she half-heartedly surrendered my insane lunch provisions to her father-in-law.

As those of you who work with family and friends know, it's not all sunshine and seafood crêpes. Working with family and close friends can be, without a doubt, complicated at the best of times. Like a suc-cessful marriage, it's about responsibilities and mutual respect—ignore this and your tasty lil' business, and more seriously, your relationships, will painfully suffer bringing the ship down with them. Practice and embrace the basics, and your good ship lollipop will enjoy a layer of strength and protection that others can only dream of.

Some of the largest food companies have either been built on the broad shoulders of family power, or have crumbled because of it. To me, the greatest leg-up that working with your parent, sibling, or spouse 'should' offer you is untiring and abundant trust. My brother always has my back, and puts my needs and goals right alongside his own, if not above his own most of the time, and vice versa. It allows us to focus on making the demanding climb without worrying about how and when we'll push one another off the cliff. Equally imperative, we never go after the same bone. We rely on one another for counsel, but we're more aware that we both need to entirely own, lead and contribute something different to the mission. It helps that we have distinctive skill sets, but work with the same set of core values and a similar paradigm. Going after the same bone will eventually lead to silent competition, acrimony and one or both persons feeling undervalued.

For example, I look after most of the company's sales, but Dave is also responsible for a set of key retail chain accounts so that he can keep a firm finger on our customers' rhythm. He also governs the finances and supply partner relationships. We both tackle product development, but we each have our own brands and product concepts to flush out and to build. Be aware that roles and responsibilities also have best before dates—and because your relationship is always hanging in the balance, be honest about shaking things up before they get stale.

In the first ten years of building the business together, Dave and I found that tackling retailer and supply partner meetings together worked best—people seemed to like the 'brothers in arms' show. After a while, we felt that each meeting ended with either one of us unintentionally stealing the show causing the other to feel dejected and undervalued. As soon as I felt this problem bleeding into our time together out of the office, I became obsessed with restructuring the business so that we both felt re-energized and inspired. A couple years or so ago, we went so far as to hand the BrandFusion Presidential reins over to Dave. He was more than ready and capable to lead, and I'm ready to help contribute to our family's future via other initiatives.

Would you be okay with losing a small fortune if it meant keeping peace in the family? My family would, and here's a story—about popcorn, of course—to prove it. My younger cousin Chris (think back to the Pope corn escapade) worked with me during BrandFusion's primary years—we grew up as close as brothers. During that time, he worked with, and got to know, both the popcorn business and our partners over at Kernels Popcorn. As he grew older and gained industry experience, and an insatiable appetite for his own entrepreneurial adventures, it became clear that BrandFusion wasn't large enough to provide both a career path and the financial compensation, both of which Chris deserved.

After some time, he ventured out on his own to pursue a number of related and remarkably creative opportunities (and has been very successful since). One such opportunity was partnering with an existing small popcorn manufacturing facility out of Ottawa, Ontario called Snack Brands. His partners, Mike and Todd, built the business on producing bagged popcorn for Kernels' fundraising division that sold product to schools for kids to resell and generate funds for sports programs.

When Chris (and Kernels) asked for my opinion about his role and involvement, I somewhat hastily gave them my blessing either believing or, perhaps miscalculating, that his Kernels branded fundraising business wouldn't clash with BrandFusion's Kernels grocery initiatives—knowing that if our worlds did end up colliding it would lead to conflicting agendas and retailer confusion. Besides, at the end of the day, who'd want to deny family a chance to advance if their mission seems realistic.

Chris rolled up his sleeves, and invested a serious six-digit amount into the company to buy equipment, packaging and to improve the facility on the whole. Early in the game, it became apparent that, in order for his new company to sustainably grow, pay back his investment and turn a profit, the potential volume that we could generate in grocery would count the most. In the early going, we felt only a slight and manageable pressure to come up with ideas and concepts that could drive meaningful volume into his bourgeoning company. The issue was, and still is, that selling popped popcorn is a difficult and frustrating game—the cost of entry is laughable ($60,000 in listing fees per sku with certain National retail chains!), the margins are dangerously low, the competition is too stiff, the product's shelf life is gravely short, and the aftermath clean-up of a failed grocery launch can be financially crippling.

Unfortunately, or perhaps inevitably, we just couldn't come up with a breakthrough item that could stick. As the pressure to produce in order to survive mounted, Chris was put in a precarious, and obvious, position. If BrandFusion couldn't find a concept winner, he had to do what he could without us in order for his company to live. And yes, I would've totally done the same thing if the cross was mine to carry. The drawback was that BrandFusion's most coveted asset was, and quite frankly still is, its licensing agreement with Kernels that grants it the right of first refusal to represent the brand's pre-packaged retail products outside of its normal channels of operation (i.e. kiosks in shopping malls and fundraising related activity).

It was only later that we all realized that Snack Brands had inadvertently succeeded in getting Kernels to sign a somewhat similar, and regrettably conflicting, agreement allowing them to produce and sell its namesake popped popcorn directly to retailers. To explain, although we had no immediate plans to sink our teeth into creating and selling popped popcorn into grocery stores pre Snack Brands, the decision of when, how and why rested exclusively with us. What's more, should we have decided to launch a popcorn product, Snack Brand's agreement prohibited us from shopping our concept around to other contract packers, irrespective of unfavourable pricing and manufacturing capability differences. Under the new arrangement, we'd be shoved into launching a product for the wrong reasons, at an inopportune time, and potentially with an ugly balance sheet. Suffice it to say, neither Chris or I had duly thought through the potential complications before pulling the trigger. In any case, the seeds were sown.

We shook our head in disbelief: *'How could this have happened?'* Rest assured, Chris, Dave and I lost many nights sleep over this one. Feeling the gravity of the situation, I started to bring the burden home which, for me, is rare. My Grandmother taught me at an early age to *'hang your problems on the problem-tree outside the house before you walk in the door'*—which, incidentally, sounds much cooler in her Sicilian dialect —*'they'll be waiting for you to claim the next morning.'*

It began to get ugly as Chris and I tried to navigate our respective companies through the murky waters knowing full well that, if we weren't dealing with a close family member, we'd both take a much more forceful position. It got well beyond the point of being able to sit restfully at the family table together—a ritual we practiced often since birth and both respected immensely. It was agreed that we had to nip things in the bud before someone took a more regrettable and irreparable route. Despite not being able to drum up consistent and worthwhile volume for Snack Brands, we half-heartedly decided to buy Chris's share of the company. Chris half-heartedly agreed to sell it to us knowing full well that if it was anyone else he would've dropped the Sicilian hammer. We all realized that it was imperative in order to regain family balance, control of the wheel and our sanity.

Aside from a handful of heated debates and empty disparaging threats, we settled on a number—a large number that resulted in a very serious six-digit hoof to the family jewels for both sides. The purchase felt more like we had bought a money pit cottage when we should've been focusing on making mortgage payments on our principal residence. Our new partners Mike and Todd proved to be hard working, agreeable confidants in the battle to see the company triumph. Despite our best efforts, serious additional cash infusions, and fifty percent of our time (backed by no salary, of course), we eventually closed the corporation down a year or so later. Our accountants used the losses as best as they could to minimize the throbbing financial sting.

In the end, we justified our actions on two critical fronts. We managed to uphold our exclusive sales and distribution rights, unshackling my cousin from the peculiar predicament he was unfairly placed in; and, much more importantly for Chris, Dave and I, we still can enjoy sitting at the family table with one another. Actually, my relationship with Chris is stronger today than it ever was. To be frank, he's developed into quite the unshakable and formidable warrior. He's the one dude you want at the helm should you go into battle, not the guy you want to see coming through your binoculars. For those of you still cross-examining our actions, you haven't met Chris's father (my Mum's big brother, my second father, and our family's undisputable moral compass)—having disappointed him by choosing power and money over family would've stung way, way more.

The moral here isn't that losing small food fortunes is okay if it means saving Easter lunch with your next of kin. It's about reminding yourself to challenge your logic before making your lil' sis the social media marketing guru of your company, or partnering with Pops to launch his legendary sweet potato home fries. Cousin Chris and I have a uniquely staunch relationship that implored us to go Dutch on our wild and crazy-expensive outing and then eventually call it a day. If you were parked in a similar predicament with your blood, could you call it a day and move forward? Before you start handing out jobs or commitment letters to your family make sure you're partnering with, or hiring them because they have the right talent and aptitude, or at least potential talent. Think about what type and size of impending conflict tomorrow might bring, and ask yourself if you'll be emotionally equipped to navigate through it. Have no doubt, on the road to profit, conflict is inescapable and with it comes the responsibility to govern your emotions.

Make sure that your company is, or can become, large enough to adequately support you and your posse. We work closely with two very well respected, prominent and successful family-owned companies. One generates enough volume and opportunity to employ and sufficiently reward parents, siblings, spouses, children, cousins and even neighbours—but, each has a key role in the company that reflects their specific talent and temperament. The other is run by three equally sharp brothers and their larger-than-life and lovable father. Before their collective eleven children were old enough to need a career, the family agreed that treating everyone equal was the mission; and given that the company tree wasn't large enough for each of the children to suitably harvest from, it was decided none of them would be given a career opportunity. That's not to say that each of the brother's children didn't work at the company during a few summers to earn money and valuable experience—in fact, I imagine slugging it in the factory was a mandatory rite of passage. And, most importantly, the intent of this chapter was to rightfully brag about the insane calibre of my office lunches.

Let it Simmer ~

1. *Are you partnering with a close friend or family member because you make a strong team together, or because it's comfortably convenient and could be exciting?*

2. *Do you unintentionally upstage friends or family at the negotiation table? If so, do you know when to take a backseat to let them shine and to maintain balance in your more important relationship outside the office?*

3. *If you're in a position where involving a close friend or family member feels inescapable, have you documented the difficult discussion about expectations, boundaries and consequences?*

4. *Is your company large enough to permanently support the friends and family members currently working there? Would it be healthier to provide them with a clearly defined contract opportunity so that you both can assess a longer-term fit?*

5. *What's in your office lunchbox?*

CHAPTER 33

Putter or Butter?

Networking

I'm a ghastly golfer so despite the chance to forge a deeper relationship with my supply partners and retailers, I don't attend too many—well, actually not any—of the many golf tournaments I'm invited to. I don't mind playing sports, especially with my own three kids, but for me, playing or worse yet, watching most sports is like watching the apartment lobby camera channel—it's fun and exciting for about 5 minutes. Cooking, eating, watching and learning about food, however, is pure pleasure for me.

I'd trade a primo set of TaylorMade® golf clubs for a set of Wüsthof® Chef knives any day. So when JP, my Uncle El, Milan, Just-a-Pinch (Gourmet Salt) Mario and my brother formed a Brotherhood dedicated to 24-hour food excursions, I knew I'd discovered front row season tickets worth investing in. The bi-monthly outings look something like this: We pick a showcase, occasionally rare, ingredient (à la *Iron Chef*) —something like white truffles or Kobe beef. Each person submits an ambitious dish contribution to Dave one week before the outing so that he can organize a structured full day's gorging where gluttony becomes a sport.

At 2 p.m. on a Friday, we leave the office and rendezvous at one of two hush-hush locations, both an hour out of the city. Copious amounts of gorgeous Italian wines, a giant leg of Iberico ham, a hand-forged-iron stone pizza oven and monogrammed cutlery are indispensable essentials. We cook, eat and drink until around midnight. We then dust off a bottle of Brother Milan's homemade plum brandy and then finally retire to bed. By 6 a.m. the premises are cleaned, and we're back on the road and home to our families by breakfast. We usually have a new pledge each time—typically a supply partner or a customer from the food biz. It's my chance to forge a deeper relationship, but over a glass of wine and a leg of imported pork instead of over a hot dog at the halfway house. Hey hey, now that's more my speed.

CHAPTER 34

Chew Your Food

Tale of the Triple Pants

Onward and upward. It's high time to take a solid crack and bust open any crusty hesitations that are holding you back from moving forward with your quest. Protect yourself. Move sensibly by defining and then playing within your risk tolerance threshold, but move forward. Carefully structure your game-plan so that, if you should nose-dive, you'll easily be able survive the fall. If and when you do fall, take time to let the situation simmer and then apply the learnings and try again—and again. Create and embrace the self-pressure that comes along with involving supply partners and prospective retailers in your mission. If nothing else, consider that a little well-placed stress is both healthy and necessary to keep you travelling in the right direction.

I started this book by confessing that your fight will be about surprising, and sometimes unplanned, successes as well as carefully planned product launches ending in agonizing failure. Full disclosure: I'll be the first one to admit that I've had more food fiascos than tasty triumphs. For clarity's sake, let's call it five to one, respectively. And believe you me, I'm still sitting on a colourful cornucopia of more untold whoppers that I haven't shared for either legal or future tactical motives—remind me to tell you about the popular 80s seltzer that we struggled to resurrect. But hey, to the quote the Chairman of the Board: *'Regrets I've had a few, but then again too few to mention.'*

The flip side of the coin is that, for every five or six letdowns, we've had one hell of a sweet ride. Consider that most everyone you know has secretly had a viable idea at some point in his or her life. It's startling then to recognize just how very few folks choose to act on their burning ambitions. To breakaway from this pack of overly-cautious nonstarters, you'll need to flush the idea out of your system and be cleansed of that nagging blueprint that you've been telling people about for longer than you care to remember. Go for it. Be all in. Sound the bell. Strap on a pair of mitts, step into the hot and sticky ring and throw the first punch to instigate your food fight.

'Son, please chew your food! Breathe in between bites. Slow down, no one is chasing you!'

I can't tell you how many times I've heard these cautionary words in my life. But damn it, I'm hopelessly addicted to the flavour rush too damn much despite the imminent risk of passing indigestion. Want proof? I'll let you in on my top-secret triple-pant-size strategy to prove just how much I love to food, can unleash my appetite and just flat-out go for it. When I travel on vacation, I'm always prepared to accommodate my culinary curiosity and ravenous appetite. I'll pack three different waist sizes of pants because I know what to expect. After years of practice, I'm all too familiar with the rapid transformation and damage that I'll wreak on my waistline, so deploying what I call the *34-6-8* routine is mandatory if I'm to function comfortably.

Hold your judgment and give me the chance to explain. Six or so weeks leading up to my travel, it's all about the pregame training. You see, I know I'm about to be all in at the all-inclusive buffet so doubling down on trips to the gym and cutting serious calories will be my fleeting obsession. When it's time to go, I'm dialled in. I'll step off the plane in my 34" Levi's feeling like an Olympian. Halfway into the voyage, after having put back one too many beachside cervezas and hot chicken wings, I'll slip on a pair of 36" khakis to let the belly breathe a bit better. By the end of the week, after having totally invested myself into the experience, I'll need to strap on my emergency 38s to survive the flight home.

However, the very moment that I touchdown on Canadian soil, it becomes all about the control of knowing it's time to unplug, step away and to rebalance. Within a week, I'm sporting my Levi 511's again and looking back on the adventure with a nod and a smirk. I suppose you can call it eating in extreme moderation. Or you can just call me un-controllably crazy. Either way, it's how I'm built.

When an opportunity to create and launch a food product comes my way, I attack the situation with the same ferocious appetite and veracity. I'm all in, baby. Look, don't over-think the jump too much—think of it more as a well-organized expedition than as a blind leap of faith. If you want it, go for it with a purpose and without regret. Avoid the energy-vortex that comes from analysis-paralysis. Assess the situation as you go without waiting around for every light between your starting point and the finish line to turn green. Otherwise, you're bound to grow weary and then leave your car parked in your driveway. Go for it with a sharp aware-ness and the responsibility of knowing when to put your fork down, get up from the table and then properly digest until it's time to dig in again.

It's a common characteristic and philosophy that serves to separate the corporate soldiers from the entrepreneurial warriors. Learn to think quickly and to operate freely with no reservations. Relish in the last minute magic and the exhilaration that comes as a result of string-ing together a clever and imaginative opportunity with only a few uten-sils at your disposal—this is the mark of a genuine entrepreneur's spirit and ultimate ability.

My most memorable and prized meals were never associated with scoring a rare reservation at the hottest and hippest restaurants. Whether it was barbecuing short ribs on the beach in Maui while watching surfers carve up the waves, or brown-bagging a silky Pinot Noir while enjoying a fresh focaccia on a vineyard bench in Napa, it was never about over-thinking the menu options. Nah, it's all about embra-cing the last minute opening and then totally giving into the experi-ence. Imagine being able to dream up a product idea in the morning, and then have it become your reality to pursue by dinner.

When obsessing over your work comes naturally, onlookers will de-scribe it as passion. For me, if it's about food, I'm instantly excitable. Food is my medicinal marijuana. These days, I've slowed down a touch because I've had to as my stomach isn't ironclad anymore. Dramatic binging followed by erratic weight fluctuation have thankfully also slowed. Admittedly, I'm also a tad more responsible when I operate, but still take on more challenges than most. I've finally dropped the danger 38" waist zone from my arsenal and can now proudly travel with only a couple pairs of 34s—and, of course, a pair of emergency 36s. But I guess that comes with a little experience and one too many generous slices of humble pie à la mode.

As with any recipe, there are numerous interpretations and techniques that can be used to prepare a successful dish, but it's the final product that matters most. Whichever industry you're attempting to conquer, be sure to lean heavily on the fundamentals. Let my lemons help to serve as a careful reminder that it takes more than one attempt to pull off a perfect dish. Add your own flair. Mix it up in your own way, but don't change or challenge the basic ingredients. Like every pizza dough, a product launch plan will demand a lot of kneading before the final pie presents itself. Keep battling and know that you may have to survive ten unwelcomed flops before busting the game wide open with your eleventh swing. Play hard, but play smart. If you're new to the product launch game, try to resist up and quitting your day job until that triumphant eleventh wallop comes through. Play the game on the side until there's enough traction to transfer all of your energy and effort into the same pot. Keep your head down, keep your cash burn rate way down, and keep chopping away. Have faith, it's not a matter of if it'll happen, it's much more about when it'll happen and then ensuring that you're properly suited up for battle.

To be completely honest with you, what keeps me going is the fear and discomfort of not being able to repeat the process, for that would mean I'd have to actually find a job for a living. Ugh! Nope, not me. I'm hopelessly addicted to three tasty vices: chocolate, coffee and napkin sketches.

Let it all Simmer ;)

Acknowledgements

To my wife Lisa (fresh pasta fanatic) for her unwavering enthusiasm & encouragement for every new road I unexpectedly decide to travel; to my little meatballs Gabriel (steak hunter), Eliana (bacon addict) & Lea (salmon sashimi ninja); to my Mother (lemon meringue mama) for her unforgettable spirit; to my Father (hot pepper maniac) and Brother (master pizzaiolo) for the nearly 3,000 superb homemade office lunches, complete with a daily helping of integrity; to my Nonna Iole (arancini artist) for her endless nourishment; to Uncles El (burnt & butterflied sausage Baron) and Lou (pecan pie specialist) for fueling my appetite for something more; to my Mother-in-Law Marisa (queen of brunch) for entertaining my unpredictable appetite; to my childhood friend Christine (poutine predator) for her commitment to seeing this book completed; to BrandFusion warriors Febe Ann (chocolate dreamer) and Archie (popcorn Picasso); and to my business partner Joe (King of Alaskan King crabs) for the bottomless cups of vino and wisdom.

The Dead Stroll

Edward L. Mercer

authorHOUSE®

AuthorHouse™
1663 Liberty Drive
Bloomington, IN 47403
www.authorhouse.com
Phone: 1-800-839-8640

First published by AuthorHouse 4/12/2011

ISBN: 978-1-4567-2046-9 (e)
ISBN: 978-1-4567-2045-2 (sc)

Printed in the United States of America

Foreword

In 1968 computers were the size of refrigerators, police cars had no air conditioning, cell phones didn't exist and DNA had never been heard of. Only the largest departments had crime labs or crime scene technicians. In most cities, homicide detectives did it all. They processed the scene, took photographs, collected evidence and talked to witnesses. An identifiable fingerprint was the most solid piece of physical evidence one could hope for and such a print didn't turn up very often. Most cases were solved by talking to people, asking hundreds of questions and by cultivating informants. The label "serial killer" had not come into vogue yet and criminal profiles came only from the minds of detectives who remembered previous cases. This story takes place during a period of turmoil in the history of our country and the city of Louisville. It is my attempt to show what homicide cops did in those days and how they responded to the pressures on them from the job, their families and their environment.

This story is not autobiographical. Certain characters such as Dr. Martin Luther King, Jr. and his brother, Rev. A. D. Williams King obviously played parts in the events that are the backdrop for the story. Other characters such as noted restaurateur Ed Hasenour and musicians Freddy George and Bob Rosenthal are real people. However their words and actions in this story are entirely mine and never actually took place. All other characters are the products of my imagination and not based on any actual persons, living or dead.

I would like to dedicate this work to the men and women of the Louisville Division of Police Homicide Squad, with whom I had the pleasure and privilege of working for several eventful years.

Chapter One

Louisville, Kentucky. Sunday, May 10, 1964, 8:38 p. m.

The girl was there on the corner, right where she had been on the previous nights. She was standing on the lot of the Star service station at 18th and Osage, talking to a couple of other hookers in an animated way. She was young, not more than eighteen, with a light complexion and a definite looker. There was too much light from the station's floodlights. He couldn't take a chance on being noticed, even though he had switched plates from an old junked car. He did not want anyone to get a look at his car or him. But there was time. If she followed the same pattern from the other nights he had watched her, she would walk down the block before long. It needed to be done soon, however, before she made contact with another john. Dixie Highway, also called 18th Street, bisected the city from the river on the north to the southern city limits, where it became the main highway leading to Fort Knox. Usually, it was a busy thoroughfare at all hours. Fortunately, tonight was a slow night and there wasn't much traffic. The city was still enmeshed in its post-Derby lethargy

He lit another cigarette and willed the girl to shut up and move on. Finally she did, waving goodbye to her companions and turning to walk north on 18th Street. He waited until she had gone a block, then pulled out of the side street and pulled along beside her. She stopped and came over to the passenger window of his car.

" Hi, sugar. You lookin' for a little action tonight?" she asked in a soft voice.

"Maybe" he replied. "Depending on the price for action tonight."

"You ain't no vice cop, are you, baby? They always wantin' to know what the price is first thing."

"Do I look like a cop?" he asked.

"No" she replied "but you can't always tell by looks. This don't look like no cop's car, though."

She seemed to make up her mind and, opening the door, got into the front seat.

"Drive around the corner, sugar and we'll talk business. The damn beat cops come along here and see you talkin' to me, we both in trouble."

He did as she instructed and pulled around on a side street.

"Now, then, baby," she said, "if you want a quickie or a little head here in the front seat of yo' big old car, it's twenty for each, forty for both."

"Don't you have someplace we can go?" he asked. "I'm no teenager and I don't want to do it in the car."

"Sure," she replied. "We got a crib around the corner on Grand but it will cost you twenty extra."

"Show me where" he said, pulling away from the curb.

She entered the vacant house in front of him. In the dark, she didn't notice the small canvas bag he carried. He could smell some very unpleasant odors as he passed the front room. Then he stumbled over something in the hall. He could hear a rustling noise in one of the side rooms that sounded like rats.

"Turn on some lights" he requested.

"Ain't no lights, honey. Louisville Gas and Electric don't know we moved in here. I got some candles in the back room," she replied.

He knew very well from his previous observations of the girl and her habits that there was no electricity in the vacant house. He also knew that the whores took turns using the place, that they wouldn't be interrupted. That suited his needs perfectly.

He heard the scratch of a match being struck and then the dim light of a candle illuminated the girl's face. She lit two more and placed them on either side of a mattress on the floor. Sitting down on the mattress, she pulled her shoes off and began to pull her panties down her slim bare legs. Looking up at him, she smiled.

"Get your pants off, honey. We ain't got all night."

Looking down at her, he could feel the blood pounding in his temples. This was the moment that he thought about constantly He dropped his bag on the floor behind him and continued to stare at her ripe young body, as she slipped her short dress over her arms, revealing firm breasts with large dark nipples.

"What's the matter, sugar? Can't get it up. Let little Angel help you."

She scooted on her knees across the mattress and began to grope for the zipper of his fly. He pulled back from her grasp, exclaiming

"Don't touch me, you filthy whore."

Astonishment flashed in her eyes. With the blood still pounding loudly in his head, he reached down, grabbing her arms and pulling her to her feet. She started to yell as he spun her around and slipped his right arm about her neck in a practiced motion, cutting off her yell. He pushed her neck forward into the crook of his elbow and brought his left arm across the back of her neck, applying intense pressure to her carotid arteries. In just a few seconds, she lost consciousness and sagged in his arms.

He placed her body on the mattress and positioned her on her back with her legs spread. He fumbled on the floor for his kit. Removing adhesive tape and rope from his bag, he quickly bound the girl hand and foot and gagged her with the tape. She slowly regained consciousness and gradually realized that she was tied up tightly. Her eyes widened in fear as he stood looking down at her. He removed the cheap overalls and the rubber gloves from his bag, along with the canvas sneakers. Quickly donning the garments, he reached for the Rapala filet knife. It was time to get down to serious business. He had work to do.

* * *

"Car 406, at 18th and Grand. See the lady about an injured person," the police dispatcher intoned in a bored voice.

"10-4, radio. From 34th and Market," Officer Charles Newman responded into the microphone.

Hanging it back on the hook, he said "That's way the hell over on 3's beat. Where are they?"

"They got a fire run down in Parkland, while you were eating," his partner, Officer Scott McAllister, responded.

"Car 406. Make your run code three. The lady says the injuries are very serious." An obvious note of urgency was apparent in the dispatcher's normally emotionless voice.

"10-4," Newman shouted into the mike over the growl of the siren mounted on the front fender of the Dodge station wagon, as the vehicle sped up.

"Know where we're going?" he asked McAllister.

"South of Broadway a couple of blocks, isn't it?" McAllister replied. He was less than two months out of the academy and still learning his way around the district, as well as many other facets of the job. This was only his third emergency run and the first one to occur while he was driving. He had to admit it was quite a rush pushing the old black Dodge down the street with the red light reflecting off the buildings they passed and cars pulling over at the howl of the approaching siren.

Newman, a ten year veteran, was paying close attention to each intersection they approached, leaning forward in the passenger seat to get a clear look at cross traffic.

He was a conscientious and methodical officer. McAllister felt fortunate to have drawn him as a regular partner. When he thought about a couple of the men he had ridden with right after graduation from the academy, their lackadaisical approach to police work and the petty corruption they engaged in, he was doubly grateful. His first partner was an old veteran whose major concern each day was picking up a free pack of cigarettes from each of several bars on their beat. The man's do nothing attitude frustrated McAllister to the point that he seriously considered resigning.

Fortunately, those assignments only lasted a couple of weeks and then he found himself working with Newman. Newman was honest, patient and painstaking in teaching the job and McAllister absorbed his instructions avidly. He was infatuated with police work, with the city, and with the department. He took his off days grudgingly and rushed back to work. He regarded each shift as a new adventure and could not wait to see what dramas would be played out before him on the stage of the 4th Police District. Fortunately, Newman had the patience to encourage him to temper his eagerness with common sense and solid police procedure.

As they drove south on 18th Street from Broadway, passing the giant Phillip Morris cigarette plant and Brown Forman Distillery, Newman told McAllister to slow down. Just ahead they could see a young black woman waving her hand at them from the curb.

As they pulled to the curb and the siren wound down, Newman motioned the woman to the car.

"Oh, God, Oh, Jesus." the woman screamed. She's dead! She's dead!"

"Slow down, sister. Who's dead? And where?" Newman queried.

"It's Angel. She's dead. There's blood all over the place."

"Show us" Newman commanded, getting out of the car. He followed the hysterical woman around the corner on Grand Street to a house just on the other side of the alley. McAllister pulled to the curb and grabbed the first aid kit and his flashlight and started after his partner.

The woman would only go on the porch.

"There, in the back room" she said.

The two policemen moved slowly through the garbage cluttered hallway, shining their lights on the floor. Looking in some of the side rooms, they noted filthy mattresses in a couple of the rooms.

"Crib house," Newman said, "where the whores on the stroll bring their johns."

Reaching the end of the hall, they each shined their lights into the back room.

4

McAllister let out an audible gasp and felt the gorge rising in his throat. The nude body of a young black girl lay spread-eagled on a mattress in the middle of the room. Her legs were splayed apart and her vaginal orifice gaped wide. There appeared to be some sort of object inserted in her vagina. Where her breasts should have been were two red circles of tissue. There was blood covering the entire mattress and most of the floor in the room. As they played their lights up her body, the reason for the extensive blood spill became obvious. Her throat had been cut, nearly severing her head. Her spinal column appeared to be the only thing still connecting her head to her body. As they looked further, they could see that her abdomen had also been cut open and her entrails were draped across her stomach. The thick fetid smell of blood permeated the air.

Feeling the nausea overcome him, McAllister turned and ran back through the house. Jumping off the front porch, he spewed vomit into the bushes alongside the house. Bending over gasping for breath and trying to control his heaving stomach, he heard two young boys talking in the alley beside the house.

"Man, did you see that cop puke?" one asked the other.

"Sure did," the other replied, "and it must be bad if it makes the police sick."

Looking up, he saw Newman standing on the porch looking at him quizzically.

"You all right?" Newman asked.

"I think so. I just never saw or smelled anything like that before."

"Well, get used to it. It can get worse. Can you go call this in while I make sure nobody else gets in here? You know who to notify, don't you?"

"Yeah. I'm okay now." Scott replied. "The homicide squad and the coroner, right?"

"Notify 420, too. We'll have to have some help here to secure the area and probably do a canvass."

McAllister went back to the car and made the request for the dispatcher to make the necessary notifications. While he was getting his and Newman's notebooks, he heard the homicide unit and the 4th District supervisor, Sgt. Marvin, acknowledge the dispatcher's message. Marvin then instructed the dispatcher to send Car 404, the adjoining beat car, to assist at the scene.

Going back to the house, McAllister met Newman on the porch and handed him his notebook. They looked across Grand Avenue, where a small crowd was beginning to gather, attracted by the police car's flashing red light.

"Reckon that girl who flagged us down is still around?" Newman asked. "We need to get her name."

"She's over there by the alley with those other two girls. They all look like hookers." McAllister replied.

"This time of night, on Dixie Highway? Hell, son, they are all hookers." Newman said. "I'll go talk to her. You stand by here and make sure nobody goes in before the homicide dicks get here."

A few minutes later, a battered unmarked Dodge sedan noised to the curb in front of the house. Two white men, obviously detectives from their rumpled suits and "stingy brim" straw hats, got out of the car and walked up to the porch. The one in the lead, a tall husky man with sandy hair, flashed a small gold badge at McAllister and said,

"Detective John Craig, Homicide. This is my partner, Detective Bailey. What have you got here, Officer ..." He paused to squint at McAllister's name tag in the dim light and then finished "McAllister?"

McAllister quickly explained how they had received the run and what they had found on arrival. He told them that Newman was across the street interviewing the person who had evidently found the body. Bailey, a heavy-set man in his fifties with a florid complexion and a thick crop of gray hair, pushed past him and started into the house. He paused to flick a light switch on the wall. When nothing happened, he snorted and, turning on his flashlight, started down the hall. Craig and McAllister followed him.

"Jesus Christ!" Bailey exclaimed, stopping short at the doorway of the back room.

Looking over his shoulder, Craig shined his light over the girl's body.

"Not much sense in checking for vital signs, is there, Vern?" Craig asked. "Looks like she bled out real quick. That cut got both carotid arteries. All this other shit is probably post mortem. Something sharp made those incisions."

"Didn't happen too long ago." Bailey surmised. "The blood hasn't clotted much. I'll get some help on the way and start the canvass, if you want to handle it in here."

"Okay, and contact the fire department. Get a couple of those big portable lights of theirs so we can see what we're doing. Officer McAllister, can you give me a hand in here until we get some more people on the scene? Hold the light for me. Try not to step in the blood or disturb anything"

Voices in the hallway proved to be Sgt. Marvin and Officers Roberts and Sorenson, Car 404.

"Just stay right there, guys." Craig commanded. "We don't need any more big feet in here. Sarge, can you put a guy on the door and have somebody assist my partner with the canvass? Nobody else in but the coroner and photographer and the other guys from homicide. McAllister is going to help me out until they get here."

"Will do." Marvin, a short, stocky, no-nonsense supervisor turned and went back to the porch. In a moment, his voice could be heard issuing instructions to the others.

Controlling his revulsion, McAllister played his flashlight where the big detective indicated and watched with interest as Craig moved, catfooted, around the girl's body, scribbling notes and talking to himself under his breath. Gradually, McAllister became so interested in the detective's examination of the scene that he found himself able to put aside the horror of the girl's appearance and the awful smell and concentrate on the work that was being done.

"This son of a bitch had lots of fun and games with this poor girl," Craig told him. "Looks like he cut her throat, then disemboweled her and did what ever else he did to her. We'll have to wait for the autopsy to see what that is he rammed up her. Looks like a bottle."

In a few minutes, additional detectives arrived along with the deputy coroner and police photographer. Craig thanked McAllister for his help and the young officer gratefully left the room. Newman was standing by their car, talking to Detective Bailey. As McAllister approached, Bailey turned and walked back toward the house.

"Lose your lunch, rookie?" he asked sarcastically as he passed. "Next time, try not to fuck up my crime scene, okay?"

"He noticed the mess in the bushes," Newman said. "I had to explain to him that it wasn't really part of the crime scene. Fuck him, don't worry about it. You didn't mess anything up."

His face flushed with embarrassment, McAllister sought to change the subject.

"Did you find out who the girl was that found her or who the victim is?" he asked.

"Our victim is Angela Johnson, also known as Angel. Age eighteen and lives in the 1400 block of Catalpa Street. She has two prior arrests as a juvenile, for runaway and habitual truancy. She's been busted once as an adult for soliciting prostitution. Showed up on the stroll out here about six months ago and has been going strong. No pimp that I can find out about. Just a little girl trying to get along in the big city."

"Pretty impressive." Scott said. "How did you find all that out?

"Believe it or not, that phone booth on the corner actually works. I've been on the phone to records and the Youth Bureau once I got her name from the complainant, who, incidentally, is Margaret Sistrunk, alias Sissy, a veteran Dixie Highway whore. She says that she saw Angel talking to a john in a big black car up the street around 18th and Garland. Then she got into the car and they drove to the house they all use as a crib. Sissy says she didn't think anything about it, that they usually use the house one at a time. She evidently had a little action in a car back in one of the alleys, then picked up a real sport who wanted to do it on a mattress. They charge extra for that. More like true love, I guess. Anyway, she didn't see the car in front of the house, the one she saw Angel get into, so she figured the mattress was available. She took her john in there, lit a candle and found Angel's body. She went to the phone booth and called it in."

"What happened to her john?" Scott asked.

"Beat feet back to his car and laid rubber all the way to Oak Street. Guess he didn't want to explain to momma how he got involved in a murder investigation at 18th and Grand, when he was supposed to be at the Elks Lodge."

As word spread in the police department, a stream of curious cops began to arrive at the scene, including the night chief of police, Major Dolan. He and all the others were met by Craig at the front door and diplomatically refused admittance.

As the scene investigation progressed, the crowd grew bored and began to drift away.

A fire department service truck stirred up some interest when it delivered two portable, battery powered flood lights to the scene. When they were set up inside the house, a bright glow could be seen from the street and the detectives cast long shadows on the windows as they moved back and forth inside.

Around ten o'clock, a hearse from the funeral home with the county contract pulled up to the curb in front of the house. Craig signaled to Newman and McAllister from the door, as the two attendants from the funeral home entered the house with their collapsible gurney.

"Can you give us a hand loading her up?" he asked. "We're done here and ready to move her to the morgue."

All of the other police and detectives seemed to have faded away as the two officers entered the room where the girl's body was lying. The funeral home attendants were unwrapping a sheet and stretching it over the gurney, just past the area of the blood spill. The harsh glare of the portable flood lights gave the whole scene a surreal appearance.

"Watch where you're stepping" Craig cautioned. "Let's each get an arm or leg and somebody's going to have to steady her head or it'll fling blood all over us."

Grunting with the strain, the men maneuvered the girl's mutilated body onto the gurney. Wrapping the sheet around her, the two funeral attendants wheeled the gurney out the door.

"General Hospital?" one of them queried as they were leaving.

"Right," Craig replied "We'll meet you at the morgue."

Looking around at the room, Craig seemed lost in thought for a minute,

"This is one sick, evil motherfucker who did this," he stated. "And I'm afraid he's just getting started. We put out a pickup on the car with the best description we could get, big black sedan, maybe a Lincoln, but nobody got a look at the guy inside."

"Won't he have blood all over him?" Newman asked.

"Maybe" Craig replied. "But he was smart enough to take the knife and all his other equipment with him. We found enough trace evidence on the body to tell that he taped her mouth with adhesive tape and tied her hands and feet. But, no rope, no tape, no knife. He left a bunch of footprints in the blood but they look like sneakers. He brought all his gear with him and took it away with him. Ten to one he's smart enough to get rid of his clothes and shoes too. The whole thing has the look of being planned out by an asshole who really enjoys this kind of thing. Well, thanks for your help, guys."

Driving back to police headquarters, McAllister asked his partner

"Do you think they'll catch this guy?"

"I don't know." Newman replied. "Doesn't look like they have a lot to go on right now. But, Craig is supposed to be the best of the bunch in the homicide squad. So maybe he'll get lucky."

"What about the fat guy, Bailey?" McAllister asked.

"He's just marking time till retirement. He used to be a pretty good cop but he got on the jug a few years back and is pretty much worthless now. They say the only way he stays in homicide is that he and the Chief of Detectives are lodge brothers. I know that the homicide lieutenant has tried to move him a couple of times but the Chief of Detectives has always overruled him"

"What we need to do," Newman continued "is keep our eyes open for a big black Lincoln around the stroll there on Dixie. If this guy likes to cut up whores, that's the most logical area for him to go back to."

"Be kind of hard for us to do, won't it?" McAllister asked. "Seeing as how Dixie Highway is about two miles off our beat."

"Scott, you know those two old farts that ride 403 are off the air all the time doing 'tavern checks'," Newman replied. "We get half their runs anyway. We'll just make sure we travel up and down Dixie a lot while we're covering for them. I'd love to catch this bastard."

"Homicide looks like an interesting assignment," McAllister said as they pulled into the parking lot by headquarters.

"Yeah, well, if you're thinking about a career in homicide, you'd better learn to control your stomach muscles," his partner replied as he got out of the car and gathered his equipment. "They probably frown on a detective puking all over their crime scenes."

"Hey, Charlie. Kiss my ass."

* * *

In a vacant farmhouse in a remote part of Oldham County, to the northeast of Louisville, the killer watched as the flames of his small fire consumed the coveralls, sneakers, rope and tape. Only now was he beginning to get his breathing under control and his pulse rate to return to normal. It had been even more exhilarating than he had envisioned. The actual feel of the girl's flesh was indescribable, even through the rubber gloves. He could actually feel her fear and the sensation of absolute power that it gave him, the mastery of life and death. And the rest, the aftermath, that would be something to be savored in his darkest, innermost thoughts. He also relished the thought of the police at the scene, their bafflement. He could see them asking each other "Who would do something like this?" Well, fuck them. What did they know – about life and death, sin and mortality, good and evil for that matter? He intended to cause them more puzzlement in the future. This was his work. He had been called to do it.

He had to leave for a while. While he was gone, perhaps he would find other places to work, practice and hone his skills. But he would definitely be back. Louisville needed him.

Chapter Two

Louisville, Kentucky. Tuesday, April 17, 1967, 6:45 p. m.

McAllister was sweating profusely through his light blue uniform shirt. He twisted the 36 inch riot baton nervously in his hands. Even though it was only April, it was already hot and humid in the Ohio Valley. He and the other cops watched as the U-Haul-It trucks pulled up to the entrance to Iroquois Park and began to discharge their loads of young black demonstrators. They milled about in the street while some of their number began unloading signs from the trucks. A group of older black men in suits and ties got out of cars that had pulled in after the trucks. McAllister identified the Reverend A. D. Williams King in the group. They were joined by a group of white people who had been waiting on the lot. An Episcopal priest was visible in the crowd.

The younger brother of Martin Luther King had come to town several months ago to serve as pastor at the Zion Baptist Church. He had soon become involved in the controversy over open housing that was generating nightly demonstrations in the white neighborhoods of the city's South End. Now he was leading those demonstrations regularly. His better known brother had been here once already to preach at Zion Church and there were rumors that he would be returning to Louisville soon to assist in the drive to compel the city's aldermen to pass an open housing ordinance.

From McAllister's point of view, that was all they needed. The sight of the groups of young blacks marching down Southern Parkway brandishing their signs and singing "We Shall Overcome" was already driving the area's quota of knuckleheads into nightly frenzies. If the famous civil rights leader was added to the mix, McAllister was sure a full scale riot would be the result.

This was the third night in a row that McAllister and his partner, Dave Randall, had drawn crowd control duty for the demonstrations. It had become repetitious: the demonstrators would arrive, get out of their trucks in the park, and march north on Southern Parkway, singing and chanting. The local residents of the all-white neighborhood, augmented by a large number of representatives of white-supremacy groups like the Klan and assorted rubber-neckers, would gather across the street and shout obscenities and racial slurs at the marchers. Every night this group got bigger. Eventually, rocks and bottles would start flying, and the police would move to disperse the two groups. The demonstrators would persist long enough to ensure that the television news crews had plenty of footage and then return to their trucks. At least that was the game plan.

The past two nights, the white crowd had gotten increasingly loud and threatening. Some of the young black men began to react and there were several confrontations that had resulted in arrests. Tonight the police had formed up in two lines stretching along Southern Parkway, a wide tree-lined street with older middle-class homes on both sides, set back from the street. The white crowd of hecklers was directly across the street from them. The open housing demonstrators had passed out their signs and were moving in a group from the park entrance, obviously intending to march down Southern Parkway as they had the two previous nights.

McAllister's attention was drawn to a strikingly beautiful black woman in the front rank of demonstrators. She had a moderate Afro hairdo and was wearing a mini-skirt and light colored knee length boots. She made such an attractive appearance that she stood out vividly from the rest of the crowd.

"Look at that black goddess," McAllister said to his partner.

"Huh?" Randall replied. "Oh, yeah. She's a fox, all right. Wonder what she's doing with this bunch. She looks a little out of place."

"There's the chief," Randall said, pointing to a group of police supervisors nearby, distinguishable by their white uniform shirts. "Looks like they're trying to come up with a plan."

"Here comes the county," McAllister said. Down the side street near where they were standing, a group of about forty Jefferson County police officers were marching toward them in a loose formation.

"I hope they hang on to their fucking tear gas tonight." Randall complained. "That shit made me sick as a dog last night."

"It would help if we had gas masks," McAllister replied. "You know, I heard that the city has six gas masks to its name."

"It's a cinch no blue shirt has got one," Randall said. "Hell, the chief's probably got all six of them in his car trunk."

Across Southern Parkway, the crowd of whites began to move toward the park. The noise of individual curses and threats swelled as they moved. A large red-headed white man moved from the sidewalk into the street.

"Niggers, go home and take your nigger-lovers with you," he screamed.

Flecks of spittle could be seen flying from his mouth as he repeated his cry. A group of young white males detached themselves from the body of the crowd and moved after him.

"Niggers, go home! Niggers, go home," they began chanting.

The Reverend King and several of the adult leaders of the demonstrators stepped off the sidewalk and began moving toward the red-haired man. A beer bottle sailed over the heads of the crowd and smashed in the middle of the street. It was followed by several more. Rocks and bricks began to appear in the mix. The red-haired man pulled a whiskey bottle from his pocket and hurled it at the oncoming demonstrators. It smashed to the street in front of them.

"Captain, move your men out," McAllister heard the chief say. "Get in between them, there."

"Yes, sir," the captain replied. "Squads one and two move out."

McAllister and Randall and their fellow officers began filing into the street between the oncoming demonstrators and the rapidly increasing crowd of hecklers that had surged forward. A barrage of rocks, bricks and bottles sailed into the street from the rear of the crowd of hecklers. Two officers were struck by objects and fell to their knees. All of the police were wearing regulation uniform hats that provided no protection. The city didn't own any riot helmets either, although there were rumors that some had been ordered.

Two more squads of officers were sent into the street, which had become a melee of shouting, cursing people from both sides. The police officers were punching and jabbing with their riot batons as they attempted to keep the two groups separated.

"Dave, let's get that red-haired asshole," McAllister shouted as he tried to work through the crowd toward the big man.

The red head saw McAllister coming toward him and spat a wad of phlegm toward his face. McAllister jerked his head to one side and the mess struck his shoulder. As the man swung a big fist at his face, he sidestepped and, with both hands thrust the riot baton deep into the man's protruding belly. He had the satisfaction of seeing him drop like a stone to his knees. Randall, one step behind him, swung his club across the back of the man's neck in a sweeping arc and he pitched forward on his face. Reaching down, they each grabbed an arm of the stunned man and began moving out of the melee with him. Reaching the relative security of the sidewalk, they threw the man on the grassy median. McAllister knelt down and, pulling the man's arms behind him, quickly snapped handcuffs on him.

The two of them pulled the big man to his feet and moved him toward the big paddy wagon parked in a nearby driveway. A uniformed captain stepped in front of them and looked at the man's face.

"Good job," he said. "Put his ass in the wagon and charge him with inciting to riot. That's the son of a bitch who got all this started."

"Yessir," they chorused and propelled the man toward the wagon.

One of the officers assigned to the wagon handed McAllister a book of arrest forms. He reached in the big man's hip pocket and removed his wallet. The red-headed man was slowly recovering from the affects of the blows he had received and stood there shaking his head.

"Harold Swanner, that your name?" McAllister asked, looking at his driver's license.

"Fuck you," the man mumbled.

"Okay, Mr. Fuck You, we'll book your ass as John Doe. Then they won't set bond and you can lay in jail until you remember your name."

"Yeah, I'm Swanner. Why ain't you guys out there locking up them niggers instead of harassing me?" the man answered. "I'll remember you, McAllister, and you too, Randall."

The department had not had much experience with disorderly crowds and officers still wore their nametags on their shirts. Later, as their experience level grew, nametags would disappear and badge numbers would be taped over.

McAllister ignored the rest of the man's tirade, finished filling out the forms and turned the prisoner over to the wagon driver and guard, switching his handcuffs for one of the several sets they carried. By now, other officers were approaching with prisoners.

The melee in the street continued without letup and the two partners started in that direction. A loud report was heard off to their left, then two more. They watched as tear gas canisters, launched from shotguns by the county police, sailed into the middle of Southern Parkway. The prevailing wind began blowing the clouds of gas over the struggling crowd. Soon everyone, including all the city police officers, was scrambling o get clear of the fog.

"C'mon, Scott," Randall urged, grabbing his partner's arm. "Let's get clear of that crap."

They moved back to the intersection of Taylor Boulevard and Southern Parkway, their eyes stinging, and watched as demonstrators, hecklers, and police officers ran in all different directions, trying to escape the acrid fumes.

"That county commander gets his rocks off coming out here every night and gassing the shit out of the city police," Randall fumed as he tried to turn his head into the wind and blow the gas out of his eyes.

"Don't rub your eyes, Dave," McAllister cautioned. "It only makes it worse." He had been exposed to tear gas during his army hitch. "There's a water spigot on the wall of the school where we parked. We can rinse our eyes out."

In a few minutes, the chaotic situation began to sort itself out. The hecklers had seemingly dispersed and the open housing demonstrators were getting back into their trucks and cars. The captain they had encountered before came by, telling everyone to assemble back where they had parked their cars, on the lot at Iroquois High School.

McAllister went quickly to the water spigot on the side of the school building. While they were waiting for the commanders, he and Randall flushed the remnants of the tear gas from their eyes. Around them, others were doing the same. McAllister also took the time to wash off his shirt where the red-haired man had spit on him.

They assembled in a circle around the chief of police. A portly man with white hair and a red face, he reminded McAllister of Santa Claus without the beard. Tonight, his eyes were as red as everyone else's and he looked angry.

"You men from the districts can return to your beats. The detectives are following Reverend King and his people to make sure they're done for the evening and going back to the west end. If they don't and try to parade at another location, we'll call you back."

"Chief, who got hurt?" a voiced from the rear of the group asked.

"Collins, from the 1st District, and Adams, from the Parks Unit," the chief replied. They both just have knots on their heads and should be okay."

"Chief, when are we going to get helmets and fucking gas masks?" a disgusted officer in the front rank asked. "I'm tired of this shit, doing this duty with no protective equipment and the county gassing us every night."

The chief peered at the man.

"Sidebottom, isn't it?" he asked. "Well, Sidebottom, I'd like to have those things too. I've asked the Board of Alderman to make an emergency appropriation to get some helmets, masks, and some other riot gear, but it takes time to get things done."

Turning on his heel, the chief started toward his car. One of the captains who had been standing by him turned to the crowd of officers.

"You people get back to your beats," he instructed.

Grumbling aloud, the group of weary officers began to disperse toward their own cars. McAllister and his partner reached their own vehicle and started north on Taylor Boulevard with Randall driving. As McAllister reached for the radio microphone to call them back in service, Randall said,

"Let's swing by the White Castle at 7th and Algonquin and get a sack of sliders before we head back to the district."

"Good idea," McAllister replied "but I thought tear gas made you sick. Sure you can handle sliders tonight?"

"I'm in good shape. Let's eat," his partner said.

McAllister had been working with Randall since the preceding November. His former partner, Charles Newman, had been promoted to Sergeant last August and was now languishing in undisguised boredom as the late watch supervisor in the city jail. McAllister had worked as a relief man for several weeks after Newman's promotion, riding every beat in the 4th District on the regular men's off days. Although he enjoyed the variety, he missed the camaraderie of the relationship with a regular partner.

Then, in October, his watch commander, Lieutenant Hendricks, had informed him he would be assigned to beat 403 on a regular basis and would be getting a recruit to train as a partner, when the next Academy class graduated in November.

Although McAlister was pleased by the prospect of riding a regular beat again and the opportunity to teach a new officer, the assignment to beat 403 created a new set of problems, one he had not faced before. The corruption that permeated certain aspects of work in the city police department was more evident on some beats than others. His only other permanent assignment, beat 406, had been relatively "clean." There were no locations on the beat that engaged in the practice of paying off the assigned officers for overlooking certain violations, usually related to gambling. 403, on the other hand, had several such locations. This put McAllister in a dilemma. His Scots Presbyterian upbringing had conditioned him to believe without question that such practices were wrong. However, officers who didn't go along with the status quo frequently found themselves with less than desirable assignments.

He wanted badly to ride 403, to break in a new partner, to take advantage of the opportunities that working in that area would provide him to make a lot of felony arrests, to make a name for himself as a police officer, and to achieve his ultimate ambition, to become a detective. He solved the problem for the time being by taking the assignment and ignoring the places that were paying off, unless he got a run there. If he did get such a run, he handled whatever he found there as properly as he knew how. So far it had worked. He was still there and no one had approached him about the fact that he and his partner were not picking up their share.

McAllister found that he enjoyed teaching the job to Randall as much as he had enjoyed learning it from Newman. He had quickly grown to like the impulsive young rookie but was a little embarrassed by the attitude of deference his partner showed toward him. Randall was bright and eager to learn, much as McAllister himself had been. His major problem was a quick temper that flared whenever he sensed a challenge to his authority or encountered a belligerent subject, a situation that occurred daily in the volatile area in which they worked. McAllister had lectured him several times on the necessity of keeping cool and he appeared to be making major efforts to control himself in a better manner.

They picked up their orders of hamburgers and sodas from the small white restaurant and headed west on Algonquin Parkway toward the city's west end. As they approached the traffic light at 16th Street, a dark Pontiac GTO blasted through the red signal and sped north on 16th.

"Better pull him over," McAllister said, flipping on the red emergency lights. He reached for the radio and reported their unit back on the air, along with the information that they were making a traffic stop. Randall tapped the siren switch with his foot and it admitted a low growl as they pulled in behind the Pontiac. They could see at least two people in the back seat of the car looking back at them. The Pontiac slowed and pulled to the curb. McAllister called in their location, description and license number of the car. Taking his flashlight, he approached the right side of the vehicle as Randall went to the driver's side. Shining his light into the car, he could see four people, a man driving and a woman beside him in the front seat and two men in the back seat. As he observed the occupants, McAllister realized that the woman was the striking black female he had noticed earlier at the demonstration. The faint odor of CS tear gas came to his nostrils through the open car window.

"Let me see your operator's license," Randall told the driver.

"What is this shit, man?" the drive responded in a belligerent tone. "You honkies ain't got nothing to do tonight but harass black people."

"That's about it," Randall replied. "Especially when they bust a red light right in front of me like it wasn't there. Now, shake out that license."

The man's tone caused McAllister to bend down and take a closer look at him through the car window. He appeared to be a muscular black male in his twenties, with a large bushy afro hair style. He continued to mutter under his breath as he extracted his wallet from his hip pocket and produced his license.

"Let's everybody show some I. D.," McAllister told the woman and the two black males in the back seat. "Where are you people coming from?"

"We been to the south end, man, demonstrating for our rights," the driver said. "You got a problem with that, honky?"

"Nope," McAllister replied evenly. "But I do have a problem with your attitude and the way you're addressing me. Keep it up and you'll get a free ride downtown."

He collected the licenses from the other three people and waited while Randall wrote out the citation for the driver. Then he carried all the licenses back to the police car and asked the dispatcher for warrant and wanted checks on each subject. Somewhat to his surprise, all the checks were negative. He walked back to the Pontiac and handed the licenses to the woman. To his amazement, she smiled at him and thanked him in a soft voice. He listened while Randall gave the driver the usual cautionary speech and they went back to their car while the Pontiac pulled away. The driver was evidently not interested in pushing his luck as he drove off at a normal rate of speed.

"Let's see that citation," he asked Randall as they continued back to their assigned patrol area.

Randall handed him his citation book and he flipped it open.

"Jerome Lewis, and he lives on our beat, 2810 Virginia," McAllister mused. "Might be a good one to remember. He has a whole bunch of attitude."

"Hell, man," Randall replied. "Doesn't everybody down here in the west end? I've never felt so unloved in my life."

"The goddess didn't seem to have one," McAllister said. "She even smiled at me and thanked me when I gave her the license back."

"You're shittin' me," Randall responded. "Must be your movie star good looks. Who is she , anyway?"

"Name's Phyllis Johnson. Lives on our beat, too. 1436 Catalpa. Born in 1943, let's see. That would make her twenty-four."

"Just the right age for you, Scott," Randall teased. "Why don't you go down there and ask her out. I'll bet her parents would be tickled to death to see their daughter going out with a honky cop."

"Get real," McAllister replied. "She is a good looking woman, though."

"Car 403," the dispatcher interrupted their conversation. "18th and Oak. See the man about a prostitute robbing him."

"10-4, radio." McAllister replied as Randall sped up and they headed north on 18th Street.

Chapter Three

Louisville, Kentucky. Tuesday, March 12, 1968, 7: 38 p. m.

Detective John Craig leaned back in the rickety swivel chair and plied a toothpick industriously to his rear molars. The remnants of a stromboli steak sandwich were on the desk in front of him. At the other desk in the small office assigned to the homicide squad, his partner, Rick Rovinelli, finished off the last of his meatball sandwich. It had been a quiet night so far, for which Craig was thankful. Outside, a blustery wind was blowing off the Ohio River. The thought of venturing out was not pleasant to either detective. They both had reports to write, anyway, from follow-up interviews on an open case which they had conducted that afternoon.

A few minutes later, the two detectives working the overlapping eight-to-four shift, Wilson and Colbert, entered the office. They were the only black detectives assigned to homicide. Their assignment had occurred three years ago after an extensive investigation failed to solve the murder of a black female prosecutor in a branch of the city police court. Her body had been found in the Ohio River after she failed to return home from a visit to her hairdresser. The squad had worked hundreds of man-hours on the case with no luck. Wilson and Colbert had been temporarily assigned to the unit because the investigation focused primarily in the city's black community. The police command staff had hoped that black investigators would be more successful in getting information from black witnesses. The two men approached the task with diligence but had no more success than their white counterparts. The commander of the homicide squad, Lieutenant James Garrard, had been impressed with their efforts, however, and requested their permanent assignment to the unit.

"What's going on?" Colbert asked as he took off his topcoat. He was the younger of the two, in his late twenties with an afro hairstyle that pushed beyond the limits of the department's uniform and grooming regulations. He dressed in a mod style, tending to favor double knits and bell bottomed trousers. His ties were usually wide and wildly patterned. Colbert had an edgy personality and tended to take offense at any slight, intentional or not. He was, however, a meticulous and hard-working investigator. He respected Craig's abilities and got along better with him than he did most of the rest of the squad. He and Rovinelli, an edgy Italian-American, disliked each other intensely.

Wilson, his partner, was older and more laid-back, both in his approach to life and to his work. His knowledge of west end hoodlums was encyclopedic, however, and his stable of informants was legendary. He had walked a foot beat for years in the Walnut Street area that had been the center of black night life in Louisville. The process of urban renewal had changed all that during the early 1960's, acquiring all the property along Walnut Street, tearing down the buildings for future development and moving a large segment of the black population into the west end of the city. During that time, the police department was totally segregated. Black officers worked for black sergeants and policed black neighborhoods. No black officer held any higher rank than sergeant. In 1962 the department became desegregated to some extent and two black sergeants were promoted to lieutenant and given command over units that contained white officers. It was still rare to see a black officer and a white officer riding together as partners, although manpower requirements had made it necessary in some instances.

"Pretty quiet night so far," Craig replied to Colbert's question. "We did some follow-up on the Hatcher shooting and came back here to write it up. There's two interviews on the follow-up sheet that need to be done on that rape case last week."

"We'll get them after we read up," Wilson said. It was the responsibility of each oncoming shift to read all of the reports that had been prepared since the end of the last shift they had worked. Through that process, every detective in the squad knew all developments in every case being worked by the unit. Solution was the goal, and team playing was required. An individual glory seeker soon found himself transferred to another unit where the stakes were not so high.

It was crowded with four large men in the small office. Craig gathered his notes and prepared to move into one of the small interview rooms down the hallway where a typewriter was available. Secretarial help was non-existent in the homicide squad. Each detective typed his own reports. Typing skills were considered a perquisite for transfer to the unit.

The phone rang and Colbert picked it up.

"Homicide squad, Detective Colbert," he said. "Hey, sarge. What's the address?"

Scribbling notes on a pad, he asked a couple of more questions as the other detectives stood poised in expectation.

"Dead body in an empty house at 1756 Dumesnil," he said to the others. "Some wino found it. The beat car is standing by."

"Let's hit it," Craig said. As the senior detective on duty, he was the de facto supervisor.

Pulling up behind the parked beat car, Craig noted with some satisfaction that the blustery weather appeared to have kept any onlookers indoors. On the porch, two uniformed officers were talking with an elderly black man. As the detectives came up to them, Craig noticed that one of the officers was Scott McAllister, whom he had encountered several times in the past couple of years. Craig knew the young officer was conscientious and didn't anticipate any problems with the way the scene had been protected.

"Hi, Scott," Craig said. "What have you got here?"

"Hey, Detective Craig," McAllister replied. "We have a dead body inside this house. Mr. Wilburn here was looking for a place to get out of the wind and crash for the night, went in and found the victim. He says he went right to the tavern on the corner of 18th and Dumesnil and called it in. The victim is a young black female and, Detective Craig, it looks like she's been mutilated like that girl we found back in '64, at 18th and Grand. Remember? Angela Johnson, I think her name was."

"Good memory. That was her name. AKA Angel. Still unsolved," Craig said. "Let's take a look. Ask your partner to stay here and keep anyone else out. Rick, can you take Mr. Wilburn to our car out of the wind and get his interview?"

"Will do," Rovinelli replied. "Come on, Mr. Wilburn."

The three detectives and McAllister entered the shotgun style house and proceeded to the back room. Although the house was apparently vacant, there were some odds and ends of furniture in several of the rooms. As they entered the back room, which was the kitchen, their lights fell on the nude body of a black female spread-eagled across a kitchen table. Her throat revealed a gaping wound literally from ear to ear and copious quantities of blood covered the table and ran off on the floor. Her abdomen had been slashed open and her intestines were draped across her lower body. Both breasts appeared to have been excised. The similarity of her wounds to those of Angela Johnson was obvious to Craig. It was as if the killer intended to replicate the earlier crime.

Craig knelt and shined his light under the table. Footprints were visible in the blood. He examined the blood closely and noted that it appeared to have partially congealed.

Touching the girl's leg, he found it cold. He attempted to flex her leg slightly and found that she was in full rigor mortis.

"She's been here a while. Full rigor and the blood is partially clotted," he told the others. "Larry, can you and Wallace start checking the neighbors? See who owns this place, how long it's been empty. Find out if the girls on the stroll use it to turn tricks," he asked Colbert and Wilson.

Colbert had been examining the walls of the room with his light.

"John, look at this," he said, shining his light on what appeared to be writing on the plaster wall.

All four of the men shone their flashlights on the area Colbert pointed to.

"I AM DOWN ON WHORES" was written on the wall in what appeared to be blood.

"What kind of freaky shit is this?" Colbert asked.

"You called it. Freaky shit," Craig replied. "I've got the feeling I've seen that statement somewhere before."

"An old case of yours?" Colbert asked.

"An old case but not mine," Craig replied. "Remember Jack the Ripper in London, back in the 1800's? If I'm not mistaken, he used that same phrase in a letter he sent to the newspaper after his first couple of killings." He broke off when he noticed the other three men staring at him.

"How do you remember that shit?" Colbert asked. "Something in a letter some dude wrote a hundred years ago."

"Hey, I read a lot, okay?" Craig replied somewhat defensively.

"That's John Craig, folks," Colbert said in an admiring tone. "A cat could be shooting at him and he'd tell you the make and caliber of the bullet."

"Do you think this guy is deliberately trying to make us compare him with Jack the Ripper?" McAllister asked.

"Could be," Craig replied "but Jack would have to be over a hundred years old by now if he were still alive. Whoever this asshole is, maybe he's an admirer of his work or maybe he's just trying to fuck with our heads - or both."

"Well, he's succeeded in fucking with mine," Colbert said. "Wallace, let's go do the canvass. We'll contact the complaint desk too, John, and get the coroner and the photo lab started."

"Better ask the desk sergeant to notify the boss, also. He may want to roll on this one," Craig replied. "Tell the photo lab to bring those new portable lights."

"You got it," Colbert said, leaving the room with Wilson.

"Looks like her clothes here in the corner," McAllister said to Craig, shining his light on a pile of clothing. "I think there's a purse here too."

"Okay," Craig replied. "Let's leave it until the photographer gets here. Then we'll see what's there."

"This is a whole lot like that other case, isn't it?" McAllister asked.

"Too much like it," Craig said. "That other case didn't get much publicity and none of the stories mentioned the mutilations. These are so similar it almost has to be the same guy. We ran out every lead we could get on the Johnson case and came up with zilch. But, if it's the same guy, where's he been the last four years?"

*　*　*

At 6:00 a. m., John Craig pulled his old Ford into the driveway of his home on Kenwood Hill in the south end. He sat behind the wheel rubbing his eyes, which felt full of grit. His mouth had a foul taste, from too much coffee and too many cigarettes. The investigation at the homicide scene had lasted until 1:00 a. m. Then he and Rovinelli had returned to the office to process the clothing and other physical evidence collected at the scene and write their original report. Colbert and Wilson had accompanied the victim's body to the morgue and finished the processing there, photographing and fingerprinting the victim for identification purposes and getting a complete description of her wounds. An autopsy would be performed in the morning, attended by one of the day shift detectives.

They had tentatively identified the victim as Vanessa Richards from the driver's license in her purse. A search of arrest records had turned up seven arrests for solicitation of prostitution under that name, all in the Dixie Highway area and one for loitering for purposes of prostitution, at the Executive Inn near the airport. A comparison of fingerprints later that morning had confirmed the identification. Their victim was twenty-three years old and had lived on Southwestern Parkway, near Shawnee Park.

The day shift would be checking her home address and known associates, getting as much background on her as possible. Craig would report back to work at 3:30 p. m. and pick up the case from that point.

Glumly, he stared at the dark house. Of course, there weren't any lights on. There hadn't been any lights on awaiting his arrival since Susan, his wife, had taken the kids and moved back to her parents' home in Valley Station, back in February. He remembered vividly the day they left. He had come home after working the day shift to find her waiting for him with suitcases packed and the kids ready to go.

"I've had it, John," she told him angrily. "I can't handle sharing you with your job all the time. Hell, there is no sharing. You come home to us when there's nothing going on at work. You haven't made a single parent teacher conference this school year, you missed Melinda's concert, and you have yet to make one of Sean's ball games. I can't remember the last time we went out, except to some fast food place."

This blast of accusations caught him completely off guard. He stammered for a reply but wound up asking her,

"What are you going to do? Are you saying you want a divorce?"

"I don't know," she replied. "Right now, we're going to stay with mom and dad."

Obviously, she had been planning this for some time. Susan was a strong willed woman and had always been decisive. But this sudden breakup of his home and family stunned him. Caught completely off guard, he had not perceived a hint that this was about to happen. Susan complained about his long hours but she had been doing that since he went to homicide seven years ago.

"Let's talk this over, Susan, before you make this move," he said.

"There's nothing to talk over, John. I've made my mind up. I need to get away from this city and from you, so I can think out what I want to do. But whatever I decide, it will be what I think is best for the kids."

"You know I want what is best for the kids, Susan. Your opinion of me can't have fallen that low that you think I don't love my kids."

"I know you love them, John," she replied "but I think you love your job more. Or maybe you just don't think about them or me very often. When you get on a case, you might as well not be here, even when you are."

"You can visit us," she went on. "I won't try to keep you from seeing the kids, and I'll let you know when I decide what to do."

Then, while he was still marshalling his arguments, she told the kids to kiss him good bye, bustled them into her car, loaded up Buster the dog, and was gone.

Since then, he had made the trip to her parents home three times, picked up Sean, who was ten, and Melinda, eight, and taken them out for movies and ice cream. They were both confused by the situation and didn't at all understand why their parents were living apart or why they had to move. Each time, both he and the kids parted feeling more frustrated. Susan, on the other hand, appeared to be adapting quickly to her new life and showed no indication to reconcile with her husband. Her response when he attempted to question her about her intentions was that she was still examining her options.

Craig got out of his car and entered the empty house, flicking on lights as he moved through to the kitchen. The house was another issue that was going to have to be addressed soon. It had taken both his salary and Susan's teaching salary to qualify for the loan to buy the place. They had lived there less than three years. Their dream home – that was a joke. Their dreams seemed to have turned to shit. Now, since Susan was contributing nothing to the mortgage payments, he would probably have to sell the place soon.

Pulling his clothes off, he brushed his teeth and fell into bed, remembering just in time to set the alarm. He needed to be back in the office by 3:00 p. m. This case was going to be a bastard, just like the Johnson case. Mulling it over, he fell asleep.

Across town, in his two-room apartment in the Highlands neighborhood, McAllister was also trying to get some sleep. He went back on duty at 2:30 p. m. and daylight was approaching fast. He and Randall had stopped in the Lollygog, a bar across from headquarters, after their shift ended and had wound up closing the place. As usual, the job was their main topic of conversation. This latest homicide had given them plenty to talk about. After the bar closed at 2:00 a. m., they had gone to the Toddle House on Bardstown Road for breakfast and had ended up staying there until 5:00. McAllister was reasonably sure that Randall's wife would be very unhappy with her husband when he finally did arrive home. McAllister had no such worries but he did have a sergeant to answer to if he were late for work the next day. Consequently, he was trying to shut his mind down and get to sleep. The remembrance of the mutilated body of the murdered girl stayed with him, however and, so far, sleep had eluded him.

McAllister had found this apartment while he was selling floor polishers door-to-door and waiting to begin the police academy. He had come to Louisville in 1963 after his discharge from the army. He had gone to work for a small loan company in his home town of Owensboro, in western Kentucky, when he first got out of the service and the company had transferred him to one of their branch offices in Louisville.

A month or so in the finance business had convinced him that his career interests lay in other directions, so he resigned his job. He found the bustling, sprawling city on the Ohio River fascinating, however, and decided to stay there and find another job. Hearing an advertisement on the radio one day about applications being taken for the city police department, he had applied and taken the employment examination. With a high score and his military background, he was promptly offered a slot in the recruit class that would form after January 1 of 1964. This left him at loose ends for four months before he would start the class and begin drawing a regular salary. Consequently, he became by default a door-to-door floor polisher salesman, and not a very successful one.

McAllister was living in a third floor sleeping room in a turn of the century brownstone house on Third Street, near the University of Louisville campus. Its main advantages were that it was cheap and centrally located. Its disadvantages were many and centered around the other residents, most of whom came and went at all hours and loudly. Domestic disputes were frequent and often ended with blows, screams and threats of retribution. McAllister had decided quickly that he needed to find another place to live.

One beautiful fall day in October, he had made a sales call on a lady named Minnie Turner, who owned a large home on Windsor Place, just off Bardstown Road in the Highlands area. Mrs.Turner didn't want to buy a floor polisher but she did have a second floor apartment with an outside entrance for rent. There was one other lodger, an elderly piano tuner named Henry who had no vices to speak of. She and McAllister were favorably impressed with each other; a deal was struck and he had been a satisfied tenant for over four years.

For McAllister, the four years since his graduation from the police academy had flown by. His fascination with the sweeping panorama of human conduct that he observed and with which he interacted on a daily basis never left him. However, his latent ambition had begun to assert itself recently. He longed to do more than apply the stopgap solutions to problems that were available to police patrolmen. He wanted to solve big cases, clear heinous crimes and send murderers to prison. He had watched with envy and admiration as certain detectives, like John Craig, had investigated crime scenes and interviewed witnesses. He had seen the respect that Craig was accorded by his colleagues and by his commanding officers. He wanted that kind of respect for himself and he wanted the satisfaction of being able to work a case to its conclusion. He decided that he would actively seek a transfer to the homicide squad. However, he wasn't exactly sure how to go about it. Maybe Craig could give him some advice on how to proceed. The big detective always seemed to be friendly and approachable when he encountered him and always treated him like an equal. McAllister decided that he would seek an opportunity to talk with Craig soon and ask for his advice.

Having made this decision, he turned over and composed himself to go to sleep. The thought crossed his mind that his weekends off were coming up and he sleepily thought that he would check out a few bars this Friday. His love life was pretty dormant lately and, who knew? Maybe he might meet a datable girl. With this pleasant thought, the visions of Vanessa Richards' mutilated corpse slipped from his conscious memory and he slept.

*   *   *

26

Vanessa Richards' killer was also having thoughts of her that morning. The kill had been extremely satisfactory. The girl had been beautiful, her fear had been palpable, and the aftermath had been highly exciting. He was particularly proud of the quote from Jack the Ripper. If the cops didn't release that information to the paper, he intended to find a way to make sure they learned of it. He wanted to be sure that every whore in Louisville knew what fate awaited her. His work had been interrupted for a few years but he was back for good now. He had been able to perfect his techniques on a number of women while he was away. But this was the city he had been chosen for. Louisville was full of whores and he was there to deal with them. Humming a classical tune, he carefully knotted his tie and prepared for the new day.

Chapter Four

Louisville, Kentucky. Wednesday, March 13, 1968, 3:03 p. m.

Craig parked his car in a vacant slot on the parking lot that the Fraternal Order of Police leased from the city. The scene of numerous late-night drinking sessions after the 3 to 11 shift ended, it was affectionately known as the "Gravel Lounge." He stepped around several mud puddles and headed across the street to police headquarters. It had rained most of the night and the weather was cold and blustery.

The three story building, with a façade of Vermont marble, was twelve years old and already was bulging at the seams. The rapidly expanding department was running out of room quickly. The homicide office on the second floor, a space about twenty feet long and eight feet wide, was big enough to contain two desks and a row of filing cabinets. In this limited area, nine detectives and two supervisors functioned in an intricate ballet of space sharing. Fortunately they were assigned to four shifts. When a major case was working, however, it was not uncommon to find most of the squad there at one time.

It was crowded today as Craig entered the office and hung his topcoat in a large cabinet in the corner. The detective sergeant, Tom Howard, had the three day shift detectives gathered around his desk, where the crime scene photos from last night's case were spread out in vivid array.

He looked up as Craig entered and said "The lieutenant wants you in the Chief of Detectives' office, John. It's about last night's case. The major is in an uproar over it."

Nodding acknowledgment, Craig turned and walked down the hall to the spacious, wood-paneled office occupied by Major Farley M. Bishop, Chief of Detectives. A large, completely bald man built like Humpty

Dumpty, Bishop was widely known to be politically ambitious and to covet the job of Chief of Police with all his soul. He was seated behind his huge desk when Craig knocked on the open door.

"Come in, Craig," he said, motioning toward a long conference table where Lt. James Garrard, commander of the homicide squad, was seated, along with Captain Emmett Hall, assistant Chief of Detectives. Craig gingerly took a seat alongside Lt. Garrard and opened his notebook.

"What about this killing last night?" Bishop asked. "Do you think it is connected to the unsolved you had back in 1964?"

"Sir, the mutilations are almost identical, the victims are both prostitutes and it's only a couple of blocks from the other one, in another vacant house. I'd say it almost has to be the same guy. The Johnson case didn't get much notice in the press, as you remember, so the details of the crime didn't get released to the public. If the same guy didn't do them both, he has to have told someone all about it and that someone has copied his style exactly."

"Either way, we have a serious problem on our hands, if the press picks up on the fact that we have two cases so much alike," Bishop said. "Garrard, did you ever come up with a viable suspect on that Johnson girl?"

"No, sir," the lieutenant replied, "but not from lack of trying. We put in several hundred hours on that case. There just wasn't much to work with."

"What's this about some kind of writing on the wall?' Bishop asked. "I was told, Craig, that you think the guy is quoting Jack the Ripper."

"He is, Major," Craig said. "I looked it up in a book I have on the Ripper murders before I came in today. It's an exact quote from one of the letters attributed to Jack the Ripper that was sent to a London newspaper."

"That will be all we need, if the *Courier Journal* finds out that we have a killer who is imitating Jack the Ripper," Bishop responded. "Keep this information to yourselves. Craig, who else besides you and your partner saw this writing on the wall?"

"Colbert and Wilson, sir, and the two beat men, McAllister and Randall. Also, the deputy coroner, Bill Anderson, and the fingerprint and photo techs," Craig said.

"Get a hold of them all, Garrard. Tell them that this is a direct order from me. They are not to discuss that bullshit writing with anyone. If they do, they'll all be walking a foot beat in Southwick housing project. Do you understand me?" the Major growled.

"Yes, sir," Garrard replied. "I'll call the deputy coroner, too. He's a good guy. He won't be a problem."

"Nobody had better be a problem," Bishop said. "Craig, get busy and solve this case before the press does find out and plays it all out of proportion. The fact that it's nothing but a couple of black whores will be lost in the shuffle if that happens. And I don't like reading about myself or my bureau when it's not favorable to us. Do I make myself clear?" He focused a hard glare on each of the three other men.

"Yes, sir," they all said together and left his office. Captain Hall stopped at the entrance to his office and turned to the two homicide detectives. A quiet, soft-spoken man with a backbone of steel, he was admired by the men who worked for him and respected as Bishop would never be.

"Let me know what you need on this, Jim," he said to Garrard. "If you need to borrow people from some of the other squads, I'll arrange it."

"Thanks, Captain. I'll work up a game plan and get with you," the lieutenant replied.

"John, get in contact with those two beat men and pass on the Major's orders," Garrard said as they entered the homicide office. "I'll call the photo and fingerprint labs. It's a good idea to hold that kind of stuff back, anyway, in case we get some kook wanting to confess."

"Okay, boss," Craig replied. "What about putting the word out among the hookers on Dixie Highway that there's a screwball loose, probably posing as a john? I'd hate to have another victim turn up."

"Do it on the Q. T.," the lieutenant said. "Word of mouth only. Don't those two beat men you mentioned ride the stroll? Ask them to help spread the word. But, God help us all if the newspaper gets wind of it. I don't think the Major was kidding. He takes his public image pretty seriously."

"Yes, sir. Most of the stroll is on their beat. I'll get them to contact the girls and try to warn them off. I doubt it'll do much good, though. Since the war in Viet Nam heated up and Fort Knox expanded, that stretch of Dixie Highway has been busier than hell. Those women are making some serious money out there. It'll probably take more than Jack the Ripper to keep them off the street." With these words, Craig went off to find a vacant desk and telephone.

Louisville, Kentucky. Friday, March 15, 1968, 9:30 p. m.

McAllister finished his beer and looked around at the few customers in the Office Lounge (Slogan: 'Tell them you stayed late at the Office.') Located inside a mid-town shopping mall, the bar was usually one of Louisville's most popular. Tonight, everyone seemed to be some place else. The few people that were there were couples seated at the piano bar listening to Freddy George tickle the ivories. The diminutive pianist wore his black hair in a pony tail and carried a beaded purse, which was pretty far out for

Louisville but, when he sat down at a piano, people stopped talking and listened. McAllister was a fan of Freddie's but tonight he was in the mood for female companionship.

He had broken up with a nurse he was dating, several months ago. Since then he had not had a date. He had worked a lot of extra duty since Christmas and it hadn't seemed important at the time. Tonight, however, he had the feeling that talking to somebody cute and personable about something other than dead bodies and dog bite reports might be what he needed. He decided to check out some other bars in hopes of finding a livelier crowd and perhaps some attractive woman. He left the bartender a dollar tip and, waving at her and at Freddy, went out the door.

Turning his '67 Mustang south on Bardstown Road from the mall parking lot, McAllister was debating his choices when he noticed a sign in the window of a small bar.

The sign read 'Bob Rosenthal tonight.' The place was called The Shack and McAllister had never been inside. It had a reputation as a hippie hangout, which wasn't his forte normally. However, he had met Rosenthal, a guitar-playing folk singer with a penchant for arm-wrestling, a couple of years ago and liked both the man and his music. Making up his mind, McAllister pulled to the curb and parked.

The club was very dark when he went inside, except for a small spotlight shining on the pony-tailed singer at the back of the room. McAllister groped his way to the bar and ordered a beer from the long haired bartender. As his eyes became accustomed to the darkness, he discovered that the walls appeared to be covered with some sort of burlap sacking, adorned with large peace signs and other counter-culture emblems. He also noticed that someone in the darkened room was smoking a pretty potent joint. The semi-sweet smell of a good grade of marijuana hung heavily in the air.

Rosenthal was beginning a spirited rendition of *Whiskey in the Jar*, an Irish folk song that McAllister particularly liked. He was humming along with the music when he noticed a beautiful girl a couple of stools down from him. She too was singing along. Her long brown hair, parted in the middle in the current style, hung past her shoulders. Her peasant blouse and bell bottomed jeans were *de rigueur* for the time and place but she appeared to his jaundiced eye to be classier than the average hippie chick. Foe one thing, she looked a lot cleaner. In fact, she had a look of fresh scrubbed wholesomeness that McAllister found captivating.

Rosenthal concluded his number and hit a series of discordant notes on his guitar.

"Pause for the cause. Be back in about fifteen," he told the applauding crowd.

Walking quickly to the bar, he took a beer from the bartender and, turning, noticed McAllister sitting next to him.

"Hello, Scott," he said in a pleased tone. "What brings you out among the natives wild?'

"I saw your name on the window and decided to see if you'd ever learned all the words to *Froggy Went Acourtin'*," McAllister replied.

"Hell, you know I do, but that song might be a little advanced for tonight's crowd – except for this lovely lady. Hello, Jenny. Nice to see you," the singer said to the girl seated down the bar.

"Hi, Bob," she replied. "I'm really enjoying your music."

"I'm glad. Do you know my friend, Scott McAllister?"

"No, I don't. Hi, Scott. Jenny Holcomb. Nice to meet you," she said with a smile that seemed to light up the room.

"Hi, Jenny. Nice to meet you," Scott replied. "Bob, have you been playing here long?"

"Just a week," Rosenthal said. "One more week to go, then I'm at the Holiday Inn on Zorn Avenue for a month."

"Cool," McAllister replied. Turning back to the girl, he asked her "Jenny, are you a folk music fan? I saw that you knew the words to *Whiskey in the Jar*. That's not exactly a top forty tune, so you must be, a fan I mean."

She nodded enthusiastically.

"That's one of my favorite songs. How could I not like a song about a girl named "Sportin' Jenny'?" she replied. "I've loved folk music since I was a little girl. I minored in music at Western and my main interest was folk songs. Then, when I moved to Louisville last year, I heard Bob at a folk festival at Bellarmine College. Since then, I try to go hear him at least a couple of times wherever he plays." She flashed another one of those amazing smiles at Rosenthal and he raised his beer glass in salutation.

"What about you, Scott? Are you a folk music fan or just a Rosenthal fan?" she asked.

"Both, really," he replied. "I learned to like folk music while I was in the army. The Kingston Trio, Peter, Paul and Mary, they were kind of the sound track for my time in the service. I met Bob a couple of years ago and I really like his music. Don't ever arm wrestle him, though. The man is unbeatable."

"All these compliments are turning my head," Rosenthal said. "But I'd better make a pit stop and get back to work. It's good to see both of you. Jenny, can I play something for you?"

"Play *Blowing in the Wind* please, Bob," she said. Nodding, the singer turned and headed toward the rear of the bar.

"Where do you work, Jenny?"

"I'm a legal secretary for a law firm downtown," she replied. "I came up here after college and got a job. I lived with my aunt for about six months and then, just before Christmas, a couple of the girls I work with asked me to share an apartment with them.

So now, I'm a Highlands resident. We live over on Cherokee Road, close enough to here that I walked over. We've even adopted a cat. She was a stray hanging around our back porch and we started feeding her. I guess you could say she adopted us. Her name is Matilda." Then with a laugh, she said

"I'm sorry. When I get started, sometimes I just run on for hours. Tell me about you, What do you do, Scott?"

"I work for the city," he replied. "I'm originally from Owensboro. Got out of the army and came up here to find a job. I like Louisville, so I've stayed."

They were deep in conversation when the outer door opened and a group of young people entered, talking loudly. Several of the patrons turned to give them annoyed stares which they ignored. There were four men and three women, all in their late twenties and well dressed with flushed faces that, along with their loud conversation, indicated that this was not the first stop of the evening for them.

One of the men, a tall slim individual with blonde wavy hair, wearing a dark expensive-looking suit, noticed the girl at the bar and made his way over to them. Turning his back to McAllister, he interspersed himself between them at the bar.

"Hello, Jenny. How have you been?" he said to the girl.

"Hi, Michael. Where have you guys been tonight?" she replied.

"Oh, just hitting a few spots, having a few drinks and some laughs. Say, if you're not doing anything important, why don't you join us? It would even out the numbers and I'd love to get a chance to talk to you," the man said in an off-hand, almost insolent manner that irritated McAllister immediately.

"Nice of you to assume that talking to me wasn't important," he said to the man, who looked around at him with a surprised air. He had an angular face with sharp features and a pointed nose.

"I wasn't aware that any part of my comments was directed to you," the man replied.

"No, you were doing a pretty good job of acting like I wasn't sitting here talking to Jenny. But I am and we intend to finish our conversation. So why don't you rejoin your friends, and tell them to hold it down so other people can hear the music?" McAllister said, standing up and looking the man in the eye.

"Oh, are you the bouncer or something?' the man said.

"All right, boys. That's enough," Jenny interjected. "Michael, I'm talking to Scott. Thanks for the invitation but no thanks. I'll probably see you downtown next week. Maybe we can have lunch."

"I'll hold you to that. I'll call you," the man said and, turning, walked back to the table where his friends were sitting.

Turning to McAllister, the girl flashed another smile at him and pulled him back onto the barstool.

"Calm down, Scott," she said. "That's just Michael's way. He can be rather – imperious, I guess would be the word."

"Smartass would be my word for him," Scott replied. "Who is that jerk?"

"I'm surprised you don't know him," she said. "He works for the city, too. He's the new assistant Director of Safety. Michael Renyard is his name."

"I've never seen him before," McAllister said. "Where do you know him from?"

"His best friend works in the law firm I work for. He's over there a lot and – well, he asked me out a couple of times."

McAllister felt an instant flash of jealousy. "Hold on a minute," he told himself, "you just met this girl. You have no right to get jealous." This line of reasoning did not serve to calm the intense dislike he had immediately formed for Mr. Renyard. He was not normally prone to make snap judgments of people or to form sudden antagonisms. He could only attribute his behavior to the strong feelings that Jenny Holcomb aroused in him.

"Scott," she interrupted his reverie. "Would you like to go to a party? A friend of mine lives on Eastern Parkway near here. She's giving a party tonight. I didn't want to go by myself but, if you wouldn't mind taking me, it might be fun."

"I'd love to take you, Jenny," he replied.

They waved goodbye to Bob Rosenthal and started out the door. As they departed, McAllister noticed that Renyard was staring at him with a look of hatred.

"Well, bud, that makes two of us," he thought as he steered Jenny toward his Mustang.

He drove to the address she pointed out on Eastern Parkway, a few blocks away. There were a lot of cars in the area and they had to search for a parking place. Finally locating one on a side street, they entered a large three story house that had been subdivided into apartments. The party was going on in a third floor apartment and spilling out into the hall and stairwell, as they came up the stairs. Grace Slick and Jefferson Airplane could be heard wailing *The White Rabbit* out the open door of the apartment and, once again McAllister's nose was assailed with the pungent smell of marijuana. Only here it was so strong that it was overpowering.

Jenny gave McAllister a sideways glance and a grimace.

"Too much pot smoke," she said. "I don't like to smell the stuff. Oh, here's my friend, Linda. Hey, Linda, this is Scott."

A statuesque redhead draped with beads came out of the crowd and hugged Jenny. She looked appraisingly at McAllister, whose hair was by far the shortest in the room.

"Hi, Scott," she said in response to Jenny's introduction. "What will you have? We've got beer and wine and I think there's some whiskey left in the kitchen. Anything else, you're on your own."

"Thanks, beer would be fine," McAllister replied and steered Jenny in the direction that Linda pointed.

Beads seemed to be the central decorating theme of the place. They were hung in every doorway. There didn't seem to be much furniture other than lots of pillows and bean bag chairs. Strange looking lamps provided dim light through the haze of cigarette and marijuana smoke that permeated the apartment.

They maneuvered their way through the crush of people into the kitchen. There they snagged a couple of bottles of beer from a tub in the kitchen and worked their way back through the throng to a spot near a glass door which led to a large wooden porch across the back of the building. The air was thick with smoke and the music was so loud that conversation was impossible.

They scrambled through the door and joined a smaller group on the porch. Stairs led down to the second and first levels and had obviously been added as a fire escape when the building was converted to apartments. Now they were serving as overflow space for people seeking relief from the overcrowded apartment. It was a cool evening and the outside crowd was much smaller than that inside.

"Do you know most of these people?" McAllister asked Jenny.

"No, just Linda and a couple of her friends," she replied. "She's a graduate assistant at U of L, in the Sociology Department. I think her roommates go to school, too."

"Quite a party," McAllister commented, looking around at the couples near them. He was already nervous about the amount of pot being smoked at this gathering. He had visions of the Narcotics Squad storming up the stairway and locking everybody up. That would pretty well end his police career before it really got off the ground. If not for the fact that he was so smitten with the girl beside him, he wouldn't come near a gathering like this. Even now his common sense told him to take her and get out.

Just then, a girl inside the apartment shrieked in a loud voice and began babbling about bats and rats. Two young men took her by the arms and led her off to another room.

"That was Meagan. She told me she was going to try acid tonight. Looks like she made it," a girl standing near McAllister and Jenny told her companion.

"Yeah, and she's not the only one," the boy replied. "There were two or three guys in the bathroom cutting up some windowpane when I went in there a couple of minutes ago. This party may get freaky."

McAllister bent near Jenny's ear and whispered,

"I think we should get out of here. This place is ripe to get busted."

"I'm with you," the girl replied. "All this smoke is giving me a headache anyhow."

They went down the wooden stairs to the rear of the building and walked to his car.

"Jenny," he said as they drove away, "there's something I should have told you before but I didn't know how you'd take it and I really wanted you to keep talking to me. I'm a cop."

She turned to look at him and flashed another of her smiles.

"I kind of figured that from the short hair and the way you acted with Michael," she replied. "Did I put you in a bad spot by taking you to that party?"

"It could cost me my job if I got caught there," he said. "But I wanted to spend as much time with you as possible. I just didn't know how you would feel about police. We're not popular with a lot of people these days."

"Scott, my dad is a Captain on the Bowling Green Police Department," she said. "I've been around police officers all my life and my dad is the finest man in the world. I don't do drugs and never will. I couldn't face my father. But, everywhere you go these days, everybody is smoking pot and doing a lot of other stuff, too. It's either sit at home all the time or go out and try to ignore it. I choose to go out sometimes."

"How about something to eat?' McAllister asked her. "It's only a little after midnight."

"I'm famished," Jenny replied. "Where should we go?"

"Hasenour's is right up the street. They're open until 2:00," Scott said and turned toward the restaurant.

"Have you eaten here?" he asked Jenny, as they entered the well-known restaurant.

"No, but I've heard a lot about it," she replied. "Isn't it awfully expensive?"

"It can be but poor folks like us can usually get a booth in the bar here and get a good cheeseburger or hot brown without breaking the bank," Scott said.

They found a vacant booth and slipped into it, ordering burgers and glasses of Heineken draft from the waitress. Soon they were deep into their food and into their continuing conversation. The high backed booths gave a sense of privacy and intimacy that seemed to fit the mood they were in. They were quickly discovering that they liked each other.

Later, over the remnants of their meal, he asked her to go out the following night.

To his disappointment, she replied,

"Scott, I can't. I've already got a date. How about Sunday?"

"I have to work Sunday on the 3 – 11 shift," he said. "But I'm off again next Saturday. How does that sound?"

"It's a date," Jenny smilingly replied. "I'll give you my address and phone number."

She scribbled the information on a cocktail napkin and gave it to him.

"Now, don't lose it," she chided.

"Not a chance," he replied, tucking it into his shirt pocket. "I've already got it memorized."

*   *   *

Several miles away, on the parking lot of an elementary school at 18th and Wilson Streets, he sat in his car, feeling the frustration build in him. The usually busy stretch of Dixie Highway was void of foot traffic. There were a couple of hookers hanging out in front of the White Owl Liquors, just down the street from where he sat. But they were accompanied by a large black man, obviously their pimp and he was closely examining each car that pulled up to do business with the girls, looking into the windows as the cars pulled onto the well lighted parking lot.

The police had definitely spread the word. There had been just a short item in the newspaper about his latest work and no mention had been made of the earlier kill. But the cops had probably made the connection and put the word out on the street. Now his normally thriving hunting grounds were almost deserted.

A police station wagon, one of the new white ones, passed in front of him going north on Dixie. Although he was parked in the shadows, he was certain that the passenger officer had looked over and seen his car. They would drive around the block and come back to check him out. He put the car in gear and pulled to the corner. Sure enough, he could see the tail lights of the cop car as it turned west on Wilson. He pulled out and turned south on Dixie Highway and floored it. He didn't intend to be in the area when they came back around.

He would just cool it for a couple of weeks. It was a matter of economics. The whores would heed the cops for a couple of days and then, when nothing happened, they would return to the streets. They wouldn't be able to give up the money they would lose, with the weather getting warmer and the Derby approaching. They would be back out in droves. He would make his selection then and continue his work. The next time, he would make sure the newspaper and television stations knew all about it and about the other ones too.

Thinking about it, he decided that he would continue to tie Jack the Ripper into his work. After all, the Ripper did two in one night. That would be a real test of his skills, two in one night. He had some time now to scout for two new locations, two new places where he could work undisturbed. He would have to bring the other car. He didn't want this one seen in the area too much. Two in one night. That would drive the fucking cops crazy. Just thinking about it gave him a pleasurable feeling as he drove away.

Chapter Five

Louisville, Kentucky. Thursday, March 28, 1968, 2;10 P. M.

McAllister muttered under his breath as he reached to the back of the top shelf of his locker. He was trying to find his ball point pen which, so far, was eluding his grasp. Then his fingers brushed it, down behind a stack of used citation books he had rubber banded together and thrown up on the top shelf. As he retrieved the pen, he examined a smear of dust and grime on the sleeve of his uniform shirt.

"Damn these light blue shirts, anyway," he muttered to himself. "They show everything you come up against and this is my last clean shirt. Marvin will eat my ass out if he notices this."

He went into the adjacent restroom and was busily trying to scrub the dirt off his shirt at one of the sinks. Intent on what he was doing, he didn't notice the short, rotund officer who approached him until he spoke.

"Doing your own laundry, Mac?" the officer said. "Most people take them off before they wash them."

"Hi, Mike," McAllister replied. "I'm trying to get enough of this dirt off to get by at roll call. Anything exciting going on in Parkland today?"

The other officer, Mike Kowalski, and his partner Lloyd Meyers were assigned to beat 403 on the off-going day shift. McAllister and Randall would be relieving them after the 2:30 p. m. roll call.

"Not much happening," Kowalksi replied. "Say, Mac, I need to ask you something. I was in the Copper Lantern today, down at 32nd and Hale, and Roscoe Brown mentioned that he never sees you and your partner. He says you never stop by."

"Yeah, okay. So what?" McAllister said. "I've been in there two or three times, once this month on a fight run."

"He's not talking about that, Mac. He says you all never come in to get a coke and you haven't never made a pickup." He leaned closer to McAllister and said in a quieter tone "He's good for ten bucks apiece a week just to run his little old card game and let a couple of girls work out of there."

"I'm not interested in that shit, Mike, " McAllister replied, " and neither is Dave. You and Lloyd can have our piece."

"It don't work that way, Mac, and you know it. You've got Brown all nervous and a couple of the other joint owners on the beat, too. They think because you don't stop in that you're setting them up to get knocked off by vice or somebody."

"Why would they worry about the vice squad?" McAllister asked. "Hell, they're in every one of those joints every week, getting their piece of the action."

"Yeah, well. They're still nervous. I mentioned it to Sgt. Marvin and he said you all should stop in and see these people, reassure them that everything is all right."

"Thanks a lot, Mike. If Marvin wants me to do that, he can tell me himself," McAllister replied.

"Look, Mac," Kowalski said. "We have a pretty good deal going on this beat. There's eighty or a hundred bucks a week tax free out there for each of us. All we got to do is not pay any attention to a couple of things nobody gives a shit about anyway. And it's all square right up the line. Even city hall gets some of the action. All I'm saying is don't screw things up for everybody."

"I'm not trying to screw things up for anybody," McAllister replied. "All I want is to do my job and I don't give a damn who's paying who what. If they break the law in front of me, they're going to jail."

"Don't be such a smartass, McAllister," the older officer said. "There's people a lot bigger than Marvin interested in these places and they won't like it much if you rock the boat. I'm trying to do you a favor and give you a headsup but if you're too smart to listen to me, fuck you." With that, Kowalski spun on his heel and went back into the locker room.

"Yeah, well, fuck you too, buddy," McAllister muttered as he dried off his hands. He had been anticipating an encounter like this since last year when he was assigned to the beat. He had even warned Dave Randall to expect it. He didn't care whether or not Kowalski approved of him but if the district commanders were involved, it was a different matter entirely. His future suddenly looked a lot more complicated.

He didn't have a chance to speak to Randall privately before Sgt. Marvin gave them the command to fall in for roll call. The sergeant read off the radio car assignments quickly and then commanded "At ease, the lieutenant wants to say something to you all."

Lieutenant Hendricks, a tall cadaverous looking individual who wore his trousers and gun belt high up under his arms, stepped forward. His nickname among the troops was "Long Zipper."

"Men, as you're all aware, there has been a lot of racial trouble in other cities recently. Martin Luther King and his friends are stirring up things down in Memphis right now, the way they stirred them up here last year," Hendricks said. "Things have been quiet around here for some time but the natives are getting restless down in the projects. Last night 408 made a domestic trouble run to 38th and Von Spiegel in Southwick. They got a bunch of rocks and bottles thrown at them before they could get out of there. With warm weather coming, we'll probably have more of this sort of thing. So keep your cool out there. Don't do anything to create an unnecessary confrontation and back each other up if you hear a bad run come out. I'm not telling you that you have to take any shit off anybody. Just don't start it yourself. That's all, Sergeant."

"Yes, sir," Marvin replied. "Platoon, attention! Fall out. McAllister and Randall, see me in the office before you go out."

As the shift broke ranks and started toward the door of the roll call room, all the white officers were surreptitiously watching Congrove and Lewis, the only two black officers on the platoon, to see their reaction to Hendicks' speech, especially the part about the restless natives. Both men had virtually unreadable poker-faced expressions as they went out of the building.

"Wonder what this is all about," Randall queried, as they headed to the sergeant's office across the hall.

"I think I know," McAllister replied. "I didn't have a chance to tell you before roll call. Just listen for now. I'll fill you in later."

"You wanted to see us, Sarge?" McAllister asked.

"Yeah, Kowalski tells me that some of the joint owners on your beat are saying they never see you guys except when you get a run there," the sergeant said. "These guys want to be cooperative. They want you to stop in every now and then, get to know them. Makes you a better cop when you know the people on your beat."

"Frankly, Sarge," McAllister said, "We stay out of those places because we hear there are some activities going on there that aren't exactly kosher but are sanctioned by higher ups. We're not too comfortable with that."

Marvin looked sharply at the two young patrolmen.

"I don't know what you're talking about, McAllister," he growled. "I'm not telling you to overlook anything illegal. I'm telling you to get to know your beat. You heard the lieutenant talking about racial problems. Well, these people can be very helpful to us in seeing that that kind of thing doesn't get out of hand here. So get your ass out there and do what you're told."

"Yes, sir," McAllister said and he and Randall turned to leave the office. Lieutenant Hendricks was coming in the door and glanced at the two young officers sharply as he passed them.

As they drove west on Jefferson Street, headed to their beat, Randall was pointing out that their bosses' attitudes toward them seemed to have changed overnight.

"Hell, Hendricks has always been real cordial toward me and Marvin, too. And I was sure you were their fair haired boy. But Hendricks stopped me in the hall before roll call and chewed my ass out over my hair cut. Marvin didn't sound very friendly today, either."

"I think Kowalski probably went straight to Marvin after our conversation in the locker room and told him what I said," McAllister replied. "He probably passed it on to the Lieutenant. Neither one of them wants anybody rocking the boat. They've got a sweet deal going down here and you can figure that they're each making a nice chunk of change. Let's see. There's eight beats in the district. At least six of them have got joints, bootleggers, card games, or whorehouses on them that are paying off. There's no action on 406 that I know of and 408 is just housing projects. So figure that the bosses are getting money from each of six beats, that would amount to some pretty good money each week and all tax free."

"What are we going to do, Scott?" Randall asked

"Dave, I don't know about you but I can't do it. It's not right and I could never look my father in the face if I started taking payoffs. I'm not judging what anybody else does but I've got to be able to live with myself."

"They make it seem normal," Randall said. "The bosses, the district detectives, the chief's office, city hall – Hell, they're all in on it. And this piss-ass salary they pay us, it's almost like they want you to take the money. God knows I could use it, with one kid and another one on the way."

"Where does that leave you, Dave?" McAllister asked.

"I'm with you, buddy," Randall replied. "Hell, these people on our beat dislike and disrespect us enough as it is. I don't think I could work down here if I was getting paid off to look the other way at some of the shit going on."

"You realize we'll probably get moved off this beat," McAllister said. "They'll put us on 6 or 8 or have us riding extra and replace us with somebody they can count on. My hope is to get transferred to the Detective Bureau before long and get out of all this crap."

"Where do you want to go, the Vice Squad?" Randall asked with an impish grin.

McAllister shot him an extended middle finger as they sped westward to the area where they both loved to work but where nobody loved them.

Later that evening, they were eating dinner at the Chop Shop Restaurant at 26th and Broadway. In a break from procedure, they were both out of the car and eating at the same time. McAllister had invested $19.95 plus shipping and handling in a device he had ordered from a police supply catalogue. It was called a "Little Tiger" and was about the size of a box of kitchen matches. Attached by rubber bands to a transistor radio and tuned to a certain frequency, it converted the transistor into a police radio receiver, capable of receiving the calls broadcast by KIB 695, the city police radio station.

If they got a run, one of them would have to dash out to the car to okay it, but it still allowed them to both be away from the car at the same time.

Thinking about this, McAllister was wishing that the department had two-way "walkie-talkies" such as he had seen on the news being used by larger departments. The Louisville Division of Police seemed to always be four or five years behind when it came to getting equipment. They had just recently been issued so-called riot helmets, which had been badly needed during the open housing demonstrations the preceding year. These helmets were more like Little League batting helmets than any serious protective gear. There was some talk about everyone being issued a gas mask, although none had materialized yet.

"What about Jenny?" Randall interrupted his thoughts. "Are you still seeing her?"

"We've had two dates and I've taken her to lunch a couple of times," McAllister replied. "My off days haven't worked out with her schedule very well. I'm hoping when we get on day work next month, things will get better."

"Is she still dating that high muckety-muck in the Director of Safety's office?" Randall asked.

"Yeah, I think so," McAllister said. "I saw her having lunch with him at Holly's one day. There is something about that guy that rubs me the wrong way but I'm trying to play it cool."

"Hung up on this girl, aren't you, pard?" Randall said.

"I really like her," McAllister answered "but, at this point I'm afraid if I start coming on too strong, I'll scare her off."

"Well, good luck, buddy. If you can figure women out, let me know how you do it. I can use some help at home, sometimes."

A television set behind the counter was tuned to "I Love Lucy". Then an announcer broke in, saying that a demonstration in Memphis that evening led by Dr. Martin Luther King Jr., had turned violent, resulting in a riot. The network showed footage of Memphis police officers charging demonstrators and hosing down crowds of people with fire hoses.

"Jesus," Randall said. "Look at that. What's that all about?'

"It started with a garbage workers strike," McAllister replied. "They've been marching for several days. Looks like the Memphis cops have their hands full."

"Car 403, at 32nd and Greenwood, outside the liquor store, a large crowd fighting in the street." The police dispatcher's voice sounded distorted and tinny through the static on the little transistor radio. They both abandoned their half-eaten meal and bolted for the door.

When they arrived at the location a few minutes later, it was obvious that there was, indeed, a large crowd in the street. McAllister tapped the siren switch with his foot and it gave forth a low moan. Usually this was enough to make a crowd disperse but this crowd appeared determined to stay put. Several of the people on the fringes of the crowd began yelling obscenities at the two officers.

"Call for backup," McAllister told Randall, who grabbed the microphone off the dash and spoke rapidly into it.

"Car 403 to radio. Request assistance in handling large disorderly crowd at 32nd and Greenwood."

"10-4, Car 403. All Fourth District units. Car 403 requests assistance at 32nd and Greenwood with large disorderly crowd. Units responding, advise."

As McAllister and Randall got out of their car with their nightsticks and flashlights, they could see a group of three or four men pummeling another man who was down on the sidewalk. The prostrate man was bleeding profusely from his face and was attempting to shield himself with his arms. As they started toward this group the assailants turned and melted into the crowd. Randall turned back to the car and grabbed the first aid kit.

They approached the downed man and knelt beside him to determine the extent of his injuries. As they did so, a bottle smashed on the sidewalk beside them. This set off a barrage of rocks and other debris, targeting both them and their station wagon. A group of young black males climbed on the police unit and began rocking it up and down.

"Honky motherfuckers. Get yo' white ass out of here." A tall black male with an afro hairdo yelled at them from the street. Others took up the cry.

"Honky motherfuckers. This ain't Memphis. Kill the honkies!"

They grabbed the injured man under his arms and dragged him up against the wall of the liquor store. McAllister interspersed himself between the man and the crowd, while Randall attempted to stem the flow of blood from a large jagged cut on the man's face. Staring at the sea of hostile faces, McAllister felt a cold wave of fear rush over him. The situation was rapidly deteriorating and, for the first time in his police career, he was uncertain as to his next course of action. It was beginning to look like they might have to fight their way out of this crowd at gunpoint.

Just then, McAllister heard a sound as sweet as any he had ever heard in his life. The moaning wail of police sirens could be heard rapidly approaching the intersection. In a few moments, flashing red lights lit up the area as four cars arrived almost simultaneously. Terry Vogel, a large bear-like officer with a well-deserved reputation in the district for violent behavior, got out of his car with a short-barreled, twelve gauge Remington shotgun in his hands. Looking directly at the people in the forefront of the crowd, he deliberately racked the slide of the gun back and loaded a shell in the chamber. He then leveled the weapon at the crowd, which parted like the Red Sea before Moses.

People began pushing and shoving to get out of the way. Those on the fringes melted into the yards and alleys. A group of officers lined up on the sidewalk in front of McAllister, Randall and the injured man. In a few moments, the police were the sole occupants of the intersection, although shouted curses and threats could be heard from the retreating mob. Periodically, a bottle or brick would be thrown over the houses on 32nd Street to land with a crash in the intersection.

Sergeant Marvin pushed his way through the line of officers to where McAllister and Randall were standing.

"What is this shit all about, McAllister?" he demanded.

"You've got me, Sergeant," McAllister replied. "We got a run on a crowd fighting in the street. When we got here, they were still fighting. Three or four of them were working on this guy and we could see he was bleeding pretty good. So, we went to him and they started rocking us. Looked like a bunch of them were trying to turn over our car. Frankly, I felt like Custer at the Little Big Horn until you guys showed up. When Terry produced that twelve gauge, it changed the whole situation."

"Who is this guy?" Marvin inquired.

"He's my clerk, Lawrence Johnson," a short, balding Jewish man stated as he came up to the group. " We caught a kid trying to shoplift a pint of Jim Beam and Lawrence chased him outside. When he did, a bunch of the usual low-lifes that hang on this corner jumped him and started beating him up. Then everybody got into the act. They've all been looking for an excuse to raise hell all evening. Everybody that's come in the store is all fired up about Martin Luther King and Memphis. Sergeant Marvin, you need to keep these low-lifes cleaned off this corner better. Hell, there's forty or fifty of them hanging around here every night, stealing me blind and leaving trash all over the street.

"Yeah, okay, Abe," Marvin replied. "We'll take care of it. How about your man there? Is he going to need to go to the hospital?"

"He's going to need stitches, Sarge," Randall said, arising from beside the injured man. "I got the bleeding stopped but that gash on his head will have to be cleaned out and sewed up."

"Okay, 403, you take him to General. 404, you all stand by here for a while to make sure it stays quiet. The rest of you get back on the air," Marvin ordered. "By the way, McAllister, you didn't pay much attention to what the lieutenant said at roll call, did you?"

"What are you talking about, Sergeant?" McAllister replied.

"If you had handled this run a little better, we wouldn't have all had to come running over here to pull your asses out of a jam, would we?" Marvin said.

"I don't know what we could have done different, boss," McAllister said. "We had just got here and saw this guy getting beat up when all hell broke loose and we-"

"Just get moving, get this guy to General, and get your ass back on your beat," the sergeant brusquely cut him off.

As they pulled away from General Hospital after delivering Johnson to the emergency room and taking a report from him, Randall turned to his partner.

"Doesn't seem to be much doubt that we are number one boys on Sergeant Marvin's shit list, does there?" he asked.

"Nope and I figure we will have a hard time doing anything right," McAllister replied. "We'll be on day work in a couple of days. Maybe things will cool off a little."

"I hope so," Randall said 'but, man, I hate day work. Getting up at five o'clock doesn't go well with me. The only good thing is I get more time with Janet and the kid in the afternoon. And, if we can find a sitter, we might even go out for dinner and a movie this month. Are you planning on improving your love life next month?"

"Maybe," McAllister replied. "I've got a date with Jenny next Wednesday night to go to some play she wants to see at Actor's Theater. I'm hoping to see her a lot next month."

"Good luck, buddy. Maybe we can double date some night. Janet would like to meet Jenny and she thinks you hung the moon," Randall said.

"Even after I kept you out all night?" McAlister asked.

"Janet knows how I am when I get started. She didn't blame you but she sure chewed my butt. Anyway, want to try to get together one night next month?"

"Sounds good to me," McAllister said. "You want to call us 10-8 before Marvin finds out we're clear from the hospital and writes us up for staying off the air?"

Chapter Six

Louisville, Kentucky, Monday, April 1, 1968. 6:25 a. m.

The first day of day work – and double back day, also. 6:30 a. m. roll call for odd cars, 7:00 a. m. for even ones. McAllister and Randall stood yawning with the rest of their platoon in the roll call room, waiting for the sergeant or lieutenant to come in and give them the command to fall in. It was a cinch both of the bosses wouldn't be there. They never were on double back day. One of them would hold the oncoming roll calls and then go home early. The other would come in late and hold the off going roll call. "Not a bad setup," McAllister mused to Randall. "Hell, let's all be bosses."

They had been scheduled to end their shift last night at 10:30 p. m., which figuratively gave them eight hours off before coming back on day work, doubling back as it was called. However, McAllister and Randall had been stuck at General Hospital's psychiatric unit until 11:30 with an elderly man on a mental inquest warrant taken out by his daughter. Finally, the psychiatric resident on call showed up, talked to the man for fifteen minutes and declared him sane. They then had to return the man to his home and book him by proxy through the city jail. This was all accomplished by 1:00 a. m. So their eight hours of off time had been considerably shortened.

To make the matter worse, the subject of the warrant didn't live on their beat. However, they had been ordered by Sergeant Marvin to come to headquarters and get the warrant and serve it, even though car 402, whose beat the man actually lived on, was in service at the time. When McAllister attempted to point this out, Marvin brusquely told him that he had another assignment for 402. This was taken by both officers as further proof that they were definitely on Marvin's list.

48

"Platoon, fall in," Lieutenant Hendricks called out as he entered the room.

The seven officers assigned to odd numbered cars formed a ragged line across the room and then straightened their rank as the lieutenant stepped in front of them. He read off the radio cars assignments quickly, gave out two subpoenas and dismissed them. Glad to avoid any further extra assignments, which they had been half-way anticipating, McAllister and Randall hurried down the back steps to the parking lot.

Later that morning, they were finishing a report run on Garland Avenue regarding a stolen lawnmower. As they got back in the car, Randall began to propose possible choices for lunch. McAllister held up his hand for quiet and called the radio dispatcher to report them back in service. He was rewarded for his trouble by receiving another run immediately to "see the man at the tavern, 32nd and Hale."

McAllister okayed the run and turned to Randall. "That's the joker Kowalski was talking about last month, the one who got all this crap started with Marvin."

"Well, let's go see what he wants," Randall replied, pulling into traffic.

The Copper Lantern was a two-story frame structure. The bar and lounge occupied most of the first floor, along with a small kitchen. The upstairs was taken up by what purported to be apartments, although their actual purpose was to provide places for additional entertainment for patrons seeking more than a watered down highball.

As they entered the bar, their eyes adjusted to the dim light and they could see four black males gathered at a round table in the rear of the front room. A younger black man was behind the bar and a short, light-complexioned black man with gray hair was hastening toward them, extending his hand.

"Come in, officers. Glad to see you. I'm Roscoe Brown," the man said in an obsequious manner. "What'll you have? Tyrone, get these officers something to drink."

"No, thank you," McAllister said. "Did you call?"

"Yes, sir, I did," Brown replied. "I wanted to get to know you officers better. All the other men on this beat, they stop in all the time, get a beer, get a pop, have a chicken sandwich. But you fellows never come by. I got the best fried chicken in town, ain't that right, boys?" He waved his hand toward the four men in the back, who gave a chorus of assent. McAllister could see that they were all older men in their fifties or sixties and that Tyrone, the bartender, was the youngest man in the group.

"We're glad to know you, Mr. Brown, and, if that's all you need, we'll be on our way," McAllister said.

"No, no, no," Brown protested. Grasping McAllister by the elbow, he attempted to pull him off to the side. McAllister pulled away from the man and stared at him.

"Listen, son. I told Sgt. Marvin to send you by. I got something for you boys. Here, take it."

The man thrust his hand into McAllister's and he could feel a folded wad of paper being placed in his hand. Looking down, he saw that it was currency. Looking over the man's shoulder, McAllister noticed that all the other people in the room were interested observers of this scene. Cynical smiles were on all their faces. Watching the crooked cops come to get their weekly payoff was evidently a spectator sport to these guys. McAllister's face grew red, first with embarrassment, then with anger. He reached out and stuffed the wad of money into Brown's shirt pocket with such force that he tore the material.

"What are you doing?" Brown demanded. "You can't touch me. You tore my motherfuckin' shirt. I'm gonna call downtown about you. Jive ass motherfucker, come in here, tearing a man's clothes off."

"Okay, pal, that's it," McAllister said. "You're under arrest." Grabbing the man by his shoulders, he spun him around and pushed him up against the bar. "Put your hands on the bar and spread your legs. Dave, line those other guys up and keep an eye on them."

Randall moved to the rear of the room and motioned the bartender out with the other four men. He unsnapped the restraining strap on his holstered service revolver.

"Everybody line up on the wall and stand still," he commanded. "Don't make any sudden moves or I'm liable to get real nervous." The four men quickly complied.

McAllister by this time had put handcuffs on Brown and pushed him into a chair at the front table. "Get their ID's, Dave. We'll run warrants and wanted on all of them."

Gathering all the men's identification cards, McAllister moved to the telephone on the corner of the bar. Standing where he could see the entire room, he called the police records section and quickly ran through the six men's names and dates of birth. Somewhat to his surprise, the only warrants that were found outstanding were two misdemeanor bench warrants for Roscoe Brown. The records clerk advised him that they had been returned to the warrants desk after attempted service by Officer Kowalski, marked "subject not known at this address."

"Pull them out, Juanita. We're bringing Mr. Brown in," he told the woman.

Hanging up the telephone, he turned to Brown.

"Do you want to close up or let your bartender keep it open?" he asked the man, who still appeared dumbfounded over the turn events had taken. "You're going downtown."

"Tyrone, keep the place open," Brown called to his bartender. "I'll be back in a few minutes. Call my old lady and tell her to get ahold of Claude Benbow and get me out."

"Okay, Mr. Brown," the bartender replied. "What's the charge, officer?"

"Attempted bribery, for one," McAllister replied. "And he has two outstanding warrants for traffic violations."

They placed Brown in the back seat of their car and belted him in. McAllister got in the back seat with the prisoner and Randall pulled away, radioing the dispatcher that they were 10-7 to the booking clerk.

"Man, are you just plain crazy or what?" Brown wanted to know. "Getting mad like that just because I try to take care of you."

"You tried to shove money in my hand in front of all your buddies there to show them all what a high roller you are, paying off the police. Well, pal, you picked the wrong boys this time. We don't want your damn money. But I will need that wad you tried to give me for evidence." With this, he reached over and took the folded bills from the man's torn shirt pocket. He unfolded them and found two ten dollar bills.

"You are crazy", Brown sputtered. "Don't you know I'm okay with everybody down the line?" I wouldn't be operating if I didn't have the go-ahead from the district and that gets cleared through city hall. You don't know the shit you are stirring up. You boys are going to be in some serious trouble before this is over. Look, I tell you what. Just drop me off at the house and we'll forget this happened. I won't say anything to anybody downtown and there won't be any trouble."

"Mr. Brown," McAllister replied. "Let me see if I can explain this to you. You tried to bribe us. We arrested you for it. You're going to jail. Now, if you want to stand up and tell the judge about all the people you've got paid off, that's up to you. I doubt that will make your big time friends real happy with you but it's up to you. Now, shut the fuck up."

Brown subsided and, except for muttered curses, was silent for the rest of the ride to the basement of headquarters. Randall took him into the holdover area while McAllister went upstairs to the records section to pick up the warrants. Juanita Collins, the supervisor of the section had them ready for them. She was a short, vivacious woman in her thirties with a voluptuous figure that attracted cops like flies. Her ability to exchange wisecracks with them and fend off offers of sexual gratification was well known throughout the department. McAllister was one of her favorites.

"Juanita, honey," he asked her as he took the warrants from her, "when are you going to quit fighting fate, admit we're made for each other and give me a little?"

"McAllister, I wouldn't mind giving you a little, because you're kind of cute," she replied. "But you cops can't keep your mouths shut. You'd tell everybody in the Fourth District and then I'd never be able to get any work done for all your friends up here wanting me to give them a little, too. So, sorry, honey. You'll just have to keep dreaming. By the way, baby, come here a minute." She beckoned him to the counter and, lowering her voice, asked him,

"Are you in some kind of trouble with the bosses in your district?"

"I don't know for sure," McAllister replied, "but probably so. What have you heard?"

"Just that Sergeant Marvin was trying to get rid of you and Randall. He was telling somebody that you all weren't team players. What have you done, honey?"

"Just my job, Juanita," McAllister replied, "but that doesn't seem to satisfy my sergeant. After I serve these warrants, he's probably going to be even more unhappy with me."

"Watch yourself, baby," she said. "George Marvin can be a backstabbing little SOB when he wants to."

"Thanks, Juanita," he said. "I'll see you later, and call me if you change your mind."

McAllister took the warrants back down to the holdover and he and Randall finished the booking process. As they ushered Brown through the barred door into the custody of the jail guard, he turned to them.

"This ain't the last of this, by a long shot," he told the two officers.

"See you in court, Mr. Brown," Randall replied, shoving the big door closed behind the man.

As they returned to their beat area, McAllister told his partner about his conversation with Juanita Collins.

"Looks like the wolves are closing in, Dave," he said. "Juanita usually has good sources of information and if she's hearing that they're trying to move us, it's probably true."

"We knew it was going to happen, Scott," Randall replied. "This deal today will probably speed up the process but I wouldn't have it any other way. Man, that was fun. Did you see the look on that little bastard's face when you told him he was locked up? And those other yaps were all about to piss in their pants."

"Yeah, well, hang on to that memory," McAllister said. "We'll use it to amuse ourselves while we're walking a foot beat over in the bricks."

When they returned to the district that afternoon for off-going roll call, Marvin was waiting for them. His face a fiery red, he jerked a preemptory thumb at them, signaling them into his office.

"I've received a complaint from Roscoe Brown that you assaulted him, tore his clothing, and falsely arrested him this morning. Also, that you used profanity and threatened the other people in the place. Have you two idiots lost your minds?" he asked heatedly.

"Sergeant, the man tried to bribe us in full view of five other people," McAllister replied. "Then he called me a jive-ass motherfucker. I had no choice but to arrest him. I'm not going to take that off anybody."

"Well, I'll tell you what you're going to take, both of you," the sergeant said. "You're going to take your ass over to those typewriters and write a full account of this to the captain. This is going to Internal Affairs. Roscoe Brown has always been a good friend to all the police in this district. "

The sergeant moved closer to McAllister and looked up at him. His eyes were bulging out of their sockets and he appeared almost on the verge of a stroke.

"Who the fuck do you think you are, McAllister, some kind of do-gooder super cop trying to clean up the world?" he hissed. Flecks of spittle came off his lips. "Well, you've stepped on your dick this time, super cop. Now get busy. I want those reports before you go home. You'll be lucky to keep your jobs."

Shrugging their shoulders, the two men went into the roll call room and began their reports.

Thursday, April 4, 1968. 4:35 p. m.

McAllister stepped out of the doorway leading to Police Court and stopped to light a cigarette. It was a gorgeous spring day and he had spent most of it indoors. Stretching his arms, he shook off the effects of sitting on a hard wooden bench in Traffic Court for four hours. He had been summoned on his day off to testify in a drunken driving trial. He and Randall had transported the defendant to jail for the two motorcycle officers who made the arrest. The defendant's attorney had subpoenaed them to court, along with the arresting officers. Randall was out of town visiting his wife's parents, so he had escaped being served. McAllister had not been so lucky. Consequently, he found himself spending a large portion of his off day listening to attorneys argue with each other. The outcome had been a verdict of guilty from the six-person jury, who were collectively as eager to get the proceedings over with as McAllister was.

Now, he stood at the corner of 6th and Jefferson streets examining his options. Jenny was in Bowling Green for a long weekend with her family. He was in civilian clothes since he had been called in from home. He could stop and have a beer and get something to eat or go home and throw something together in his small kitchen. As he considered, he noticed a familiar figure in a rumpled suit going into the City Hall Bar across the street- John Craig. He had wanted an opportunity to talk to the big detective and this looked like a good one.

The City Hall Bar was appropriately named since it was directly across the street from City Hall. It was frequented by judges, lawyers, politicians, cops, bail bondsmen and other assorted court house hangers-on. It was said that more city business got transacted in its scarred booths and at its bar than in the real city hall. Everett, the amiable and ancient bartender, had been a silent witness to many high-level and low-level transactions during the years he had worked there.

McAllister entered the bar, which was long and narrow. There were booths on the left side and a long bar ran almost to the rear of the room on the right. The predominant smell was a mixture of stale beer, cigarette smoke and grease from the kitchen. After his eyes adjusted from the bright sunlight outside to the dim interior, he saw Craig seated at the bar near the rear of the place. Sitting down next to him, he said,

"Hey, John. How are you doing? Can I buy you a beer?"

"Hi, Scott," Craig replied. "Yeah, thanks. Let me have a Blue Ribbon, Everett."

"Make that two, Everett," McAllister said. "How's your case going, John? Any leads on that girl on Dumesnil yet?"

"Not much going on that," Craig replied. "We've found her pimp and interviewed him but he hadn't seen her since about eight o'clock the night before. The coroner's office figures she was killed sometime after midnight. Last contact anybody had with her was another hooker who was talking to her at 18th and Grand about nine p. m. She thought she saw her talking to a john in a car at 18th and Oak a little after that but she was a block away and couldn't tell anything about the car or the driver. She thinks it was a big black car but that's all she knows. Nobody else seems to know a damn thing. I spent the afternoon down in Parkland talking to a nut case who claimed he did her and twelve others. Only problem was he strangled them all. I guess somebody with a knife showed up later and did all the mutilations."

His frustration was evident in Craig's voice as he gave this information to McAllister.

"I didn't see anything in the paper or on the news connecting that case with the one back in '64," McAllister said.

"Yeah," Craig replied. "Evidently, no reporter has made that connection yet and the Chief of Detectives is keeping a pretty tight lid on information coming out of the department. But – if he hits again, and he will, it'll be really tough to keep that lid on. Then, we will take heat for not telling the public that a crazed killer is running around killing women and cutting them up."

"Well, we did spread the word among the girls that work Dixie Highway," McAllister said. "And with you guys down there every day questioning them, they should all know about the guy.

"Yeah, but you know what," Craig said. "That helped for about two days. Then nothing else happened, the weather got pretty and now they're all right back out there."

He took a long pull at his beer and set the bottle down.

"Let's change the subject," he said. "What are you doing in here this time of day? I don't believe I ever saw you in here before."

"Never been in here before," McAllister said. "I just got out of a DUI trial and saw you come in here. I've been wanting to talk to you so I followed you in."

"Give us a couple more beers, Everett," Craig said. "What's on your mind, Scott?"

"I'd like to get into homicide," McAllister said. "I thought maybe you could tell me the best way to go about it."

Craig looked at him musingly.

"How long have you got on now?" he asked.

"Four years last January," McAllister replied. "All in the Fourth District."

"Got any relatives in the Detective Bureau, any big brass you're kin to? Are you a Mason?"

"Nope, all I've got is a desire to do the job. I love policing and it looks to me like you guys are the best. I want to be one of the best. I was in the 82nd Airborne in the army and that was an elite unit. I liked being part of an elite unit. The homicide squad seems to me to be the closest thing to an elite unit in the police department. I'd like to be part of it."

"Well, you're right about that," Craig said. "We are pretty selective and it is one place where your connections won't help you if you can't do the job. A lot of guys can't do it. It takes some special qualities."

"Would you help me at least get my hat in the ring?" McAllister asked.

Craig looked at him for several seconds before replying. Then he picked up his beer bottle and motioned toward an empty booth.

"Let's move over here, Scott," he said.

When they had settled in, Craig lit a cigarette and blew a stream of smoke upward.

"All right, Scott," he said. "Here's what you need to do. Go see our boss, Lieutenant Garrard. Tell him you're interested in coming to the squad. I'll mention you to him when I come to work tomorrow so you won't be just a face to him when you go see him. I'll tell him you have been very helpful to us on crime scenes and appear to be a conscientious and hard-working young officer. He'll start giving you old case files to read so that you can learn how we work up a case. The next vacancy we have, he'll ask us all for our recommendations. We usually have a squad meeting and discuss all the candidates and try to settle on one. Garrard makes the final pick but he usually goes along with our recommendation. Then he takes it to the Chief of Detectives for approval. How about your bosses in the Fourth? Will they put in a good word for you?"

McAllister flushed as he answered.

"That might be a problem," he said. "Right now, neither Sergeant Marvin nor Lieutenant Hendricks is real high on me."

"What's the matter?" Craig asked. "Won't you play games with the boys down there, let them run their little operations without interference?"

"Guess you heard about it, huh?" McAllister said.

"I did hear that you and your partner locked up Roscoe Brown the other day and that Marvin was all bent out of shape about it," Craig replied with a grin. "You've upset one of George's best supporters. Yeah, I doubt that he will give you much of a recommendation, and Hendricks wouldn't go against Marvin, even if he liked you."

"Yeah, what's the deal there?" McAllister asked. "I mean Hendricks is a lieutenant and yet he seems to let Marvin run the show."

"Hendricks is just putting in time until retirement, Scott," Craig replied. "He doesn't want anything to rock the boat and is happy to let Marvin make all the decisions and run the platoon – and, incidentally, to set up all the deals with people like Roscoe Brown."

"Is the whole department set up that way?" McAllister asked. "I mean, with the card games and handbooks and whores operating out of these places and nobody giving a shit."

"A lot of that goes on, for sure," Craig replied. "But things may be about to change, with this new chief. Maybe things will get better. One thing is for sure, you wouldn't have to worry about that in the homicide squad. We just do our job, no matter who's involved."

"That's what I want," McAllister said. "Just a chance to do my job."

"Well, your bosses may be a problem, but maybe not," Craig said. "I know Lieutenant Garrard and Sergeant Marvin hate each other's guts. It may help you with him if I let him know you're not one of Marvin's boys. What we have to worry about is the Chief of Detectives. Major Farley M. Bishop is as political as they come. He doesn't blow his nose if he's not sure it's okay with city hall. So if he thinks you aren't a good little boy who goes along with the status quo, that may be a problem. However, there's a rumor that he won't be Chief of Detectives much longer. Since he didn't get to be Chief of Police this last go-around, there's some word that he's not as politically strong as he was. Plus, the new chief doesn't like him, even though they're both big in the Masons"

"Yeah, you asked me earlier if I was a Mason," McAllister said. "What's that got to do with anything? I'm not but my dad is, down in Owensboro."

"Well, Bishop and the new chief, plus a whole bunch of other bosses and a lot of detectives are all pretty active Masons. Seems to help a little in getting assignments, sometimes. Few years ago, when Malone was Chief of Detectives, it was Catholics getting all the good jobs. But we'll work with what we've got. Things may change here before long. I think you'd make a good homicide dick, now that you don't toss your cookies at crime scenes anymore, or do you?" Craig asked with a grin on his face.

McAllister felt himself blushing as he answered,

"No, I think I'm over that now. Thanks, John. I'll go see Lieutenant Garrard tomorrow."

"Okay, Scott. I was in the 101st and the 8th Airborne, myself, over in Germany. We old paratroopers have got to stick together."

"Hey, Craig," the bartender called out and pointed to the television set over the bar. "Look at this. Somebody shot Martin Luther King."

Craig and McAllister both walked over to the bar and focused on the television, where Walter Cronkite was saying that the civil rights leader had been assassinated by a sniper at the Lorraine Motel in Memphis, Tennessee. Then the scene at the motel was shown, along with coverage of police officers in riot gear trying to restrain large crowds of angry black people.

They sat at the bar for another hour, watching the television coverage of the assassination. Rioting mobs were shown in Washington, D. C., Detroit, and several other cities. National Guard units were being mobilized in Tennessee and elsewhere. It appeared that the anger engendered by the act was spreading rapidly across the country.

"What do you think, Scott?" Craig asked. "Are we going to have to deal with this kind of stuff in the west end?"

"It could happen," McAllister replied. "There are a lot of young blacks down there who would love any excuse to start a riot. We can't drive through the intersection of 32nd and Greenwood without getting a bottle thrown at us just about any night. And, if we make a run down in the bricks and make an arrest, we usually have to call in two or three more cars just to get our prisoner out of there. Even the older black people who need our help are afraid to call us most of the time. The young bucks call them Uncle Toms. So, yeah, I'd say it can happen here and probably tomorrow, if it doesn't start tonight."

"Well, if that's the case, we'd better get home and get some sleep," Craig said. "We may be busy tomorrow."

As they were walking to the parking lot, McAllister said,

"Thanks again for the advice, John, and for being willing to help me. I hope I haven't got you in trouble at home, keeping you so late after work."

"Nobody at home to worry about," the detective said gruffly. "I'll talk to Garrard in the morning and tell him you'll be in to see him soon. Catch you later."

On his way home, McAllister felt a sense of elation. For the first time in several days, he felt positive about his job. Plus, things were looking up with Jenny. His attraction for the girl was stronger than ever. He enjoyed her company more than that of any girl he had ever dated. And he felt that she was strongly attracted to him. She had told him earlier in the week that Renyard continued to ask her for dates. She had agreed to have lunch with him a couple of times but, so far, she had not gone out with him at night. McAllister hoped fervently that she would keep it that way.

He wondered briefly what Craig meant by "nobody at home to worry about." He was sure that the detective was married. Charlie Newman, his old partner, had told him that Craig was married to a gorgeous school teacher and that they had a couple of kids. Plus, Craig was wearing a wedding ring. Maybe his wife and kids were out of town or something. Turning his thoughts again to Jenny, interspersed with thoughts of a detective's gold shield, he headed out Bardstown Road to home.

Craig, too, was thinking about his parting remark, as he drove home. Susan had called him last night and wanted to meet on Saturday. She had sounded more cordial than in previous contacts and his hopes were up. He sincerely wanted his family back in one location together and was willing to make just about any concession to have that happen. Hopefully he could convey that to Susan on Saturday. Then he snorted derisively and said to himself that, with his luck running the way it had been, his mystery whore-slayer would probably strike this weekend just as the west end went up in flames from a riot. Susan would never believe it.

Chapter Seven

Louisville, Kentucky. Wednesday, April 10, 1968, 11:48 p. m.

The white Dodge station wagon cruised slowly east on Dumesnil Street at idle speed. Officer Sheldon "Sandy" Burns shined the portable spotlight on the store fronts of the businesses they passed. He gave forth a mighty yawn as his partner, Officer Ron Cavendish brought the car slowly to a halt at the red traffic light at 28th Street. Burns yawned again and said,

"How about hitting Cooksey's and getting some coffee?"

"Sounds good to me," his partner replied. "I just ---" He stopped in mid-sentence as a piercing scream split the air at the deserted intersection.

"What the hell was that?" Cavendish said.

"Sounded like a woman," Burns replied. "Around the corner on Cypress."

Cypress Street intersected Dumesnil just a few feet east of the point where 28th Street dead-ended. The intersection was surrounded by two and three story buildings housing small businesses that formed the heart of the community known as Parkland. Large residential dwellings built in the twenties were on Cypress just south of there. As Cavendish swung the car around the corner, another scream rang out.

Burns had his head out the car window and was listening intently.

"About halfway down the block, on the right," he told his partner. "It came from one of those houses. Whoever that is, she needs help."

As they approached the middle of the block, Burns caught a glimpse of a light through the front window of a large house that had been standing vacant for several months.

"There," he called as he bailed out of the car. "1328, that vacant house we chased those kids out of last month."

Burns pounded up the sidewalk to the front door of the two-story dwelling with his older, heavier partner close behind. Drawing his pistol, he pushed the door wide open and quickly stepped to one side. He then shined his flashlight down the entrance hallway. He could see a pair of feet protruding from a doorway on the left, at the end of the hall.

"Cover me!" he snapped over his shoulder. "Somebody's down, on the left!"

"Got you," Cavendish replied.

As Burns went down the hallway, he played his light across the rooms on either side. Reaching the doorway, he saw the body of a young black woman lying across the threshold with her feet in the hallway. One high heeled shoe was on her right foot. The other foot was bare. She was clad in a mini-skirt and blouse. Under her chin, a large gaping wound was visible and blood was spurting like a fountain against the wall from a severed carotid artery. Moving quickly to her side he knelt beside her just as the blood flow slackened and then stopped, as her heart ceased beating.

"Son of a bitch," Burns said aloud, realizing that he had just watched the woman die.

Cavendish approached behind him and shined his light on the body.

"Any chance she's still alive?" he asked.

"I don't think so. She just died as I got here," Burns replied. He started to say more but hesitated as he heard a noise from the rear of the house. Grabbing Cavendish by the arm, he pointed in the direction of the noise and held his finger to his lips. He then turned his flashlight off and slipped quietly through the door at the end of the hall. Moonlight filtered through windows at the rear of the house and showed him that he was entering the kitchen. He thought he saw a shadow pass across one of the windows and heard footsteps outside moving rapidly across the porch. He moved quickly through the room and onto the large rear porch. He could see the silhouette of a person running across the backyard to a gate opening into the alley. Shining his light toward the figure, he called out,

"Police officer. Hold it!"

A bright flash and then another winked out of the darkness at him, followed by the double report of a large caliber handgun. Glass shattered in the window beside where he stood and he felt splinters sting his cheek as a round struck the door frame next to him. Instinct took over and he dropped to his knees to lessen his silhouette. He peered into the darkness, trying to see his quarry but the muzzle blasts had ruined his night vision.

Then he heard a car starting in the alley. Rising, he ran quickly down the stairs and across the yard. As he came through the gate into the alley, he saw tail lights bouncing as a large car sped south in the alley to the next cross street. He raised his pistol and then lowered it with frustration, as the car turned left onto the cross street and roared out of sight.

"Sandy, you hit?" Cavendish called from the backyard of the house.

"Out here, " Burns replied. "No, the son of a bitch missed me but barely. He got into a car and got away before I could get a look at him."

Cavendish approached him and, grasping his arm, turned his face to the street light.

"You've got blood all over the side of your face," he said. "Are you sure he didn't hit you?"

"That must be splinters," Burns said. "He hit the door frame right beside me and I felt something hit my face."

"Let's get some help and call the boss," Cavendish said as he started back through the gate.

"I think help is on the way," Burns replied. The sound of the new yelping electronic sirens that LPD cars were being equipped with could be heard in the distance and drawing nearer. "One of the neighbors must have called in. Hold on a minute, Ron. Shine your light over here around the gate."

The two officers scanned the area where the gate opened into the alley.

"There," Burns said, as he knelt to examine two shiny shell casings lying on the concrete. ".45 automatic, I thought that damn thing sounded like a hand cannon."

He picked up a cardboard box from a nearby trash can and upended it over the casings. Standing upright, he began to suddenly tremble as he started to experience a delayed reaction to the encounter. Giving off a strained laugh, he said,

"I got shot at a few times in 'Nam but I believe this guy came closer. He sure made it personal."

Cavendish glanced sharply at his young partner. There had been a note in his voice that alerted the older officer.

"Let's get you in the light and look at that face, Sandy." Taking his partner by the arm, Cavendish led him back to the house.

* * *

Larry Colbert turned the corner onto Cypress Street and began looking for a parking place. Marked police cars were situated haphazardly on both sides of the street, their flashing red emergency lights causing bizarre reflections in the windows of the houses.

"Great," Colbert muttered to himself. "Fifty goddamn cops stomping all over my crime scene."

He wasn't surprised. When the dispatcher said that shots had been fired at a police officer, that insured that every available car would respond, marked and unmarked. What Colbert needed was to locate a kick-ass supervisor to help him get all of the excess people out of there, so he could conduct his investigation. To his relief, he saw the night chief, Major Dolan, coming down the sidewalk at 1328 Cypress, as he got out of his car. The big, florid-faced Irishman was not one to suffer fools lightly or to let a bunch of cops hang around a crime scene, sightseeing.

"Colbert, are you the homicide squad tonight?" the night chief asked.

"For right now, Major," the young detective replied. "601 is at the hospital on a rape case and Wallace is on vacation."

"Well, you've got a hell of a scene in there. Looks like the same asshole who killed those other girls. Cavendish and Burns heard her scream and interrupted him before he could cut her up. They weren't in time to keep him from killing her, though. Then he took a couple of shots at Burns before he got away."

"Is Burns okay?" Colbert asked.

"Got some splinters in his face from where one round hit the door but no gunshot injury," Dolan replied.

"That's good. Boss, can we get all these onlookers cleared out of here?"

"Will do," Dolan replied. "Burns is going to need to go to the hospital as soon as you can get a quick statement from him. I'll clear out these other tourists."

"Thanks, boss," Colbert said. Going up the steps quickly, Colbert entered the house and noticed two officers in the front room on his right. One of them had a first aid kit open and was dabbing at the other's face with a sterile bandage.

"Ouch, damn it, Ron, that hurts," the younger officer said.

"Okay, I'll quit. You're going to need a doctor to dig those splinters out of there anyway. I was just trying to get some of the blood off," his partner replied.

"What have you got here?" Colbert asked, stepping into the room.

"A dead girl in the hallway," Burns replied. "We heard her screaming but didn't get here in time to help her."

"Let's take a look," Colbert said.

The three men went down the hall to the girl's body. Shining his light over her, Colbert asked,

"Where was the killer when you got here?"

"We heard him in the back of the house. I went into the kitchen and then heard him going across the porch."

The young officer led Colbert through the kitchen and onto the back porch.

"Then I saw him running through the yard to the back gate. Like an idiot, I stood in the doorway and shined my light on him, yelling for him to halt."

"What happened then?"

"He popped two caps at me. One hit the window here on my left, the other hit the doorframe right by my face."

Colbert shined his light on the doorframe where Burns indicated. A splintered hole was visible in the wood.

"Then what?"

"I felt splinters hit my cheek. I got down on the porch and then heard him starting his car. I got out to the alley just in time to see him turn east on Woodland."

"Get a look at him?" Colbert asked. "Any description?"

"All I saw was his outline," Burns replied. "I couldn't even tell if he was black or white. The car looked like a Lincoln Continental, fairly new, dark color, black or blue maybe. Had a big damn gun, too, .45 automatic. We found the casings out in the alley."

"That may be the first piece of physical evidence we've found to tie this guy to a crime scene. Did you leave them there?" Colbert asked.

"I put a cardboard box over them so nobody would step on them," Burns replied. "Major Dolan sent Harrison out there to secure the area after I told him about it."

"Good job, Burns," Colbert said. "Let's take another look at the victim."

The three men went back down the hall to where the body of the girl was lying. Kneeling beside her, Colbert played his light on the wound in her throat.

"Know her?" he asked.

"I've seen her on the stroll for the last several months," Cavendish replied. "I don't know her name but they call her 'Pepper.' Hangs around the bar at 18th and Gallagher."

"Shit, I think I know this girl," Colbert exclaimed. He bent closer to her and shined his light indirectly on her face. "I went to high school with her, Beverly Watson. Damn, she was kind of wild, even in high school. But she sure didn't deserve to die like this."

He stood up and turned to the two patrolmen.

"Why don't you go on to General and get your face tended to? I'll either meet you there or at the homicide office to get both your statements. Cavendish, did you get a look at the guy?"

"I never saw him," Burns' partner replied. "I was still inside the house with the victim, heard the shots and went to find Sandy."

"Okay, when you get to the car, will you have the complaint desk call John Craig at home and ask him to respond here. Also tell them to notify Lieutenant Garrard and the coroner's office. Who's here with me?"

"404," Cavendish replied. "Harrison is out in the alley where the shell casings are. Brighton was out front a few minutes ago."

The two officers went out the front door and Colbert turned to his work, unable to reconcile in his mind the difference between the lively, spirited girl he had known in school and the lifeless corpse at his feet.

He had finished his description of the scene and was rummaging in the trunk of his car for his camera and evidence collection kit when he heard the dispatcher on his car radio.

"Radio to any homicide unit that can clear."

He went quickly to the front of the car and picked up the microphone.

"602 to radio. I'm still tied up down here on Cypress. What do you have?"

"602, 420 requests homicide in the lot behind the school on 18th between Wilson and St. Louis. They have another victim of a cutting, DOA at the scene."

"420 to radio," Sergeant Roger Johnson's harsh voice cut in. "Advise 602 this is the same kind of killing as the others. This girl has had her throat cut and been disemboweled. She's been dead several hours."

Colbert stood for a moment holding the microphone in disbelief. Then he answered, "10-4, advise 420 I'll be there as soon as I can finish up here."

"601 to radio," a new voice came on the air. "We are clearing from General. What do you have?" Detectives Noonan and Boyd had evidently decided they could finish up their rape case and help out a little. Neither of them liked Colbert, regarding him as a mouthy, militant black man. He returned their feelings with interest. In his opinion, they were a couple of racist bastards who couldn't or wouldn't pack their share of the load in the homicide squad. They had caught the rape complaint just after they came on, at 8:00 p. m. He was certain they had been letting him hang on the homicide on Cypress, rather than finishing their investigation and coming to his assistance.

"601, meet 420 at 18th and Wilson, behind the school on a homicide," the dispatcher responded.

"610 to radio," Lieutenant Garrard's distinctive voice joined in the dialogue. "I am responding from my home to 18ᵗʰ and Wilson. I'll meet 601 there. Detective Craig is on the way to assist 602."

Gathering up his camera and evidence kit, Colbert turned back toward the house. The shit would hit the fan now. News reporters from all night radio stations monitored the police frequency regularly. Unless they were all asleep, they had picked up Roger Johnson's transmission and now were in possession of knowledge that the police were working multiple homicides of women who had been disemboweled. Newspaper and television reporters would not be far behind. Colbert did not want to be around when Major Farley M. Bishop found out that the lid was off his carefully orchestrated plan to keep the news media unaware of the ongoing investigation.

Looking up, he saw John Craig's battered Ford Fairlane pulling to the curb. Meeting Craig as he got out of his car, Colbert began filling him in as they walked back to the house.

Thursday, April 11. 1968. 8:10 a. m.

The front row of the Training Bureau classroom on the second floor of Police Headquarters was occupied by the bleary-eyed detectives of the homicide squad's night shift and an equally bleary-eyed John Craig. Detectives from other squads were filtering into the room, talking loudly and animatedly about this break in their normal routine. The Chief of Detectives did not often call meetings of every detective on day work and their curiosities were aroused. The bluish haze of cigarette smoke filled the air as several men stood by the big ash trays near the doors, getting in one last smoke before the meeting started.

Craig turned to Colbert, who was seated beside him, and quietly said

"Wonder what the great white father has in mind for this meeting?"

"I'm not sure," Colbert replied, " but I'll bet it ain't gonna be fun. I saw him coming out of the Chief's office a few minutes ago with Hall and Garrard in tow. He looked like he could chew nails. Did you see all those reporters downstairs?"

"Yeah, it looked like all the TV stations were there and the Courier sent over some high powered new female reporter. Guess they didn't think George Koper and the regular guys on the police beat could handle it. Looks like the shit is going to hit the fan, all right. Did Noonan and Boyd find anything useful at the second scene?"

"Not that I know of. They said he killed her in the entryway to the school building and cut her up right there. Her intestines were draped all over the place and her liver and kidneys were missing. Looks like it happened before the one on Cypress. She had been dead several hours. A couple of kids cutting through the school yard found her. We may get lucky on one of the shell casings from our scene, though. Patterson in the fingerprint lab says there may be an identifiable print on one of them. Plus, the slugs we recovered are in pretty good shape. There's enough striations to make a comparison if we can find the gun."

"Good," Craig replied. "Now, if we can just keep quiet about that, maybe the scumbag won't dump it."

"All right, listen up." Major Bishop strode into the room and stepped to the podium at the front. He was followed by Captain Hall, Lieutenant Garrard and all the other bosses in the Detective Bureau who arranged themselves in chairs along the side of the room.

The portly Chief of Detectives did not look happy. He glared at the assembled group as he shuffled some papers on the podium.

"I'm forming a task force to work on the killings of these black whores in the west end," he announced without preamble. "It will be under the command of Captain Hall, with Lieutenant Garrard as second in command. I'm assigning four homicide dicks, along with two from robbery and two from the storehouse and safe squad, for right now. Additionally, the chief is going to assign a couple of men from the Fourth District to work with us. If it turns out we need more men, we'll get them. But I expect to get this thing cleared up in a couple of days. The rest of you people will have to pick up the slack in your squads. Additionally, I want all of you working your snitches to come up with some leads on this character. Give any information you come up with directly to Lieutenant Garrard. Any and all statements to the news media will be made by me or through my office. I will personally have the ass of anyone who shoots his mouth off about this case to the media. Any questions?"

The group of detectives remained silent, so Bishop turned to Captain Hall and said "Read off your detail and get them started, Captain."

Abruptly he stalked from the room.

Hall moved to the podium and unfolded a piece of paper.

"The task force will be Craig, Colbert, Rovinelli, and Boyd from homicide, Bristow and Parsons from robbery, and Thompson and Birdsong from storehouse and safe. Those men remain here for a minute. The rest of you can get back to work. Remember what Major Bishop said about working your informants. We will need all the help we can get on this case. Thanks for your attention."

The eight men named by Hall gathered in the front of the room.

Garrard and Sergeant Howard joined them. Hall pulled a chair over and sat facing them.

"Let me recap the situation," he said. "We have four dead women, Angela Johnson in 1964, Vanessa Richards back in March, Beverly Watson and Margaret Sistrunk last night. All known prostitutes, known to frequent the Dixie Highway area known as the stroll. All killed the same way. Their throats cut with a very sharp instrument. Three of them were disemboweled. Watson was not because the beat car ran the killer off before he could get started. He also carries a .45 caliber automatic and is evidently ready to use it, considering that he nearly hit Officer Burns last night. He left a message in blood at the Richards scene which John Craig thinks, and I agree, is a quote from one of the Jack the Ripper letters sent to a newspaper editor in London in the 1880's."

He paused for a moment and then, shaking his head, opened up another piece of paper.

"This is a copy of a note delivered to the *Courier Journal* at 6:00 a. m. this morning. It reads:

'I was not codding dear old boss when I gave you the tip, you'll hear about Saucy Jack's work tomorrow double event this time number two squealed a bit couldn't finish straight off. Had not time to get ears for police. Thanks for keeping last letter back till I got to work again.

Jack the Ripper'

As far as we can tell, this is an exact copy of a note allegedly sent by Jack the Ripper to a newspaper office on October 1, 1888 with the exception that 'number one' has been changed to 'number two.' It is written in red ink as the original was. We are definitely dealing with a madman here who is emulating Jack the Ripper."

"Did we get the original note from the newspaper, Captain?" Craig asked.

"After some intense discussion, they turned it over to me," Hall replied. "Of course everybody in the news room had handled it by then. I sent it to the lab anyway, in hopes of getting some prints. You can expect to see a full blown feature in the *Louisville Times* this afternoon and I'm sure it'll be the lead story on all the TV stations. In the meantime, we've got a lot of work to do. I want a complete workup on each of the victims, their families, school and work history, every arrest they've had, who and when they were locked up with. We will need to do a canvass on Dixie Highway tonight and see who we can turn up that might have seen either victim last night. Lt. Garrard will be the coordinator for this case. Funnel all your reports through him. Craig is the senior detective, so he will be the acting sergeant. He'll do the scheduling and assign follow-up work. We've pulled five cars for you to use and, for the time being, we will use this classroom as our office. Communications will put some extra phone lines in here today and I'm having some desks moved in. Let's start a picture board and do a time line on each case. Any questions? Yes, John?"

Craig said "Captain, this is probably a coincidence but the first victim last night, Margaret Sistrunk, was the complainant on the Angela Johnson case, back in 1964. She found her body."

"Okay, maybe we shouldn't be surprised at that, if she continued to be a prostitute," Hall replied. "Was there any indication that she had any contact with the killer in that case?"

"No, sir. She saw the victim getting into a car but couldn't see the driver. I've had a couple of follow up contacts with her recently, after the Richards case. She didn't say anything to make me think she knew any more than she told us originally. And, she was still working the stroll."

Hall looked at his watch and said "I have to go brief the mayor and safety director on this. Let's get started. Jim, I talked to Captain Hanson about getting two men from his district to work with us. He said we could have who we wanted. Get me a couple of names today."

"Yes, sir," Garrard replied. Hall left the room and Garrard turned to the other detectives. "Any suggestions?"

"Boss, that young officer I mentioned to you a few days ago that wants to come to the squad, Scott McAllister. I think he came in to see you a couple of days later. He would be a good man, I believe. And it would give you a chance to evaluate him."

"Isn't he the one that's on Marvin's shit list for locking up Roscoe Brown?" Garrard asked.

"Yes, sir, but—" Craig replied but stopped when Garrard held up his hand.

"Sounds like my kind of guy. I'll ask for him. Anybody else?"

"This kid, Burns, that the guy shot at last night, handled himself pretty well. He was sharp enough to find those shell casings and secure them," Colbert said. "I've worked with him at some other scenes, too. He's got a good head on his shoulders. He would definitely be more help than some old hairbag."

"Coming from you, Larry, that's high praise, indeed," Garrard replied. "Okay, anybody else want to suggest someone? If not, I'll tell the Captain we want McAllister and Burns. Burns should have a vested interest in catching this guy. Okay, John, you and Larry bring these guys from the other squads up to speed on all the cases. Boyd and Rovinelli, you two get up to General and cover the autopsies on last night's two victims. Then we'll start doing backgrounds on all the victims. You may as well call your wives and tell them they won't see much of you for the next few days. Just hope we can catch this creep before he hits again or life is not going to be too pleasant around here. Let's hit it."

The nine men turned to their tasks while, in the downstairs lobby, Major Farley M. Bishop was sweating profusely as he tried to fend off the persistent questioning of a mob of shouting reporters. The Louisville Ripper case was definitely picking up steam.

Chapter Eight

Louisville, Kentucky. Thursday, April 11, 1968, 6:25 a.m.

McAllister was in a bad mood to begin with. He and Jenny had gotten into a furious argument the night before, the first one they had, but it was a good one. It had started when he asked her to go out the following Saturday. She told him that she couldn't but didn't initially give him a reason. After he pressured her for an answer, she finally told him that she was going to a bar association dance that night with Michael Renyard. McAllister's dislike of the man overcame his better judgment and he said a lot more than he should have. Jenny had responded in kind and the evening ended with neither of them speaking as he drove her to her apartment. She had gotten out of the car without a word and did not look back as she went to her door. He had gone to a neighborhood bar and drank four beers before going home and spending the rest of the night tossing and turning. Now, as he prepared for roll call, his mouth tasted like the Russian Army had camped in it overnight and his head throbbed painfully. Dave Randall gave him a quizzical look as he came into the roll call room. Before they could speak, the sergeant and lieutenant walked in. Marvin gave the command to fall in.

Sergeant Marvin scowled as he looked at the ragged line of sleepy patrolmen lined up in front of him. Behind him, Lieutenant Hendricks leaned against one of the roll call tables and watched as Marvin called the shift to attention. Then, instead of commanding them to stand at ease while he read off the lineup, as was his usual practice, he barked,

"All right, listen up. We're starting a new beat configuration today. Because of all the crime down in the projects, we're going to put extra coverage in that area. There's going to be a new beat added to the district, beat 409. It will overlap the areas of 404 and 408 that have housing projects on them. In other words, it'll cover Cotter Homes and Southwick projects. 404 and 408 will be backup to this new car but it will be dispatched first on all runs in the bricks."

An almost inaudible murmur ran through the line of patrolmen as they looked with sideways glances at each other, wondering to themselves who was going to get the shaft of this piece of shit assignment. McAllister was pretty sure he knew.

"McAllister and Randall, you're assigned to 409. We weren't able to get a station wagon for you to use, so it will be a cruiser beat. You won't have to make any hospital runs, but you'll probably be pretty busy anyway. There's a map in the office that will show you the outlines of your new beat."

Marvin read off the other assignments rapidly and gave the command to fall out. Davis and Carter, two old timers, were now assigned to 403. As the officers broke ranks and headed out the door, McAllister and his partner stopped in the district office to check the map Marvin had mentioned. The new beat was outlined in red and covered the areas of the two large public housing projects that were adjacent to each other. There was nothing on the beat but brick tenements – no stores, no restaurants, no businesses, nothing.

"Looks like the games have begun," McAllister said as they walked down the hall.

Marvin and Hendricks walked out of the roll call room and glanced at the two as they started into the office.

"Any questions?" Marvin asked harshly.

"What car are we supposed to use, Sarge?" McAllister asked.

"You'll find it on the lot. It's already been marked for your beat. It was the director of safety's old car. You two hotshots stay on your beat, you hear me. Don't let me catch you off of it."

"Yes, sir," McAllister replied.

Coming onto the parking lot in the rear of headquarters, they noticed a boxy black sedan parked on the lot. It was a four or five year old Nash Rambler. The standard department shields had been affixed to both doors, replicas of the Louisville police badge, with the numerals "409" on them. Large rust spots were visible on the front and rear fenders. A "bubble gum machine" red light had been attached to the roof and a large old style siren hung on the right front fender. It looked like something a bunch of clowns in police uniforms would pile out of at a circus.

"Don't tell me we're supposed to drive this piece of shit!" Randall exploded.

"This asshole has it in for us big time. He's put us in this junker and put us in the middle of the projects where we can't mess up any of his deals he's got going. But we ought to catch a lot of crooks. They'll be laughing so hard when they see us coming they won't be able to run," McAllister replied.

They loaded their gear in the car and Randall got behind the wheel, griping continuously. He turned on the ignition which produced a clattering noise under the hood and a large cloud of greasy blue smoke belched forth from the exhaust. Randall looked at the speedometer in disbelief.

"This crate's got 157,000 miles on it," he said, shifting into first gear. "Hope it holds together for at least one shift."

They drove off the lot and headed west, trailing a cloud of blue smoke as they went, with the valve lifters clattering away. As they passed by the front of headquarters, two traffic officers coming out of the front of the building stopped and pointed at their strange vehicle. As Randall looked in the rear view mirror, he could see both of the cops doubled over with laughter.

"This is the bottom of the barrel," Randall said. "It's bad enough to get a beat where you can't even get a ham sandwich to go but to have to drive this junker on top of it is just too damn much."

"I knew Marvin was going to get us somehow but I didn't think he'd be this creative," McAllister replied. "I figured he'd have us riding extra. This is worse. This is embarrassing."

"Why haven't we heard from Internal Affairs about the Roscoe Brown deal?" Randall asked. "I figured Marvin would try to get us five or ten days suspension over that."

"My guess is they couldn't get Brown to come in and sign a complaint. I checked on his court case when we didn't get subpoenaed after we booked him. The prosecutor recommended amending the charge to disorderly conduct and the judge went along with it. Roscoe paid a fifty dollar fine and walked. I would say he didn't want to call any more attention to himself by signing a formal complaint. We might start squawking about his felony charge being amended and get some more shit started. Instead, Marvin takes this subtle little method of sticking it up our ass."

"Yeah, well, it hurts," Randall replied. They were stopped at a traffic signal and the blue haze of exhaust smoke was beginning to surround and fill the interior of the car. "Look at those kids on the corner laughing at us. Little bastards. Why aren't they in school?"

"They're waiting for the school bus, Dave. It's only a quarter to seven. And you can't blame them. This is a funny looking contraption. We probably can't get it going fast enough to wreck it, so we'll have to come up with some other way to red line it.

Now swing by 26th and Broadway, so I can get some coffee and an Alka-Seltzer. My head is killing me."

"Only if you let me park around the corner," Randall replied. "I don't want any of the girls to see me driving this hunk of junk."

* * *

A couple of hours later, Sergeant Marvin was getting a second cup of coffee from the pot in the district office. He was feeling pretty pleased with himself over his handling of McAllister and Randall. The two troublemakers were now assigned to an area where they couldn't cause any more problems, and it had taken them down a notch in the eyes of their fellow officers. Yes, getting that old junker fixed up and assigning it to them had been a stroke of genius. Policemen were conscious of their image and riding around in a rattletrap like the old Nash would be a blow to both of their young egos. Well, they would learn not to fuck with George Marvin.

Marvin had sat down at his desk when the district commander, Captain John Hanson, stuck his head in the office door.

"Sergeant Marvin, let me see you a minute," the Captain said.

Marvin followed him into his office, his notebook poised expectantly.

"Get in touch with Officer McAllister," Hanson said. "Tell him he's been assigned temporarily to Homicide. Tell him to report tomorrow morning to Lt. Garrard up in the dicks' office. Also, call that kid, Burns, on Johnson's platoon and tell him the same thing. He's on late watch so you'll have to call him at home."

"Yes, sir, but….. but" Marvin sputtered.

"What's the problem, Sergeant? Didn't you understand what I told you?"

"Yes, sir, but I just assigned McAllister to that new beat in the projects this morning," Marvin replied.

"Well, I guess you'll have to assign somebody else," Hanson said. "This detail came out of the chief's office. I told Emmett Hall he could have whoever he wanted and he asked for those two. They're forming a task force to work on these prostitute killings. So get it done."

Marvin went back into his office and hurled his notebook at the wall. This seriously pissed him off. His carefully conceived plan had just been sidetracked. Somehow, McAllister had managed to worm his way out of the hole Marvin had dug for him. However, the Captain had said it was a temporary assignment. He would be back in the Fourth District before long. These task forces never lasted for very long. And when he did come back, he'd find old Sergeant Marvin waiting for him right here.

Comforting himself with this thought, Marvin picked up the phone to call the radio room.

* * *

"Car 409, McAllister, call your district."

"Car 409, 10-4," McAllister acknowledged the call and turned to Randall. "Where do we find a phone on this beat? I'll bet there isn't a pay phone for miles that works."

"What about the liquor store at 32nd and Young?" Randall replied. "He has to have a phone. Hell, as many times as he gets robbed, he ought to have a ringdown line to the complaint desk."

They pulled up to the liquor store and McAllister went in. Randall could see him talking to the Lebanese proprietor who led him around the counter to a phone. The conversation was short. McAllister came back to the car with a puzzled look on his face.

"What's up?" Randall asked.

"That was Marvin. I've been assigned TDY to Homicide. Some kind of task force they're setting up. I start tomorrow," McAllister replied.

"Hey, way to go, pard," Randall said. "I'll bet it frosted old George's balls to have to tell you that."

"Yeah, he didn't sound too thrilled," McAllister replied. "Craig must have made this happen somehow. Marvin said to tell you that you would go on extra until I get back."

"Suits me," Randall said. "I'd rather ride extra than push this pile of junk around."

"Frankly, partner, if I can work it out any way, I don't plan to come back to the Fourth," McAllister said.

"I hear you," Randall replied. "As long as they left us alone and we were partners, I was happy. The way things are going now, I'm going to call my uncle in Traffic. He told me the other day they were going to fill five vacancies on the motorcycle squad. I think he can get me one of them."

"Good deal," McAllister said. "Maybe we can both get out of this hellhole before it blows up in our faces."

"Scott, do you think it's going to blow up down here?" Randall asked. "I mean, like Detroit or L. A.?"

"Hell, yes," McAllister replied. "Look at that bunch across the street eyeing us. They hate our guts and I think it will just take one small spark to set them off."

A group of black men in their late teens and early twenties were clustered together across Young Avenue at the end of one of the yellow brick housing units. Their hostile glares could be felt as well as seen by the two officers.

"Those assholes hang on this corner and deal drugs day and night," Randall said. "No wonder they hate us. But does everybody else in the west end hate us, too?"

"In case you haven't noticed, Dave, we don't get many friendly looks from anybody in this district," McAllister said. "The older people down here that still respect the police are afraid to say so. I think the whole west end is like a powder keg after King's assassination and all the shit going on in other cities. Everybody sees it every night on Huntley and Brinkley and they're bound to be thinking 'Why not do it here?' One incident here in the projects could get the whole thing started."

"Boy, do I feel better after listening to you. Let's get the hell out of here."

Randall put the boxy black car in gear and they went smoking and clattering out of the parking lot. The crowd of young blacks was yelling insults after them which they studiously ignored as they headed west to tour the rest of their beat.

Friday, April 13, 1968. 7:25 a. m.

John Craig, in his shirtsleeves, was holding his sport coat on the desk with one hand. With the other he was maneuvering a stapler and punching a row of staples into the lining. He looked up to see Scott McAllister standing in the door of the homicide office with a quizzical look on his face.

"The lining keeps getting torn by the hammer on my gun," Craig said with a flush of embarrassment. "I was stapling it up to keep it from hanging out the bottom of my coat. I look like enough of a ragmuffin without that."

"Makes sense to me, John," McAllister replied. "But, why don't you just get your wife to sew it up?"

"My wife has decided to go home to mommy and daddy until she decides if she wants to be married anymore," Craig replied. "So I'm doing my own tailoring these days."

Quickly changing the subject, he added "Welcome aboard. We're running the task force out of the training classroom down the hall so you'll need to check in down there. I just came in here to get some extra notebooks – and the stapler."

The two men walked down the hall together. Craig noticed McAllister was wearing a dark woolen suit with a striped tie. It appeared to be the same suit he had seen him wear to court. McAllister interpreted his glance and said

"I've only got one suit and a couple of sport coats. I wasn't sure what to wear but I figured the suit would be o.k."

"Looks pretty warm," Craig replied. "But you can take your coat off when we get on the street. Most of the guys don't dress too formally except when they have a case go to trial. Your sport coats will be fine as long as you wear a tie."

"Good," McAllister said. "I was a little concerned about not having the right clothes. I remember a few years ago, all you guys wore hats in the Detective Bureau."

"Yeah, that used to be required. Straw hats after Derby Day, felt hats after Labor Day. But we've gotten away from that the last few years."

They entered the classroom where the other members of the task force were gathered. The room had changed considerably overnight. Five battered gray metal desks had been moved in. Phones and typewriters, the working tools of homicide detectives, were on each desk. Large sheets of poster board were attached to the walls and blown up photos from each crime scene were stapled to them, ringing the room with grisly decorations. A large portable blackboard sat in one corner and a time line for each killing was being drawn on it.

Craig was introducing McAllister to the other detectives when Lieutenant Garrard came in the room accompanied by a young man in a checkered sport coat.

"This is Sandy Burns," Garrard announced to the room at large. "He'll be working with us for a while. Hello, McAllister, nice to have you with us. John, if you've got today's assignments made out, let's get to work."

Craig read off work assignments and split the homicide detectives up so that one was part of each pair of men, except for Bristow and Parsons, two veterans who had worked a number of homicide cases in the past. He assigned Burns to work with Larry Colbert and McAllister to work with him. Then he gave a brief synopsis of each case.

"We'll catch you two guys up on the details as we go along this morning," Craig said. "A couple of teams will have to work tonight and do a recanvass on Dixie Highway. So far, we haven't turned up anybody who saw either victim from night before last. We'll swap off, try to alternate night turns, keep some of you old guys from having to stay up late every night. Colbert and Burns, McAllister and me, we'll take tonight. Now, let's hit the bricks."

As they climbed into the battered Ford sedan on the parking lot, McAllister glanced up at the windows of the Fourth District office. Sergeant Marvin was standing at the window staring directly down at him. McAllister could feel the malevolence of his gaze even though fifty yards separated them. Craig looked across the top of the car at him and then glanced in the direction he was looking.

"Marvin doesn't look too happy to see you in slick clothes," Craig said as he pulled out into Congress Alley and headed west.

"No shit," McAllister replied. "If he had had his way, I'd be deep in the projects this morning. Yesterday, he moved me and my partner off our beat, onto a new one especially created for us – Cotter Homes and Southwick. He gave us a new car too, an old Nash Rambler on its last legs. Then two hours later, he had to call me and tell me about this assignment. He is seriously pissed off."

"Yeah, I saw that Nash on the lot yesterday. I though it was somebody's idea of a joke," Craig said.

"It was a joke all right and Dave and I were the butt of it. Thanks a lot for getting me this assignment, John. I really appreciate it."

"Thank the boss; he's the one who okayed it. Now, let's catch this asshole and maybe we can get you transferred in permanently."

"Can it work that way?" McAllister asked. "Can you get a permanent transfer if you're working a task force?"

"It worked for Colbert and Wilson a few years ago," Craig replied. "They were assigned to homicide for the Alberta Jones case and wound up getting transferred permanently. And they didn't even solve the case. Of course, you're not the right race to get special consideration but if we can solve this thing, who knows what might happen?"

A few moments later, Craig spoke again.

"I didn't mean to give you the impression that Colbert and Wilson don't pull their weight. They're both good detectives, Colbert especially. He's a hard guy to get to know, but he'll work his butt off. He's a little militant in his attitude about things and doesn't mind expressing his opinion. A few of the old heads mark him down as an uppity nigger who doesn't know his place but I think he's a damned effective investigator."

"Where are we headed?" McAllister asked.

"We're doing in-depth backgrounds on each victim; see if there's any connection between them or any common denominators, other than that they're all hookers. I gave us the first victim, Angela Johnson. I believe you remember her case."

"Jesus Christ, yes, I remember it. I had never seen anything like it in my life."

"Well, we're going down to her family's house on Catalpa Street. I haven't talked to them in two or three years and I want to run the names of these other girls by them, see if Angel knew them. Plus, we'll do a general interview, go over everything again. You never know, somebody may have said something to them in the past few years that may give us a lead."

A few moments later, Craig asked "Did you see the paper or the TV news stories?"

"Yeah, I caught a couple of the TV stations. They were milking the Jack the Ripper angle for all it was worth," McAllister replied. "They were calling this guy the Louisville Ripper."

"That's an attention getter, all right," Craig said. "This asshole doesn't think he really is Jack the Ripper. He knows that will get his killings more press attention, and he's going to feed on that."

They pulled to the curb in front of a neat two-story frame house on Catalpa Street, across from an elementary school. It was a beautiful sunny morning, typical of April in Kentucky. Groups of black children were playing games on the fenced-in playground. Their shouts and laughter gave to McAllister a sense of unreality concerning the assignment they were on. He asked himself if a sadistic mad man like the one they were seeking could really exist in a world that seemed to be beautiful spring days, shady streets, and frolicking children. Then he answered his own question. The dead bodies he had seen had certainly been real enough and each one of them had, at some point, been a laughing child, playing on a playground. It was time to catch this bastard before he struck again.

Craig knocked on the door of the Johnson home, which was promptly opened by a beautiful black woman. He produced his badge and ID folder and said,

"Detective John Craig, Miss Johnson. City homicide. I don't know if you remember me. This is my partner, Scott McAllister."

"Of course I do, Detective Craig. Please come in, and you, too, Detective McAllister."

McAllister felt flustered at being addressed as "Detective" but he kept what he hoped was a professional look on his face as they entered the neatly kept living room. He was churning through his memory for the circumstances in which he had seen this woman before. Then, he remembered – the traffic stop last year after the open housing demonstration, with the mouthy black guy at 16th and Algonquin. Before he could formulate his thoughts completely, the woman spoke again.

"I'm sure you've come about my sister. Have you found out who killed her?"

"No, I'm sorry to say we haven't, Craig replied. "In fact, as you may have seen on the news, there have been three other homicides recently under very similar circumstances. We believe the same man may have killed all four of these women. We'd like to talk to you and your parents, go over Angela's background again and see if she might have known any of these other girls. We're looking for any connection that might help."

"Of course," the woman replied. "I'm afraid my father won't be much help. He had a stroke six months ago and is still bedridden. He can't talk and the stroke has affected his mind. My mother is still sharp as a tack, however. I'll get her. You all have a seat."

She left the room but returned in a moment with an elderly woman in a flowered print dress, with iron gray hair. In spite of the years, it was easy to see the resemblance between her and her daughter. Craig held out his hand to her.

"Nice to see you again, Mrs. Johnson. I'm sorry we don't have any news about your daughter's case. In fact, we are hoping to go over some things again with you."

"Let's go in the kitchen," Mrs. Johnson replied. "I just put on a fresh pot of coffee."

An hour later, Craig and McAllister were headed back downtown. The interview had not revealed much new information. They had learned that Vanessa Richards had gone to high school with Phyllis Johnson but could not unearth any other connections between the first victim, four years ago, and the three recent killings. They also learned that Phyllis, who had been in college when her sister was killed, now taught at Southwick Elementary School.

"I saw you studying Miss Johnson pretty intently, Scott," Craig said. "Do you know her from somewhere or was it just because she's such a fox?"

"She is that," McAllister agreed. "But I saw her last year in one of the marches at Iroquois Park, the open housing demonstrations. Then, later that night, Randall and I pulled a car over at 16th and Algonquin for busting a red light. She was in the car, along with three black dudes. The driver gave us a ration of shit about picking on the poor black man – you know the routine. He was a real mouthy, militant type. But she was nice. Even smiled at me and thanked me when I gave her back her license."

"What was his name?" Craig asked.

"I'm not sure, John," McAllister replied. "Jerome something, Lewis, I think but I wouldn't swear to it."

Craig looked sharply at McAllister. "Is there any way we can check that?"

"Randall wrote him a citation for running the red light. The hard copy should be on file in records. It was last April. Shouldn't be too hard to find. Why is it important?"

"A man named Jerome Lewis has come up involved with two of the other victims, Vanessa Richards and Beverly Watson. He had gone out with both of them, was engaged to Pepper Watson and supposed to been real upset with her when she got hooked on smack. Broke up with her over it. Now, here's a possible connection with Angela Johnson's family. May be a coincidence, may be something else. Let's get back to the office and try to find that ticket."

Though his tone was calm, there was an edge of excitement in Craig's voice. It was contagious. McAllister felt a lift of exhilaration. Maybe they would catch this asshole soon. He would love to tell Jenny about that! He had tried to call her last night to tell her about his new assignment and apologize for losing his temper. Her roommate had told him she wasn't in but McAllister was sure she was lying. On an impulse, he left home and drove by her apartment. Her Corvair Monza was parked at the curb. Frustrated, he contemplated going up and beating on the door until she let him in. Then he reasoned that his caveman tactics hadn't worked very well so far. He decided he would give her another day to cool off and then call her at work.

Craig pulled into the lot and double parked.

"You go check records for that ticket," he said. "I'll go on up and pull the interviews where Jerome Lewis' name came up."

Excited in spite of himself, McAllister went to do as he had been told. In his mind, he could see himself putting handcuffs on Jerome Lewis and walking him past television cameras.

Chapter Nine

Louisville, Kentucky. Friday, April 13, 1968, 11:10 a. m.

John Craig shuffled through the files on his desk systematically, looking for the reports that contained the interviews concerning Jerome Lewis. He quickly found the first one, an interview done by Larry Colbert the day before with the sister of Beverly Watson. The other reference to Lewis was in an interview with Vanessa Richards' mother. Wallace Wilson had done that one, back in March.

Finding it, Craig scanned through it quickly to refresh his memory. The woman had given Jerome Lewis' name to Wilson, along with three others, as men whom her daughter had dated before she became a prostitute. She had mentioned to Wilson that Lewis had a bad temper and was extremely jealous. According to the mother, the breakup between Lewis and her daughter had been stormy. She also told Wilson that her daughter was afraid of Lewis and went out of her way to avoid him after the breakup.

Craig flipped through the pages of the follow-up list, kept on a clipboard on his desk, looking to see who had been assigned to check Lewis out. He found the notation that the task had been assigned to Detectives Noonan and Boyd on March 20th, the day after Wilson had interviewed the mother. There were no initials or date beside the item to indicate that it had ever been done.

"God damn it, those two duds wouldn't make a pimple on a detective's ass between them," Craig swore out loud. Then, he checked himself. He was as negligent as they were. As the lead detective on the Richards case, it was his responsibility to make sure all the follow-up tasks were completed and signed off. The follow-up list on the Richards case was four pages long and he simply had not noticed that the job had not been completed. The fact that this sort of thing happened a lot with Noonan and Boyd did not excuse his own neglect.

The interview with Watson's sister was also very interesting. According to her, Lewis had started dating Beverly Watson four years ago and they had quickly become engaged. Unknown to her family, Beverly had been experimenting with heroin for several months and had eventually become addicted. In order to pay for her habit, she had turned to occasional acts of prostitution. When Lewis learned about this, he became violently angry and beat her badly. She broke off the engagement and soon became a regular on Dixie Highway, plying her trade with the increasing numbers of soldiers that the escalating war in Viet Nam brought to Fort Knox and to Louisville on weekends.

"John, I found the citation on that guy," McAllister said, coming into the room with a sheaf of papers. "Jerome Lewis, 2810 Virginia, on April 17, 1967, just three days shy of a year ago. We stopped them at 16th and Algonquin. Phyllis Johnson was in the car with him, along with two other dudes. He drove a black Pontiac GTO, J-John 45-832. I pulled his city arrest records and his mug shot, too. It's the same guy I saw that night.

He's got five arrests, one for Disorderly Conduct and A. & B. Police Officer, one for plain old A. & B., one for speeding and R. D., and one for Failure to Disperse and Parading Without a Permit. That was from last year, during one of the open housing marches at Wyandotte Park, a couple of days after we cited him. He also got busted for a felony, Auto Theft, in 1965 and did eighteen months at LaGrange. That means he hadn't been out of the joint long when we stopped him last year."

"What's his date of birth?" Craig asked.

"July 7, 1941," McAllister replied. "He's twenty-seven."

"That's probably the same guy who's mentioned in these interviews," Craig said. "The age is right. Who locked him up for Assault and Battery on a Police Officer?'

McAllister fingered through the papers in his hand.

"Here it is. Back in '63. Terry Vogel and Bill Waters arrested him at 26th and Maple, in the bar there. The write-up just says he was disorderly in the bar and struck Vogel when he went to place him under arrest. Knowing Vogel, he probably went to General Hospital before he got booked, if he was stupid enough to swing at him."

"The boy we're looking at is a hothead," Craig said. "He is also supposed to have smacked two of our victims around. We need to contact these families, show them this mug shot and make sure it's the same guy. Then, if it is, we go back to Phyllis Johnson, find out what her relationship with Lewis is and if there was any connection with her sister. Interesting that he was in the joint during a good part of the time between the first killing and the rest of them."

"Hey, that's right," McAllister said. "And he was on parole until February of this year, so he may have been keeping his act cleaned up until he got off parole."

"One thing at a time," Craig said. "Let's get him identified first and then we'll see where it takes us."

They were headed out the back door of headquarters when they met Colbert and Burns coming in. Craig pulled the mug shot of Lewis out of his pocket and showed it to Colbert.

"Larry, do you know this guy?" he asked.

Colbert took a long look at the picture and handed it back.

"Jerome Lewis," he replied. "Went to Central High with me and with Beverly Watson. He's one of the names Beverly's sister gave me yesterday. She told me he went to school with Beverly and me. Said he worked her over pretty good when they broke up. I was going to work on him some today if I got the chance. You got something else on him?"

Quickly, Craig explained the possible connections between Lewis and the three victims.

"We need to get him identified by Vanessa Richards' family and by the Johnsons. If he's connected with those three victims, we may have something here."

"We'll check with the Richards family if you want," Colbert said.

"Good, we'll get the Johnsons. Advise us if you get him i.d.'ed and we'll meet you and go pick him up."

"Here's another copy of the mug shot," McAllister said, handing it to Colbert.

"Where does he live?' Colbert asked.

"Last known was 2810 Virginia last year," McAllister replied.

"2810 Virginia," Colbert said. "You know what that is, don't you, John?"

"Doesn't mean anything to me," Craig replied.

"That's the house where the Southern Christian Leadership Conference is headquartered. He may be hooked up with them."

"That would make sense," Craig said. "He was involved in the open housing demonstrations last spring and the SCLC led a lot of those. This could get real interesting."

"Yeah," Colbert replied. "We may have to get A. D. Williams King and Ralph Abernathy to okay locking him up."

"Yeah, you know that's going to happen," Craig said. "Let's get going."

Phyllis Johnson answered the door quickly when Craig and McAllister returned to the Catalpa Street address. Without preliminary, Craig showed her Lewis' mug shot.

"Do you know this man, Miss Johnson?" he asked.

"That's Jerome Lewis," she replied. "I dated him some last year. Does he have something to do with my sister's death?'

"That's what we're trying to find out," Craig said. "Did he know your sister?"

"We all grew up together, right here in this neighborhood," she said. "Jerome's family lived down the street. He was a few years older than Angela but he certainly knew her. I remember that he got very upset when he learned that she had – that she was selling herself. She told me that he met her over on Dixie Highway one night and tried to get her to leave with him. She said he was very angry. She ran away from him and some of the men, I guess they were pimps, made him leave her alone."

"When did this happen?" Craig asked.

"I think it was about a month before she died. I called her where she was staying and met her one day at a restaurant on Dixie. I was trying to convince her to come back home. My mother and father were just grieving over her and what she had become.

She asked me if I had sent Jerome after her. I told her that Jerome had come by the house after he got out of the Army and mother told him what Angela was doing. He must have took it on himself to go after her. She was afraid of him."

"You say he was in the Army?" Craig asked, with a glance at McAllister who was industriously taking notes.

"Yes, he got drafted but was only in like six months or so. They kicked him out for some reason in the early part of 1964. He was always vague about it."

"You said that you dated him some. How did that come about?" Craig asked.

"We went out a couple of times in high school but it was more like brother and sister, if you know what I mean. I had been knowing the boy all my life. Then I didn't see him for awhile. I went to college and he, well, I guess you know that he went to LaGrange. So I didn't see him for quite some time. Then, last year our church was recruiting volunteers for the open housing marches. I went to one of the meetings and Jerome was there. He was active with the SCLC then. We went to some of the marches together and then we started dating. But he got real possessive and we broke up last summer. The man has a terrible temper and I wouldn't put up with him manhandling me. So I broke it off. I haven't seen him in several months."

She glanced sharply at both men.

"Does he have something to do with these other girls that have been killed?"

"We're not sure, Miss Johnson," Craig replied. "He knew a couple of them, for sure. Can you us tell where he works or where we might find him?"

"He was working part time as an organizer for SCLC, organizing voter drives, that sort of thing. But I heard that he quit. They say that he has gotten real militant and has joined the Black Panther Party. So I don't know where he's living now."

"If he should contact you, will you call us?" Craig asked.

"Certainly, but you know, Detective Craig, I just can't picture Jerome doing those things to all those girls that I heard about."

"We're not saying that he did, yet," Craig replied. "But we do need to talk to him. We'll keep you posted. Thanks for your help."

"Surely," she replied, opening the door for them. "If you need to contact me next week, I'll be back at school, Southwick Elementary."

The two men got back into their car and Craig picked up the radio microphone as McAllister started the car and pulled away.

"602 Adam to radio," Craig said into the mike.

"602 Baker, have 602 Adam meet us at 28th and Virginia," Colbert's voice came over the radio before the dispatcher could respond.

"602 Adam, 10-4," Craig replied.

"602 Adam, 602 Baker, at 11:42 a. m." the dispatcher intoned.

Colbert and Burns were parked on the lot of a service station. McAllister pulled in beside them and all four men gathered behind the cars.

"This is the right Jerome Lewis. Vanessa Richards's sister knocked him out right off the bat," Colbert said.

"So did Phyllis Johnson and – he was over on Dixie Highway in 1964 trying to persuade Angela Johnson to repent and come home," Craig replied. "So we've got him connected to three of the four victims."

"Plus, the fourth victim, Margaret Sistrunk, she was a friend of Angela's and found the body when she was killed," McAllister chipped in. "She may have seen him when he was trying to get Angela to come back home. Could be, she recognized him again, either four years ago or night before last, or both."

Craig looked thoughtfully at the young officer.

"You may be on to something there," he mused. "Maybe our boy, Jerome, doesn't like his old girl friends turning tricks after they break up with him and maybe he thought Sistrunk could ID him and make the connections. Maybe all this other shit is just a smoke screen."

"Lot of maybes there, John," Colbert said. "But a lot of tie-ins too. Enough to pick him up and talk to him. Richards' sister says he doesn't live at the SCLC house anymore. She thinks he's joined the Black Panthers. They have a headquarters in a house in the 3600 block of Greenwood. Maybe he's staying there."

"Phyllis Johnson told us the same thing about the Black Panthers. Before we go hitting their headquarters, I'm gonna run this by the boss and get his okay. It probably wouldn't hurt to take some uniforms over there with us either. Let's head back to the office."

"This guy is a horse, John," Colbert said. "He played football at Central and was hard as a rock. He had some scholarship offers from a couple of small colleges but he got locked up a couple of times and they lost interest in him. He always had a chip on his shoulder and would fight at the drop of a hat."

"All the more reason to make sure we're prepared when we go get him. See you in the office," Craig said.

* * *

Jenny Holcomb smiled at Gloria, the receptionist, as she returned to her desk from lunch with Michael Renyard.

"I'll catch the phones if you're ready to go to lunch, Gloria. Did I get any calls?"

"Thanks, Jen. Nope, no calls. I'll be back in about 45 minutes," Gloria replied, gathering her purse and heading for the elevator.

Jenny sat down in Gloria's chair and contemplated her situation. She had half hoped that Scott would call. She hadn't heard from him since their argument two days ago. She had been to a baby shower for a sorority sister last night when he called, riding to the event with another girl. She had expected that he would try to reach her at work this morning. He had not called and when Renyard had called, asking her to go to lunch, in a fit of pique at Scott for being so pigheaded, she had agreed.

The argument they had seemed fairly inconsequential now. Scott had reacted so vehemently when she told him she was going to a dance with Renyard that she had responded in kind. Now she was sorry that she had.

She had agreed several weeks ago to go to the bar association dance with Renyard, before she and Scott had started dating regularly. She felt that she couldn't break the date, in good conscience, even though something about Renyard bothered her. He was polished and charming and his constant arrogance was interesting to a degree, but it grew old quickly. She always had the feeling that he was more interested in himself than in her.

Now, to make matters worse, Renyard had taken her agreement to have lunch as a signal that she found him much more irresistible than she really did. He was putting pressure on her to make another date for the following weekend and his attitude seemed to convey the idea that she would accept as a matter of course, even after she had said no. Renyard's self assurance and conceit seemed to her to be character flaws when viewed alongside Scott's straightforward and open approach to things.

"Oh, damn you, Scott McAllister, for putting me in this mess with your stubbornness," she thought as she chewed the end of a perfectly good Number 2 pencil.

The phone pealed sharply, interrupting her thoughts.

"Barnes, Harding, and Nelson, Attorneys at Law," she answered.

"Jenny, it's Scott. Listen, honey, I'm sorry I started that argument. I -"

"Scott, I'm sorry, too. What took you so long to call me, you big oaf?"

"I tried to call last night. Megan said you weren't home," Scott said.

"She told me. I went to that baby shower I was telling you about with two other girls."

"Listen, Jen, I've had a good thing happen. I've been assigned to homicide as a member of a task force."

"Oh, Scott, that's marvelous. Are you a detective, now?"

"Not yet, but if I can do a good job on this task force, I may have a chance to be. We're working on the murders of those prostitutes in the west end."

"I read about that," Jenny said. "The papers are calling it the Louisville Ripper case."

"Yeah, well, that's doesn't help us much. Listen, I've got to run. Can I see you tonight?'

"Pick me up about seven," Jenny said. "Let's go get a pizza and talk about all of this."

"I'll see you at seven. 'Bye, sweetheart."

Jenny hung up the phone and sat back in her chair. Suddenly, she was very happy with the way the day was turning out. She put the impending date with Renyard in the back of her mind, to be dealt with later. Right now, she intended to concentrate on strengthening her relationship with Scott.

* * *

McAllister turned away from the pay phone in the lobby and ran up the steps to the second floor of police headquarters, feeling as if he were floating up them. Jenny Holcomb's ability to make him feel on top of the world amazed him. He was beginning to realize that he was in love and now he had to figure out what to do about it. Maybe he could make some progress on that project tonight. Right now, he had work to do.

Coming into the task force office, he found all nine of the other task force officers gathered around Craig's desk with Lieutenant Garrard. Garrard was sketching the Black Panther headquarters on a legal pad and assigning teams of detectives to cover areas of the building.

Garrard glanced at him and said,

"Nice of you to join us, McAllister."

"Sorry, Lieutenant, I had to make a phone call and didn't want to tie up these lines."

"Okay, you and Craig, Colbert and Burns are going to the front door, along with two uniforms. We're getting a search warrant for the clubhouse and for Lewis himself. Judge Colson has decided that we have enough probable cause for that. Sergeant Howard is on his way back from the judge's chambers now. We'll search the place and, if we find any contraband, we'll lock everybody up and cut Lewis out of the herd when we get back here. Then Craig and Colbert will take a crack at him. Let's all get together on the lot and head that way. We'll meet the beat cars at 34th and Greenwood and move in from there."

Half an hour later, they pushed their way past the large black man who answered the door of the small frame house in the 3600 block of Greenwood and spread out inside the front room.

"Man, what is this shit? What're you motherfuckers looking for?" the man wanted to know.

"Louisville police," Craig answered. "We have a search warrant for this house. Turn around and put your hands on the wall. Scott, pat him down and show him the warrant."

The furniture in the living room consisted of five large ratty looking sofas and several broken chairs. Posters of Che Guevera, Lenin and other revolutionaries were on the wall.

Moving on through the house, they found bedrooms with mattresses and bedrolls on the floor and a kitchen piled with dirty dishes and overflowing garbage cans. Six surly looking black men were being herded into the living room by the detectives and officers who had entered through the back door. McAllister recognized Jerome Lewis as one of them.

Detective Parsons came into the living room carrying a large paper grocery sack and a rusty sawed-off double-barreled shotgun. He showed the contents of the bag to Lieutenant Garrard.

"Looks like about a half pound of marijuana, Lieutenant, and this sawed-off is definitely less than eighteen inches. This was in the back bedroom. The shotgun was under a mattress."

"Okay," Garrard said. "Load 'em up. Let's take them all downtown."

A chorus of curses broke out from the house occupants who had been made to sit on the couches. Several protested that they didn't live there but were just visiting. McAllister watched Lewis carefully. The man remained silent as he and the others were handcuffed and led out of the house.

Outside, a small crowd had gathered and was yelling curses at the police as they loaded their prisoners into cars. The two Fourth District officers who had remained outside were looking decidedly nervous as they eyed the crowd. As the detective cars pulled away, rocks and bottles began to fly into the street and bounce off the cars. Looking in the rear view mirror, McAllister saw the crowd spill out into the street as the last police unit sped away.

"Just another routine day at the office," Craig said.

"The people are done with you pigs," Jerome Lewis said from the back seat. "The revolution is coming. Power to the people!"

At that moment, the revolution seemed a real possibility to the two cops.

Chapter Ten

Louisville, Kentucky. Friday, April 13, 1968, 3:45 p. m.

Colbert and Craig sat across the table from Jerome Lewis. The small interrogation room contained a two-way mirror, behind which McAllister, Burns and Lieutenant Garrard stood. The hidden microphone broadcast the conversation in the room over a nearby speaker. The men's voices sounded tinny and distorted, like an old-time radio show.

Craig began the interview, laying a legal pad on the table and pausing to light a cigarette. Lewis folded his arms across his chest and glared at the two detectives.

"Jerome, I'm Detective Craig and I think you know Detective Colbert. We're with the homicide squad."

"I know Uncle Tom," Lewis replied. "If you and Tom are working homicide, why you talking to me? What I got to do with homicide?"

Colbert flushed under the condescending insult and a small muscle ticked noticeably behind his jaw. However, he remained silent.

"We think you may be able to help us on some cases we're working. We know that you were acquainted with three girls who have been killed in the Dixie Highway area."

"What you talking about, man? I don't have nothing to do with no girls on Dixie Highway."

"Are you saying you didn't know Vanessa Richards, or Beverly Watson?" Craig asked. Laying the two girls' mug shots on the table between them, he pointed to the pictures.

"Look at these pictures and tell me you didn't know both of these girls."

With a scornful glance at the photos, Lewis pushed back in his chair.

"Yeah, I know both them bitches, but I haven't seen either one of them in a long time. I broke off with both of them when they started selling their pussy on the street and fucking with smack."

"That make you mad, when they started being hookers," Craig asked. "or when they started using drugs?"

"Nah, man, I didn't get mad. I just got clear of them. I don't need that shit. I can't stand a woman who isn't clean, so they go their way and I go mine. Like I say, I ain't seen either one of them in months."

Colbert spoke for the first time.

"Where were you in May of 1964, Jerome?"

"Damn, Tom, you gonna' talk after all? You better ask ol' massah here if you can talk before you get in trouble," Lewis replied in an exaggerated dialect.

"Knock off the shucking and jiving, and answer the question, asshole. I don't have time to listen to your shit."

Lewis looked at Colbert with a contemptuous sneer.

"Man, how do you live with yourself? In here every day kissing the white man's ass and helping keep your own people down. You better wake up, Tom. The revolution is coming and we gonna take you out along with your white friends when it does. The day of the white man is over. The day of the black man is here."

"Spare me the Stokeley Carmichael bullshit, Jerome. Just answer the question. Where were you in May of 1964?" Colbert said.

"I got nothing else to say to you, Tom, or to your white massah here, except I don't know nothing about these girls getting killed. Besides, you haven't advised me of my rights. I want a lawyer."

"We haven't accused you of anything, Jerome," Craig said. "Why do you think you need a lawyer?"

"Yeah, right. I got nothing else to say. I want a lawyer."

"Who's your lawyer?" Craig asked.

"Daniel T. Tompkins Jr. and I want to call him," Lewis answered.

"We'll be back in a minute, "Craig said, groaning inwardly as he motioned with his head for Colbert to leave the room with him. Daniel Tompkins was a well-known local espouser of radical causes and a royal pain in the ass to the police. It was not surprising that Lewis had asked for him. He had previously represented other members of the Black Panther Party in criminal matters and was quick to accuse the police of overstepping their bounds in any case he became involved in. He was flamboyant and colorful. The news media flocked to him whenever he wanted to make a pronouncement in behalf of whatever client was the current beneficiary of his legal talents.

Garrard met them in the hallway as they left the interrogation room, trailed by McAllister and Burns.

"Did you hear it all, boss?" Craig asked.

"Yeah, looks like we've hit a wall here. Go ahead and book him on the gun and dope charges. He was in the bedroom where they found the stuff. We'll have to go at him another way."

"Let me talk to him again, Lieutenant," Colbert said. "If we can crack that militant revolutionary act he's putting on, I believe we can get a lot more out of him."

"What good will it do us, Larry?" Garrard replied. "If we talk to him now without his lawyer, after he's asked for him, it won't be admissible, no matter what he tells us. His pals have already been booked and probably made bond by now. I won't be surprised if Daniel T. shows up here any minute demanding to talk to Lewis, anyway. Forget it, book him like I said. We'll start digging into his background and his activities. By the way, the partial print from the shell casing from the Watson case isn't his. I had Patterson run it while you were talking to him."

"Doesn't mean anything," Colbert said. "Any number of people might have handled that shell before the shooter got it."

"That's true, Larry, but it sure as hell doesn't help us right now," Garrard replied. "Now go book the guy like I told you to and get back up here, so we can figure out where to go next."

The five men were gathered around Craig's desk in the task force office dividing up assignments to begin a close scrutiny of the life and actions of Jerome Lewis when the phone rang. Craig answered it, spoke briefly and turned to the others.

"Lewis just made bond. Evidently, Daniel T. got the on call judge to set bond on both charges before arraignment, even though they're felonies. He got a bail bondsman to post it and he's walking."

"Okay," Garrard said. "He's out on the street and he knows we're looking at him. That may keep him from killing some other girl. In the meantime, let's turn him inside out. Talk to everybody you can find about what he does, where he goes and with who. See if we can find out where he was during the times of the killings. I'm going to keep the other teams doing backgrounds on each victim."

"Boss, we still need to do a canvass in the Dixie Highway area tonight for witnesses on Sistrunk and Watson," Craig said. "I've got the four of us scheduled to do that."

"Okay," Garrard replied. "Go home, get some dinner and come back later tonight to get that done."

"Yes, sir. You heard the man, guys. What's up, Burns?"

"Lieutenant, my sergeant called me a little while ago and told me I was assigned to the infield at Churchill Downs for Oaks Day and Derby Day. I'm scheduled to work the Derby Parade too. What should I do about that?"

"The Derby is still two weeks off," Garrard replied. "If we clear these cases before then, you'll be back in the district, so you'll probably work those assignments. If we don't, I'll try to get the chief's office to exempt us from Derby details."

Walking to his car, McAllister felt deflated. The case against Jerome Lewis, which had looked so promising that morning, had gone no place, so far. And Lieutenant Garrard's remarks to Burns didn't leave much doubt that they would be returned to the Fourth District once this assignment was over. This would probably happen just in time for Sergeant Marvin to assign him to restroom patrol in the infield on Derby Day. So much for his big plans to be a homicide detective.

Then he remembered that he was going to see Jenny that evening. Immediately he felt better. Even though their date would be curtailed because he had to come back in to work, the thought of her company for a few hours brightened his outlook considerably.

Saturday, May 4, 1968, 7:35 a. m., Derby Day.

The crowds had begun to form long before daylight outside the gates to Churchill Downs, waiting to be admitted to the grandstand or the infield. The clubhouse patrons would arrive later in a parade of taxis and limousines, with the wealthy and the famous being escorted by police motorcycles. The early morning sun had risen high enough now to warm up the air and the people waiting in line stretched gratefully in its rays.

A few blocks north of the racetrack, Officer Pete Grisham drove car 301 randomly through the streets at the north end of his beat. He had been on duty since 8:00 p. m. the night before and still had a half hour to go. The manpower demands of the Kentucky Derby and its attendant activities required twelve hour shifts during Derby week in order to staff all the special details and still cover the regular patrol assignments.

Grisham was glad to be riding his regular assignment instead of having to direct traffic around the track or hassle with drunks all day in the infield.

In the right hand seat, his partner, Officer Matt Kelly, snored softly with his head against the door column.

Derby Eve had been busy. A special riot squad had been deployed on 4ᵗʰ Street, downtown, to deal with the rowdy mob of college students who flocked there to party and carouse. From the radio traffic Grisham and Kelly had overheard, a large number of arrests had been made. The west end had also been active, with 4ᵗʰ District cars being sent on a new run as soon as they could clear from the previous one. Disorderly crowds had gathered on several corners and bombarded police cars with various missiles. However, the night had ended without any major disturbances.

Grisham and his partner had also been busy for the first six hours of their shift but things had quieted down since 4:00 a. m. Now Grisham was hovering near the north end of their beat in anticipation of heading to headquarters for off going roll call. They would have to come back in at eight that evening for another twelve hours, so he didn't want to waste any time getting off.

As he passed Central Park, three acres of greenery in the heart of the Old Louisville area just south of downtown, Grisham noticed a white man dressed in jogging clothes waving at the patrol car from the corner.

"Matt, wake up," Grisham said. "There's a citizen trying to flag us down."

"Huh – what? Oh, yeah. I'm awake," Kelly replied groggily. Peering at the jogger, he said,

"Wonder what this joker wants? He looks agitated."

As Grisham pulled to the curb, the man approached the passenger window. He was indeed agitated.

"Officers, there's a woman in the park there who has been horribly injured," the man said in a high-pitched voice.

"Whereabouts in the park, sir?" Kelly asked.

"In the shelter, in the middle of the park. She's been – she was... My god, I have never seen anything like that. There is blood all over the place. I was jogging by and saw her. I was on the way to find a phone when I saw you."

"Okay, sir," Kelly said. "What's your name and address?"

"Lawrence Jeffers. I live at 1438 Belgravia Court, just south of the park."

"Okay, Mr. Jeffers. If you'll wait here, we'll get back with you."

Leaving the man standing on the corner, Grisham pulled the car across the curb and onto the wide sidewalk leading into the interior of the park. They quickly reached the open sided picnic shelter and got out of the car. Grisham stepped inside the structure and stopped short. The sight that met him stunned him into speechlessness. Coming in behind him, Kelly stepped around him and then he also stopped.

"Oh my God," Kelly stammered.

Before them, the nude body of a young black female was splayed across two park benches that had been pulled together. She had been slashed across the abdomen and her intestines had spilled out and off the benches onto the floor. Her throat had been horribly cut completely across from ear to ear and her head hung backwards off the bench, attached to her torso only by her spinal column. What appeared to be the handle of a police nightstick protruded from her vagina. The floor around the benches was covered in a dark pool of blood. The buzzing of flies filled the air in the shelter and the smell of rotting meat was overpowering.

Grisham forced his eyes away from the horrible scene and began to examine the surrounding area. He realized that his first responsibility was to protect this scene. There was obviously nothing that could be done for the victim.

"Matt, get on the horn and get homicide started out here. You'd better notify 320, too."

Kelly returned to the car and Grisham continued his scan of the interior of the shelter.

On the wall across from where he stood, he noticed words written on the plaster in what appeared to be blood. It had run down the wall from each letter and had dried completely. He silently mouthed the words he read,

"JACKS BACK – HAPPY DERBY"

* * *

Eight hours later, the entire task force was assembled in their office, typing reports and comparing notes. Weariness showed on the faces of all eleven men. The past two weeks had gone by in a blur of fourteen and sixteen hour days. Hundreds of interviews had been completed and added to the huge file. They had microscopically examined the life of each victim back to childhood. They had also gathered a great deal of information on the background of Jerome Lewis. They also conducted periodic surveillances on Lewis, tailing him as he left the Black Panther headquarters, usually with other members of the organization. The Black Panthers apparently spent most of their time going to meetings and holding rallies. So far, all of the detectives' efforts had led nowhere.

The events leading up to the Kentucky Derby had come and gone, mostly unnoticed by the task force members except as a minor irritant when they were trying to get from place to place. They had been exempted from Derby Festival details by special order from the chief of police. Garrard had kept them occupied day and night. The only positive result from all of this activity was that there had been no further killings – until today.

"Who had Lewis last night?" Garrard asked.

"We did, boss," Rovinelli said. "Put him back at the Panther headquarters at 11:10, along with those two dudes who came in town last week. The two the FBI were interested in, Cortez and Hawkins. There was quite a party going on. We hung around until after midnight, and then called it quits. Guess he could have gone out again."

"And we've got a time of death sometime between 10:00 p. m. and 4:00 a.m., which doesn't help much. He had plenty of time to leave there again, pick up the girl and do her, and get back with time to spare."

"Boss, I'm sorry. We had been on since eight that morning and knew we had to be back in this morning. With everybody else on Derby details, there wasn't anybody available to watch the place the rest of the night," Rovinelli said.

"I'm not blaming you, Rick," Garrard replied. "I just wish we could catch a fucking break. John, do we know who our victim is yet?"

"Yes, sir," Craig replied. "The fingerprint lab called just now. Deborah Brown, AKA Sunshine, DOB 12/14/44, last known address in Arlington Village, off Manslick Road. This girl's a little different from the others. She evidently works the downtown hotels instead of Dixie Highway. Vice has busted her three times in hotels. No arrests on Dixie."

"Okay, let's get some copies made of her latest mug shot and start hitting the downtown hotels – doormen, bartenders, waitresses, bellhops, whoever. See if anybody remembers her from last night and who she might have been with. John, contact Jack Graham in Vice when they come in at eight. See if they know anything else about her or if any of their detectives remembers seeing her last night," Garrard said.

"Okay, boss. I'd like to send Colbert and Burns back to the west end. See if they can spot Lewis at the Panther headquarters and keep an eye on him. This bastard is getting real bold. If Lewis is our man, he may –

Craig stopped speaking as the office door opened and Major Farley M. Bishop entered, followed by George Farris, the Director of Safety and his assistant, Michael Renyard.

"Lieutenant, the Director of Safety wants to speak to your squad," Bishop said in an ominous tone.

"They're all here, Major," Garrard said.

Farris, a short, pompous politician who owed his current position to the fact that his wife was a wealthy contributor to the Republican party, cleared his throat and said, quite unnecessarily,

"All right, listen up you men. I have just come from the Mayor's office and he is not happy. He has been besieged in his office all afternoon by the news media, demanding to know what he is going to do about this latest atrocity. He has instructed me to tell you that he wants this case and the others cleared up immediately. This unwanted publicity is bound to affect business for the Derby. Why, we'll be lucky if anybody comes to the Derby next year."

"Sir, I can assure you that every man in here is doing everything he can to solve these cases," Garrard said.

"That may be, Lieutenant, but that is not sufficient. This task force has been in place for over three weeks with no results. I understand you have a suspect. Was he under surveillance last night?"

"Yes, sir, for part of the night," Garrard replied. We did not have sufficient manpower to maintain twenty-four hour surveillance on the man. We are in the process of determining when the victim was killed so we can —"

Farris held up an imperious hand.

"Spare me the details, Lieutenant. Just get on the ball and get these cases cleared up. If you're not able to do so, we'll get someone in here who can."

"Sir, I work for the Chief of Police and it is his prerogative to transfer me whenever and wherever he sees fit. But I don't think you'll find anyone who could do anything differently to solve these cases."

"That remains to be seen, Lieutenant," Farris replied. He appeared to notice for the first time that every man in the room was watching this exchange between him and Garrard.

"Major Bishop, I need to speak to you and Lieutenant Garrard privately," Farris said.

"Yes, sir," Bishop replied. "My office is just down the hall."

The three men left the room. Renyard started to follow them, and then paused at the desk where McAllister was sitting.

"Officer McAllister, isn't it? I wasn't aware you'd been transferred to Homicide," Reynard said.

"Temporarily," McAllister replied.

"Hmmm, Jenny didn't tell me that. Well, don't get comfortable. If your squad doesn't catch this killer damn quick, you'll all be back in uniform and I doubt that your new assignments will be pleasant ones. You probably won't have much time to foist your attentions on the lovely Miss Holcomb."

"Why don't you let Miss Holcomb and me worry about my attentions, Renyard? We're doing very well without your help, as you've discovered the last ten times you've called her trying to get her to go out with you," McAllister said.

Renyard leaned toward McAllister and spoke in a low voice.

"If you get in my way, my impetuous friend, I promise you, you will regret it."

McAllister rose to his feet and looked Renyard directly in the eye.

"Fuck you and I'm not your friend," he said.

John Craig stepped over to McAllister's desk.

"Is there something we can help you with, Mr. Renyard?" he asked.

Renyard stepped back and looked around the room at the other men who were all watching him.

"No, I'm done here. Later, McAllister."

He turned and left the room. Craig looked at McAllister, whose face was bright red.

"What the fuck was that all about, Scott?" Craig asked.

"That asshole keeps trying to date my girlfriend," McAllister replied. "She went out with him once and now he won't take no for an answer. Keeps calling her and coming to where she works. Do you know anything about him, John?"

"He got appointed to his job around the first of the year," Craig replied. "He's a lawyer and his father is supposed to be some political bigwig in Lexington. Rumor has it that he has political ambitions and would like to replace Farris as Safety Director, for starters. Probably not the best guy you could pick to get pissed off at you."

"Yeah, well, he keeps injecting himself into my personal life, so I haven't had much choice. He and I seem to strike sparks off each other every time we meet," McAllister said.

Garrard came back into the room at that point. His face was darker than usual and he was visibly upset.

"All right, John," he said. "You know what needs to be done. Let's get started."

"Boss, are they threatening you with reassignment if –," Craig began. Garrard interrupted him.

"Don't worry about these political hacks, John. Just do what needs to be done on this case. I'll run interference for all of you. But God help us all if this guy hits again and we don't catch him."

"Okay, boss," Craig said. Larry, you and Burns set up on Lewis. Rick and Boyd, check the downtown hotels, especially the Brown, the Seelbach, the Kentucky and the Watterson. Bristow and Parsons, hit the east end hotels, Brown Suburban, Holiday Inns and so on. Birdsong, you and Thompson take the Executive Inn, Standiford Motel and the bigger motels out on Dixie Highway. Go on out into Shiveley and the county, if you don't get any leads in the city. McAllister and I will check with the Vice Squad and then we'll check with the girls on the stroll, just in case Miss Brown changed her M. O."

With little conversation, the Ripper task force dispersed to their assignments.

Chapter Eleven

Louisville, Kentucky. Saturday, May 11, 1968, 4:30 p. m.

McAllister left police headquarters and headed toward the parking lot. This was the earliest that he had left work in several weeks. It was Saturday and he was looking forward to a hot shower and having dinner with Jenny that evening.

As he crossed Jefferson Street, he noticed a dark blue Ford sedan parked at the curb. It was obviously an unmarked police car but not LPD. It had two radio antennas on the rear fender in addition to the type used by the Louisville Police Department. McAllister could not see the driver clearly but he appeared to be a white male wearing sunglasses.

"Feds," McAllister thought to himself.

The current racial unrest in Louisville had attracted a number of visitors to the city from various civil rights groups and groups with more militant agendas. The Black Panthers were holding nightly rallies in the west end and speakers from their Chicago and Los Angeles chapters had come to town to participate in those. The Southern Christian Leadership Conference was also stepping up its activities, holding meetings in west end churches, denouncing the police. Ralph Abernathy and other prominent leaders in that organization had made appearances at these meetings. These visitors had attracted the notice of the local FBI office. Agents were sent to cover the rallies each night and more FBI agents were being seen around police headquarters on a regular basis.

McAllister was driving east on Broadway from the downtown area when he noticed the blue Ford again, in his rear view mirror. The car was positioned two car lengths behind him and maintaining the same speed. It followed him out Bardstown Road, keeping the same position.

He bypassed his turnoff at Windsor Place and, continuing south, pulled onto the lot of the White Castle restaurant at Bardstown and Eastern Parkway and parked. The Ford pulled into the space beside him. McAllister got out of his car and stood by the door.

A tall, lanky, red haired man, wearing a dark blue suit, white shirt and striped tie, got out of the Ford and approached him.

The man produced an ID folder with a small gold badge affixed to the outside.

"Officer McAllister?" he said with a disarming grin. "I'm Wayne Borders, FBI. How are you today?"

"Tired," McAllister replied bluntly. "And curious as to what I've done that would cause the FBI to follow me all the way out here from headquarters."

"Just wanted a chance to talk to you. Can I buy you a cup of coffee?"

McAllister shrugged his acquiescence and the two men entered the restaurant.

A few minutes later, they were seated in a booth, over cups of coffee. Borders opened the conversation.

"I'll get right to the point, Scott. May I call you Scott?"

"Call me whatever you like, Agent Borders. Just tell me what this is all about."

"Sure thing. We've been told by other officers that you are a real straight shooter and that you're not happy with a lot of the things that you see going on in the department. We also heard that Sergeant Marvin screwed you over pretty well because of that. Would those be fair statements?"

"Sergeant Marvin and I don't agree on a lot of things. Why is that of interest to you all?"

"Look, Scott. We know what's going on in the west end and in some other areas of Louisville. We know that Marvin and others are getting paid off to look the other way on gambling, handbooks and prostitution. But we need help proving those things. What we need is somebody on the inside, somebody who is willing to help us collect evidence that can put a stop to this shit, clean this town up and put these crooked cops away."

"What do you have in mind for this someone to do, exactly?" McAllister asked.

"Well, let's say for discussion that this someone would be you. We understand that you will be relieved from your assignment in Homicide in the next few days and sent back to the Fourth District. We would want you to just keep your eyes open and tell us what's going on between Marvin and the bar owners. We'd like for you to work your way into his confidence, make him think you've changed your mind. Maybe you're pissed about not getting to stay in Homicide, whatever, but you want to get in on the action. We think you can work your way into his confidence, maybe make some pickups for him. You could easily record conversations between you and him. You could record the payoffs you get too. Then after we have enough evidence, we'll move in and make arrests. You'll have to testify, of course. But we'll have put a stop to this shit and you'll be an important part of doing that. You will do a great thing for your department. You will, in fact, be a hero."

McAllister looked for a long moment at the agent.

"Tell me, Agent Borders, where are you from?'

"Jacksonville, Florida, originally. I worked in New Jersey for four years after I joined the bureau. Been here in Louisville about eighteen months. Long enough to know it's a nice town that needs to be cleaned up."

"Do you hope to get back to Jacksonville some day?"

"Sure do. As a matter of fact, in about two years I'll be eligible to request reassignment to the field office of my choice. If I'm lucky, that'll be Jacksonville. Why do you ask?"

"So, in a couple of years you would be in Jacksonville with a nice commendation in your file for cleaning up the Louisville Police Department. However, I would still be here working with people every day who'd be labeling me as a federal snitch. I don't think that's a proposition I'm very interested in."

"The bureau would help you relocate, if that's what you wanted," Borders said, "or help you get on another department here locally, like the Jefferson County Police."

"I don't want to relocate, I don't want to transfer to another department and I don't want to be a hero," McAllister replied. "I love Louisville and I love this police department. In spite of its faults it is a great place to work with some terrific people. What I want is to solve this multiple murder case I'm working on, get a permanent assignment to Homicide, marry my girl friend and stay right here and raise kids and retire. I think I'll make more of a contribution to the city of Louisville that way than I will your way. I believe I would make a good homicide detective eventually. I don't think I would make a good undercover federal informant."

"We may be able to help with that permanent assignment to Homicide after the investigation is concluded," Borders said, "or any other assignment you prefer."

"I'm afraid you don't get it, Agent Borders. I want to do a good job and earn the respect of my peers. That would never happen if I took your proposal. No matter what the outcome, I would be labeled a federal snitch for the rest of my career. There is a big hole in your plan anyway.

Marvin is never going to trust me or believe I've changed my feelings about payoffs. He doesn't like me one bit. Besides, he's just the tip of the iceberg. Everybody says that you have to have the blessing of city hall to operate. A lot of the department brass are also supposed to be involved. You're going to have to change the whole political climate to have any real effect on the situation. Taking Marvin out won't achieve that."

"It will be a starting point. If we can get him to roll over, he can take us on up the line," Borders replied.

"I wish you luck and I hope you find someone to help you," McAllister said. "But it won't be me. I'm just not interested in screwing up my life that way."

"I'm sorry you feel that way," Borders said. "I'm going to have to report your lack of cooperation to my bosses. Let me warn you to keep this conversation completely confidential. If it leaks out, you can be charged with interfering in a federal investigation."

The agent's demeanor underwent a complete change. The folksy approach he had adopted at the start of the conversation was replaced by a noticeable effort to appear as a steely-eyed federal agent delivering a stern warning.

"I have no intention of screwing up your investigation, Mr. Borders. Like I said, I wish you luck. Thanks for the coffee and have a nice day."

Rising, McAllister left the restaurant and went to his car. Driving home, he mulled the conversation over in his mind. What really puzzled him was the question of who in the department might have fingered him to the FBI as a possible informant. He didn't especially feel complimented that someone would think him susceptible to the feds' proposal.

He also wondered about the agent's statement that he would be sent back to the Fourth District soon. He and Burns had discussed that possibility and had asked Craig that same morning if the task force was going to be disbanded soon. There had been no additional killings since Derby Day but they were not really any closer to making an arrest than they were two weeks ago. Jerome Lewis continued to be the primary focus of their efforts but they had also checked out dozens of known sex offenders living in the Louisville area. They continued to delve into the past lives of the victims, looking for common threads. They had gone over the physical evidence in each case again, looking for something that would lead them to the killer.

The media uproar over the last killing on Derby Day had abated somewhat, although they received daily inquiries from the newspaper and each TV station as to their progress.

The political uproar, however, continued on. Lieutenant Garrard was now required to report daily to the mayor's office, the chief's office and to Major Bishop on the work of the task force. True to his word, he took the heat and passed little of it on to his detectives. They felt it nonetheless and intensified their efforts, not just to vindicate themselves and the work they had done, but in the hope that a successful solution would rehabilitate the lieutenant.

Lewis continued to be actively involved with the Black Panther party in their rallies. For the last several days, he and others had been passing out leaflets at major intersections in the west end, announcing a big anti-police rally in Shawnee Park that weekend. The task force had watched the Black Panther headquarters throughout each night after Lewis and others returned from their activities. As far as they could tell, Lewis had not left the house once he came in at night.

Craig's opinion was that they had about another week to come up with something or the task force would be disbanded. He was concerned that Lieutenant Garrard would be made the scapegoat for their failure to solve the cases. He did not hold out much hope for anything good to happen to the rest of them either. McAllister figured that his hopes for a permanent assignment to Homicide were not likely to be realized. The FBI apparently didn't think so either.

Later that evening, McAllister and Jenny were finishing their dinner in a bar booth at Hasenour's, which had become their favorite restaurant. He had shared with her his pessimism about continuing in his present assignment. Jenny was trying to cheer him up and was succeeding. He usually found it impossible to be depressed around Jenny when she was using all the charm of her personality. Jenny had a smile that seemed to light up a room whenever she turned it on. McAllister was so infatuated with her that he couldn't maintain his gloomy mood. He was laughing at her description of one of the senior partners in the law firm where she worked when he spotted a familiar tall figure in a rumpled suit coming in the front door, accompanied by a pretty blonde woman.

"Excuse me, Jenny. Here's someone I want you to meet," McAllister said as he slid out of the booth and went to the door.

"John, I didn't know you ever came here," he said as he approached the couple.

Craig smiled as he recognized his young partner.

"Hi, Scott. Say, this is my wife, Susan. Susan, this is Scott McAllister who's been my partner for the past month or so."

The woman smiled and extended her hand.

"Hello, Scott. John has said good things about you. It's nice to meet you."

"Very pleased to meet you, Susan. Let me introduce you to my girlfriend."

He led them to the booth and introduced them to Jenny, who flashed one of her amazing smiles and asked them both to sit down.

"Thank you, Jenny but we have a reservation in the main dining room," Craig replied.

"It's easy to see why Scott can't keep his mind on his work half the time. You are more beautiful than he said."

"Thank you, sir," she replied, "although I think I recognize some blarney here."

"Oh, no," Craig said. "I'm a Scotsman, not an Irishman. The Scots are famous for always telling the truth."

After a few more pleasantries, Craig and his wife moved on to the dining room.

"His wife is very uptight about something," Jenny said.

"They have been separated for several months," Scott replied. "She took the kids and moved in with her parents. I hope this may mean they're getting back together. John has been totally down in the dumps over being away from her and the kids. He really loves his family."

"Oh, I hope so, too. He really seems like a nice person."

"Yeah, you're just saying that because he said you were beautiful."

Jenny promptly stuck out her tongue at him.

"Jenny," McAllister said, impulsively, "have you ever thought about getting married?" He paused, somewhat shocked that he had brought the subject up, even though he had been thinking about it for weeks. Jenny was staring at him with a stunned expression on her face. Summoning up his courage, he plunged ahead.

"I mean, we've been dating for some time now and I – I never met a girl like you before. I'm in love with you. I would love to spend my life with you."

"Scott, are you proposing to me?" Jenny asked. "It sort of sounded like it but I want to be sure." Her eyes sparkled and that smile played across her face.

"Yes, I am. I guess I backed into it. I didn't really plan on asking you this tonight but it happened. What do you think?"

"I think the answer is yes," she replied. "I'm probably supposed to be coy and say I need to think about it, according to the manual for young spinsters. But I'm not going to do that. I decided I wanted to marry you weeks ago. I'm glad you finally got around to asking me."

McAllister sat back in his seat as an indescribable feeling of happiness washed over him. His face split into a broad grin.

"I feel like I want to jump up and dance on the bar," he said.

"Don't do it," Jenny replied. "Mr. Hasenour probably wouldn't like it."

Ed Hasenour, the owner of the restaurant was passing by their booth at that moment.

"What could you two possibly do that I wouldn't like?" he asked. "You've become two of my best customers and my best customers have the run of the place."

"Scott wanted to dance on your bar, Mr. Ed," Jenny replied. He sat down beside her and faced McAllister.

"Well, if you give me a good enough reason, that might be possible, Officer McAllister," he said.

"Jenny just said she would marry me, Mr. Hasenour," McAllister replied. "I felt like something special was called for."

"I agree," Hasenour said. "That's wonderful. How about a bottle of champagne, instead? It'll be less wear and tear on the bar and on Shorty's nerves. Shorty, let us have a bottle of champagne and some glasses over here," he called to the bartender.

He poured three glasses of champagne and, raising his glass, said

"Here's to you both. I hope you have a long and happy life together."

The customers and waitresses in the bar broke into applause. McAllister was a little nonplussed by the sudden burst of attention but his sense of euphoria was so strong it overcame all other feelings. He had absolutely no regrets and, looking at the laughing girl across the table from him, he thought that this was surely the best night of his life.

In the main dining room, Craig and his wife had ordered their meal and sat in a strained silence waiting for their salads. Susan had called him earlier in the day, suggesting that they meet for dinner. He had quickly agreed, hoping that this might be the preliminary move toward a reconciliation. She had arranged to meet him at the restaurant and had little to say after they had exchanged greetings. He inquired about the children and her answers were short and terse. Craig tried to maintain a light tone in the conversation but finally fell silent and sat looking at her.

"All right, Susan," he said. "What's on your mind?"

She continued to look into her martini glass, poking with the toothpick at the olive in the bottom of the glass. Then she appeared to make up her mind and sat up with a sudden shrug.

"John, I want a divorce. I've been trying to figure out a nicer way to put it but I can't. These last few months have shown me that you and I are better off apart."

Craig sat stunned for a moment, trying to comprehend why his life was falling apart all at once.

"How are we better off, Susan? The last three months have been the most miserable of my life. I don't want to lose you. I want you and the kids back home. I can make whatever adjustments you want. I'll transfer out of Homicide and get a day work job, whatever you want."

She glanced at him before replying,

"It's beyond that point now. Besides, you would never be satisfied if you gave up the Homicide Squad and you'd blame me for it. That would just make a bad situation worse. We need to make a clean break and get a new start. I'll let you have plenty of time with the kids and I won't be a bitch about a property settlement. But I've got to do it, John. For my sake and the kids' sake."

"Sounds like you've thought it all out," Craig said, bitterly. "Nice of you to give me so much input in a decision that affects us both so greatly. What is going on here, Susan?

Three months ago, you grab the kids and the dog, load up and walk out of the house, giving me about two minutes to get used to the idea. You stay at your folks and I hear from you once a week about when I can see the kids. No talk about us, what we're going to do, are we going to try to work it out. Then tonight, you call me up, meet me and say you want a divorce. I thought our marriage was a partnership but it looks like you're the CEO. You're the one making all the decisions. What the hell is going on?"

"I knew you'd react that way," Susan replied. "You only see your side of the issues and you think that's all there is to it. Well, there's more, John, a lot more."

"How am I supposed to see your side when I never see you or hear from you, until tonight and then that's just to receive the word that it's all over?"

"John, how many dinners have you showed up late for or missed altogether? How many games and concerts and recitals have I had to take the kids to because you were tied up with your damned Homicide Squad and your dead bodies? And I was supposed to be the good little police wife and say 'That's all right dear. I know the job comes first.'

Well, I'm tired of the job coming first. I want me to come first and I intend to see that I do from now on." She stopped speaking suddenly and averted her gaze. Her hesitation and her demeanor confirmed to Craig what he had been suspecting since the conversation started.

"I'll be damned," he said. "You've got a new man on the string, don't you? How long has this been going on? Were you seeing him before you moved out? Hell, of course you were. That must have been the reason for the increased interest in taking night classes at U of L. Who is it, Susan? Anybody I know?"

Her flushed face and her body language told Crag all he needed to know. He had interrogated too many suspects not to know a guilty countenance when he saw one.

"I didn't come here to discuss my personal life," she said quickly. "I came here to tell you I want a divorce. I've done that. I see no reason to continue the conversation."

She stood up suddenly and picked up her handbag.

"My lawyer will be in touch with you. It's J. Miles Dempsey," she said as she turned to leave.

"Why, of course it is," Craig replied. "What would J. Miles do if he didn't have all the police wives to represent and take their husbands to the cleaners?"

Their voices had risen and diners at nearby tables were staring at them. Susan noticed this and abruptly said,

"This is getting us nowhere. Goodbye, John."

She strode out of the dining room. Craig sat for a few moments, feeling his anger build. He motioned the waiter over, cancelled their orders, flung some money on the table and stalked out of the room. He was conscious of the curious stares from the other diners and it only added to his frustration and anger.

As he came into the bar, McAllister saw him and went quickly over to him.

"John, come have a drink with us and congratulate us. Jenny and I are engaged. We want you to …" He stopped speaking and looked intently at his partner.

"What's the matter, John?"

Craig raised his hand in a gesture of helplessness.

"Scott, I'm not fit company for anybody. My wife is leaving me and I just can't – I can't… It doesn't make any sense. I've got to go."

He turned and went quickly out the door of the restaurant, leaving McAllister staring after him.

Sunday, May 12, 1968. 2:32 a. m.

He reached out with the poker and stirred the fire in the fireplace. Its light caused shadows to leap across the walls of the old farm house. The light was also reflected in the terrified eyes of the woman who lay bound and gagged against the opposite wall. Her short dress was torn in several places, reflecting the struggle that she had put up before he got her here. Her lower lip was split and bleeding and her swollen right eye was almost closed.

This would be a first for him. The first time that he had carried one of his subjects, as he thought of them, to a completely remote spot where he could work undisturbed. The deserted farm house was miles from the nearest neighbor and there was little chance of interruption. He had used it before to dispose of clothing and other things but tonight it would be put to a much more important use. His curiosity had grown as he had disemboweled his previous subjects and he wanted a chance to remove some organs intact, perhaps send one of them to somebody like his distinguished predecessor had done. To accomplish that, he had to have more privacy and more time.

He had first seen the girl in the bar at the Executive Inn. By now, he was as experienced at spotting a hooker as any vice cop. She had given him an inviting smile as he sat down next to her and offered to buy her a drink. An hour later, she met him on the parking lot, as he had arranged before leaving the bar. He had told her that they were going to his room at the nearby Holiday Inn. The struggle had occurred when he drove past the place. She had tried to get out of the car vigorously, forcing him to pull into an alley and beat her unconscious. Then it had been a simple matter to tie her up and gag her before bringing her to the old farm.

He stood up from the fireplace and turned up the sputtering Coleman lantern sitting on the floor. Removing a plastic tarp from his bag, he spread it across the floor. He then grabbed the woman by the shoulders and dragged her onto the tarp. He ripped the tape from her mouth with a quick jerk and she let out a piercing scream.

"Scream all you want, slut," he told her. "There's nobody within miles of us here. That's why I chose this place, so we can work undisturbed."

Working quickly, he untied her legs and fastened them to the handcuffs he had affixed to the steel rings in the floor earlier. Then he did the same with her arms, warding off with ease her attempts to strike him. When he finished, she was spread-eagled across the blue tarp and fastened hand and foot so tightly that she could only turn her head from side to side.

She began to alternately curse him and plead with him. He ignored both as he took the razor sharp filet knife and ran it up the side of her dress, slitting it open. He quickly cut her panties off of her and then stood up, studying her naked body.

"It will be interesting to see how much of this procedure you can endure before you lose consciousness. I had to cut the others' throats to keep them quiet but that's not a factor here. So let's begin, shall we?"

Kneeling beside her, he quickly slashed the knife across her abdomen, opening a long incision. She screamed loudly as blood welled from the vicious cut.

"Scream your head off. It will do you no good. You are going to provide the most worthwhile service of your worthless life."

Bending to his work, he continued cutting and probing as her screams grew to a crescendo, then faded away and stopped altogether.

Chapter Twelve

Louisville, Kentucky. Sunday, May 12, 1968, 7:55 a. m.

The early morning churchgoers stepped up their pace as the bells of the Cathedral of the Assumption pealed out from the steeple above them, calling them to Mass. Several of them stared with curiosity at the bundle wrapped in a blue plastic tarp, lying on the sidewalk at the foot of the stairs, just below the main entrance.

"Probably some trash from the construction next door," Sam Jenkins told his wife, Doris. "I'll pull it out of the way so somebody doesn't trip over it."

Bending over, he grabbed the edge of the tarp and gave a tug. When he did, a bloody human hand flopped out of the tarp. Doris let out a scream that echoed off the downtown buildings. Other parishioners quickly gathered as Sam pulled back more of the tarp, exposing the head and upper torso of a young black woman. Her sightless eyes were wide open and trickles of dried blood ran from each corner of her mouth.

"Oh, my God," Sam exclaimed. Quickly he flipped the tarp back over the staring eyes of the woman. "Somebody call the police, now!"

Father Sean Ryan, who was assigned to do the early Mass that morning, came to the door after hearing Doris scream. Sam saw him and motioned for him to come down the steps. He quickly did so and, seeing the look on Sam's face, asked quietly,

"Sam, what is it? What's the matter?"

"There's a dead black girl in this tarp, father. She's been cut to pieces. Some devil has done this and left her here for us to find."

"May God have mercy on her soul," the priest said. Kneeling beside the body, he uncovered her head and passed his hand across her eyes. Crossing himself, he began to administer the last rites of the church. In the distance, the yelping wails of police sirens mingled with the clanging of the cathedral bells as a crowd gathered around the kneeling priest.

* * *

Craig and McAllister got out of the car on the rear parking lot of police headquarters and began collecting the paper evidence bags from the back seat. The autopsy had been long and thorough and they were both tired. Craig was also suffering from a lack of sleep and too much scotch, after his scene with Susan the preceding night. The investigation at the cathedral had been fruitless to this point. It was obvious that the girl had been killed elsewhere and dumped there during the night. So far, no witnesses had been located who had seen anything. The churchgoers who had discovered the body were unable to supply any useful leads at all. It was shaping up fast to look like another dead end investigation.

As they walked toward the back door, a group of men came around the corner of the building from the front. Three of the men were carrying bulky television cameras. They were obviously reporters.

"Detective Craig, how about a statement?" one of them called out.

If Craig hadn't been tired, he probably wouldn't have stopped to answer, but he did.

"Jeff, you know you'll have to get your statement from the Chief of Detectives' office," he said. "We can't comment on an ongoing investigation."

The lone black man in the group, an irritable reporter named Waycroft who worked for the *Louisville Guardian*, the only black-oriented newspaper in town, let out a sardonic laugh.

"Ongoing investigation, that's a crock of shit," he said. "Just another dead black whore, right, Detective? Just another name to file away and forget about. I mean, who cares about another dead black whore."

Craig turned and looked at the man angrily.

"I do, Waycroft, and my partner does, and every other man working on this task force. If you say anything else in that rag of yours, you're more interested in stirring up trouble than you are in reporting the truth. We will get this lunatic, I'll tell you that, and you can put that in your damn paper."

Craig spun on his heel and left, ignoring the shouted questions of the other reporters. Once inside, the building, he glanced at his partner who was regarding him quizzically.

"Yeah, I know," Craig said. "I should have kept my mouth shut. That guy gets under my skin. I just lost my cool."

"Let's hope they don't quote you," McAllister said. "Major Bishop probably won't be happy.

Starting up the stairs, Craig said over his shoulder,

"You know, Scott, at this point, I really don't give a shit. I probably will later but right now I don't."

Monday, May 13, 1968. 8:00 a. m.

Craig got off the elevator on the second floor and entered the Detective Bureau through the double doors. He was carrying a copy of the day's morning newspaper, which had a picture of him on the front page, above the fold, accompanied by the bold black headline "Another Killing – Veteran Detective Vows to Catch 'This Lunatic.'"

To make matters worse, his face and his comments to the black reporter had been on every television news program yesterday. Garrard had called him at home after the eleven o'clock news the preceding evening and warned him that Major Bishop would be upset and would want to see him in the morning.

As he went by the front desk, Collins, the elderly detective on duty there, told him "Major Bishop said he wanted to see you as soon as you came in."

Craig turned and went past Collins to the door of Bishop's office. He knocked and Bishop spun around in his chair and glowered at him.

"Get in here, Craig, and close the door."

Craig complied and went to stand in front of Bishop's desk.

"What in the hell has gotten into you, making a dumbass statement like that to the news media?" Bishop asked. "You're not supposed to be talking to the press at all, let alone make any "vows" to catch anybody."

"Major, I lost my temper," Craig replied. "The black reporter, Waycroft, was saying that we weren't trying to catch this asshole because all the victims were just black whores. I should have ignored him but I didn't. Unfortunately, all the other news people were right there and picked up on it."

"Yeah, well, the shit has hit the fan over it. The Director of Safety has already been on the phone chewing my ass, saying we look like we're emotional and incompetent. I've told you before, Craig, I don't like bad press. The situation in the west end is bad enough right now without you getting the *Louisville Guardian* on our ass. You've been a pretty good detective up to now but one more stunt like this and I'll bounce your ass back in uniform so fast you won't know what hit you. Do we understand each other?"

"Yes, sir," Craig replied. "It won't happen again."

"It better not," Bishop replied. "Now get out of here and get busy catching this guy before things get any hotter. Anything going on this latest case?"

"Not much, Major," Craig said. "We did get her identified and learned that she's a hotel hooker like the victim he left in Central Park. Looks like he may have shifted his attention to a higher priced class of girls. We're hitting all the downtown hotels tonight with her picture. Maybe somebody saw them together."

"What about that nigger, Lewis? Any connection with him?"

"Not that we know of, sir. He was under surveillance Saturday night, when this girl was most likely picked up."

"But the killer could have had her longer than that, right, before he killed her."

"That's right, sir. We don't know yet when was the last time she was seen by anybody. Hopefully, we'll find out today or tonight."

"All right. Get out of here and get busy. Tell Garrard I want regular reports."

Craig escaped gratefully from the Chief of Detectives' office and went to the task force office. Lieutenant Garrard was waiting for him.

"Well, get your ass chewing?" Garrard asked.

"Yeah, but it wasn't as bad as I expected. He seemed a little subdued, like he had something else on his mind."

"Probably sees his career going down the tubes, like the rest of us, if we don't catch this guy soon," Garrard said. "I imagine city hall and the chief's office have been on him pretty good."

"He said to tell you he wanted regular reports," Craig said.

"I only reported to him about ten times yesterday," Garrard replied. "Where's McAllister?"

"He was going to stop by General Hospital and pick up the autopsy report before he came in," Craig said.

"How is he working out, John?"

"Boss, he's a natural for this work. He catches on fast and you never have to tell him something twice. He soaks up information like a sponge. I hope we can keep him in the squad. I'd like to work with him regularly."

"I hope we can all stay in the squad," Garrard said. "The way things are going right now, it doesn't look real good. But I'll see what I can do."

The phone rang and Craig turned to answer it.

"Homicide Task Force, Detective Craig."

"Detective Craig, this is Juanita down in records. Somebody has left a kind of strange package on the front counter addressed to you."

"What kind of strange, Juanita?" Craig asked.

"You'd better come down and see for yourself. I haven't touched it."

"Be right down. Thanks, Juanita."

Hanging up, he turned to Garrard.

"Somebody left a package with my name on it down at the front counter. Juanita says it's strange. Guess I'd better see what it is."

When Craig approached the big front counter separating the record bureau from the main lobby, Juanita, the records supervisor, pointed at a package sitting on the counter. It was about the size of a shoe box, wrapped in brown paper and tied with staging twine.

Examining it without touching it, Craig saw that it was addressed to "Det. John Craig – LPD HQ" in large scrawled letters. In the upper left corner were the letters "J. RIPPER." Then he noticed that the bottom of the package was damp, as if the contents were leaking.

Juanita came over to the counter.

"John, I don't know how the thing got there. I looked up about five minutes ago and it was sitting on the counter. I saw your name on it and then I saw that it looked like it was leaking something. So I called you."

"Thanks, hon. Call the fingerprint lab, will you, and ask them to send a technician up here. I don't know what this is but we're going to treat it like it's important until I find out otherwise."

Paula Davis, a young records clerk, came over to where the two of them were standing.

"Juanita, I saw Johnny, the sandwich runner from Holly's, leave that package on the counter about ten minutes ago," she said. "I meant to say something to you but you were on the phone. Then it slipped my mind."

She looked anxiously from Juanita to Craig.

"Is it important?"

"Don't worry about it, Paula," Craig said. "You're sure it was Johnny you saw? Johnny One Eye?"

"Yes, sir. I mean – he's in and out of here ten or twelve times a day delivering food, so I didn't really pay much attention to him. But it was Johnny, all right."

Several minutes later, Craig, Garrard and McAllister were gathered around a lab table in the fingerprint laboratory as Pat Patterson, a tall cadaverous man with a pronounced stoop, unwrapped the package with gloved hands, spreading the paper out and saving the twine after cutting it away from the knots. It was indeed a shoebox. Lifting the lid, Patterson turned the box toward the detectives. It contained what appeared to be a human kidney resting on a bed of rock salt. Bloody fluid from the organ had stained the salt and had obviously leaked through the bottom of the box and the wrapping paper.

"The sick son of a bitch," Craig said involuntarily.

"Looks like a note taped to the inside of the lid," Patterson said. Carefully, he pried the folded paper free and spread it open on the table. All four men shuffled around to read it. It was printed crudely in pencil using clumsy block letters on a sheet of lined paper torn from a school notebook.

"Dear Det. Craig – Here's a little gift from the lunatic. As the original Ripper said in one of his letters, I ate the other one. It was delicious. Hope you like it. Jolly Jack."

Garrard looked at McAllister.

"What about that latest victim, Purcell? Was she -?"

"Yes, sir. I just got the autopsy report. She had had both kidneys removed, along with her uterus and some other organs. The pathologist said it was pretty amateurish, not like a trained doctor would do."

"Okay, let's get this thing in the refrigerator until we can get it to the lab," Garrard said. "Pat, can you process the paper, tape and the box as quick as possible and let me know what you find?"

"Yes, sir. I'll get right on it," the technician replied.

Back in the office, Garrard gathered his detectives together.

"All right, we have got to keep the lid on this latest thing. If this hits the news, we won't have time to deal with anything but the press and it will get the crank callers pumped up for sure. John, where do you want to start?"

Craig looked up from his notebook where he had been documenting the morning's events.

"Boss, the first thing we need to do is find Johnny One Eye and find out who got him to deliver the box and how. Hopefully, he saw the guy. Scott and I will go to Holly's and try to catch him. We'll need to get a lot of background on Doris Purcell. From her arrest record, she was a call girl, instead of a street walker. Maybe she worked for an escort service. Why did our boy change his MO, I wonder?"

"Maybe the girls on Dixie Highway are getting too jumpy," McAllister said. "There sure don't seem to be as many of them out at night."

"Okay,' Garrard said. "I'll get Colbert and Burns going on her background. You run Johnny down. Everybody keep their fingers crossed that the lab comes up with some prints off that box or the paper."

A few minutes later, Craig and McAllister entered Holly's Lounge, a block from police headquarters. It was a popular breakfast and lunch spot for lawyers, cops and city hall and courthouse workers and an after work watering hole. The owner, Holly George, was slicing thin slivers from a large ham on the bar.

"Hey, John. Long time since you've been in. Where have you been keeping yourself?" he said to Craig.

"Working a lot these days, Holly. Is Johnny around?"

"I just sent him over to Fiscal Court with an order. He should be right back. What has he done now? He told me yesterday that he was still on the wagon."

"He's not in any trouble, Holly. We hope he may have seen something to help us in a case," Craig replied.

"Well, here he comes," Gabriel said, pointing with the butcher knife he was holding.

A diminutive man entered the bar. His right eye was missing and the empty eye socket gave a caved-in look to the right side of his face. His clothing consisted of a filthy shirt that had once been orange and a pair of striped dress trousers several sizes too big for him. The trousers were held up by a grimy pair of suspenders and a belt that was at least a foot too long. One of his tennis shoes was bound together with duct tape. Johnny One Eye looked as though he had received seven years bad luck all at once.

"Hi, Johnny. Can we talk to you a minute?" Craig asked.

"Detective Craig. Sure thing. Did you get your package all right? I put it right where the guy told me to," the man replied.

"That's what we want to talk about, Johnny. Let's set down over here."

Craig led them to a corner table.

"This is my partner, Scott McAllister, Johnny. We need to ask you about that package. Who gave it to you to deliver?"

"I don't know his name," Johnny One Eye replied. "He called here this morning and wanted to talk to me. He told me he wanted to deliver a surprise to you. Said I could find it by the back door and there was ten bucks in it for me. I looked out the back door and, sure enough, there it was, with a ten spot stuck under the string. I took it over and put it on the counter, like he said to. Looked like it had spilled, whatever it was. The bottom was all wet. Hope it didn't get ruined."

"Johnny, did the guy give you a name?" Craig asked.

"Nah, he just said he was a friend of yours and wanted to surprise you. He talked kind of funny. Didn't sound like he was from Louisville."

"Would you know his voice if you heard it again," Craig asked.

"Maybe. Can't say for sure but maybe," Johnny said.

"Could you tell if he was black or white?" McAllister asked.

"Oh, he was a white guy, all right. He didn't sound like no nigger," Johnny replied.

"Did I do something wrong, Detective Craig?"

"No, Johnny. It's okay. Do you still have that ten spot?"

"Yes, sir. Got it right here." The little man pulled a fist full of change and a couple of wadded up bills from his pants pocket. He fished a ten dollar bill out of the collection and held it up.

"Only ten spot I've had in a while. Do I have to give it back?" he asked in an apprehensive tone.

"Just swap it to me for this one," Craig said, handing him another bill and taking Johnny's bill. He put it an envelope and placed it in his coat pocket.

"Now, show us where you found the package."

Johnny One Eye led them to the rear door of the bar and opened it. He pointed to the stone step below the door's threshold.

"It was sitting right there," he said. "On the stoop."

"Was there anybody around back here when you found it?" Craig asked.

"Nobody but me," Johnny replied.

"Okay, thanks, Johnny. We'll catch you later," Craig said.

The two detectives were in a small alleyway that ran behind the building. Directly across from them was the blank wall of a building housing bail bond offices. The alley led north to the rear of a building that faced onto Market Street and south to Congress Alley, which ran beside city hall, the police court and police headquarters. It was blocked at that end by a large dumpster. The back door of Holly's was not visible from any of those buildings.

"Looks like he picked a good spot to leave it without being seen," McAllister said.

"That's for damn sure. This asshole is crafty but he's getting real cocky. Maybe he's screwed up and left prints on some of this stuff."

"Well, if your friend Johnny can be believed and this is our guy, we've wasted a lot of time on Jerome Lewis. Guess I set us off on a wild goose chase."

Craig turned to face his young partner.

"Scott, that's the way it happens sometimes. You have to run leads out and go where it takes you. Besides, we all thought Lewis looked good too. And he still does. Johnny's brain has been pretty well pickled. He's not the most reliable witness in the world. We can't scratch Lewis off the list just on his statement."

"What happened to his eye, anyway?"

"He used to be a pretty good jockey. Rode at Churchill Downs and some of the other good tracks. Then a horse broke down on him. Threw him into the rail and broke it. The jagged end tore his eye out. Jocks don't have much insurance, so they just sewed it up. He couldn't ride any more, so he started drinking. Now he's a sandwich runner."

Craig stepped back into the bar and approached the owner.

"Holly, did you take the call when a man called for Johnny this morning?" he asked.

"Sure did," Holly replied. "Johnny doesn't get many phone calls. In fact I think that's the first one he's ever gotten here. Actually, the guy called twice. Johnny was on a run the first time. I told him to call back in about fifteen minutes and he did."

"What time were the two calls?' Craig asked.

"The first one was about 7:15 and the second one about 7:30. Johnny was running coffee and two sausage and egg sandwiches over to Tom Denton in police court, so I knew he wouldn't be gone long."

"What did the caller say?" Craig asked.

"He just asked to speak to Johnny. I think he said Johnny the food runner or something like that. The second time, he just asked if Johnny was back yet."

"He didn't ask for Johnny One Eye?"

"Nope, I'm pretty sure he said Johnny the food runner. Why? What's going on?"

"The man who called may be a suspect in one of our cases," Craig said. "Did he sound like a white man to you?"

"Oh, yeah, definitely, and an educated white man at that. He didn't really have a Louisville accent, if you know what I mean. Sounded more like from back east somewhere."

"Would you know his voice if you heard it again?"

"Yeah, I think I would. His accent was unusual. You know, I'm from Detroit, so all you local people sound funny to me. But this guy's voice was different, more clipped. I might know it if I heard it again."

"Well, if you do, give me a call, Holly," Craig said, handing him a business card. "Right away. It could be important. Listen to your customers at lunch and after work. If you even think you hear the guy, let me know."

"Will do, John."

Out on the street, the two detectives looked at one another.

"Beginning to look more like a white guy, isn't it, John?" McAllister said.

"Yeah, I guess. Let's go give the boss the good news. Not only does it look like we've been focusing on the wrong guy but we don't have a clue what the right one looks like. Our hope of a positive ID depends on a one-eyed ex-jockey and a Lebanese bartender from Detroit. I hope Patterson has come up with something off that packaging. We definitely need a break."

Chapter Thirteen

Louisville, Kentucky .Tuesday, May 14, 1968, 10:54 a. m.

Doris Purcell had lived in a three story apartment house on West Broadway, near Shawnee Park and the river. Her apartment was on the second floor in the rear of the building. Craig and McAllister had just completed an exhaustive search of the apartment. They knew little more than they had when they started.

Purcell had a closet full of expensive clothes and at least thirty pairs of shoes. She had six bottles of beer, a dozen eggs and a pound of butter in the refrigerator and two cans of soup on a shelf. Her liquor cabinet was well stocked, however, and there were signs that she occasionally used the apartment for entertaining clients.

One of the drawers in her bedroom contained dozens of condoms and a dog leash and collar. There were also whips, chains and masks of various types and sizes. Miss Purcell was apparently well prepared to cater to the needs of her clients, whatever they might be.

The apartment was clean and well kept. Once the fingerprint technicians had finished their work, the detectives had gone through the accumulated mail in her box and found nothing of interest. There was very little of a personal nature in the entire place. It seemed as though the woman might have slept there and entertained there and little else.

The day was hot and muggy and the ancient air conditioner wheezing in one window did little to help out. Both men's shirts were sweated through and sticking to them. They had shed their sport coats long before. Craig sat down heavily in an overstuffed chair in the living room and wiped his streaming forehead. McAllister was examining the record collection beside the expensive hi-fi console.

"It looks like Miss Purcell was doing very well for herself in her line of work," Craig said. "This is a little more uptown than the average street whore's pad."

"No address book or list of clients anywhere," McAllister said. "Probably in her purse, wherever it may be. It's pretty clear he didn't cut her up here. Maybe in a hotel room somewhere?"

"Maybe, although you'd think the maids would have found it by now. There had to be a hell of a lot of blood, even if she was on that tarp when he did her. I think he's got a safe house some place that he took her to. He's getting more complex as he goes along.

You know, he starts out snatching girls off the street and cutting them up right in the same area, then moves to Central Park, then to where we don't know. Now he's taking pieces away, sending them to me. His rage is growing and he's putting more organization into his kills."

"Nobody came up with anything last night from the hotel canvass?" McAllister asked.

"Not a thing, although we need to do it again tomorrow night. A lot of the people who work on Saturday nights are off Monday and Tuesday."

The outer door opened and Colbert and Burns came into the apartment. They had been canvassing the other apartments and the neighboring houses. Colbert flopped down on the sofa with a loud sigh.

"Nada, nada, nada," he said. "Nobody knows nothing, nobody saw nothing. The neighbors in the building all thought Purcell was a dance instructor for Arthur Murray. That's the story she put out. They've seen her bring men home a few times but didn't make anything of it. Just thought she was having dates like any normal red blooded girl."

"Yeah, well, if they got a look at her tool chest in the bedroom there and her supply of condoms, they might get a different picture," Craig replied.

"Oh, really," Colbert said with a grin. "Our girl has some toys, does she?"

"Just the usual collection of whips, masks and so forth," Craig said. "We're done here. Let's grab some lunch."

As they drove east on Broadway, headed downtown, McAllister noted large groups of young black males congregating on several street corners. The looks directed toward the two obvious unmarked police cars were decidedly hostile.

"You know, John, it is really getting bad down here in the west end," McAllister said. "I talked to Dave Randall the other day and he said they can't make a run at night without getting shellacked with rocks and bottles.

He's getting transferred to Traffic effective tomorrow and he's a happy boy to be getting out of the Fourth District."

"Yeah, I'll bet he is," Craig replied. "I think it's just a matter of time before the whole place blows up. What's Randall going to do, ride a bike?"

"Right, Sergeant Donaldson's his uncle. He got Dave assigned to motorcycles. They're evidently taking on five new guys."

"What about you?" Craig asked. "Sounds like a better deal than working for George Marvin. You interested in riding a cycle?'

"Nope, I'm interested in being a homicide detective and hoping like hell I can wrangle a transfer before this temporary assignment is over."

"If we could catch this guy, it wouldn't be a problem," Craig said. "Right now, we're all on everybody's shit list. I just wondered if you'd thought about a fallback plan, in case it doesn't work out."

"Not really. Guess I just keep hoping we'll get lucky. If it doesn't work out right now, maybe it will later on."

"You and Jenny set a date yet?" Craig asked.

"In the fall sometime. With my seniority, that's about the only time I can get a vacation. We're going to go shopping for rings tonight."

"She's a beautiful girl, Scott, and what she sees in you, I can't imagine."

"Yeah, I'm no bargain for sure."

"Just kidding, partner. I hope you two have a long and happy life together."

"What about Susan, John? Any chance of getting it worked out?"

"I heard from her lawyer yesterday," Craig said. "Looks like she intends to go through with the divorce. I'm pretty sure she's got a new guy on the hook. Knowing Susan, I hope for his sake he's well heeled. I think - -"

Craig stopped speaking in mid-sentence and focused on the radio. An electronic tone had been sounded, indicating a holdup in progress.

"All cars in the vicinity of Royal Bank, 8th and Broadway, an ADT silent holdup alarm. Cars responding, use caution," the dispatcher said.

"That's the next block, Scott," Craig said quickly. "Turn left here and let's go through the alley."

McAllister whipped the old Dodge into a tight turn and headed east in the alley. In his mirror, he saw Burns and Colbert following closely behind him. The piercing tone came over the radio at ten second intervals, adding to the tension.

The two cars pulled to a stop across 8th Street from the rear of the bank. There were no pedestrians in front of the building. A battered Buick was parked beside the bank. Its smoky exhaust spewed fumes into the air. A lone black male was visible behind the wheel.

"602 Adam, we're in the rear of the bank with 602 Baker. A tan Buick parked in front headed south on 8th, one black male driver. L28-187 Kentucky tags. Nobody else visible."

"10-4, 602 Adam. Be advised they do not answer the phone at the bank. All cars, be advised plain clothes detectives are at the scene."

"Scott, get over there and cover the driver," Craig ordered. "Come in behind him, if you can. Larry, you and Sandy get behind those parked cars on this side ."

McAllister looked up and saw a Louisville Transit bus coming south on 8th. He grabbed Craig's arm and motioned toward it. As it drew abreast of them, the two men ran across the street behind it, using its bulk for cover. Craig went to the corner of the building by the alley where he could cover both the driver and the door of the bank. McAllister approached the Buick from the rear on the passenger side.

McAllister's pulse was pounding so loudly in his head that he was sure the driver of the Buick could hear it. He had a cold metallic taste in his mouth. From the moment he got out of the car, he experienced a heightened sense of awareness of all his surroundings. It was almost like he was looking at a movie of himself doing these things. His short barreled Smith and Wesson .357 magnum was in his hand and he realized that he was ready to shoot, even though he didn't remember drawing it from his holster.

Coming up on the open passenger side window of the Buick, he saw that the driver was a young skinny black man wearing a "do-rag" on his head and sunglasses. He was drumming nervously on the steering wheel with his left hand. His right hand was by his side, clutching a chrome plated pistol. He was staring at the door of the bank intently, unaware of McAllister's presence.

McAllister jerked the door of the car open and pointed his pistol at the man's right temple.

"Police! Freeze, asshole! Don't even blink."

The man jumped visibly but made no other move.

"Take your hand off the gun and put both hands behind your head. Do it now!"

The driver started moving his hand away from the gun toward his head. At that moment, the door of the bank burst open and two men carrying long guns came running toward the car. They had masks made from nylon stockings over their faces. As they exited, a loud alarm bell on the wall of the building began ringing. McAllister reached in and grabbed the driver by the shirt and, with a convulsive jerk, dragged him from behind the steering wheel and half out the open door.

He heard Craig yell, "Police, drop your guns!" The final syllables were lost in the roar of a shotgun, followed by a burst of gunfire. He dragged the driver the rest of the way out into the street and knelt on the man's chest. The driver's hands came up grabbing at his throat. With a vicious backhanded swing, he brought his heavy pistol against the side of the man's head. It was as hard as he had ever hit anyone. The man's hands dropped and he went limp.

Kneeling beside the car and looking through the window, McAllister could see one of the robbers had backed into the offset entryway of the bank. Evidently, the people inside had locked the door because he was pulling fruitlessly on the handle. Giving up his effort, he opened the breech of his double-barreled shotgun, kicking two empty hulls out. He plugged two more shells into the weapon and stepped out of the entryway.

Glancing to his left, McAllister saw Craig on his knees by the body of the other gunman. His face was bleeding and the right sleeve of his shirt was bloody. His short barreled Smith and Wesson was hanging limply in his right hand. With his left hand, he was reaching for the gunman's weapon, which was lying on the sidewalk beside him. McAllister recognized it as a military .30 caliber carbine.

The gunman by the bank door raised his shotgun and pointed it at Craig. Without conscious thought, McAllister leaned across the top of the car and fired six shots at the man as fast as he could pull the trigger. The first round would have been enough. Striking him just above the left ear, it passed through his skull and exited the other side. A red mist erupted from the side of his head, forming a nimbus around it. His lifeless body toppled to the sidewalk, the other rounds striking him as he fell.

Falling back against the car, McAllister fumbled for his speedloaders on his belt and reloaded his pistol. His ears were ringing from the gunfire. His nose was full of the pungent odor of cordite. Then he noticed another figure lying in the middle of the street. Gradually his mind began to recognize the brightly patterned sport coat. He realized that the prone figure was Sandy Burns and that his body was lying in the middle of a rapidly spreading pool of blood. Larry Colbert was kneeling beside him, attempting to stanch the flow of blood with his own sport coat.

McAllister looked up to see Craig standing beside him, his bloody right arm hanging loosely at his side.

"Thanks, Scott. You saved my ass for sure," Craig said. "Can you get cuffs on that asshole you're sitting on? I can't use my right arm."

"Yeah. What about the guys on the sidewalk?"

"They're both dead. Sandy broke from cover when you went after the driver as they were coming out of the bank. I guess he was coming to help you. The guy with the carbine hit him in the chest before he could get across the street. Larry and I both opened up on him. He went down but the other guy hit me as I was trying to get to him and get that carbine away from him. A ricochet, I think, but I can't raise my arm."

McAllister rolled the unresisting driver onto his stomach and quickly cuffed his hands behind his back. The street was rapidly filling with police cars and uniformed officers were hurrying toward them. Several men were loading Burns onto a stretcher. His face was waxy and lifeless looking. His shirt and the front of his sport coat were covered in blood. Quickly, a station wagon backed up to the group and they loaded Burns in. Colbert climbed in the back with him and the car pulled away with the yelp of its electronic siren adding to the unreality of the situation.

McAllister stood beside the old Buick, trying to come to grips mentally with what had happened. Five minutes earlier, he, Craig and the others had been on their way to lunch. Now he was standing near two dead men. Craig was wounded and Burns was critically injured, perhaps dead. He had killed a man. It was the first time he had ever used his weapon in the line of duty and he couldn't quite fathom how so much violence and death had happened so quickly.

A uniformed patrolman took custody of the driver from him and led him away.

Suddenly, he realized that Lieutenant Garrard was there, in the middle of the street, directing detectives in the act of preserving the scene. Burns' pistol was lying in the street next to Colbert's blood drenched sport coat. On the sidewalk, someone had spread sheets over the bodies of the two gunmen. Craig was seated on an overturned garbage can with his shirt off while a patrolman wrapped a bandage around his right arm. The occupants of the bank were being shepherded into police cars to be taken to headquarters for their statements. A group of police supervisors were clustered in the middle of the street, their white uniform shirts stark in the sunshine. He saw all this through a haze like he was watching a movie that was slightly out of focus.

"Scott, you all right?"

He realized that Garrard was standing before him with a quizzical expression on his face.

"Yeah, I'm OK, boss. Just trying to get my head together."

"Well, John Craig says you had it together a few minutes ago. He says the one guy would have killed him for sure if you hadn't dropped him when you did. Good work!"

"I couldn't let anything happen to John, boss. He owes me lunch," McAllister replied.

"Let's get you down to the office and get your statement. I'll take it myself. Don't talk to anybody until I get there."

"Yes, sir. What about John? Is he hurt bad?"

"Looks like he got some buckshot in his arm and some cuts on his face. Part of the buckshot ricocheted off the bank wall. He'll be all right. I'm sending him to General."

"And Sandy? Is he--"

"They say he had a pulse when he left here, Scott. We'll just have to see. Go on to the office. Take your car. I'll send John to the hospital in another one. I'll be there as soon as I can."

"Hey, Lieutenant Garrard, you need to see this. You, too, Scott."

The caller was Rick Rovinelli, who was kneeling by the body of the man McAllister had shot. He had pulled the nylon mask up, exposing the man's features. It was Jerome Lewis.

"Son of a bitch," Garrard said. "I guess he decided to get a head start on financing the revolution."

"Boss, I had no idea who it was," McAllister said.

"Scott, don't sweat it. His ass was paid for when he put on that mask and picked up that shotgun."

* * *

Garrard switched off the tape recorder and laid down his pen. He stood up and stretched, easing the kinks in his back.

"Okay, Scott," he said. "That'll do it for now. I'll get it typed and you can stop by tomorrow and sign it."

"Stop by? Boss, I figured on coming to work tomorrow. We've still got a lot of leads to run down and I don't think John will be able to work. So I ----."

"Scott, you're on administrative leave until we can finish the investigation. It was a righteous shooting, so it shouldn't take but a day or so. Nonetheless, you, Craig and Colbert need to stay home for a couple of days. I'll have to wrap it up and present the case to the Commonwealth Attorney for his review. You can't come back to work until he says it was a righteous shooting."

"But, boss, what about the task force? Hell, that's half of us off the case."

"We'll get it done. Why don't you run by General and check on John and Sandy, then head home? I'll call you tomorrow when your statement's ready. And, I'll need your gun to send to the lab. Stop by the supply room and get them to issue you a replacement until we get yours back. Is that departmental issue or your personal weapon?"

"It's mine, sir. I have a letter on file to carry it."

"Okay," Garrard said. "I picked up your casings where you dumped them beside the car. All .38 special, so there's no problem there. The press likes to make a big thing out of it when police use .357 magnum ammunition in a shooting. I'll see you tomorrow."

"Yes, sir."

Garrard gathered up his notes and started down the hall to the homicide office.

Major Bishop called out to him as he passed the open door of the Chief of Detectives' Office.

"Garrard, I need to see you."

The lieutenant changed his direction and went in. Bishop was standing by the window. He turned and said,

"Have you cleared those cases yet?"

"Rovinelli is booking the two dead guys by proxy right now, Major. Bank robbery, attempted murder, malicious shooting and wounding on both of them."

"What about the murder cases on those whores? Have you charged that nigger, Lewis, with those yet?"

"Major, we don't have enough to make a case on Lewis for those charges."

"What the hell do you mean? Wasn't he your main suspect? Haven't you been following him around for a month? Why can't you make a case on him?"

"Major, like I told you yesterday, we stopped surveilling him when it became obvious he couldn't have killed Doris Purcell and it was looking more and more like a white guy was involved."

"Garrard, nobody gives a damn about that now. He's dead and he won't put up any argument. Clear some of those first cases on him and say we're looking at him for the others. Gets the heat off of us and gets us some good press for a change."

"What happens if the Ripper hits again after we do that?" Garrard asked.

"We call him a copy cat killer. Say he's just trying to pick up where Lewis left off. Hell, use your imagination, man. Besides, there's a good chance Lewis was the Ripper. Even if he wasn't, we can make it look like he was. Takes some of the wind out of these loudmouth nigger preachers who're going around saying we aren't working hard on these cases because they're just black whores."

"Major, I can't go along with that. I know Lewis wasn't the Ripper and I can't stand up and say he was."

"If you can't, I may have to find me a homicide lieutenant who can. You may not find being back in uniform much to your liking. Shift work, no take home car and all that."

Garrard stepped up close to the big man, who took an involuntary step back.

"Bishop, it's the prerogative of the Chief of Police to decide where I work. If you can get me transferred, so be it. But, if you try this bullshit you're talking about, I promise you I'll give the whole story to the news media and blow your fat ass right out of this big office you're so fond of. You've known me twenty years and you know I'll do it. So keep that in mind."

The angry lieutenant turned and stalked out of the office. Behind him, a shaken Bishop sat down heavily in his oversized swivel chair. He composed himself, then picked up the phone and dialed a number.

"This is Major Bishop. We're going to have trouble with Garrard. He threatens to go to the media if we stick with the story on Lewis."

He listened for a moment, then replied.

"Yes, sir. I'll take care of it tomorrow."

* * *

McAllister stood with Jenny and Craig in the hallway outside the intensive care unit at General Hospital. Craig's right arm was in a sling and his face was discolored in several spots where the emergency room crew had painted his wounds with betadine. Jenny gave an involuntary shudder when she looked at Craig's face.

"John, you look like all the guys from 'The Spirit of '76' rolled into one. All you need is a fife, a drum and a flag," McAllister said.

"Scott, be quiet," Jenny commanded. "He's here in one piece, thank the Lord."

"Thanks to your boyfriend, too, Jenny," Craig said. "If it weren't for him, I wouldn't be here. So I'll let him get away with a couple of cracks for the time being."

Larry Colbert came through the double doors at the end of the hallway. He was in his shirtsleeves and his shirt was darkened with blood stains in several places.

"Any new word on Sandy?" he asked.

"He's still holding on," Craig replied. "The surgeon came out a little while ago and told us the bullet missed his heart but nicked his subclavian artery. They've got everything sewed up and think they have all the bleeding stopped. If he makes it through the night, they think he's got a chance."

"The hall in the ER is full of cops," Colbert said, "wanting to donate blood. Do they need any?"

"They went though several units before they got it stopped," Craig replied. "So, yeah, they could use some."

"I'll put out the word. John, are you all right?" Colbert said with a questioning look.

"A little sore but I'll make it. How about you?"

"I can't stop to deal with it yet. I couldn't believe it when I saw him break from cover and start running across the street. I know he wanted to help you, Scott but, hell, you were handling it. You didn't need any help."

"Did they identify the other guy yet?" Craig asked.

"Yeah, Luther Williams. He was in La Grange at the same time Lewis was. Doing ten years for armed robbery. Guess he was trying to teach our boy the trade."

"Who was the driver?" McAllister asked.

"Albert Mucker AKA 'Sweet Pea'. He has several misdemeanor arrests, gambling and so forth but this is his first felony bust. He's down on the prison ward with a serious concussion. You sure took the starch out of him, Scott," Colbert said with a grin.

"Yeah, well, it seemed like the thing to do at the time. Garrard take your statement yet?" McAllister wanted to know.

"Just finished up a few minutes ago. Our boss is seriously pissed about something."

"Over this shooting?" Craig asked.

"No, I think it's got to do with the headquarters brass. He had nothing but good things to say about us and the way it went down. Says he's putting us all in for a Mayor's Award."

Craig snorted. "That and a dime will get us a small coffee at White Castle."

"Still, it's nice of him to do it," Colbert replied.

Craig looked suspiciously at Colbert. "Are you feeling all right? I never heard you say anything a boss did was nice before this."

"Hey, man, I like Garrard. For a honky lieutenant, he's a standup guy. I may make him an honorary brother."

"Larry, did Sandy ever mention any family to you?" McAllister asked. "Personnel has nobody listed as next of kin."

"He was an orphan. Raised in the Masonic Widows and Orphans Home up on Frankfort Avenue. We went up there one day to see an old teacher of his. I think his only relative is an old aunt who lives down in Glasgow. He said he hasn't seen her in years. Guess we're his family. I'm going to go spread the word about the blood donations."

Colbert started off and then stopped and turned to McAllister.

"Scott, my man, you did a hell of a job out there today. I want you on my side in any firefight I ever get into."

"Thanks, Larry. Let's all get some coffee. I'll tell the ICU nurse where we are. If there's any change, she can call us in the coffee shop."

The four of them left the hall. Behind them in the darkened ICU ward, the monitor over Sandy Burns' bed beeped periodically and the green line of his tenuous hold on life danced across the screen.

*   *   *

Later that evening, McAllister and Jenny sat over the remains of a pizza at Kenny Pastor's Pizza Parlor. Garrard had come to the hospital with two detectives from the Homicide Squad's late watch. He posted them outside the ICU and chased Craig and the others away, promising to call them if there was any change in Burns' condition.

McAllister had been staring out the window without speaking for several minutes. Finally he turned back and smiled at Jenny.

"Penny for your thoughts, mister," she said.

"I'm afraid they're not worth that much. I was just trying to make some sense out of all that went on and I can't do it. I killed a man today and, although I can't feel bad about it, I'm sorry it had to happen."

"Scott, you had no choice. The man was going to kill your partner. John said he was pointing his gun right at him."

"I know, Jen, and I accept that fact. I just wish it didn't have to go down that way."

Jenny was looking over McAllister's shoulder at the rear door of the restaurant.

"Oh, God, here comes Mike Renyard. Now, Scott, keep your cool," she said.

"Don't worry. I'll stay as cool as he does. Maybe he won't want to speak to us."

However, Renyard walked directly to their table.

"Well, it's the lovebirds. I hear you had a busy day, Officer McAllister."

"You could say that," McAllister replied.

"Yes, well, we'll be taking a close look at your actions starting tomorrow. The Director of Safety has assigned me to conduct a complete inquiry into the shooting. I hope for your sake everything is above board. With the tense situation in the west end, we can't tolerate any trigger happy white cops killing black men."

McAllister flushed at the insulting tone the man used.

"Sounds like you've already made up your mind, Renyard. Inquire all you want of me tomorrow. Tonight, I'm off duty and I don't feel like talking to you. So take your bullshit somewhere else."

"I'll have plenty to ask you tomorrow. So be in the Chief's Office at 9:00 a. m., in uniform. You can consider that an order. And you might as well get used to wearing that uniform again. You'll be in it for quite a while, if you get to keep your job. Nice to see you, Jenny. You're as lovely as ever."

Renyard turned and walked back to the group he had come in with. Jenny looked at McAllister with a bemused expression on her face.

"You know, Scott, I don't think he likes you very much."

Both of them burst out laughing. Then Jenny sobered and said,

"He's going to try to do something to you. It's because of us. He called me yesterday and tried to talk me into going out with him again. I told him we were engaged and he really went off on me. He told me I was a fool and that you didn't have a future in the department. He wound up telling me he'd be around when I came to my senses. Sometimes I think he's not quite right in the head. He just ignores what he doesn't want to hear. I'm afraid of him and what he might try to do."

"Well, the only living witnesses to the shooting that I know of are John and Larry. Sandy was down before I shot Lewis. I don't think Renyard's going to be able to get them to say the shooting wasn't righteous. But he probably can get me reassigned off the task force. We'll just have to wait and see. Lieutenant Garrard is on my side and he's well respected throughout city government. Let's get out of here."

They paid their tab and walked out the rear door, passing Renyard and his party. He looked up as they passed and gave them a flippant wave of his hand, making a remark to his companions that caused a burst of laughter from them. Jenny grabbed McAllister by his arm and urged him out the door.

* * *

Wednesday, May 15, 1968. 4:34 a. m.

The green life line on the monitor over Sandy Burns' bed flattened itself out and the intermittent beep changed to a loud, constant tone. The ICU nurse came running to the bed, felt for a pulse and then hit a bedside button, sending a Code Blue alarm to the ICU team. She began to perform CPR on the young officer and was joined by the members of the team in a matter of seconds. They worked feverishly for several minutes. Finally, the chief resident stepped back and pulled off his mask.

"We couldn't save him," the doctor said. "Too much internal bleeding. Put the time of death down as 5:04 a. m. Somebody tell the cops out in the hall and call the coroner."

The team dispersed and the young ICU nurse pulled the sheet up over the young cop's face and walked back to her desk. A single tear fell on the chart as she made the time of death notation.

Chapter Fourteen

Louisville, Kentucky. Wednesday, May 15, 1968. 9:00 a. m.

Scott McAllister, wearing his uniform as Renyard had ordered, went in the main entrance of police headquarters. As he went up the stairs to the lobby, he passed the bronze plaques listing the LPD officers who had been killed in the line of duty. The Detective Bureau desk man had called him earlier that morning and advised him of the death of Sandy Burns. The thought that Sandy's name would soon be added to those plaques was more than he wanted to deal with. His mind still couldn't reconcile all the events of the preceding day. In addition to that, he was headed to what seemed to be shaping up as a serious session of after the fact second guessing, conducted by a man whose hostility toward him was evident. With these unpleasant thoughts in his mind, he opened the door into the outer office of the Chief of Police. The uniformed sergeant seated behind the counter glanced up at him.

"Officer McAllister, you are to report to Lieutenant Garrard in the Detective Bureau. He has orders for you."

"I was instructed by the assistant Director of Safety to report here at nine," Scott replied.

"That interview has been postponed. Mr. Renyard is in with the Chief now. They will contact you later."

McAllister left the office and went to Garrard's office on the second floor. The lieutenant was seated at his desk with a dark look on his face.

"Come in, Scott and close the door," he said. Then he picked up a document from his desk and handed it to McAllister.

"This is a personnel order relieving you of your temporary assignment to Homicide and transferring you to the Parks and Special Services Section, effective today. You will be assigned there until a determination has been made as to whether your actions yesterday were lawful and in compliance with departmental regulations regarding the use of force."

McAllister stared at the expressionless face of the lieutenant, puzzled by his formal tone and the bureaucratic phrasing of his words. He reached out and took the letter from Garrard's hand.

"I was ordered by the Chief of Police just thirty minutes ago to tell you that in just those words, Scott. The assistant Director of Safety, Renyard, is heading up an investigation into the shooting. He seems to think you did something wrong. Anyway, they are putting you in this assignment rather than sending you back to the Fourth District, because of the possible fallout if it turns out that you killed a black man without justification."

Scott exploded. "Lieutenant, this is total bullshit. This jerk, Renyard - - "

He stopped speaking as Garrard held up a warning hand and pointed upward to the air vent above his head. He then shoved a scrap of paper toward McAllister, who picked it up and read it.

DON'T TALK HERE. MEET AT CUNNINGHAM'S – NOON.

"Yes, sir. Who do I report to in Parks?" McAllister asked.

"Sergeant Arthur has been notified of your transfer. He's expecting you. You know where their office is?"

"Yes, sir, I think so. Down at the other end of the hall on this floor, isn't it?"

"That's right. Scott, you did a good job for me and I'm sure this will all turn out right for you. It is tragic that we lost Sandy Burns. He was a fine officer. Good luck."

Garrard extended his hand and McAllister shook it. He left the Detective Bureau and went down the hall to the small office housing Parks and Special Services. Commonly called "The Squirrel Police," the unit was reputed to be a dumping ground for misfits, alcoholics, and old timers who wanted to retire in place. It was the last place McAllister ever wanted to work.

Sergeant Arthur, a stocky little man with porcine features and a flattop haircut that looked like a scrub brush, did not invite him to sit down.

"Well, brother, seems you have your ass in a jackpot, hmm? So they send you down to the old Sarge to straighten out. You just do what you're told and we'll get along fine, brother. You turn out on the evening shift today, riding 516. Your beat is the east end Parks, especially Cherokee and Seneca. You'll be riding with John Zarnecki, the mad Polack. Any questions, brother?"

"What time is roll call, Sergeant, and what exactly does Parks do?"

"Roll call is at 5:45 p. m., right here in this office. There's only two cars on our evening shift, and Zarnecki is the acting sergeant. Do what he tells you and you'll learn what Parks does, quick enough. And to get along in here, you take care of the old Sarge and he'll take care of you. Know what I mean, brother? Now, I'm awful busy, so see you later."

Puzzled by the abrupt and strange turn of events, McAllister went to his car and drove to his home, then changed into civilian clothes for his meeting with Garrard. He called Jenny at work and explained what had happened that morning.

"Scott, that is so unfair. How can they say you did anything wrong when you saved John Craig's life? And they're doing this after Sandy Burns died at these people's hands. What could they possibly be thinking?"

"I believe our friend Renyard is trying to jam me up and nobody in the department seems to have the balls to stop him. But I think Lieutenant Garrard is a straight arrow. I'm anxious to hear what he has to say. I'll call after we meet and tell you what went on. Love you."

At 11:55, McAllister pulled into the parking lot of Cunningham's Restaurant at 5ᵗʰ and Breckinridge. A couple of blocks south of downtown, the sprawling building had started life as a livery stable in the late 1800's. It had also been a whorehouse, a speakeasy, and finally a restaurant. Its back section and upper floors were divided into small rooms that had originally been cribs for the working girls in its earlier existence as a house of ill repute. Now they were private dining rooms seating six or eight people. It was an extremely popular eating place and a good location for a private meeting.

As he went toward the back entrance, McAllister saw Larry Colbert beckoning him from the doorway.

"We've got a room upstairs. Come on," Colbert said and led him up the stairs to a room at the very back of the building. Garrard was in the room, along with Craig and, to McAllister's surprise, Captain Emmett Hall. He had only met the Assistant Chief of Detectives on a couple of occasions. He knew, however, that both Craig and Lieutenant Garrard thought highly of him.

"Come in and sit down, Scott. Let's order some lunch and then we'll get down to business."

The five men ordered lunch and then Garrard began to speak.

"First of all, the task force is being restructured. We're all off of it and back to our original assignments, except for you, Scott. I've been ordered to turn over all the files to Lieutenant Dan Bittner, who is coming in from Internal Affairs to take over. He is bringing six detectives with him from I. A., none of whom would know a homicide investigation from a church social. John here is to work with them for a week, while he is recuperating from his injuries, and bring them up to speed on what we have done so far. Then he goes back to Homicide with the rest of us."

He paused and looked at the others with a whimsical expression on his face.

"Sir, who is Lieutenant Bittner?" Scott asked. "Is he an experienced investigator?"

Garrard smiled.

"He's the Director of Safety's fair-haired boy. He spent most of his career so far working nights in the record bureau and going to college, also studying for promotion exams. He came out number one on both the sergeant's and lieutenant's tests. When he made Lieutenant six months ago, they put him in I. A. Since they work out of the Director's office, he has evidently convinced Mr. Farris that he is the reincarnation of Sherlock Holmes."

"What's this all about, boss?" Colbert asked. "What the hell is going on? They act like they don't want to solve these cases."

"Oh, they want to clear them all right and they're not too particular who they clear them on," Garrard replied. "Major Bishop tried to order me last night to clear all the cases on Lewis, in spite of the fact that we couldn't begin to prove it. He said if we had other killings after that, we could call them the work of a copycat. I balked on him, so this morning, the Director of Safety orders the Chief to take me off the case, along with the rest of you, and hand it over to Bittner. Bittner reports directly to Bishop, taking Captain Hall out of the loop. The order to send you to Parks, Scott, came right out of the Director's office. Your friend, Renyard, seemed to enjoy conveying it. He seems to have it in for you in a big way."

"It's over my girlfriend, boss. He keeps trying to date her and she keeps shutting him down. I guess he thinks if he makes me look bad, it'll make him look good to her. But she can't stand him."

"Where does the Chief stand on all this?" Craig asked.

Captain Hall spoke for the first time.

"He's got his hands full with the situation in the west end right now. He's got a month in the job and he's afraid his city is going to blow up in his face. So he's not inclined to try to buck the Director of Safety on this issue. I don't believe he thinks you did anything wrong yesterday, Scott, but he's just not ready to fight that battle right now. He thinks it might be a good idea to put you out of sight for a while."

"The main issue is that it looks like Bishop and Renyard are cooking up some kind of deal to clear these cases whether they can prove it or not," Garrard said. "Bishop would sell his soul to the devil if he thought the devil would make him Chief of Police. The rumor is that Renyard wants to run for Mayor next time and he may be promising our boy Farley the top job. Farris is an old fool who is not going to stand up to a strong guy like Renyard, so Renyard is pretty much running the show right now."

"Lieutenant, what were you trying to tell me in your office this morning?" McAllister asked.

"I'm pretty certain that Bishop has my office bugged and several other offices in the Bureau," Garrard replied. "Quite a few times, he has known about things that were said in there that I thought were unknown to anyone but me and the person I was talking to. He's famous for taping all his phone conversations and he usually wears a pocket recorder to any meeting. I guess he's trying to mold himself after J. Edgar Hoover. Anyway, you should assume that anything you say to him will be recorded. Do you know Sergeant Morris, the one they call 'Whispering Bill'?"

"Little short guy, looks like a weasel?" McAllister asked.

"That's him. He's Bishop's phone tap and bugging man. Comes and goes when he wants to and reports only to Bishop."

"So what do we do, now?" Colbert asked.

"Sit tight, do our jobs and see how this starts to play out. They'll have to tip their hand before long. Both Captain Hall and I have some contacts within city government that we are going to keep informed of this situation. In the meantime, I intend to continue to try to solve the killings of these six girls. I don't think the task force is capable of doing it and this bastard needs to be caught," Garrard said.

"What if they try to stop you from doing that, boss?" Craig asked.

"John, I've got twenty-eight years on the job. I can retire any time I want to. If they want to play games, I may do just that. But I'll take them down before I go."

"Yeah, but what about this bullshit investigation by Renyard of the shooting yesterday?" Colbert asked. "John, Scott and I have got to stay around for awhile. We can't afford to be sandbagged by some fucking politician who's trying to make a name for himself."

"Larry, we'll have to wait for them to show their hand" Captain Hall replied.

"Hopefully, it's just Renyard trying to impress Scott's girl, as he mentioned. If it goes further than that, we'll have to come out swinging. If they try to do anything other than hang medals on you men and on Sandy Burns, I'll be calling my own press conference."

"What shift did they assign you to, Scott?" Garrard asked.

"Evenings, working the east end with a guy named Zarnecki," McAllister replied.

"Ah, yes. The mad Polack," Garrard said. He, Hall and Craig all burst out laughing.

"What's the deal?" McAllister asked. "That's what Sergeant Arthur called him."

"Let's just say you're in for an experience," Garrard said. "You know my home and office numbers. Keep in touch and don't get discouraged. You have the ability to be a good detective. Captain Hall and I intend to see that you get the chance."

The waiter brought their orders and conversation dropped off, while they ate.

"Lunch is on me, gentlemen," Captain Hall said. They all stood and prepared to leave.

Colbert squeezed McAllister's bicep hard as they walked out together.

"You're a good man for a honkie, McAllister. I may make you an honorary brother, too," he said.

* * *

At 5:30 p. m. that day, McAllister reported to the Parks office. His uniform was impeccable and his shoes and leather gear gleamed. He wasn't sure what was in store for him in this new assignment but he wasn't going to get called down over his personal appearance. A glance at the three men seated in the small office told him that any worries on that account were groundless. Their uniforms were rumpled and their shoes and leather looked as if they had been buffed with a brick.

A short, thickset man, bald as a billiard ball, looked up from the paperwork on the desk before him.

"You must be McAllister. Come on in. I'm John Zarnecki. This is Reeves and Gladstone, the other half of our merry band."

Gladstone, a fat black man whose gun belt sagged almost to his knees, raised a hand in greeting but said nothing, continuing to eat the large sandwich he held in one hand. A good portion of its contents seemed to have been deposited on his shirt front.

Reeves, whose gray hair was as long as a rock star's, gestured toward a vacant chair at the small table, where teletype reports were scattered across the surface.

"Welcome to the last bastion of lost souls, the elite Parks and Special Services unit, although nobody knows what special services we're supposed to perform," he said, in melodramatic tones. "What did you do to be sentenced to our little group of exiles?"

Before McAllister could speak, Reeves answered his own question.

"Oh, yeah. McAllister. You're the hero from yesterday's bank robbery.

Hell of a way to treat a hero. You must have pissed some big cheese off drastically to get sent here."

"Richard, shut your mouth," Zarnecki said, tonelessly. "All right, you and Gladstone are 512, as usual, covering everything west of I-65. McAllister and I will be 516 and handle the east end. Remember to chase everybody out of the parks at midnight and keep an eye out for that dick shaker that's been working the lower road in Shawnee Park."

To McAllister, he said, "This wacko takes off all his clothes and sneaks up on couples parked down by the river. He knocks on the window and when they look up, he jacks off on their car, then takes off like a striped-ass ape. We've got a dozen complaints on him.

Okay, let's hit the bricks."

As they stored their nightsticks, flashlights and other paraphernalia in the Ford station wagon, Zarnecki said,

"I'll drive the first half and show you around. You got any questions, just ask me."

"Okay," McAllister said as they pulled out of the lot. "Just what is it we do?"

Zarnecki took a huge bite from a plug of chewing tobacco before answering.

"Primarily patrol the parks in our sector. Write some tickets every now and then, mostly for speeding and parking on the grass. Handle any runs that come out in the parks.

Other than that, we just ride. Evening shift is good. We usually ain't real busy and we don't have to put up with our dickhead sergeant, Arthur. Parks close at midnight, so we have to go through and chase everybody out. That's why we don't turn out until six o'clock."

They made a trip through each of the two major parks in their sector, Cherokee and Seneca. Zarnecki then drove through two smaller parks on River Road. He told McAllister that there were several smaller parks in the sector but most of their time was spent in the bigger ones.

Several hours later, McAllister was contemplating being bored to death for the first time in his police career. They had not received a single run and Zarnecki, after stopping at a small, neighborhood tavern for dinner, seemed to be content to cruise repeatedly through Cherokee park at a steady twenty miles an hour. It was a hot night and McAllister could feel the sweat coursing down his sides from under his arms. The back of his shirt was dampened clear through. His attempts at conversation with his partner were met, for the most part, by monosyllables and grunts.

Promptly at ten p. m., Zarnecki pulled the car to the side of the road.

"Your turn to drive," he said.

McAllister gladly climbed behind the wheel, grateful to have something to do.

As he pulled away, Zarnecki, still wearing his uniform cap, rested his head against the door post. In just a few minutes, he was snoring softly.

McAllister decided to have a look at Seneca Park for a change of scenery. Hanging his left arm out the window, he headed in that direction. Suddenly, he became aware of a damp feeling on the underside of his left arm. Stopping the car, he yanked his arm in the window and raised it. He could see a dark stain on the light blue uniform shirt and on his upper arm. He opened the car door and, with the dome light on., saw that both his shirt and arm were stained with tobacco juice. The driver's door on the white car was heavily streaked with the same stains.

"Damn it, Zarnecki, can't you spit any further than that?" he asked his recumbent partner, who raised his cap brim and eyed him with an oblique glance.

"Oh, yeah. I meant to tell you about watching out for that. But, don't worry, it washes right out."

He went promptly back to sleep, leaving McAllister fuming and contemplating what was starting out to be a very long assignment.

*　*　*

Later that evening, Craig sat morosely in his recliner, contemplating his empty house. His shoulder and his face were hurting like hell and he was just about ready to pour himself another scotch on the rocks, strictly for its analgesic effect. The first two had not helped but maybe the next one would.

His soon to be ex-wife had called him earlier, expressing concern over his injuries and wanting to know what to tell the children. Her concern was obviously tempered by her desire to learn if his physical condition was going to prevent him from keeping the appointment in her lawyer's office the next day to sign the divorce papers. Upon learning that he wasn't in any danger of dying and that he planned to be there, she cheerfully rang off with an admonition for him to take care of himself. The phony concern in her voice was almost more than Craig could bear. He wondered how he could have known so little about a woman he thought he knew so well.

Gingerly pushing himself to his feet, he went to the breakfast counter and clumsily splashed another three inches of Chivas Regal into his glass and added a couple of ice cubes. He was already tired of having to use his left hand to do everything.

He reached over and flipped on the small television set on the counter. In a few seconds, the evening anchor man on WAVE TV filled the screen.

Then the scene shifted to a reporter interviewing a group of young black males. They were gathered outside a bar on West Broadway and were shouting at the reporter and camera man. From what he could discern, they were angry about the shooting of the two bank robbers. Several of them had their clinched fists raised in the black power salute made famous by the Black Panther party.

Abruptly, Michael Renyard's face came on the screen. He was being interviewed in front of police headquarters. Craig listened in disbelief as Renyard made reference to a "surprise witness" who "gave a different account" of the shooting. He promised a full and complete investigation and assured the station's viewers with great sincerity that the city would not tolerate any excessive use of force by its police department. No mention was made of Officer Sandy Burns or of Craig's injuries.

Renyard continued to talk, describing the "new" task force that had been established to work on the Ripper homicides and lavishing great praise on Lieutenant Dan Bittner and his hand picked team of detectives. Bittner was standing beside him, freshly scrubbed and trying to look modest. No mention was made of Lieutenant Jim Garrard or the team of detectives who had been working on the case for weeks.

Craig slowly set his drink down on the counter, resisting the temptation to throw it at the television set. It would do no good and would just make a mess for him to clean up, one handed. Besides, what he really wanted to do was throw something at Renyard, like a left hook. The smarmy bastard was playing political games with homicide cases, which tore at the center of Craig's professional soul. He could not conceive anyone leaving anything undone to solve a murder, any murder. This asshole was not only doing nothing to solve them, he was impeding their solution. There had to be a reason for his actions, more than just political ambition. There was too much that could backfire on him.

Craig's strong affection for Scott McAllister was a factor in all of this, also. He believed that McAllister had the ability to be a great detective. In addition to that, he was a good person, strong and loyal with better instincts for the street than Craig had ever seen in so young a man. The fact that he had unquestionably saved Craig's life had a bearing on the situation too. A Scotsman did not take a debt such as that lightly. He wasn't sure just why Renyard seemed to dislike Scott so much but he intended to do everything he could to help his friend keep his ass covered.

Craig determined that he needed to know more about Renyard, a lot more. But he would have to step carefully. The man evidently had a lot of political clout.

Turning off the television set, Craig went to bed. But, in spite of the three highballs, sleep did not come easily or quickly. He had always been able to put his personal problems aside and concentrate on his job. But those problems were becoming more distracting every day. The job wasn't going all that great either. He saw himself and McAllister as the good guys in this situation. At the moment, it seemed that the bad guys were winning.

Chapter Fifteen

Louisville, Kentucky. Tuesday, May 21, 1968, 8:08 p. m.

He sat on the couch with his collection spread out on the cushions beside him. He fingered each item pensively and recalled some little fact about its original owner; a mole on the cheek, a scar by her eye, or in a couple of instances, a tattoo. He had taken an item from each one of his subjects, even the one the police had nearly caught him with. In her case, he just had time to rip an earring from her left ear. Officer Burns had interfered with that operation, but Officer Burns would interfere no more. He was dead, as dead as any of his subjects, and, though he himself had nothing to do with Burns' death, he reveled in it. God, how he hated cops! Almost as much as he hated whores. They were always telling somebody what to do, throwing their weight around, just like his father.

His father should have been a cop. He would have made a good one. His greatest joy was telling people what to do and punishing them if they didn't. His father's punishments could be quite creative, too. He had several scars to prove it, both inside and out. But he had evened that score.

He gathered up his collection and reluctantly put it away. Each one had been special, even the girls in Nashville and in Bowling Green. The police pressure had gotten so heavy here in Louisville that he had been forced to go out of town to seek new subjects. After he had deposited the girl on the cathedral steps, street whores had basically vanished from the streets and call girls were only doing business with customers they knew.

Another thing that sent him out of town was the mood in the west end. It was getting dangerous for a white face to be seen west of 12th Street after dark. The shooting involving Burns had stirred up some animosity, even though the two dead men were obviously robbing a bank and had killed a cop doing it. But what had every young black man on edge now was an incident a couple of days ago. Two white cops had stopped a black man on Broadway and run a warrant check on him. When they determined that a warrant was outstanding, they started to take him into custody. He began to object loudly. A crowd gathered and one of the white officers took the man's arm to arrest him. He broke away and, in the ensuing scuffle, the officer slapped him. A near riot followed and the police chief had suspended and then fired the two officers involved, and suspended two more who were present.

Rumors were rampant in the west end that the city intended to put all the officers back to work. A number of rallies had been held and things were tense. Several white motorists driving down Dixie Highway had had their vehicles damaged by thrown objects. Two young white males cruising Dixie looking for some action had been beaten and robbed.

He would just have to wait it out. Economics would prevail. The hookers would have to have money to feed their habits and satisfy their pimps. When they returned to work, so would he. Right now, the main thing was to be cool. He would start checking the bars again soon. The call girls would be back on the job first and he could continue his work with them. If the urges got too strong, he could always go to Cincinnati or back to Nashville, for that matter. Nashville had a lot of whores. It might be a good place to move to if Louisville got too hot.

Suddenly, another possible source of subjects occurred to him. Up to now, once the street whore traffic had dropped off, he had been looking in the hotel bars and cocktail lounges where higher class call girls plied their trade. But there was another class of bars and juke joints that had their own set of hookers. The bars along Jefferson Street in downtown Louisville had lots of whores hanging in them. Since most of their clientele were rednecks and white trash types, they wouldn't be worried much about the Ripper. After all, he just preyed on street whores and black ones at that, didn't he? Well, he could change all that. He could be a redneck, or anything else he wanted to be. The girls in those places deserved some attention, too. A whore is a whore.

These thoughts entertained him as he stowed his collection in its special hiding place. The urge to be about his work was strong, however. He had to guard against himself, against being incautious. He had to do some scouting, check out the scene on Jefferson Street. Then he could select his next subject, wait until the situation was right, and then make his move. After that, he would send Detective Craig another little memento. This time, he would make sure the newspaper and the television stations learned about it. The cops were trying to keep his handiwork quiet. He wasn't about to let that happen. The more that people knew about and feared his work, the greater the challenge and the greater the accomplishment.

Louisville, Kentucky. Monday, May 27, 1968, 3:15 p. m.

McAllister drove slowly through Shawnee Park, in the extreme west end of the city, next to the river. It was hot and humid and the warm air coming in the open windows of the car did little to cool him off. He could feel his shirt sticking to his back. Beside him, John Zarnecki was immersed in the department's daily bulletin, his lips moving slowly as he read. They had been instructed by Sergeant Arthur to come in early and ride the west end parks, Chickasaw and Shawnee until 5:00 o'clock. Then they were to go to 28th and Grand Streets and block traffic for a rally at 28th and Greenwood Avenue. Car 512 had to do the same thing at 28th and Kentucky, north of the rally site.

The black community had been fermenting since the slapping incident on Broadway the preceding week. Four "organizers", all from out of town and claiming to be from the Student Nonviolent Coordinating Committee and other groups, had been holding meetings and rallies for several days. The rally that evening was called to protest the potential reinstatement of the officers involved in the incident. Posters had shown up all over the west end and young men had been passing out handbills on major street corners for several days. The Intelligence Squad had advised that a large crowd was expected.

McAllister mused that the rationale he had been given for his transfer to the Parks Section didn't seem to be holding up. He had been told that they wanted to keep him out of the west end until things cooled down. Today he was deep in the west end and things weren't cooling down a bit.

Four days earlier, he had been ordered to appear before Michael Renyard and a panel of high ranking police officers to be interviewed about his part in the shooting of Jerome Lewis. One of the members, Major Bishop, had seemed openly hostile toward him and expressed skepticism that the shooting had occurred as he said it did. The other two commanders, Deputy Chief Milligan and Major Caudell, the Record Bureau commander, seemed to be friendly and inclined to accept his account of the events. Renyard had been at his sarcastic best and had questioned him at length, asking why he had not called out a warning before firing at Lewis. He snorted in disbelief when McAllister replied that there hadn't been time, that Lewis had already shot Craig once and was obviously preparing to do it again. Renyard also made an issue of the fact that McAllister had fired six shots, calling it "overkill." This did not appear to set well with Milligan and Caudell.

The upshot was that he had been told that they would be back in touch with him. According to the departmental rumor mill, the committee had engaged in a bitter argument after all the interviews were completed and Caudell and Milligan had refused to go along with Renyard's wish to discipline or terminate McAllister. So far, no report had been released by the committee and McAllister hadn't heard from them.

John Craig had been keeping McAllister abreast of the Ripper investigation. The task force had made no progress in any of the cases. Bittner had returned Craig to the Homicide Squad after two days, where he was riding a desk and chomping at the bit while his wounds continued to heal. He had gone to dinner with McAlister and Jenny the night before. The only good thing to come out of all of this, he confided to them, was that there had been no further killings since the murder of Doris Purcell. He described Lieutenant Bittner as "a lost ball in high weeds." His hand picked detectives were no better, according to Craig. Their intentions were good but they simply did not know how to conduct a homicide investigation. Bittner had held a press conference two days earlier at which he strongly hinted that the killer was a black male and that the task force was nipping at his heels, with an arrest expected any moment. No one was quite sure just what he had based this astounding announcement on.

McAllister's thoughts were interrupted by the squealing of tires. They had just reached the southern end of the park. A battered Buick made a left turn off Broadway, in front of them, and sped south on Southwestern Parkway, going at least 60 miles an hour.

McAllister flipped on the red light and pulled across Broadway after the speeding car. As he approached it, they could observe that there were at least four people in the car. He pulled directly behind the Buick and flipped on the siren. Its electronic yelp caused the driver of the Buick to glance in his rear view mirror. He pulled the car to the curb.

"516 to radio. Stopping K – King 46-823 on Southwestern Parkway south of Broadway," Zarnecki told the radio dispatcher. Both officers got out of their car and approached the Buick, Zarnecki on the passenger side and McAllister on the driver side.

The driver, a slender black man with an afro, was getting out of the car as they approached. He eyed McAllister over the top of his granny glasses and said, in a belligerent tone,

"Man, what are you stopping me for?"

"You were speeding," McAllister replied. "Let me see your driver's license."

"Speeding, my ass. You got a lot of nerve pulling me over down here in the middle of the ghetto."

On the other side of the car, the front seat passenger opened his door and made a move to get out of the car also.

Zarnecki pushed the door hard against him, propelling him back into his seat.

"Just keep your ass right where it is, chief," he said. "He don't need your help, and you guys in the back seat stay put, too."

The passenger all stayed where they were. The mad Polack had a wild look in his eye that was intimidating. McAllister was surprised. He had not seen Zarnecki move that fast since they had been riding together. He judged that Zarnecki had the situation under control and turned his attention back to the driver.

"Got that driver's license?" he asked.

"Man, this is so much bullshit," the driver muttered as he grudgingly pulled out a wallet and produced a tattered Illinois operator's license.

"Is this your car, Mr. Brown?" McAllister asked. "And do you live in Kentucky now?"

"Nah, it belongs to a fried of mine, Delores Gibson. She's lettin' me use it while I'm in town."

"I'm going to give you a citation for speeding. Get back in your car and wait for me."

McAllister walked back to the squad car and got his ticket book. He called the dispatcher and found that she had already obtained registration on the car. It was indeed registered to Delores Gibson on Fordson Way and had not been reported stolen.

Zarnecki was examining the identification cards of the other three men. McAllister asked for a warrant and wanted check on Lawrence Brown, the driver. He toyed briefly with the idea of running checks on all four of the men in the car but decided against it. The situation was already tense enough.

"Car 516, no warrant or wanted on Lawrence NMI Brown," the dispatcher said.

"10-4, radio," he replied.

McAllister walked back to the car and handed the ticket and license back to Brown, who was still standing beside his car. He told him that his court date was in two weeks and began explaining how to prepay the citation. The man grabbed his license back and, crumpling the ticket, tossed it in the car's open window. McAllister was surprised at the intensity of the hatred he saw in Brown's eyes. All this for a speeding ticket?

"In two weeks, honkie, you may not even have a police station for me to pay this at. The brothers may burn it down around your cracker asses," Brown said.

"Just take the damn ticket, Lawrence, and let's go," the passenger behind Brown in the rear seat said. "We've got more important things to do than argue with this guy."

"Keep it under 35," McAllister said evenly.

The two patrolmen stood and watched as the Buick pulled away and turned east on Greenwood.

"James Sanchez, Paul Crosby, and Walter Kidwell," Zarnecki said, reading the names from the daily bulletin he had scribbled them on. "All from Illinois. Those are the guys who have been holding all the meetings about Clifton and the other guys who got fired."

"Yeah, they're probably headed for the rally we're supposed to work," McAllister said. "Think we ought to tell the boss about this?"

"Tell Arthur?" Zarnecki snorted contemptuously. "That shithead could care less about anything we do unless it would keep him from collecting his rent."

"Collecting his rent?" McAllister looked quizzically at his partner.

"Hell, yes. He owns ten or twelve of those rundown shotgun houses over in Portland. He spends most of his on duty time collecting rent or evicting the ones who won't pay.

Trust me, Arthur don't want to hear from us. Let's make a pass through Chickasaw Park and head for our detail. Who knows, maybe we'll run into Huey Newton or Bobby Seale."

* * *

At five minutes before five o'clock, McAllister and Zarnecki pulled up to the intersection at 28th and Grand. Two blocks north of them, they could see a large crowd gathering on the sidewalks and spilling into the streets at 28th and Greenwood.

"710 to radio, have all cars on traffic detail shut down their intersections," the Traffic Bureau lieutenant transmitted. The dispatcher repeated his order and received acknowledgements from the units on the traffic detail.

"Can any unit at 28th and Greenwood advise the situation for Car 1?" the dispatcher queried.

"Car 400, advise Car 1 that there are several hundred people here, probably two to three hundred," Captain Hanson, the 4th District commander answered. "Right now everything is peaceful but the speeches haven't started yet. There are several people on the roof of the dry cleaners on the southwest corner. I talked to the owner. He says he let them climb up there. No problems, right now."

"10-4, Car 400."

McAllister pulled car 516 out into the intersection and turned on the red roof light. He and Zarnecki got out of the car and began directing traffic in and out of the cross street.

There was a lot of foot traffic as people headed toward the rally. The crowd had grown considerably and now completely filled the intersection. He could hear someone shouting through a bullhorn, evidently haranguing the crowd. The crowd was responding with shouts and chants. He noticed the people Captain Hanson had mentioned on the roof of the cleaners. They were also on the roof of the adjacent restaurant.

To his amazement, McAllister saw a green and yellow Louisville Transit Company bus coming south on 28th Street, north of the crowd. The driver obviously intended to drive through the intersection. The crowd reacted predictably. He could hear Captain Hanson shouting over the radio, telling someone to halt the bus. It continued on, however, right into the intersection where the press of people made it impossible for it to continue forward. McAllister could hear glass breaking and then the crowd began rocking the huge vehicle from side to side, attempting to turn it over. Even from where he stood, McAllister could see the windows of the bus being broken as missiles were thrown at it.

"Car 400 to radio, have all units in the area respond to 28th and Greenwood."

"10-4, Car 400. All units, all units in the area, respond to Car 400 at 28th and Greenwood."

"Let's go, John," McAllister yelled. Zarnecki jumped in the car and they sped north to Hale Avenue, where the crowd made it impossible to go further. McAllister turned west on Hale and then north in the alley. This brought them to the lot in the rear of the cleaners and restaurant. People were running toward 28th Street where the crowd was still trying to turn the bus over. McAllister pulled onto the sidewalk beside the cleaners and they grabbed their night sticks and bailed out of the car.

McAllister saw a police officer in a white shirt, on his knees, across Greenwood, beside the tavern on the northwest corner. Blood was running profusely from his head.

With a shock, McAllister realized that the injured officer was Captain Hanson. Two other police officers helped him to his feet and pulled him inside a cordon of cops gathered in front of the tavern.

The scene was chaotic. Hundreds of people were bunched in the intersection, screaming epithets at the police. A constant barrage of rocks, bottles and other missiles came sailing over buildings and from the rear of the crowd. Other people, more opportunistic, had broken out the windows and door of the liquor store on the northeast corner and were industriously looting its contents. Two or three police officers were futilely attempting to stop the looting. As soon as they turned toward one group, another group would run behind them and enter the store. No one seemed to be in charge of the police, who were mostly standing around waiting for orders.

A flat bed truck was parked in front of the cleaners and McAllister saw the four men from his earlier encounter standing on the bed. One of them, Sanchez, was holding a bullhorn. They all looked delighted at the bedlam around them.

McAllister turned back to the car and grabbed the first aid kit from the back. He ran across the street to where Captain Hanson was being helped inside the tavern by a patrolman. McAllister went in the tavern after them. Bill Wright, the owner of the bar, was standing by the door holding a double barreled shotgun. Behind him, several older white men were standing by the bar. Most of them were brandishing firearms of one sort or another. McAllister remembered that this bar was still patronized by whites, long time west end residents, even though the neighborhood had succumbed to "white flight" and had been taken over by blacks several years earlier.

Wright looked at McAllister belligerently.

"Them black motherfuckers ain't burning my place down. I'll send a few of 'em to hell first," he said.

"Just hang on, Mr. Wright," McAllister replied. "Nobody's burning anything down yet."

"Huh," Wright snorted derisively. "You cops all standing around out there with your thumbs up your asses, lettin' them jungle bunnies go wild. They start in here, they're going to get a big dose of buckshot."

McAllister moved over to Hanson, who was seated at a table. There was a large gash in the left side of his head and blood was seeping from it and running down his face and neck. The left side of his white shirt was saturated with blood. He looked dazedly at McAllister, who turned to the bartender standing nearby.

"Can you get me some wet towels?" McAllister asked.

The bartender went behind the bar and quickly returned with several towels. McAllister cleaned the wound as best as he could and wrapped a pressure bandage around the captain's head.

"What happened, boss?" he asked.

Hanson shook his head, bewildered.

"A brick, I think. I never saw it. I was headed toward that damn bus and something hit me."

"You need to get to a hospital. That wound needs stitches. I'll get somebody to take you. Who's in charge?" McAllister asked.

"Lieutenant Allen, I guess, unless the chief or deputy chief has showed up," Hanson replied. "I'll come with you."

Hanson stood up quickly, then tottered and put a hand on the table to steady himself. He sat back down again.

"Maybe I better wait here," he said.

"Good idea, Captain. I'll come back for you or send somebody."

McAllister went out the door of the bar and found that the scene had rearranged itself in a bizarre fashion. The police, in two groups, occupied the northwest corner of the intersection by the tavern, and the southeast corner by the pool room. The other two corners, by the liquor store on the northeast and the cleaners on the southwest, were held by large crowds. He saw Sergeant Joe Phillips, a 4th District platoon sergeant, standing a few feet away. He went over to him and said,

"Captain Hanson's in the bar here. He's got a hell of a gash in his head. I got a bandage on it but he needs stitches. Can we get him to the hospital?"

Phillips glanced at him briefly, then turned and yelled at Mike Kowalski, who was backed up against the wall of the tavern, clutching his nightstick and casting nervous looks at the crowd.

"Kowalski, where's your vehicle?"

Kowalski pointed to a station wagon parked at the curb on 28th Street.

"Right there, Sarge."

"Get Meyers and you two take Captain Hanson to General. He's in the bar here."

"You got it, Sarge," the short, pudgy cop replied with alacrity. He quickly grabbed his partner and they went in the bar, emerging in a moment with the Captain between them. They helped him into their car and pulled away. As they cleared the large part of the crowd north of the intersection, they turned on their lights and siren and sped away from the area.

Phillips looked at McAllister with a wry grin on his face.

"I haven't seen Kowalski move that fast in twenty years. You don't think he was glad to get out of this shit, do you?'

Before McAllister could reply, a loud explosion occurred behind him and a blast of heat struck his back. Wheeling around, he saw that an unmarked police car parked a short distance away had burst into flames.

"What the fuck happened?" Sergeant Phillips demanded of a young officer standing nearby.

"Must have been a Molotov cocktail, Sarge," the officer replied. "I saw two guys run out of the crowd across the street and throw something in the window of the car. Then it went up like gangbusters. They ran back into the crowd over by the cleaners."

"Shit," the sergeant swore. "Everybody get back from that car. The gas tank could go any minute. Somebody call the fire department."

The blazing car worked the crowd up to an even greater degree of frenzied activity. Phillips began grabbing police officers and shoving them into a line facing the bulk of the crowd which was still gathered by the dry cleaners.

"Everybody line up," he shouted. "We're going to clear that corner. Get ready and when I give the word, move out in a line. Bust 'em if they won't move."

McAllister found himself in the line between Zarnecki and Gladstone, the big black Parks officer, who stood stoically, gripping his nightstick and not speaking. His lips were set in a thin line and his eyes were angry. Much of the crowd's invective was directed at him and the few other black officers in the line. The heat from the burning car felt like the open door of a furnace

A loud siren announced the approach of a fire department pumper truck. It parted the crowd in the street by its imposing bulk and the noise it made. The line of police moved back to the sidewalk to let it pass. The truck pulled ahead of the burning car and the firemen quickly dismounted and unrolled the hose from the pumper's internal tank. They rapidly extinguished the fire, leaving the car a smoking, burned out hulk.

This action was greeted by an increased barrage of rocks, bricks and bottles directed at the firemen. The pumper's captain approached Sergeant Phillips and said,

"Joe, it's out. We're hauling ass before somebody on my truck gets hurt."

"Looks like you may have some more work down the street," Phillips replied, pointing west. A block or so away, a billowing cloud of black smoke was rising skyward and flames could be seen coming through the roof of a building there.

Just then, the fire truck's radio crackled with a call.

"Quad 5, a working fire at the Atlas Plaster Company, 2936 Greenwood. Engine 17, can you clear?"

The fire captain ran back to the cab of his pumper and acknowledged the run.

"Engine 17, we are clear and responding to Atlas Plaster. We're a block away."

Sergeant Phillips pulled two of his officers out of the line and directed them to get their car and accompany the fire truck. He resumed his efforts to organize the twenty or so officers still at the scene into a formation.

A gunshot cracked loudly from behind them and a bullet ricocheted off a metal mail box on the corner. All of the police nearby instinctively ducked for cover.

McAllister caught Phillips' attention and pointed north on 28th street.

"It came out of the second floor of one of those houses near Kentucky, Sarge. I saw a muzzle flash. Sounded like a .22 rifle."

"Take your partner and see if you can find the guy," Phillips said.

McAllister grabbed Zarnecki by his shirt sleeve and pointed north.

"Let's go see if we can locate that sniper," he yelled.

Zarnecki nodded agreement and they moved quickly up the street, keeping in the yards on the opposite side of the street from where McAllister had seen the muzzle flash. They used porches and shrubs for cover as they ran from yard to yard. When they neared the last house on the block, McAllister knelt behind a parked car and pulled Zarnecki down beside him. He pointed across the street.

"The house next to the hardware store. It looked like the guy was shooting out of the second story window."

"Let's wait a minute and see if he shows himself," Zarnecki replied.

Several minutes passed. Then they saw the silhouette of a man in the window. He pointed the barrel of a long gun out of the window and aimed south toward the crowded intersection. Zarnecki's revolver went off twice beside McAllister's ear, followed by glass breaking in the window.

Half deafened, McAllister ran across the street and up on the porch of the house. He drew his own revolver and kicked the front door open. The house was obviously uninhabited. There was no furniture in any of the rooms that he could see. A stairway in the front hall led to the second floor. He cautiously climbed the stairs and edged his way along a wall to the front room overlooking the porch. The room was empty. On the floor, a box of .22 caliber long rifle cartridges had spilled out on the rug. Four or five spent cartridge hulls lay on the floor by the window, surrounded by broken glass. Both of Zarnecki's shots had hit the upper part of the window. But the shooter was gone, taking his rifle with him.

McAllister and Zarnecki searched the rest of the house. It was unoccupied. The shooter had evidently gone through a rear window on the second floor onto the roof of the back porch. From there it was an easy drop to the ground.

The two men returned to 28ᵗʰ and Greenwood. The police were still lined up by the tavern but had not made any move to disperse the crowd, which seemed to have grown in the last several minutes. Police cars were parked haphazardly all over the area. A large parking lot behind the cleaners served a small convenience store. This lot was filled with people, all of them yelling and gesticulating at the police. The bottle barrage continued and the street was littered with broken glass. A pall of smoke from the fires hung over the entire area.

They reported their lack of success to Sergeant Phillips, who shrugged his shoulders.

"Just stand by here," he told them. "Colonel Milligan has taken charge and we're negotiating with Reverend King and his bunch."

McAllister saw the deputy chief and several other police commanders standing by the pool room, talking to A. D. Williams King and three other black men, who were all wearing suits and hats. He recognized all of the men as ministers who had been involved in the open housing marches the year before.

Deputy Chief Milligan left the group and came to where Sergeant Phillips was standing.

"Have all your men return to their vehicles and pull out of the area, Sergeant. Have them go to the school lot at 26ᵗʰ and Kentucky and stand by there."

"We're pulling everybody out, Colonel?" Phillips asked.

"Reverend King and the other ministers are going to appoint marshals to control the crowd," Milligan replied. "They claim we're provoking the situation by being here, that we're inciting the crowd. They say they can control them better and get them to disperse if we pull out."

"With all due respect, Colonel, the person inciting the crowd was that jackass with the bullhorn, telling them that Stokeley Carmichael had flown in to make a speech to them and that the police wouldn't let his plane land. They were all fired up and when that idiot bus driver pulled into the intersection, all hell broke loose."

"Be that as it may, Sergeant, I've got my orders, straight from city hall, and now you've got yours. We'll probably be back in here in fifteen minutes but, right now, we're pulling out. Leave one car down the street a ways to observe and send the rest to 26ᵗʰ and Kentucky."

Phillips turned to the line of patrolmen, who had all been listening to the exchange between him and the deputy chief.

"All right, you heard the man. Everybody get to their cars and reassemble on the school lot at 26th and Kentucky. 404, you pull down there in the 2700 block of Greenwood and keep an eye on the situation. Let's move out."

McAllister and Zarnecki crossed the street to the spot where their car was parked. The front windshield had been broken out with a brick. The brick and the bulk of the broken glass were in the front seat. McAllister used his citation book to sweep the glass out of the seat while Zarnecki broke the remaining glass out of the frame with his nightstick.

"What a clusterfuck this is," Zarnecki said. "Look at these assholes all whooping it up and laughing at us. They really think they've done something."

"Let's get out of here, John," McAllister said. "If we can get organized, we can move back in and deal with it."

"I don't like the idea of these shitheads thinking they can run us off," Zarnecki replied. "It will just make them bolder. We're going to have to kick some ass to get this situation under control."

They headed west on Greenwood to 29th Street. They could see five fire trucks battling the blaze at the plaster company, which seemed to have engulfed the entire business.

"There's brilliance for you," Zarnecki said. "Guy that owns that business employs about forty people, most of them black. Because he's white, they set his place on fire. Now, nobody's got a job."

McAllister turned east on Kentucky Street and headed toward the school. The wind coming through the missing windshield brought a lot of smoke, ash and dirt back into their faces. He hoped they could get the situation under control. Being so outnumbered by so many angry people was a scary situation, made more so by the failure of the police commanders to take any positive action to restore order. He had been taught for four years now that preserving the peace and protecting life and property were his principal responsibilities. Today, the police department didn't seem to have had any success in accomplishing any of those goals.

Chapter Sixteen

Louisville, Kentucky. Monday, May27, 1968, 5:50 p. m.

John Craig shifted his weight on the small stool uncomfortably. He wanted a cigarette badly but knew he would catch hell from the nurse if he lit one here in the emergency room. They were doing him a favor to begin with and he didn't want to mess that up. So he waited. He had come to General Hospital upon leaving work, hoping to get one of the emergency room doctors to examine him and pronounce him fit for duty. Now he was waiting to hear the results.

It was quiet for a change in the emergency room area. There was just one other patient, in the cubicle across from his, a wino getting his injured hand attended to. The usual collection of injured street people and indigents that made up most of the hospital's emergency cases seemed to be somewhere else tonight.

The charge nurse pulled back the curtain that closed off the section where Craig was seated. She had a large X-ray envelope in her hand along with Craig's chart. A short, buxom brunette, she was a favorite among all the police who visited the General Hospital emergency room daily. They brought the lower echelons of society here to be treated and they came here to be treated themselves. All cops knew that, if you needed emergency medical care in a hurry, there was only one place in Louisville to go – General Hospital.

There was a strong bond between the police and the medical people at General. Each group looked after the other. If an injured cop came to General, they would pull out all the stops to help him. By the same token, if there was a disorderly drunk or violent psychiatric patient at the hospital, police response occurred in a matter of minutes – if they weren't already there.

"Your X-rays are okay, John," the charge nurse said. "And your wounds seem to have all healed nicely. Doctor Thompson signed your release to return to regular duty. But I wouldn't be in any hurry if I were you. Sounds like they're burning down the west end."

"What's going on, Olson?" Craig asked. "What are you talking about?"

"I just saw a little bit of it on the TV in the doctor's lounge," Olson replied. "They've got a big riot going at 28th and Greenwood. The guy on Channel 32 said they had set a couple of buildings on fire."

They were walking toward the emergency room doors when Kowalski and Meyers came through them, leading Captain Hanson by the arms. His white shirt was covered with blood and there was a bloodstained bandage around his head.

"What happened to you, Captain?" nurse Olson asked.

"He got hit with a brick," Kowalski replied. "Knocked him to his knees."

"God damn it, Kowalski, I can talk," Hanson said. "Thanks for the ride. Now you and your partner get back down there. Those guys are going to need all the help they can get."

Kowalski and Meyers appeared less than thrilled with these instructions.

"Are you sure you don't want us to stick around, Cap?" Kowalski asked. "You'll need a ride back to the district when they get done with –"

"You heard me. I'll get back on my own. Go back to 28th and Greenwood and tell Lieutenant Allen I'll be back as soon as they get me sewed up."

Reluctantly, the two beat cops left the emergency room. Nurse Olson took Hanson's arm and led him to a chair in one of the treatment areas.

"Sit down, Captain, and let me get your wound cleaned up. Then we'll get some x-rays."

"What happened, boss?" Craig asked.

"A damn riot broke out, John. That's what happened. They were having a big rally in the street about this deal with Mike Clifton and the other guys. This guy, Sanchez, started yelling over a bullhorn that Stokeley Carmichael was trying to get to Louisville to address the crowd but that the police wouldn't let his plane land. That got everybody fired up. Then some idiot bus driver tries to drive a city bus through the intersection and all hell breaks lose. I was headed for the bus when somebody clobbered me with a brick and I went down. It gets a little confusing after that."

Olson directed Hanson toward a sink.

"Bend your head over here, Captain, and let me irrigate that cut," she said. Then she turned to Craig.

"John, your release form is on my desk if you want to get it."

"Thanks, Maggie. I'll do that," Craig replied. "Captain, did you see Scott McAllister down there anywhere?"

"Yeah, as a matter of fact, he patched me up and got the bleeding stopped. I hope the chief is calling out the off-duty people. This thing could turn into a real mess."

"Yeah, I'd better check in with my boss. Take care of him, Maggie."

"You know our motto, John. 'Best care anywhere,'" she replied. "Don't be a stranger. You could stop by and see us once in a while."

"I'll do that, Maggie. Thanks again."

Craig left the emergency room and went to his car, parked outside the door in a space marked "For Police Vehicles Only." He started the engine and turned on the radio, switching to WHAS, which usually had the best news coverage. An excited reporter on the scene at 28th and Greenwood was saying that the police were pulling back from the area. Evidently an agreement had been reached with several black ministers to let them try to control the crowd.

Craig pulled into a service station and dropped a dime in the pay phone. He dialed the police department's free number, getting his dime back when the operator answered. He asked for Homicide. Lieutenant Garrard answered the phone.

"Boss, this is Craig. I just got checked out at General Hospital and they okayed my return to full duty. Where do you want me to go?"

"Come on into the office, John. They're calling in off duty people to form a back up force if they're needed down there. I'm not sure if they are going to use detectives or if we are going to get another assignment. Maybe I'll know more by the time you get here."

"I'll be there in five minutes," Craig responded. When he got back in his truck, the excited news reporter was saying that looters had broken into several stores in the Parkland business district, a few blocks south of Greenwood at 28th and Dumesnil. Police units were responding and shots had been fired. It sounded as if the plan to control the crowd hadn't worked very well.

When he got to the homicide office, Craig found a large number of his fellow detectives gathered in or just outside the door of the small room, smoking and talking among themselves. There was none of the jocular conversation that usually went on when they all got together.

Garrard came out of the office with a lineup sheet in his hand.

"Okay, here's the deal. Two four-man cars, 601 is Noonan, Boyd, Mason

160

and Patrick. 602 is Craig, Rovinelli, Colbert and Wilson. 602 works until 4 AM, 601 goes off at midnight unless we're tied up on something. 601 is back in here at 8 in the morning, 602 come back in at 8 tomorrow night. Twelve hour shifts until further notice. Take your hard hats. If a shooting comes out, we all make the scene and handle the hospital later. Otherwise, ride the west end and try to stop the looting and arson. Sergeant Howard and I will be in 610, along with Boyette. Any questions?"

"What's going on at 28ᵗʰ and Greenwood, boss?" Noonan asked.

"We went back in when they kept looting the stores. Right now, they're trying to hold the crowd back. The county police are sending a detail to the area. They've set up a command post in the schoolyard at 26ᵗʰ and Kentucky. The Chief is meeting with the Mayor about calling in the National Guard. Anything else? Okay, let's hit it."

Craig and his partners made their way to the parking lot and found their car.

Colbert opened the rear door and climbed into the back seat.

"Wallace and I'll ride back here and let you two honkies drive. Maybe the brothers will think you all are chauffeuring us and leave us alone," he said.

Rovinelli shot him a venomous glance and started to reply. Craig shoved him toward the driver's seat.

"Lighten up, Rick. We've got a long night ahead," he said.

As they drove west on Walnut Street toward the heart of the 4ᵗʰ District, they saw roving bands of black youths in almost every block. The windows of the grocery store at 15ᵗʰ and Walnut were shattered and their contents gone. A marked 4ᵗʰ District car was at the curb in front of the store. It was owned by a Jewish man, who stood on the sidewalk in the midst of the shattered glass talking to the two uniformed cops.

They passed 16ᵗʰ Street, noticing that the glass in the door of the liquor store there had been broken out. The Lebanese owner and his son could be seen inside the store. Both of them were holding shotguns. The police radio under the dashboard spewed out an unending litany of runs involving break-ins and looting. Most of the calls were in the west end but the trouble was beginning to spread. They heard cars being dispatched to similar runs in Smoketown, east of the downtown area, and in the area of Churchill Downs.

"Man, look at these fuckers," Rovinelli muttered, half to himself. "They think they can get away with anything tonight."

"They're just doing what they've seen everybody else doing on the six o'clock news," Colbert replied. "The real problem is, with all these guns, somebody is going to get killed before the night is over. Then the shit will hit the fan."

"Any car in the area of 18th and Chestnut, a break-in now at the liquor store" the dispatcher said.

Craig picked up the microphone and replied,

"602 to radio, we're a couple of blocks away. We'll respond."

"10-4, 602. All cars, plain clothes detectives responding to a break-in now at the liquor store, 18th and Chestnut."

Rovinelli turned south on 18th Street and floored the Dodge sedan. In a matter of seconds they were almost to the intersection of Chestnut Street. They could see people clustered on the sidewalk in front of the store and others inside handing bottles and cartons of cigarettes out to them through the broken glass of the front door. As they approached, the crowd on the sidewalk dispersed in all directions, yelling "Po-lice! Po-lice!" Two young black teenagers climbed out through the door frame and began running south on 18th.

Rovinelli slammed the car's gear shift into Park and jumped from the vehicle almost before it stopped. He began running after the fleeing teenagers, yelling at them to halt.

This seemed to only give wings to their feet. They dodged into a yard and vanished from sight, with Rovinelli in hot pursuit.

Craig called the dispatcher and asked her to contact the owner, while Wilson and Colbert checked the inside of the store to make sure no lingering looter had been overlooked. Colbert climbed out of the broken door frame and came over to Craig.

"Why is that crazy dago chasing those kids, John?"

"I don't really know, Larry," Craig replied. "I think he's offended by the fact there's so much looting going on."

"Shit, man, they're just kids. They –"

Two gunshots from the direction of the alley in the rear of the store interrupted Colbert in mid-sentence. He and Craig stared at one another. Wilson came out of the building and joined them.

"Was that shots I heard?" he asked.

Rovinelli appeared from the rear of the building, his big nickel-plated Colt Python hanging from his hand. Casually, he opened the cylinder of the revolver and punched out two spent shell casings. He then reloaded the two empty chambers before snapping the cylinder shut and holstering the gun.

"Little fuckers got away," he said. "But I put some fear in their asses. They just thought they was running until I shot at them. Then they took off like stripe-assed apes."

"You shot at those kids?" Colbert asked incredulously.

"Sure, I shot at the little bastards. They're nothing but thieves, fleeing felons."

"For Christ's sake, Rovinelli, they're thirteen, fourteen years old," Colbert protested. "What if you'd hit one of them?"

"So what? Just another dead thieving nig – Negro," Rovinelli replied.

Colbert swung at him with his right hand, a roundhouse punch that struck him on the side of his head, staggering him and driving him back against the wall of the cleaners.

Dazed, he shook his head and then, slipping a black leather slapjack out of his pants pocket, he started toward Colbert.

"All right, motherfucker, you want to sucker punch me," he said. "Now let's see how you do while I'm looking at you."

Colbert threw his hands up in a boxer's stance.

"Come on, you asshole. I'll stick that slapjack up your ass," he hissed.

Craig grabbed Rovinelli around the shoulders from behind and pulled him into a bear hug. Wilson stepped in front of Colbert and, using his bulk, forced him back from the conflict.

"You two knock it off," Craig yelled. "We've got enough going against us tonight without fighting each other."

Wilson caught Colbert by the elbow and steered him toward the car.

"Get a grip on yourself, Larry. You lettin' that dumbass cracker get to you. You can't be duking it out on the damn street in front of all these people," he said in a low voice.

However, Rovinelli heard him.

"You calling me a cracker, you fat asshole?" he yelled, struggling to break away from Craig. "I'll show you a fucking cracker. I'll –"

Craig picked him up bodily and slammed him against the wall of the building.

"God damn it, Rick. Shut your fucking mouth,' he shouted.

"John, there's a beat car coming down the street," Wilson said.

A small crowd had gathered across the street and they were hooting and catcalling at the four detectives. A marked car with four uniformed officers pulled in behind the detectives' car. They all got out and joined the men in front of the cleaners. They gave strange looks at Rovinelli and Colbert, who were both visibly agitated.

Craig gave the uniformed cops the little information they had on the break in and he and Wilson herded the other two detectives into the car. Craig got behind the wheel and pulled away.

The atmosphere in the car was thick with tension as Craig headed west on Broadway. Colbert and Rovinelli avoided looking at each other, each of them staring out the window on their side of the car. No one said anything for several blocks. The radio continued its uninterrupted chatter. The dispatcher frequently called for any cars that could clear from their current run to make another priority call.

As they neared the Parkland area, they could see the glow in the sky from the fire at Atlas Plaster Company. They knew from the radio transmissions that the fire department had called for extra engines there and that it was now a three alarm blaze. At least two other fires had been started in vacant houses in the area and a thick pall of smoke hung over the whole neighborhood.

"Car 420 to radio," Lieutenant Allen, the 4th District supervisor's voice came over the radio in a hoarse croak.

"Go ahead, 420."

"The county police have arrived. They tear gassed the entire area. The crowd has dispersed for the time being. Most of the police have dispersed, too. Nobody has gas masks. Advise the Chief's office that 28th and Greenwood is pretty clear right now."

"10-4, 420. The Chief's Office advises that the National Guard has been requested and is being mobilized. They estimate their arrival in two to three hours. Kentucky State Police have also been notified. They estimate some units to arrive in two hours,"

"Okay, radio. I'm pulling all our cars out of this location and back to 26th and Kentucky to set up four man cars for patrol to try and stop this looting."

Craig continued south on 28th Street and soon they were at the intersection where the riot had started. It was basically deserted. The acrid smell of tear gas mingled with the smoke in the muggy air. The yellow nimbus of street lights shone dimly through the haze and glistened off the broken glass that covered the streets and sidewalks. West of 28th Street, the smoking remnant of an unmarked police car was at the curb, setting on its wheels with the tires burned away. They could see the flashing red lights of the fire equipment at Atlas Plaster, two blocks away. Their red glare reflected off the smoky haze and gave the entire scene a spectral look.

The owner of the Greenwood Tavern, Bill Wright, was standing in the doorway of his business holding a shotgun. His building was intact but the liquor store across the street had every window and the glass in the front door broken out. It looked as though a large part of the stock inside the store was gone, also. A marked car was parked in front of the store and the officers could be seen inside talking to the owner. There was not another police unit in sight, other than theirs.

Craig continued driving south down 28th Street. He was mulling over in his mind the changes that had taken place in the relationships between him and the other three men in the car in just a couple of hours. Rovinelli had always been a hothead and his racial remarks had always been a source of turmoil in the squad. But his hatred had boiled to the top this evening. Craig judged his behavior as erratic to the point of stupidity. He now believed Rovinelli could not be counted on to behave rationally in any tight spot they might find themselves in, if race was a factor.

The relationship between him and the two black detectives had changed that night, also, although with more subtlety. He now realized that they both regarded themselves as black men first and cops second and that they both looked at him as a white man first and a cop second. Colbert was the more vocal of the two but Wilson was a definite factor. He was not sure how all this was going to play out. Craig was feeling pretty isolated, riding through a riot area with three other men he had doubts about.

* * *

Wendell's 234 Bar was going strong. The redneck joint at 234 West Jefferson, next to the Trailways Bus Station, was a downtown Mecca of the seedier side of Louisville night life. Truck drivers, warehousemen, and factory workers mingled with winos, homeless people and run-down hookers, throwing down shots of Jim Beam, chasing them with a bottle of Falls City. They hugged the bar and turned the air blue with smoke from Luckies and Camels, or two-stepped around the small dance floor while a five piece band thumped out country songs, one after another. Several customers were gathered around the television set at the front of the bar, watching the local news reports on the riot going on in the West End. One thing was noticeable right away. There wasn't a black face in the place.

He sat at a booth in the back and nursed a beer. His appearance was altered considerably. He wore a dirty work shirt with a Standard Oil logo over one pocket and the name "Walt" over the other, faded blue jeans, work boots and a greasy baseball cap pulled down over his eyes. Three days growth of beard covered his chin and he had artfully affixed a long scar to the right side of his face below his eye with theatrical makeup. Dark horn rimmed glasses completed his ensemble. No one who had seen him on Dixie Highway would recognize him, not that there was anyone alive to do so. Nor would the bartender from the Executive Inn who had described to the police the urbane, well dressed guy that he had seen talking to Doris Purcell the night before her body was found on the Cathedral steps.

He had already picked out his subject. There really wasn't a lot to choose from. Most of the women in the place were skanks, with missing teeth and lots of tattoos. This one, however, was a little younger than the average Jefferson street whore, and better looking.

She had long dark hair and her short skirt flattered her shapely legs in spike heels. She had on a red blouse that was showing lots of cleavage. She had made two quick trips across the street to the Milner Hotel with customers while he had been setting there, so he was sure she was a whore.

"Want another beer, honey?" the fat gum-chewing waitress asked him, breaking into his thoughts.

Before he answered, he saw the girl in the red blouse walking out the door with another john. Making up his mind, he scooped his change off the table and handed the fat waitress a dollar bill.

"No, thanks, sweetheart. Gotta go," he replied, picking up his bag and heading for the door.

He reached the street in time to see the girl and her companion disappear in the front door of the Milner Hotel. She was turning them over quick tonight. Crossing the street quickly, he looked through the door and saw the couple getting into the elevator. He went around to the Third Street side of the building and into the Milner Pub, a small bar on that side of the building. It was crowded and no one paid any attention to him as he walked through the bar and out the back door leading into the main hallway of the hotel. He opened a fire door leading into the stairwell and stepped inside, leaving the door slightly open so he could see the elevators. He didn't think he would have long to wait. The desk clerk couldn't see down the hall from his location in the lobby, so no one knew he was in the building.

Twenty minutes or so went by, and then he heard the elevator doors open. Looking out, he saw the john getting off the elevator by himself and going out the street door. Five more minutes went by and then the elevator opened again and the subject stepped off. He came up behind her and cleared his throat, then spoke softly.

"Excuse me, miss. Uh – er, could I ask you something?"

She turned and smiled brightly at him. She had pretty brown eyes but, up close, he could see that she was older than he had first guessed her to be. Heavy makeup on her face concealed lines that had not been visible in the bar.

"Sure, honey. What do you want to know? How much pussy costs?" she said.

"Well, uh, I saw you in the bar across the street and I was wondering –" he stammered, keeping up his cornpone act.

"Yeah, I saw you watching me in Wendell's. I was wondering if you'd get up the nerve to ask me," she said.

"I've never done this before but I've got a little money," he said.

"Thirty bucks for the pussy, ten bucks for the room," she said. "It's right upstairs."

"That sounds reasonable," he said.

She turned and pressed the elevator button.

"What have you got in the bag, honey?" she asked. "Presents for me?"

"Oh, just some tools for my work," he replied.

The elevator door opened and they stepped inside.

Chapter Seventeen

Louisville, Kentucky. Tuesday, May 28, 1968, 1:38 a. m.

Craig and his companions were drinking Salvation Army coffee from the mobile canteen parked at the police command post. The large playground lot of an elementary school at 26th and Kentucky had been commandeered for that purpose. City, county and state police cruisers filled the lot. In the past hour, National Guard trucks and jeeps had begun arriving. The Salvation Army had shown up about an hour after the police arrived and began dispensing coffee, hot dogs and doughnuts to a large group of tired, dirty and hungry cops.

The mayor had announced a city-wide curfew at eight p. m. He had also ordered all establishments licensed to sell alcohol to close and remain closed. It had taken a while for the word to get out but by midnight, there wasn't a place open to get a cup of coffee or buy a pack of cigarettes. The cops who had smokes shared them with the ones who didn't.

Things had quieted down in the last couple of hours. The homicide detectives had continued to patrol the West End, responding to several reported break-ins and other runs. They had seen several roving gangs of young blacks but there were no large concentrations of people at any location. During the entire time, Rovinelli had not spoken a word to either Colbert or Wilson and they likewise ignored him.

Finally, tired of the unspoken tension, Craig had pulled into the command post lot and parked. Getting out of the car without a word, he went to the big mobile canteen and received a cup of hot coffee from the worker there. Turning away, he saw the other three men coming to the canteen, Rovinelli walking several feet apart from the two black detectives.

Craig headed toward a group of officers sitting on folding chairs under a large tree at the edge of the lot. He saw Scott McAllister at the edge of the group and went up to him.

"What did you get started down here, Scott?" he asked.

McAllister looked up and his sooty countenance broke into a grin.

"Hey, John. You seeing how the other half lives?"

He got up and shook hands with Craig and they walked a few steps away from the group. Craig fished around in his pocket and located his pack of Pall Malls. There were two cigarettes left. He gave one to McAllister and held his lighter for them both. McAllister drew deeply on his cigarette and exhaled nosily.

"Thanks, John. I ran out about midnight and my partner chews tobacco, so he was no help."

"Well, this is the last of the Mohicans for me, so enjoy," Craig replied. "What happened after Hanson got hit, Scott?"

"You heard about that, huh? They pulled us out and sent everybody over here to the school. Reverend King and his bunch were appointing marshals to control the crowd and stop the looting. When we got here, they had hard hats and riot batons for everybody that they brought from headquarters. They were handing those out when Oscar Maloney in 404 came on the radio and advised that the marshals were looting the stores at 28th and Dumesnil. Lieutenant Allen had left Oscar and his partner in the area to observe."

"So we all jumped back in our cars and went hell bent for leather back to Parkland and, sure enough, they were carrying everything away that wasn't nailed down. So, some of the guys started popping caps at them. You know, shooting in the air mostly.

Then, eventually we all wound up back at 28th and Greenwood facing off against a big mob of people. About thirty of us and five hundred of them. I was scared shitless. The bosses were lining us all up in a riot formation when the county showed up."

"The county commander didn't ask our bosses anything. He just turned to three guys that had shotguns fitted with grenade launchers and said 'Disperse that mob.' They started lobbing CS grenades across the street and pretty soon we all had to haul ass out of there, cops and rioters, too."

"Zarnecki and I got back to our car and from then on, we just rode around responding to runs and trying to stop the looting. They've pretty well stripped every whiskey store west of 14th Street. It was pretty lively up until about twelve or one o'clock but it's quieted down a lot since then."

McAllister paused and looked at Craig.

"That's my story. What have you been doing to earn your pay?"

Craig quickly told him about the scuffle between Colbert and Rovinelli. McAllister shook his head in disbelief.

"I know they're both hotheads but fighting on the street, jeez, that is stupid."

They were interrupted by Sergeant Phillips who came up to the group of cops, carrying a clip board.

"Listen up. The following units are relieved for the night; Traffic, 3rd platoon; Parks, 3rd Platoon; 3rd platoons from all four districts; any 2nd platoon people who came in or were called back in. Contact your commands about when and where to report tomorrow. All off days and vacations are cancelled until further notice."

McAllister and Craig walked back toward the parking lot.

"Guess I'd better find Zarnecki," McAllister said. "He's probably sacked out around here somewhere. The drive back to headquarters should revive him, though, with the wind in our faces."

Seeing Craig's quizzical look, he laughed and explained.

"They put our windshield in the front seat while we were out of the car. Makes for a breezy ride. Gave us a nice snoot full of tear gas, too, while we were getting the hell out of there."

"Keep your head down out there, Scott," Craig said. "This shit could get a lot worse before it gets better."

"Yeah, you too, John. See you later."

They separated and Craig walked back toward the canteen, looking for the other three detectives. A lieutenant from the Traffic Bureau yelled at him from his car.

"Hey, Craig. They're calling you on the radio."

Waving his thanks, he reversed his course and went back to his unmarked unit.

"602 to radio. Are you trying to contact us?"

"10-4, 602. Can you meet Car 230 at Wendell's Tavern, 234 West Jefferson?"

"10-4, radio. Can you advise what he has there?"

"602, 230 advises it's complicated and he'll explain it when you get there."

"10-4, 602 on the way."

Spotting Colbert and Wilson walking toward him, he waved them on over.

"We've got a run. Where's Rovinelli?"

"Haven't seen him since we got here," Wilson replied.

"He's probably somewhere ironing his sheet for the Klan meeting," Colbert said derisively.

Craig directed a sharp look at Colbert, who ignored him. Then he saw Rovinelli talking in an animated manner to a group of uniformed cops standing in the shadows by the school building. They were all laughing loudly.

"Hey, Rick, we've got a run," Craig yelled at him.

Rovinelli came to the car. As he got into the front seat, the sour sweet smell of bourbon whiskey came to Craig's nostrils. That explained the loud laughter. Some cops could always come up with a bottle.

When they pulled up to Wendell's Tavern, the 2nd District sergeant's cruiser was parked at the curb in front of the darkened bar. They could see two people in it. Then Sergeant Pat Hayes got out of the car and came back to Craig's window.

"John, I've got Big Lucy Reynolds in my car, there. You know Big Lucy? She says she knows you."

"Sure, Sarge, she shot her common law boyfriend last year. Dooley Reynolds. Shot him in the balls as I recall, to cure him of running around on her."

"That's the lady. Well, she and some of her girlfriends have been working out of Wendell's here, turning tricks over at the Milner Hotel. One of them took a truck driver over there about eight o'clock and didn't come back. You know these deals usually take twenty minutes, half hour at the most. She says this girl, Lorraine, would definitely have come back to get her before she went home. They rode up here together in Lucy's car."

"Maybe the john took her home, wanted an all nighter," Craig said.

"I asked her that. She says no way. She says Lorraine didn't do all nighters and wouldn't have gone off without telling her. We closed all the joints on Jefferson Street about ten o'clock after the Mayor's order came out. Lucy went over to the grill in the bus station and waited for a while, I guess figuring Lorraine would show up. When she didn't, Lucy tried to find out what room she was using at the Milner, but they changed shifts at eleven and the night guy, Raymond, said he didn't know. I've got everybody on my shift tied up on runs or detailed to the 4th District. I thought that, with this bastard killing all these whores, you might want to check into it."

"Why not? We got nothing better to do," Craig replied. He got out of the car and walked back to the sergeant's cruiser. A woman six feet tall with flaming red hair, dressed in a top and mini skirt two sizes too small for her, got out of the car at his approach.

"Hi, Detective Craig. You remember me?" she said.

"Sure I do, Lucy. How's Dooley doing these days?" he replied.

"Keeping his sorry ass at home, that's how he's doing. Listen, you were nice to me that night and I want you to find out what happened to Lorraine.

She's my best friend and I know she wouldn't just go off without telling me. We look out for one another, you know how it is."

"Yeah, well, we'll see what we can find out. What did the john look like that she went off with?"

"He was a big old skinny boy with jug ears. I see him in Wendell's all the time. I'm pretty sure Lorraine has tricked with him before. He came back in the bar about a half hour after they left together. When she didn't come back, I asked him where she was. He said he left her in the room, washing up."

"Did you go look for her then?" Craig asked.

"Nah, because I figured she maybe went in the pub in the hotel there and met another john, did a double, you know. So I didn't really get worried. Then when the cops came in and closed the bar, I figured I'd better find her. But that dumbass Raymond kept saying he didn't know what room she was in, she hadn't registered, all that shit. Then I seen Bill Jones, manages the pub, you know, and he said he hadn't seen her in there all night. So I knew something was wrong. I called the police but they were real busy and I couldn't get them to send anybody for a long time. I seen Sergeant Hayes driving down Jefferson Street so I flagged him down."

She delivered this information in a breathless rush, then paused and smiled at Craig, revealing several missing teeth.

"Let's see what Raymond has to say," Craig said, starting across the street. The other three detectives had gathered around them listening to the conversation. Rovinelli grabbed Craig's elbow.

"What are you doing fooling with this shit, John? It's almost quitting time and who cares about a missing whore?" he asked.

"Rick, if you don't want to help, go sit in the car and take a nap or you can walk back to headquarters. It's only four blocks. I'm going to check this out. If this is another Ripper deal, I'm not passing up a chance to catch the bastard."

He shook off Rovinelli's hand and crossed the street, going into the lobby of the old hotel. Colbert and Wilson followed him, tailed closely by Big Lucy and the sergeant. Rovinelli stood uncertainly by himself on the sidewalk for a moment, then followed the others

The Milner Hotel had been built in the 1920's and catered primarily to transients and traveling salesmen. Rooms were available by the day, week, month or hour. The rundown lobby, with faded carpet worn through in many places, furnished with broken down sofas and chairs and reeking of cigar smoke, proclaimed the nature of its business.

Craig walked up to the registration desk and gave a couple of sharp raps to the bell sitting there. A wizened little man with a few strands of stringy gray hair and a mouthful of bad teeth stuck his head out of the back office.

"Help you?" he asked.

Craig flipped his ID folder open and showed his badge.

"City detective, Raymond. Let's talk a minute."

The leprechaun came out of the office slowly and approached the desk with reluctance.

"I don't know nothing about that girl that Lucy was in here asking about, if that's what you want. She ain't checked in here."

"Yeah, that's what I heard. But you see, Raymond, I know what the deal is here. I know that you and Woodrow, the 3 to 11 guy, have got two or three rooms you let these girls use on a cash and carry basis. They don't sign in but you give them a key and then they give you five bucks every time they turn a trick in there. So what I need from you is the room numbers of those two or three rooms and your passkey. We look in those rooms, we don't find anything, we're on our way."

"I can't do that, Detective. My boss would –"

"The other option is, we start at the top floor and roust everybody in the hotel so we can check all the rooms. Probably pulling the fire alarm would be the best way to do that. Then, if I do find this girl and something has happened to her, your sorry ass goes to jail for hindering my investigation. So, how do you think your boss would like that?"

Craig smiled disarmingly at the little man. Raymond nervously cleared his throat.

"I'll need to call the boss," he said.

"Go ahead. When you get him on the phone, let me talk to him. Maybe he knows the room numbers you and Woodrow use to run whores in here," Craig replied.

"Let me at him, Detective," Big Lucy boomed from behind Craig. "I know which rooms they are and I'll get the key."

"Take it easy, Lucy. I think Raymond is going to cooperate with us, aren't you, Raymond?"

The leprechaun looked apprehensively at Big Lucy, swallowed twice and licked his lips. He reached under the counter and produced a key attached to a plastic tag.

"341, 343 and 441," he said. "At the back of the building. Please don't disturb the other guests."

"We'll be as quiet as the mice that infest this place," Craig said, picking up the key.

They tried the two rooms on the third floor first. Both were empty but showed signs of heavy usage, with rumpled bed clothes and towels on the floor in the bathrooms. As they approached the fourth floor room, Wilson came up beside Craig and spoke in a low voice to him.

"I got a bad feeling about this, John. This place smells like death."

Craig nodded in agreement. The fetid odor of blood was strong in the hallway. He turned to Sergeant Hayes, who was just getting off the elevator.

"Pat, take Lucy back down to the lobby and wait for us there, will you?"

Hayes looked at him with surprise, then nodded agreement and turned back to the elevator. The detectives could hear Lucy protesting as the door closed.

Craig inserted the pass key into the lock. Pulling rubber gloves from his pocket, he put them on and turned the knob. The room was dark. He felt on the inside wall and flipped the switch. Light flooded the small room.

The girl's headless torso was spreadeagled on the bed. Her wrists were bound to the bed frame. She had been completely disemboweled and her intestines were pulled out of her body cavity and draped across her chest and over her left shoulder. Her severed head had been placed between her spread legs, sightless eyes staring at the detectives, surrounded by a tangled mass of bloody hair. The entire surface of the bed was covered with thick, clotted blood. The wall beside the bed displayed splotches of blood which had run down the wall before partially drying.

A folded sheet of note paper was on the nightstand beside the bed. "*Detective Craig*" was printed on the outside of the sheet in block capitals.

"Holy shit, what kind of maniac is this motherfucker?" Rovinelli gasped as he saw the extent of the carnage.

"The kind we need to catch, Rick," Craig replied through clenched teeth, "and catch quick. Wallace, get on the horn and get the lab boys and the coroner started. Call the boss and tell him what we got."

"10-4, John. What about this bullshit task force? We going to notify them?"

"Tell the boss and let him make the call. If we do notify them, it'll take them a while to get here. They're probably nestled all snug in their beds. Maybe we can get the scene processed before they can get here and fuck it up."

Colbert came out of the bathroom.

"Looks like he washed off in there. There's bloodstains all over the place. I'll go get the crime scene kit. Give me the keys."

Craig flipped the car keys to him and returned to his scan of the room.

"Rick, check the rest of the rooms in this wing. See if anybody heard or saw anything," he told Rovinelli. "Then start canvassing the rest of this floor and the one above and below."

Alone in the room, he pulled out his ball point pen and, using it and his gloved hands, opened the folded sheet of paper. It was printed, like the outside, in clumsy block capitols. As he read its content, the hair rose on the back of his neck and he felt a sudden chill.

Craig-
Hear you're lonesome these days. Thought you might like some head.
Your pal
Jack

He was unsure how long he had been staring at the note when he heard Wilson come into the room behind him. The big man looked at the note with interest. Then he looked at Craig quizzically.

"How you reckon he knows about your personal situation, John? And why is he writing to you? Been a lot of people involved in this investigation."

"I don't know, Wallace. Maybe he's closer to us than we think. Something I've done seems to ring his chimes though. He wants to be my pen pal. What did the boss say?"

"He said he'd have to get here and evaluate the situation before he decided whether or not to call in the task force. Said it might just be a copy cat and he wouldn't want to waste their ex-per-tise. He's responding from home. Said for us to go on and do our thing in the meantime."

"You gotta love a man like that, you know," Craig said. "Let's get started."

"Okay, lab boys and the coroner are on the way. I'll do a sketch if you want to do the scene write-up," Wilson replied.

Colbert returned then with the Yashica camera that they used for crime scene photography and began popping flash bulbs as he started outside the door to the room and worked his way in. The intermittent bright flashes illuminated the body of the dead girl and her severed head in stark light, giving a macabre aspect to the scene.

The three detectives worked quickly and efficiently, talking little. The earlier tension between them all had vanished, lost in the viciousness of the crime and their unified desire to solve it. They were interrupted briefly when Sergeant Hayes brought a uniformed officer up to the room to help secure the scene and keep onlookers back. The big sergeant recoiled in horror when he saw what had been done to the girl's body.

"Good God Almighty. That filthy, rotten bastard −" he sputtered.

"Yeah, we agree, Pat," Craig said. "But we've got a lot of work to do here. Can you identify her? Is that Lorraine?"

"Yeah, that's her. Lorraine Carter. Been hanging on Jefferson Street for a couple of years now. Lives out around First and Oak. I can get her exact address from Big Lucy."

"Yeah, do that, if you will. Also, have one of your guys take Lucy down to the Homicide Office and stay with her until we can take her statement. Can you have somebody check all the stairwells, elevators, garbage cans and dumpsters for anything this asshole may have tossed? Bloody clothes, knife, anything like that."

"I'll do it myself, John. I've only got four cars. The other two are on detail to the 4th District."

"Thanks," Craig replied. He turned to the young officer with Hayes, who looked as if he was trying hard not to lose his dinner.

"Officer Benson, I need you to station yourself by the elevator and where you can see the stairwell door. Nobody gets on this floor but homicide detectives, the lab crew and the deputy coroner. Likewise, nobody leaves this floor that's staying in a room here until we give you the okay. Got it?"

"Yes, sir," Benson replied, swallowing hard. He bolted from the room. Craig returned to his examination of the scene. Wilson had finished the preliminary sketch of the room and he and Colbert were taking measurements of the entire room.

"John, look at this," Colbert said. He was crouched by the head of the bed holding one end of the steel tape measure. He pointed with his flashlight to a spot under the edge of the bed. A strip of what appeared to be flesh colored rubber lay on the floor in the beam of his light. It appeared to be about four inches long and an inch or so wide. Hunks of flesh toned material clung to its edges. A dark line ran down the middle of the strip intersected by several short lines.

"What is that?" Craig asked.

"I think it's a fake scar," Colbert replied. "You know, the kind actors put on their face in a play. You attach it with a kind of spirit gum and then cover the edges with flesh colored make up."

Craig stared at Colbert.

"Larry, don't ever say anything again about me knowing bits of trivia. How in the hell do you know about that?"

Colbert appeared embarrassed.

"Well, I work some with the Little Colonel Players out in Pewee Valley and I did some theater in college. I've seen these things before."

"Well, I'll be damned," Craig said. "Okay, be sure that we collect this thing after we finish processing the scene. Hell, it's rubber. It may have prints on it."

"Looks like it's got blood on it, too," Colbert said. "Don't know if it's his or hers."

"You know, she may have pulled this damn thing off his face. She may have scratched him, too. Make sure we do fingernail scrapings on her. Maybe this son of a bitch has finally fucked up enough to give us something to work on."

Rovinelli appeared in the doorway.

"John, you need to hear what this guy in room 410 has to say," he said.

Craig followed Rovinelli down the hall to a room across from the elevator. The detective rapped on the door and it was opened by a small man in his sixties, dressed in pajamas and a worn bathrobe. He motioned the two detectives into the room and closed the door.

"John, this is Mr. Earnest DePaul. He lives here in the hotel. Mr. DePaul, this is Detective Craig. He's in charge of this investigation. Would you mind telling him what you told me/"

"No, I don't mind," DePaul replied. "Like I was telling Mr. Rovinelli, I've been living here for the better part of a year. Retired from the K. & I. Railroad five years ago, then my wife died. Didn't need a big house after that, so I sold it. Moved in here. Bill Jones, runs the Milner Pub, he's a good friend of mine. Helped me get a real reasonable rate."

Craig perched on one of the chairs and prepared to listen. It was obvious that DePaul was going to tell his story in his own way and in his own time. Craig had found that he usually learned more by just letting people talk.

"Anyway, I hang over at Wendell's and Nick's Big Six a lot, as well as the pub. I know most of the girls that work out of them joints. Every now and then I do a little business with one of them. Lorraine's special. She was always real nice to me, didn't act like I was an old man. When I'd get my check, first of the month, we'd have a little party. Man gets lonesome living by himself, so I – Well, I like her a lot."

"You noticed that my room's right across from the elevator so I can see who's coming and going if I want to by looking through the peephole in my door. Well, them girls use a room at the back of the hall a lot, 441. I seen Lorraine come up there earlier tonight with Jimmy Mudd. He hangs in Wendell's all the time. He's a bricklayer by trade. Ain't a bad guy. Homely as his last name, so he don't have much luck with women. Has to buy it most of the time."

"Anyway, he comes back out by himself after a few minutes, then

Lorraine comes along in five or ten minutes by herself. I wanted to talk to her but I didn't have my teeth in, so I didn't open the door. Then two or three minutes later, I hear the elevator again. I look out and here she comes again with a guy I didn't know. But I seen him earlier tonight over at Wendell's. He was sitting in a booth by himself. Hadn't ever seen him in there before. He was still there when I left and came home."

"Well, I figure she picked him up in front of the hotel or something. They go on back to the room. I goes and puts my teeth in, figuring she'll stay behind and wash up after he gets done. Maybe I can catch her leaving and see if she won't come over to my place for a little while."

"About an hour goes by, maybe longer. Then I hear the elevator bell ring. I look out and the guy is leaving by himself. Got a canvas carryall in his hand, which he had when they first came up. So I wait for Lorraine but she never comes along. I figure I just didn't hear the elevator and she must have left first. I go to bed and then Detective Rovinelli knocks on my door. Is she dead?"

"I'm afraid she is, Mr. DePaul. Listen, now, this is real important. Can you describe this guy?" Craig asked.

"That son of a bitch," DePaul said. "She was really a nice girl."

"Yes, sir. I get that impression. Can you tell me what the guy looked like?"

"Yeah, about your height but skinnier. About thirty years old. Brown hair, had on black glasses, ball cap, work clothes. When I saw him at Wendell's, looked like he had a scar or something on his face."

"Where on his face?"

"Let's see. Right side, long scar about three - four inches, in front of his ear. I tell you what, Ella waited on him. She can probably give you a real good description."

Craig glanced at Rovinelli, who was writing furiously in his notebook.

"Do you know Ella's last name?" Craig asked.

"Just Ella's all I know. Hell, she's worked at Wendell's for a hundred years. Wendell can tell you."

"Okay, tell me about this bag he was carrying."

"It was just a canvas carryall. We used to call them AWOL bags in the army. It was green with brown trim."

Craig nodded.

"I know exactly what kind of bag you're talking about. That's what we called them, too," he said. "Did he act like it was heavy?"

"It had some weight to it, from the way he was carrying it and the way he hefted it when he threw it in his truck."

"In his truck?" both detectives said simultaneously. "What truck?" Craig asked.

"The truck he drove off in," DePaul said. "I looked out my window after the guy went downstairs, while I was waiting for Lorraine to come along. I could see the guy walking down 3rd Street. He opened the door of a truck parked across the street, threw the bag in it, got in and drove off."

"Could you tell what kind of truck it was?" Craig asked.

"Sure could. It was a 1963 Chevy pickup. Used to have one just like it. It looked like it was light green or gray. Hard to tell under the street lights. Had writing on the door."

"Could you tell what kind of writing?"

"Nope, looked like the name of a company or something."

"You've been a great help, Mr. DePaul," Craig said. "Would you know this guy if you saw him again?"

"I think I would, but I bet old Ella would know him for sure. He was just different, you know. Didn't look like he belonged in Wendell's but he looked like he was trying to."

Returning to room 441, Craig and Rovinelli found that Lieutenant Garrard had arrived, along with the fingerprint crew. Quickly, Craig filled Garrard, Wilson and Colbert in on the information DePaul had provided. Garrard nodded in satisfaction.

"Sounds like we may finally have something solid to go on," he said. "Rick, you head on back to the office and get a statement from Big Lucy. Take this DePaul along with you, get his statement down, and have both of them look at mug books. See if she saw this guy last night in Wendell's. Also, see if she knows Ella's full name and where she lives. If not, have somebody roust Wendell out and get the information from him. Put out a pickup for the Chevy truck and a white male with the description we've got. Investigation of homicide. Don't make any reference to the Ripper cases. We'll finish up here and canvass the other floors in the hotel. John, what's the other desk clerk's name, the 3-11 guy?"

"Woodrow Wilson, boss. No relation to the late president or to our esteemed colleague, Wallace."

"Okay, let's find out where he lives and get him in for a statement. I'll contact that art professor out at U of L to come in and do a sketch, if nobody picks this guy out of the mug books. Tomorrow morning we'll start running down this fake scar. Can't be too many places around here that sell stuff like that."

"Boss, what about the task force? Are we going to turn thus over to them?" Craig asked.

Garrard flashed a wolfish grin.

"I called Bittner at home. Woke him up as a matter of fact. I think being a task force commander is losing some of its luster for our boy. Anyway, he said if we didn't mind doing the preliminary investigation, he and his team would check with us later. They've been working a lot of long hours lately and he didn't want to roust them out if it turned out not to be the Ripper."

Craig snorted in derision.

"Sounds like he's got the makings of a top homicide cop."

"Don't look a gift horse in the mouth, John. Let's run with this as far we can. Then, if we're on the brink of breaking it, I can go to the chief and maybe get this task force disbanded. He is less than enchanted with their work so far. I hear the Mayor's not real happy with Renyard and company either."

"You got it, boss. Okay, guys, you heard the man. Let's rock and roll."

Garrard pulled Craig to one side as the detectives dispersed to their assignments.

"John, what about this note? Do you have any idea what he means? Is he referring to you and Susan breaking up, and, if so, how does he know about that?"

"I don't have a clue, boss. It's no secret that Susan and I are getting a divorce but I don't think it's widely known outside the department. Maybe somebody shot their mouth off in a bar or something and he overheard it, or maybe he's –" Craig paused and Garrard finished his unspoken thought,

"Maybe he's a cop."

Chapter Eighteen

Louisville, Kentucky. Tuesday, May 28, 1968. 9:55 a. m.

Craig was typing his report, or attempting to. The adrenaline rush had worn off and he found himself frequently dozing off with his fingers poised on the typewriter keys. He looked up with a start as Lieutenant Garrard entered the office. Colbert, who was dozing in the lieutenant's chair waiting for a typewriter to be freed up, also sat up and yawned.

"Okay, here's what we've got so far," Garrard said. "We've interviewed Ella, Ella Mae Snyder her full name is, and her description tallies with the one Mr. DePaul gave us. She doesn't remember ever seeing the guy before in Wendell's. She also noticed the bag. Says he carried it out with him when he left, which was right after Lorraine left with Jimmy Mudd. She saw them going out the door together and then our boy left right behind them. Tipped her a dollar. She called him a cheap son of a bitch. She says he didn't look right in Wendell's, so everybody was watching him. They thought he might be an undercover cop. I'm not sure why they thought we would have somebody in there undercover. Hell, Wendell pours enough free booze all night for on duty cops. I guess they thought he was internal affairs or something."

"Anyway, Sergeant Howard and Boyette found Jimmy Mudd and interviewed him a little while ago. He says he went back to Wendell's after he and Lorraine did their thing, which tallies with what we know. Didn't see anybody fitting the description of our boy on the way in or out. But here's where it gets interesting. Mudd says he didn't stay at Wendell's but a few minutes the second time, then went to his truck to go home. He was parked around the corner on 3rd. Says there was a gray Chevy pickup parked in front of his with writing on the door. He noticed it because it was the same make and model as his father-in law's. Says the writing was the name of a farm named after some kind of flower but he can't remember what kind. Boyette's getting a book with names of flowers and going back to see him, hoping to jog his memory."

"Now for the fake scar. There's three places in town that sell theatrical supplies. Noonan and Boyd are hitting all three of them this morning with pictures of the scar, so maybe we'll get lucky there. There was blood on the piece of rubber, type AB+. The girl is type O-, so it's probably his. We're starting to get some physical evidence on this guy, if we can come up with a name to go with it. I talked to the chief –"

Garrard broke off in mid-sentence and looked toward the door of the office. Craig and Colbert both swung around to see Lieutenant Bittner standing there.

"Can I help you, Dan?" Garrard asked.

"Yes, I thought I would just stop by and pick up whatever reports your men have finished on their preliminary investigation from last night. My team is standing by and anxious to get started on this new case. Hopefully, this time you've been able to find something that we can work with," Bittner replied.

"No, I don't think so, Dan," Garrard said. "I think we'll work this one ourselves. Thanks just the same."

Bittner stood there with a baffled look on his face.

"But you can't do that. I mean – you've been ordered to turn everything over to my task force. Assistant Safety Director Renyard specifically told you, in my presence, that you were –"

"I don't work for Assistant Safety Director Renyard, Dan, and neither do you. We both work for the Chief of Police, who works for the Mayor. And about fifteen minutes ago, I was instructed by the Chief of Police to conduct this investigation as I saw fit. And I don't see fit to hand it over to you and your 'team.' You haven't done shit with anything else we've given you, so we'll take it from here. Now we've got a lot of work to do, so if you'll excuse us –"

Garrard walked over and closed the office door in Bittner's shocked face. He turned and winked at his two detectives who were doubled over with almost silent laughter.

"How long do you think it will take him to get to Major Bishop's office?" Craig asked when he regained some composure.

"Oh, he's there by now," Garrard replied. "But he won't find Farley at home. He's downstairs in the Chief's Office trying to save his job. Seems like in the middle of all this other crap, the Chief learned that Bishop and Renyard had been working on the Mayor, blaming the riot on the

Chief and trying to get the Mayor to fire him and Farris. They wanted him to make Renyard the Safety Director and Bishop the Chief. Well, it backfired. The Mayor called the Chief over to his office, told him all about it and told him he had his full confidence. Things are not looking well for the plotters right now."

"So we don't have to worry about turning anything over to the task force?" Colbert asked.

"There is no task force anymore. Bittner is just a little late in getting the word. Now let's get busy and solve this damn case. You guys finish up your reports and get a few hours sleep and get back in here. I'm going to leave Noonan and Boyd on days, twelve hours, Mason and Patrick nights, twelve hours, you two and Rovinelli and Wilson work this case till we clear it."

Craig looked thoughtfully at his lieutenant.

"Come on, boss. There's more to this than meets the eye. You and Captain Hall said you had some friends in city government. You all didn't by any chance clue the mayor in, did you?"

"John, one of the hallmarks of a good detective is knowing when to shut up and quit asking questions. Now, get busy."

"Yes, sir. Say, boss, what about McAllister?" Craig asked. "Any chance of rescuing him from Parks, since that asshole Renyard may be on the outs? You know the only reason he got transferred was because Renyard wanted to fuck over him."

"I'll see what I can do, John. We could use the help but everybody is yelling for warm bodies right now. Maybe if the situation in the west end quiets down, we can get him back up here. He's a good kid."

* * *

The discordant ring of the telephone brought McAllister up out of a sound sleep. Groggily, he fumbled around on the nightstand beside the bed, finally finding the receiver, yanking it off the base and to his ear.

"Hello?" he croaked.

"Scott," Jenny said. "Did I wake you? Honey, I'm sorry."

"Hi, babe. Yeah, I didn't get in 'til almost four and then couldn't go sleep for a while. Finally dropped off sometime around daylight. I'm glad you called, though. I need to get moving. What time is it?"

"About 11:30. I saw all the footage on TV," Jenny said. "I think I saw you once but it was hard to tell with those helmets on. Are you all right?"

"Yeah, I'm fine, just tired. Jen, it was pretty hairy for a while there last night. I wasn't sure how we were going to get out of that mess. We were so outnumbered and disorganized for the first few hours. It got better after they broke up the mob at 28th and Greenwood and we started patrolling in four man cars. We had to use the other Parks car. They broke the windshield out of ours."

"While you were in it?" Jenny asked.

"Nah, it was parked by the cleaners there on Greenwood. We were across the street. What's on the news this morning? Is it still going on?"

"The National Guard has been called in and I saw them on TV lined up across the street with rifles with bayonets on them. I'm not sure where that was though, somewhere in the west end."

"Well, I've got to go at work at 3:00. Do you want to have lunch?"

"Sounds like a great idea. Pick me up?"

"Outside your building in about forty-five minutes. See you then."

"Okay. Oh, Scott, there was another killing of a prostitute last night at one of the downtown hotels. Lieutenant Garrard was on television this morning."

"I heard them put out a pickup early this morning for a Chevy pickup truck for investigation of homicide," McAllister said. "Maybe they've got something going on the case. Did you say Garrard was on TV?"

"Uh-huh. I didn't catch it all because I was at work."

"Okay. Maybe I can hook up with John later and he'll fill me in. I'll see you in a few minutes. I love you."

"Love you, too. Bye, honey."

McAllister got out of bed and was headed for the shower when the phone rang again.

"Scott, you awake?" Craig's voice rasped at him from the receiver.

"Just got up, John. What's going on? You sound like you haven't been to bed yet."

"That's about the size of it. We had another homicide last night, white prostitute this time, at the Milner Hotel. We've got some good leads we're working on. But, listen, the good news is there's been a palace revolution. Your buddy, Renyard, has stepped in some shit and he and fat ass Farley are on the outside now. The task force has been disbanded and Homicide is back in the saddle. I talked to Garrard about your situation. He and Captain Hall are going to try to get you transferred back to Homicide as soon as the west end settles down. Garrard says keep quiet about it and keep your nose clean and he'll let you know something in a few days. That okay with you?

"Man, I'll say. Can I go wash his car, shine his shoes or something?"

"Nah, just hang tight and keep your fingers crossed. We may be getting some breaks on the Ripper. Call me in the office this afternoon. I've gotta be back in at 4. I'll fill you in then."

"Thanks, John. I'll do that. Take care."

McAllister headed for the shower. His fatigue seemed to have vanished. Things were looking brighter. He began whistling off key as he lathered his face to shave.

* * *

At 2:45, McAllister reported to the Parks office. Sergeant Arthur instructed him to take Car 516 to Louisville Auto Glass and get a new windshield installed, and then come back to the office to pick up Zarnecki. Arthur seemed to blame McAllister personally for the car's windshield being broken. He sent him out the door with a caustic comment about taking better care of equipment.

Not even Arthur's attitude could dampen McAllister's spirits at this point. He had just finished a terrific lunch with the woman he loved and it was beginning to look like his exile to Parks might not last much longer. Besides, as Zarnecki had pointed out, their rotund supervisor had been nowhere to be seen the preceding evening. While every available unit was being sent to the 4th District, he had managed to be somewhere else the entire time. Any respect McAllister had felt for the man because of his rank was diminishing fast.

The glass shop replaced the missing windshield in a matter of a few minutes and McAllister returned to the parking lot beside Headquarters. Coming in the back door and up the steps to the second floor, he decided to look in the Homicide office and see if Craig had reported back to work.

The detective was seated at the sergeant's desk at the front of the office. His suit looked more rumpled than usual and his bloodshot eyes gave him the appearance of having been on a long drunk. His face was ruddy from a recent shave and he was squinting at the report he was holding through a haze of cigarette smoke.

"Jesus, John," McAllister said. "You look like death warmed over."

"Yeah, well. You get two hours sleep in two days and see how you look. Sit your ass down here and let's talk."

McAllister pulled a chair over to the desk as Craig shuffled through some of the papers he was holding.

"Okay, victim was Loraine Carter, white female, 35, single, lived at 110 West Oak. One arrest for prostitution during a convention last year, at the Watterson Hotel. She's been working out of Wendell's 232 Bar, turning tricks at the Milner Hotel across the street, which is where our boy did her in. He used a few new tricks this time, and he's making it real personal to me. He's definitely a white guy, Scott, and he knows something about my family situation."

Speaking rapidly, Craig outlined the details of the killing and the contents of the note. He went through the investigative steps that had been done so far and the leads that had been run down. Then he paused, sat back in his chair and rubbed his eyes.

"What's got me really stymied, Scott, is how this asshole knows about my personal situation. I mean, I haven't kept it a secret that Susan and I have split up but I haven't announced it either. Other than the guys in the squad, you, Jenny and my folks, I don't think I've told anyone else about it. Except my lawyer, of course, and I don't think he would broadcast it. Hell, Carl and I went to high school together. You got any ideas?"

"I honestly don't. Jenny and I have talked about it with each other but I haven't mentioned it to anyone else. And Jen doesn't talk about other people's business. But, John, you know this department is just a bunch of old women when it comes to gossip. If one of the guys in the squad told somebody else in another unit, it could be all over the department in a day."

"Maybe, but you'd think, if that were the case, it would have come back around to me, and it hasn't."

Lieutenant Garrard came in the office door. He smiled when he saw McAllister and extended his hand.

"Hello, Scott. Good to see you. I understand John called you earlier. Hopefully, I can give you some good news in a few days. I wish we had you today. We've got plenty of work to do."

"Yes, sir," McAllister replied. "Thank you very much, Lieutenant. I really appreciate your help."

"I'll be in touch, Scott, as soon as I can get it okayed. John, I'll be in the Chief's office for about half an hour. What have you got going on?"

"I'm waiting on Rovinelli to come back from General with the preliminary autopsy report, boss. I sent Colbert and Wilson to Wendell's to start interviews with the bartenders and waitresses on the evening shift. We'll head for the Milner and try to catch the people we missed last night, as soon as Rick gets back."

Garrard nodded, and then went out the door. McAllister was about to resume his seat when he saw the pear shaped form of Sergeant Arthur in the doorway.

"McAllister, what are you doing in here? Get your ass down to the parking lot. Zarnecki's waiting for you. You two have to report to 28th and Kentucky right away. The National Guard is catching hell down there and you're up here fucking off."

"I'm on the way, Sarge," McAllister replied, heading out the door.

"You're just a goof-off, brother, hanging around up here when there's work to be done. Now get your ass in gear."

McAllister had, by now, had his fill of the fat sergeant. He turned suddenly and walked toward Arthur, who took a step backwards.

"By the way, Sarge, are you going to be supervising us down there at 28th and Kentucky? We missed your leadership last night while we were fucking off at 28th and Greenwood, dodging bricks and bottles. I thought sure you'd be there, since they were calling for all units to respond to that location. What happened to you?"

Arthur turned and scurried back down the hall toward the elevator, talking over his shoulder.

"You just get on down there, boy, and don't worry about me."

"You got it, Sarge, and if I need any help, I'll call for you. Car 510, isn't it? I mean, rent's not due until the first of the month, so you should have plenty of time, right, Sarge?"

By now, McAllister was shouting at Arthur's bulbous backside. The detectives standing by the reception desk were all laughing as he beat his hasty retreat. McAllister looked in the Homicide office door at Craig, who was reared back in his chair, laughing uproariously.

"I'll talk to you later, John."

"Okay, Scott, and thanks for the uplift. That did me almost as much good as seeing Garrard shut the door in Bittner's face this morning."

Several minutes later, McAllister and Zarnecki parked their car on Kentucky Street near a group of police officers who were standing on the sidewalk. They were wearing the blue plastic helmets that had been issued and carrying 36" riot batons. A line of National Guardsmen wearing steel helmets and with bayoneted rifles was stretched across 28th Street facing north. A large group of young black males faced them in the street. They were yelling obscenities and catcalls at the Guardsmen and police. From the rear of the group, a barrage of rocks and other objects was being launched in the direction of the line of soldiers. Two police officers were standing behind the line of guardsmen talking to a National Guard officer wearing major's insignia.

McAllister found Lieutenant Allen and Sergeant Phillips, the 4th District bosses on the evening shift, standing with the group of police on the sidewalk.

"We were told to report to you for assignment, Loot," McAllister said. "We're from Parks."

"Oh, yeah," the lieutenant replied. "I sent your other two guys over to the C. P. at 26th and Kentucky. Report over there and hook up with a state or county car and respond to some of these radio runs. They're trying to help out but they don't know the streets. We're sending two cars on every run. You know the west end, don't you?"

"I worked down here for four years, Loot."

"Good and I see you've got the Mad Polack as a partner. I know he knows his way around."

"What's the deal with the National Guard, boss? Why are they just standing out there letting the crowd throw all that shit at them?"

"Beats me," Allen replied. "Their C. O. lined them up across the street about twenty minutes ago as a 'show of force', he said. I'm not sure what the objective is."

Just then, the National Guard major, who was standing behind the formation, began bellowing commands.

"At port arms, forward, march!"

The line of soldiers began moving north toward the crowd. This caused both the verbal and physical barrage to increase in intensity.

"On guard," the officer commanded and the line of soldiers extended their weapons, pointing their bayonets at the crowd. McAllister noticed that the bayonets still had their scabbards on them. As they neared the crowd, the mass of people began moving back away from the soldiers. Rocks and bricks were thrown from the rear of the crowd in a constant stream.

A guardsman was hit squarely in the face with a large brick and fell to his knees, his steel helmet falling off and spinning away on the concrete. Blood began flowing from a long gash in his cheek. The crowd roared in triumph. The two police officers who had been standing in the street sprinted forward and half dragged the injured soldier over to the sidewalk. A guardsman, wearing a medic's armband and red crosses on his helmet, came running to their side and began tending the injured man. While the two cops were kneeling beside him, a brick struck one of them in the side of the head, knocking his plastic helmet off and sending him sprawling. McAllister realized that the downed man was Oscar Maloney, who had worked in the Fourth District for years. The crowd of rioters cheered wildly.

Maloney staggered to his feet and shook off his partner, who was trying to help him. He moved to a police car parked on the street and, opening the rear door, dragged a sawed off pump shotgun from the back seat.

Suddenly, the burly officer ran back and pushed his way through the rank of guardsmen. McAlister heard Allen beside him, saying

"What the hell is Oscar doing?"

Maloney answered that question quickly.

"Cheer about this, you black bastards," he yelled. Jacking a round into the shotgun's chamber, he fired it into the street in front of the crowd. The lead pellets, bouncing off the pavement, became tiny whirring buzz saws, striking the legs of the people in the front of the crowd. People began screaming in pain and running to get away from the line of fire.

Maloney fired three more rounds in the same fashion, while the assembled police commanders stood and gaped. By the time the last round was fired, the street immediately in front of the guardsmen was empty. A number of men were limping away from the scene as fast as their injuries would allow.

The assembled cops broke into applause and cheers. Several of the guardsmen broke ranks and were patting Maloney on the back. Sergeant Phillips grinned at McAllister and Zarnecki.

"This shit has been going on all day. Every time we'd grab some of the ringleaders and get ready to take them downtown, a bunch of those black reverends would run over and negotiate with Colonel Milligan. Then we'd get ordered to turn 'em loose."

He looked over McAllister's shoulder.

"Here comes the brass. The shit will hit the fan now."

Lieutenant Colonel Edmund "Big Hand" Milligan was walking rapidly toward 28th Street, accompanied by A. D. Williams King and several other black men in suits and hats. His face looked purple enough to explode. The black ministers were all shouting loudly and gesticulating.

"Allen, get that man under control and get that damn shotgun away from him," Milligan shouted. "I want him suspended immediately. Get him out of here."

Allen shrugged his shoulders and started toward the crowd of guardsmen gathered around Maloney in the middle of the street. The guardsmen began booing and catcalling at the police commanders.

"Come on, McAllister, let's get out of here," Zarnecki said. "We've been in enough shit lately. Let's go do what the man told us to."

The two cops went back to their car and pulled away. As they left the area, McAllister looked in the rear view mirror at the group of people milling around in the intersection.

"Think Oscar's in much trouble, John?" he asked.

"Nah, I doubt Milligan will do much after he gets him away from there. He was just trying to pacify those nigger preachers. Old 'Big Hand' and Oscar go way back. Hell, they used to ride together on the Haymarket. They'll keep him inside and out of sight for awhile, that's all. For that matter, he can claim he was temporarily deranged when that brick hit him and didn't know what he was doing. And there won't be any complainants. Who's going to come in and say he was hit by police birdshot while he was engaging in a riot?"

Unable to fault Zarnecki's cynical logic, McAllister headed toward the command post.

Chapter Nineteen

Louisville, Kentucky. Tuesday, May 28, 1968, 7:05 p. m.

Susan Craig stirred and stretched languorously. A breeze from the air conditioning vent in the hotel room blew across her naked body and gave her a momentary chill. She reached over the edge of the bed and tugged the sheet and bedspread they had thrown off in their haste up to cover herself. From the bathroom, she could hear the noise of the shower running. Momentarily, she toyed with the idea of getting up and joining Mark in the shower. But she put the idea aside. Right now, she just wanted to lie there and enjoy her feeling of sexual fulfillment. God! How many times had he made her come? She had lost count after five. For the first time in her life, Susan felt she knew what sex was supposed to be like.

This thought caused the image of her soon-to-be ex-husband to pop into her mind. John had been a pretty good lover when he could take time off from his precious homicide squad to pay her the attention she needed. But he couldn't hold a candle to Mark when it came down to it. Mark didn't hesitate to use his mouth and tongue in all the right places. He intuitively knew what it took to bring Susan to orgasm again and again.

She had seen John on the news at noon. He looked like shit, unshaven and bleary-eyed, as if he hadn't slept in days. And he probably hadn't. They evidently had another whore killed and no arrest. She couldn't understand why John would care about a bunch of whores getting killed or why anybody would for that matter. But he did and she bitterly resented the time he devoted to his thankless job instead of to her.

When she first met Mark, she thought he was extremely attractive. At that point, she hadn't made up her mind what she was going to do about her marriage. Mark appeared as a guest lecturer at the night class she was taking. He asked her to go for coffee after class and she had agreed. She found herself excited by the thought that this good looking man was interested in her. She was thirty-five and the mother of two kids but that didn't mean her life had to always be in a rut. If her workaholic husband couldn't keep her satisfied, maybe it was time to find someone who could. Maybe it was time to explore some new horizons.

One week later, Mark had her moaning with delight in a room at the Executive Inn. A month after that, she had taken the kids and moved out. Moving in with her parents had provided her with a pair of ready made babysitters whenever she wanted to get away for a tryst with Mark, which was often. And, to make matters even better, her lawyer had just told her that John wasn't going to fight the divorce. She would get the house and the station wagon. John would get to keep his old Ford and would pay child support. In return, she had had to agree to relinquish any claim on his pension benefits. That was all right, though, he couldn't draw his pension for another twenty years. By then, she and Mark might be in Paris or London. Besides, Mark had plenty of money. She wouldn't need John Craig's paltry police pension. And Mark was going to marry her. He hadn't said that in so many words but she knew it.

The bathroom door opened and Mark came out, toweling his hair dry. He had another towel wrapped around his waist. She admired again his lean muscular body, tanned by his regular visits to the pool at the Louisville Country Club. Here again, she compared him to her ex-husband and John came up short in her mind. John was built like a tall refrigerator, square and bulky and hard. Mark was like a panther, lithe and sensuous. Plus John would never go near the country club and they wouldn't let him in if he did.

Mark looked at her and smiled.

"You'd better get a shower and get dressed if we're going to make that dinner at the club," he said.

"Just admiring the view," Susan replied, coquettishly. "I'll be ready in a jiffy."

She sprang from the bed and went into the bathroom. Behind her, she heard the television set come to life. An announcer was talking about the ongoing disturbances in the West End. Police and firemen were being fired on by snipers as they responded to calls. More National Guard troops were being activated and the curfew was in force again tonight.

"Do we have to listen to all that?" she called out

"I guess your husband's in the middle of it," Mark said.

"Oh, who cares?" she responded petulantly. "He'd rather be there than any place else. Besides, he won't be my husband in a few more days. That stuff is so boring."

Turning the shower on full blast, she stepped in and began washing the residue of her love making from her body.

Tuesday, May 28, 1968, 8:05 p. m.

"Car 516, at 38th and River Park Drive, a working fire in a dumpster outside the convenience store. Fire department has been notified," the police dispatcher intoned.

"516, 10-4, radio, from 26th and Broadway," Zarnecki said into the microphone and returned it to the dashboard.

McAllister pulled away from the Chop Shop parking lot and headed west on Broadway. Zarnecki along with Reeves and Gladstone in the back seat juggled their hot cups of coffee to adjust to his driving. The restaurant, although closed to the public, was providing sandwiches and coffee to the police officers and firefighters who could take time to go by there.

"Can't even get a few minutes to drink a damn cup of coffee," Zarnecki groused.

"Finish your coffee, John. I'll drive slow," McAllister said, grinning at his grumpy partner. He had learned in the past few days that the Mad Polack was a good man to have around in a tight spot. His idiosyncrasies were many but he was absolutely fearless. You didn't have to look around to find Zarnecki when you were in a sticky situation. He would be right beside you.

"Car 516, the fire department advised that they have shots fired at their truck at 38th and River Park. Step on your run," the dispatcher said.

Zarnecki tossed his coffee cup out the window and grabbed the microphone.

"516, 10-4, we're at 34th and Broadway."

From the back seat, two more coffee cups went out the window as McAllister stepped on the accelerator. Zarnecki flipped on the emergency lights and the electronic siren began its piercing yelp.

"Any unit in the vicinity that can back up 516, I have shots fired at the fire department at 38th and River Park," the dispatcher said, his higher pitched voice reflecting increased tension.

"406, we're clearing from this run on Market Street. We'll make it."

"771 and 772, we'll make it," two motorcycle officers chimed in.

It was a short haul to 38th Street and then McAllister turned north, pulling to the curb a short distance south of the T intersection with River

Park Drive. A large fire truck was in the middle of the intersection and several firemen were crouched down behind it. Across the street, a two story apartment complex was located next to the small convenience store. The apartment building was in a U shape with the arms of the U extending southward, enclosing a small court yard. A dumpster was sitting beside the store with wisps of smoke coming from it. A small crowd of young blacks, both male and female, was standing to the east of the convenience store and they appeared to be jeering at the crouching firemen.

As they got out of the car, the fire captain waved at them from the front of the truck. McAllister and Zarnecki, crouching low, ran to join him. Reeves and Gladstone took positions behind a parked car.

As all three of them crouched behind the big front wheel of the fire truck, the fire captain pointed in the direction of the apartment building.

"Shots came from there," he said. "Second floor, I think, but I'm not sure. We were unrolling hose on the auxiliary pump when he started shooting. Everybody dived for cover."

"He fired any shots since then?" Zarnecki asked.

"Every time somebody shows their head, he cuts loose. I climbed up in the apparatus to grab the radio so I could call for help and he bounced one right off the dash board."

McAllister glanced to his left and saw a large oak tree in the nearby yard. He grabbed Zarnecki's arm and pointed.

"I'm going to get over there and see if I can spot his location," he said.

"Watch your ass," Zarnecki warned.

"Don't worry, I will."

McAllister bolted from the shelter of the fire truck and dashed across the street into the yard. As he threw himself behind the tree, he heard the whine of a ricocheting bullet off the concrete behind him, followed by the flat crack of a rifle. He pulled himself closer to the bole of the tree and cautiously peered around it. In a moment, he saw the silhouetted outline of a person in one of the upper story windows. While he watched, the gunman stuck the barrel of a rifle out of the window and fired three rounds rapidly toward the fire truck. In the gathering dusk, McAllister could see the muzzle flashes quite vividly. The flat sound of the weapon told him that it was most likely a .22 caliber rifle, semi-automatic, from the rapidity of the shots.

He figured the range from his vantage point to the window to be about forty or fifty yards, a long distance for a handgun. However, he drew his .357 and prepared to fire at the sniper the next time he showed himself. He counted the windows and determined that the man had appeared in the third window from the left in the center wing of the building. Hopefully, somebody would arrive with some firepower better suited to the situation.

As an answer to his wishes, a National Guard two-and a-half ton truck drove up 38th Street at that moment and parked behind the police car. Several guardsmen clambered out of the rear of the truck and began running toward the fire truck.

A young soldier armed with a large Browning Automatic Rifle ran up into the yard where McAllister was hidden. He flung himself down beside the police officer and squinted down the barrel of his impressive weapon. His oversized steel helmet fell over his eyes and he had to push it back. He looked to be about fifteen years old.

"He's in the third window from the left, second floor," McAllister yelled at the young soldier. "If he shows himself again, put a few rounds in that window. He's been sniping at all of us."

The guardsman turned and looked at McAllister quizzically.

"I don't have any ammo," he said. "They wouldn't give us any."

"Great!" McAllister said. "What do they expect you to do? Throw rocks?"

The sniper appeared in the window at that point and fired three more shots in rapid succession in the direction of the growing group of vehicles on 38th Street. He was gone from the window in a second, before McAllister could line his sights up in the growing darkness.

"This is great," McAllister thought to himself. "This asshole will keep this up until he finally hits somebody and all we can do is hide behind this tree."

A yelping siren announced the arrival of another police car. McAllister watched as car 402 drove right up behind the fire truck. Terry Vogel got out of the vehicle cradling a weapon in his arms. McAllister recognized it as the Schmeisser 9 mm. machine gun that Vogel had shown him several months ago when he bought it. A German infantry weapon of World War II vintage, it was a potent firearm.

"Terry," McAllister yelled at Vogel. "Second floor, third window from the left in the middle of the building. He's got a .22 semi-auto."

Vogel stepped to the front of the fire truck and raised the machine gun to his shoulder. He fired a long, rattling burst across the front of the building's second story. Window glass shattered, shards of plaster flew from the walls and wood chips came from the window sills. The roar of the machine gun was deafening. The crowd of hecklers disappeared instantly.

Makeshift white flags popped out of several windows in the building.

McAllister, Zarnecki and several other cops charged the front door of the complex and pounded up the stairs to the second floor. Counting from the end of the hall, Zarnecki raised his big foot and kicked the door of apartment 2E in with one hard kick. A young black woman screamed as the cops ran into the apartment. She was lying on the floor in the living room, holding a baby in her arms.

The cops moved past her, into the bedroom and began searching the room. Zarnecki and a 4th District cop named Deatrich dragged a muscular young black male from under the bed and pulled him to his feet. They threw him on the bed and cuffed his hands behind him. McAllister poked through the clothes hanging in the closet and extracted a .22 rifle that had been hidden behind them.

"Here's the weapon," he shouted.

The barrel of the rifle was still warm to the touch. McAllister could see spent shell casings on the floor by the open window, lying among pieces of broken glass. One of Vogel's rounds had come through the top of the window and buried itself in the opposite wall.

Deatrich struck the young black man in the face with his fist, knocking him to his knees.

"You motherfucker, I oughta kill you," he ranted.

"Fuck you, honky," the man replied through bloodied lips.

Deatrich slipped a black jack out of his pants pocket and raised it to strike the man. Zarnecki grabbed his arm and stopped his swing.

"Cool it, Jack," he cautioned. "We got enough shit going on. Let's get him to the booking clerk."

The other cop glared at Zarnecki, who was holding his arm in an iron grip. Zarnecki stared back at him impassively. Then Deatrich subsided and took the prisoner by the arm, shoving him toward the door.

As the cops exited the building with their prisoner, the firemen were just finishing extinguishing the fire in the dumpster. Vogel was still standing by the fire truck, holding the Schmeisser. The rest of the street was deserted except for a small group of police officers. McAllister gave the .22 rifle to Partlow, Deatrich's partner, along with his and Zarnecki's code numbers, so they could receive credit for assisting in the arrest. As they walked back toward their car, McAllister noticed Dave Randall standing with the group of police. His former partner was all decked out in the riding breeches, boots and white helmet that motorcycle officers wore.

"Hey, rookie, don't you know that white helmet makes you a better target?" he yelled at Randall.

The young cop turned around and his face split into a wide grin.

"Hell, man, I go so fast they couldn't hit me if they tried. It's better than driving an old Nash Rambler. What are you doing down here, Scott? I thought you were working in the East End."

The two men shook hands warmly.

"Well, there I was, keeping Cherokee Park safe for squirrels and picnickers and the next thing I know, I'm back in the West End," McAllister said. "How do you like Traffic?"

"Man, it beats the hell out of working for Sergeant Marvin. All I have to do to keep my sergeant happy is write a few tickets every day. You know that was never a problem for me. How about you, are you stuck in Parks? I know you wanted to go to Homicide real bad. But, if you want, I can talk to my uncle and see if he can get you transferred to Traffic."

"Dave, I appreciate it but hopefully things are going to work out for me before long," McAllister replied. "How's your family doing?"

"Everybody's good, Scott. My wife is going bananas over me having to work in the West End while all this is going on but she'll be okay. What about you and Jenny? Are you still seeing her?"

"Yeah, as a matter of fact, we're going to get married," McAllister said.

Randall smiled broadly and clapped McAllister on the back.

"Way to go, buddy. Let me know when and I'll be there."

"Oh, you'll know," McAllister said. "I want you to be involved."

The loud sound of a motorcycle engine revving up interrupted their talk. Across the street, Randall's partner was beckoning him impatiently.

"Looks like Mike wants to go," Randall said. "He's not happy about having to ride in this end of town anyway. Let me know about the wedding."

"Will do, buddy, and remember, shiny side up on that Harley."

Randall waved in acknowledgement. In a moment, the two motorcycle cops left in a loud burst of noise and blue smoke. The four Parks cops went back to their car.

"Let's follow 406 downtown and help them book that guy," Zarnecki said.

McAllister looked at him inquiringly.

"Deatrich is a real hot head. If he starts tuning that guy up in the booking clerk, he could get carried away and hurt him. Then we're all in the shit if there's a complaint. I generate enough shit on my own. I don't need to be involved in somebody else's."

"You got it, partner," McAllister said as he turned the car toward headquarters.

Wednesday, May 29, 1968, 3:30 a. m.

Craig pulled into his driveway and turned the ignition off. Too tired to move at the moment, he slumped in his seat and rubbed his itchy eyes. He ached all over. They had interviewed more than two dozen people at Wendell's and the Milner Hotel. Nothing significant had come from any of the interviews to add to what they already knew. When they had returned to the Homicide office, Garrard had looked at their haggard faces and sent his Ripper detail home for the night. Craig, like the others, had reached the point of exhaustion where he was just going thought the motions. Hopefully a few hours sleep would get him back on his game.

Reluctantly, he dragged himself out of the car and into the house. Shedding his sport coat and tie as he went, he headed for the bedroom. He needed a shower but at this point, he needed sleep more. Discarding the rest of his clothes, he flopped across the bed.

The discordant jangle of the telephone on the bedside table shocked him awake. Grumbling aloud, he answered it.

"Craig. Whattaya want?"

"Good morning, Detective Craig," a deep male voice said. "How's your investigation coming along?"

"Who the fuck is this?" Craig answered.

"Oh, we haven't met, as of yet. But you've seen a lot of my work lately. You don't seem to appreciate it. In fact, you called me a lunatic to the press. That was unkind of you, most unkind. The fact that you don't understand the value of my work doesn't mean I'm a lunatic, it just means you're ignorant and closed-minded."

"Are you saying you're the Ripper?" Craig asked.

"That unfortunate appellation has been given me by the press, just as they gave it to my distinguished predecessor, almost a hundred years ago. But, yes, I'm Jack. Are you surprised to hear from me?"

"I get a lot of crank calls. You could be just another nut case for all I know," Craig said. Wide awake now, he was fumbling in the table drawer for the tape recorder he kept there. Hopefully, he could draw out the conversation long enough to get the man's voice on tape. Finding the recorder, he snapped the suction cup microphone to the telephone receiver and turned the recorder on.

"Oh, do you really think so?" the man asked. "Well, let me ask you this. Did you enjoy the little scene I set for you at the Milner Hotel? I thought it was rather droll, myself. I'm working on a follow up right now. Maybe I'll send you the next one's cunt, since you didn't seem to care for the head."

"Why are you doing this? What are you trying to accomplish?"

"Well, maybe some day we can sit down and discuss all that. I'm sure you'd find it interesting. I have my reasons, to be sure. But this conversation has gone on long enough. I don't think you can trace a call from your home but I see no need to take unnecessary chances. You'll be hearing from me again soon, and seeing the fruits of my labors. Until then, Ta Ta."

The connection broke and the dial tone came on. Craig rewound the tape and played it back. The last part of the Ripper's call was there. The man's voice was cultured, with a neutral accent. He spoke in measured tones.

Craig called Lieutenant Garrard at home and played the tape for him. They agreed that the best course was probably to submit the tape to the FBI lab for analysis. Craig advised his boss he would do that as soon as he came in that morning. He told him he would also check with the phone company, in case there was a chance of tracing the call.

"I don't think there's a hope, John. They have to put a trap in place on your phone before the call happens in order to trace a residential call. But we need to get them to do that in case he calls you back, which he probably will. He seems to enjoy communicating with you."

"Yeah, and I can't figure that out," Craig replied. "Why me?"

"We've got to catch him so we can ask him that," Garrard said. "Does his voice sound familiar to you at all?"

"I don't think so, boss. He doesn't sound like he's from Louisville, or Kentucky for that matter."

"Okay, get some sleep and I'll see you in the office."

Craig turned out the light and tried to compose himself for sleep. It was fruitless. Hs mind kept playing and replaying the conversation. Then it struck him that the man had called just a few minutes after he arrived home. Did that mean that the bastard was watching his house, waiting for him to arrive? He obviously knew his unlisted phone number, so it was likely that he also had his home address. Craig got up and parted the window curtains. The dark street outside his house looked normal. No unusual cars and no sinister figures lurking in the shadows that he could see. But that didn't necessarily mean the Ripper wasn't out there. For the first time since the separation, he was glad that Susan and the kids weren't at home.

Chapter Twenty

Louisville, Kentucky. Monday, June 3, 1968, 2:15 p. m.

The west end was much quieter. The police had clamped down tightly. The curfew was being strictly enforced and a lot of arrests had been made. Judges were setting high bonds and many of the more vocal and enthusiastic riot participants were languishing in the city jail. On Thursday night, two looters had been shot and killed; one by the police and one by a white liquor store owner. On Friday night, the streets were deserted. The mayor and police chief began discussing letting the National Guard go home.

The weather turned hot and humid over the weekend. On Monday, the mayor announced that the National Guard was being released. The state police left town and the city slowly began to return to normal. In the 4th District, the cops were still riding four man cars but the rest of the department went back to the normal patrol schedule.

Most of these events passed unnoticed by the detectives working the Ripper murders. The only benefit they derived from all of this was that the riot and the shootings had shifted the press's focus from the murders and given them a brief respite from being badgered by reporters for information. They continued working twelve and fourteen hour days, running down every conceivable lead.

Nothing seemed to pan out. The stores that sold theatrical supplies all had fake scars similar to the one they had found. Unfortunately, the scars were usually sold as part of a makeup kit which was popular with theatrical groups. To make matters more difficult, all of the stores kept lousy sales records. So far, no good suspect had turned up from the examination of those records.

Jimmy Mudd had been unable to remember the name of the farm he had seen on the door of the suspect's pick up truck, in spite of many attempts to jog his memory. Now, they were visiting all the named farms they could identify in Jefferson County and the adjoining counties, hoping to get lucky and spot the truck.

Mudd, Ella the waitress and Mr. DePaul had spent several hours with a sketch artist, an art teacher from the University of Louisville who volunteered his services to the police department. The result was a full face sketch of a white male with narrow facial features and high cheek bones. The heavy horn rimmed glasses and baseball cap obscured his eyes and hairline. It would be difficult to identify anyone from the sketch. Nevertheless, Lieutenant Garrard ordered it reproduced and distributed throughout the department and to all law enforcement agencies in a five state area. So far, no worthwhile leads had come in from the sketch.

The tape of the Ripper's phone call to Craig had been sent to the FBI laboratory in Washington. The Special Agent in Charge of the Louisville FBI office had made a personal phone call to the laboratory director asking him to expedite analysis of the tape. Southern Bell had installed traps on Craig's home phone, the homicide office lines and the special Ripper hot line. If he called Craig again, hopefully they would be able to trace the call.

The lack of progress in the case added to the tension that existed in the Homicide Squad, particularly between Rovinelli and Colbert. Rovinelli was still fuming over the fact that Colbert had struck him and he hadn't been able to retaliate. He went out of his way to antagonize the black detective at every opportunity. Craig did his best to make sure the two men worked together as little as possible.

Garrard looked up as Craig entered the office. He motioned to the chair beside his desk.

"Shut the door, John. I need to talk to you," he said. "What in the hell is going on between Colbert and Rovinelli?"

"Boss, they had a little confrontation last week. Wallace and I broke it up. No big deal."

"I heard their little confrontation involved duking it out with each other on 18th Street. Is that right?"

Craig wasn't really surprised. Garrard was an old street cop with a lot of sources of information. He had probably heard about the fight the day after it happened.

"It wasn't much of a fight, boss. They're both hotheads and they don't like each other."

"Well, they're acting like a couple of kids and it's interfering with us getting the job done. I've seen you go out of your way to keep them from having to work together. I can't have this petty bullshit going on. We've got too much at stake here. We've got to catch this sadistic asshole and we've got to do it quick."

"Boss, I - ," Craig started to say. Garrard held up his hand to stop him.

"I'm putting Rovinelli back on a shift. We're getting McAllister back tomorrow. I'm assigning him to work with you. I'm keeping you two and Wilson and Colbert on the Ripper cases for the time being."

"Lieutenant, I'm glad we're getting Scott back, but how is that going to set with Major Bishop?"

"Between you and me, John, Major Bishop is now Captain Bishop. They busted him an hour ago. His big plans to sandbag the Chief have caught up with him. Captain Hall is being named acting Chief of Detectives. You know he thinks a lot of McAllister. In fact, he went to bat for him with the Chief this morning. They're going to clear him on the Lewis shooting. Also, the Commonwealth Attorney called me and told me that he's reviewed the Lewis and Williams file, thinks it was righteous and doesn't intend to present it to the grand jury."

"Damn, things may be looking up around here," Craig said.

"Yeah, well, we'd better solve this case, John, or we may all be back in uniform."

Monday, June 3, 1968. 3:00 p. m.

McAllister found two envelopes in his mail box when he reported for duty in the Parks Office. Both of them bore the frank of the Office of the Chief of Police. He sat down beside Zarnecki at the roll call table and opened one of them.

"I'll be damned," he said aloud as he read the first memo.

"What's up, kid?" Zarnecki asked.

"It seems the Chief of Police has reviewed the Jerome Lewis case and finds that I acted properly and in the line of duty."

"What? You mean they finally got their heads out of their asses? It took them long enough. Way to go, Mac," Zarnecki said.

"I tell you what, John. I'll take it, no matter how long it took," McAllister replied.

He opened the other envelope. It, too, was brief and to the point.

To: Officer Scott T. McAllister
Parks and Special Services Section

From: Chief of Police

Effective at the close of business, June 3, 1968, you are being transferred to the Detective Bureau. Report to the booking clerk to have your photograph made in civilian clothes. You are to report to Captain Emmett Hall for specific assignment.

"I'll be double damned," he said.

"Now what?" Zarnecki asked.

Craig handed him the memo. Zarnecki scanned it and his face split into a grin.

"Well, that's just great. I'm about to get you broken in as a decent partner and you pull this shit. Now, you'll turn out to be as worthless as the rest of those dickheads running around in cheap suits."

"John, I give you my word. I won't wear cheap suits," McAllister said. "Jenny won't let me."

"I know our fat but fearless leader would like to be here to congratulate you in person," Zarnecki said. "But, unfortunately, it's still close to the first of the month and he has rents to collect, so he's taken the day off. I, as the acting sergeant, will have to do the honors."

"All right, acting sergeant, sir. Can I have a little time to check in with Captain Hall before we hit the street?"

"Take all the time you need, lad. I'm in no hurry. Oh, by the way, Captain Hall is now the acting Chief of Detectives. Did you know that?"

"No shit?" McAllister said. "When did this happen and what happened to Bishop?"

"The Chief busted his ass back to Captain this afternoon and assigned him to the impoundment lot. I guess that all may be tied into this burst of good fortune that has come your way today."

McAllister left the Parks Office and went down the hall to the Detective Bureau. He knocked on the open door of the Chief of Detectives' office. Captain Hall and Lieutenant Garrard were seated at the long conference table with files spread out before them.

"Come in, Scott," Captain Hall said. "Did you get your transfer letter yet?"

"Yes, sir. It said to check with you for specific assignment."

"Okay, you're going to the Homicide Squad. Lieutenant Garrard can fill you in on your specific assignment."

"Scott, are you working 3-11 today?" Garrard asked.

"Yes, sir. My transfer is effective at close of business."

"Can you double back and come in at 8:00 tomorrow morning?"

"Yes, sir. No problem."

"Good, you are going to partner with John Craig, at least for the time being. The two of you will be working the Ripper cases, along with Colbert and Wilson. We'll get your badge and I. D. card taken care of in the morning. Did you ever get your personal weapon returned to you after the lab finished with it?"

"They sent it back a couple of weeks ago, sir."

"Well, we're glad to have you back with us. Any questions?"

"No, sir. Not right now," McAllister replied. "I just want to thank both of you for giving me this chance. I won't let you down."

"We know you won't, Scott," Captain Hall said. "We'll see you tomorrow, then."

McAllister was elated as he left the Detective Bureau. His foremost ambition was about to be realized and he would get to work with the cop that he respected most. His life had taken a definite turn for the better. He had to call Jenny.

When he returned to the Parks office, it was empty. He sat down at Arthur's desk and dialed Jenny's work. When he told her his news, she was ecstatic.

"Scott, that is marvelous. I am so happy and so proud of you," she said. He could almost feel her warmth over the phone. They chatted for a few minutes and made plans for a date that weekend. As he was preparing to say goodbye, Jenny interrupted him.

"I almost forgot to tell you. I saw John Craig's wife last night going into Casa Grisanti with a fellow who works in my office."

"Oh, yeah?" Scott replied. "Who was that?"

"It was Mark Clayton. Haven't I mentioned him to you?"

"I don't think so, honey. I don't remember the name and you know we famous detectives never forget a name."

"Oh, bull, Mr. Famous Detective. If you're so good, how come you forgot my birthday?"

"I forgot your birth-…. Wait just a minute, your birthday's in September. What are you trying to pull?"

Jenny's laugh bubbled over the phone.

"Had you going for a minute there, didn't I? Anyway, Mark Clayton is a lawyer here. He's the one that is a good friend of Michael Renyard."

"No kidding? Maybe he's the mystery boyfriend. She wouldn't tell John who she was going out with. If he's a friend of Renyard's, he can't be much.

I hear they've transferred him to the city law department. He's working on building codes or something like that. Quite a comedown for a big wheel like him. Listen, babe, I've gotta run. I'll call you at home tonight."

Monday, June 3, 1968, 6:30 p. m.

Officer Darrell Evans sped up in a vain effort to get some cooler air circulating through the patrol car. It was futile. The air that came in through the rolled down windows and the wing vents felt like a sauna. In the passenger seat, his partner, Henry "Hank" Morrison, a twenty year veteran, was sweating buckets. Both men's shirts were soaked through and sticking to the car seats.

"Darrell, let's go to Jimmy's and get a nice cold beer and enjoy the air conditioning for a few minutes," Morrison said.

"Sounds like a plan to me, partner," Evans replied, turning the car north on 6th Street. At Magnolia, he pulled up in front of Jimmy's Bar and Grill. Grabbing their "Little Tiger" adapter and transistor radio, the two cops bailed out of the sweltering car and into the dim coolness of the bar.

Jimmy saw them coming and had two frosted mugs sitting on the bar before they reached him.

"Pretty hot out there, huh, guys?" he asked with a grin.

Morrison downed half of his beer in two gulps. Then, wiping his mouth, he replied.

"Too damn hot for a delicate creature like me, Jimbo. How about another one? This one had a hole in it."

"Are the jungle bunnies acting up tonight?" Jimmy asked as he sat two more beers up.

"Nah, it's been real quiet in the West End," Evans replied. "In fact, it's quiet all over."

The two cops bantered with Jimmy for several minutes. They all looked up as the door opened and a short stocky man in coveralls came in. Seeing the police at the bar, he walked over to them.

"Say, officers, there's a big guy out there in the middle of 6th Street directing traffic," the man said. "I think he's drunk. He's yelling at everybody and waving his arms around. Looks like he's got some kind of po-lice hat on. You better do something before somebody runs over him."

Evans and Morrison looked at one another. They had both left their uniform caps in the front seat of the car, which was unlocked with all the windows down. Setting down their beer mugs, they dashed out into the street. A very large and very dirty man was indeed standing in the middle of the intersection, waving his arms and bellowing obscenities at the cars passing him. Perched on top of his huge head was a Louisville Police uniform cap several sizes too small for him. He had procured a whistle from someplace and was blowing shrill blasts on it when he wasn't cursing.

"Oh, Gawd!" Morrison moaned. "It's Caldwell McFeeny."

"Who the hell is that, Hank?" his partner asked.

"He's a wino and a police fighter," Morrison replied. "Call us some backup."

"You think the two of us can't take him?" Evans said.

"God damn it, Darrell. Didn't you hear what I said? Look at the size of that bastard. Now, get on that radio and call for backup."

Evans went quickly to the car and picked up the radio microphone.

"Car 304 to radio. We need backup at 6th and Magnolia on a disorderly person in the street."

"10-4, Car 304. We just got a couple of calls on him," the dispatcher replied. "Car 303, back up 304 at 6th and Magnolia on a disorderly person."

"303, 10-4. From 7th and Hill."

Evans picked up his and Morrison's night sticks from the front seat and walked back to his partner.

"I think that's your hat, Hank," he said as he gave him his stick. "Mine's still in the car. 303 is coming to help us from 7th and Hill."

A small crowd of spectators was beginning to gather on the corner. They began to jeer both the police officers and McFeeny. Against his better judgment, Morrison took a tight grip on his nightstick and walked out in the street toward the man, who was at least a foot taller than he was. Evans followed him with some misgivings.

"All right, Caldwell. The fun's over," Morrison said. "Give me my hat and get your ass out of the street."

"Your hat?" the giant replied. "This is my hat. I'm the new po-lice on this beat. You go find your own beat."

He turned and yelled at the jeering crowd.

"Screw all you motherfuckers. I'm coming over there in a minute and lock all your asses up, just as soon as I get this God damn traffic directed to suit me."

Morrison reached out and grabbed McFeeny by the arm. It was like grabbing a telephone pole and had about as much effect.

The huge man turned and picked up Morrison bodily, lifting him over his head. Evans ran toward his struggling partner. McFeeny casually threw Morrison at the charging officer and the two of them went down in a tangle of arms and legs. The crowd roared.

Just then, Car 303 arrived on the scene. Snodgrass and Barnett sized up the situation quickly.

"303 to radio. This is Caldwell McFeeny over here at 6th and Magnolia and he's drunk. Send us a couple more cars."

The two officers ran into the intersection and McFeeny turned to face the latest onslaught. As he did, Evans, who had managed to untangle himself from his partner, jumped squarely on his back. He tried to apply the choke hold around the neck that he had learned in the academy. McFeeny simply pushed his chin down against his chest and refused to raise it. Evans couldn't get his arm around the man's neck. Then McFeeny twitched his shoulders and sent Evans flying.

Yelling unintelligibly, McFeeny went toward the two new arrivals. He swung a fist the size of a ham against Snodgrass's head and the cop went down. Barnett swung his stick against the giant's torso and he grunted slightly. He reached out to grab Barnett, who backpedaled rapidly.

By now, two more cars had arrived and there were nine bodies in the ongoing melee. Three of the bigger officers had managed to attach themselves to McFeeny's upper body and their combined weight was bearing him down to his knees. He had been hit in the head with nightsticks several times and his scalp was bleeding profusely. Several of the cops were also bleeding from misdirected blows.

Morrison saw the opening he wanted, as McFeeny went to his hands and knees. Quickly he got behind him and slipped one arm around the man's neck and, using his nightstick, applied a bar strangle hold, putting intense pressure on the giant's carotid arteries. In just seconds, McFeeny became unconscious and fell face forward into the street.

"Quick, get some cuffs on him," Morrison yelled. Evans quickly pulled his handcuffs out and, dragging McFeeny's arms behind his back, snapped the cuffs on his wrist. They would barely go around the man's wrists.

"Barnett, see if Jimmy's got some rope or something we can tie his feet with. Hurry up, before the big bastard comes to," Morrison said.

Barnett ran into the tavern and emerged shortly with a coil of cotton clothesline. Morrison quickly made a loop in the rope and slipped it over McFeeny's feet, yanking it tight. He wrapped the rope around his legs several times and tied it off just in time. McFeeny had regained consciousness and was attempting to rise to his feet. Two officers quickly sat on him.

"Darrell, back our car over here and we'll load him in the back," Morrison shouted.

Evans quickly backed the station wagon into the intersection and opened the tailgate. It took the combined strength of all the cops there to lift McFeeny and shove him in the car. He was cursing and bellowing like a bull. He was struggling against his restraints and the car was rocking on its springs. They got his upper body into the wagon and then he turned himself sideways and they couldn't budge him any further.

Snodgrass pushed his way through the crowd of cops and, shielded from the crowd by the bodies of the other cops, reversed his nightstick in his hand and smashed the butt of it into McFeeny's groin. The giant let out a horrendous yell and bent himself forward. The other cops seized the advantage and pulled him the rest of the way into the wagon. He had ceased struggling and was bent double, moaning softly.

"Paybacks are hell, motherfucker," Snodgrass rasped as he leaned against the side of the car. The right side of his jaw was swelling rapidly where McFeeny had struck him and his face was cherry red. Morrison looked around at the other officers there. There were torn shirts, badges and nametags ripped loose, lumps, lacerations and the beginnings of a couple of black eyes.

"Jesus Christ, what a mess!" Morrison said.

"Yeah, and to top it off, we're going to have to take this asshole to General and get him cleaned up and sewed up. The booking clerk will never take him bleeding like that," Evans said. "Don't forget your hat, Hank. It's what started all this shit."

Fuming, Morrison picked his hat up from the street and jammed it on his head.

"A couple of you all better follow us to General," he said. "We may have to do this all over again when we get there."

As they drove toward the hospital, Morrison became conscious of a strange feeling in his hairline. It felt like hundreds of little feet were crawling through his hair. Yanking his hat off, he inspected the inner lining. His suspicions were immediately confirmed by the sight of several small gray bugs crawling around in his hat. He could still feel their cousins in his hair, lots of them.

"Oh, you son of a bitch," he shouted.

"What's the matter, Hank?" his partner asked.

"Lice, that's the fucking matter. This asshole's head is full of lice and he's filled my fucking cap full. I've got the damn things all over me. That tears it. We're going to charge this son of a bitch with everything we can think of, starting with eight counts of Assault and Battery on a Police Officer."

Acting on an impulse and out of anger, Hank Morrison made a decision at that point that would have an important impact on the investigation of the Ripper murders.

Chapter Twenty-One

Tuesday, June 4, 1968, 10:15 a. m.

McAllister sat at the sergeant's desk and contemplated the turn of events since yesterday. He was alone in the office. The morning had been busy. First, he had gone to the supply room, turned in his issued service revolver, a Smith and Wesson Military and Police model with a four inch barrel, and his patrolman's badge and cap shield. In return, he had received a Smith and Wesson Chief's Special .38 caliber revolver with a two inch barrel, well used from the looks of it. Most of the bluing on the barrel had been worn away. He was also issued a worn holster, two small leather bullet pouches designed to hold five rounds each, and a small gold detective's badge, numbered 135.

Then he had gone to the photo lab and had his picture taken for his new I. D. card. With these actions, he was magically transformed from a patrolman into a detective. He had little chance to reflect on his new status, however. Once the formalities were over, Craig had immediately sat him down and gone into a detailed briefing on the Ripper murders and the things that had transpired since he was transferred to Parks. This has just ended a few minutes ago and they were getting ready to hit the street when Craig had been summoned to Captain Hall's office.

McAllister had put the Chief's Special in his locker and was carrying his own Smith and Wesson Model 19-2, a .357 magnum with a two and a half inch barrel. It was heavier and more accurate than the small framed Chief's Special and held six rounds instead of five. It felt natural riding on his hip.

He pulled the small badge out of his pocket again and looked at it reflectively. It meant to him that he had achieved an important personal goal. Now, he had to set about the task of learning his new job and being the best detective that he could be. If he could eventually be as good as John Craig, he would be well satisfied.

The shrill ring of the telephone interrupted his thoughts. There was no one around to answer it but him. He only hoped the caller didn't present a problem or ask a question that he couldn't handle.

"Homicide Squad, Detective McAllister." He spoke these words for the first time with an inward flush of pleasure.

"Hey, Scott," the caller said. "I heard you got out of the squirrel squad and got brains. Congratulations. This is Charlie Newman."

McAllister was glad to hear from his old partner and training officer. Newman had been promoted to sergeant a couple of years before and was assigned to the City Jail.

"Charlie, how the hell are you? Man, I haven't seen you in months. Are you still in jail?"

"I can't get out, man. These prisoners can serve out their time, make bond or whatever but I'm stuck here on an indeterminate sentence. About the only progress I've made is to get off the three to eleven and on straight day work, which helps the family life. Scott, is John Craig around?"

"He's in the Captain's office, Charlie. Should be back any minute. Want me to have him call you?"

"Yeah, or maybe you both might want to come up here. Do you know Caldwell McFeeny?"

"I've heard the name. Isn't he a Second District wino? Great big guy?" McAlister asked.

"Third District, mostly, but you're thinking about the right guy," Newman replied.

"He got locked up last night after fighting with a bunch of Third District cops. He came back from court a little while ago and asked me if I could get in touch with Craig for him. Says he's got some information on those murders you all are working and wants to make a deal."

"What kind of deal?" McAllister asked.

"That's all he'll say right now. He insists on talking to Craig. He's charged with eight counts of A & B – Police Officer. He went to court this morning and I think he pled guilty like he usually does when he gets charged with Drunk and Disorderly. Only there was a substitute judge on the bench this morning and he gave him ninety days. Caldwell seems to be sweating that. Says he can't do ninety days because he's got to take care of his babies."

"Babies? Does he have a family?"

"Not that I know of. I don't know what the hell he's talking about.

Maybe John can get more out of him. Caldwell says he won't talk to anybody but him"

"I'll tell John as soon as he comes back, Charlie."

McAllister hung up and was writing some notes when Craig walked into the office. McAllister related the conversation to him. Craig looked thoughtful.

"Caldwell McFeeny pickled most of his brain years ago, drinking Solax and cheap wine," he said. "I doubt that anything he's got to say will make much sense or help us out any. On the other hand, he's on the street all the time. Maybe he saw something or thinks he did. Let's see what he has to say."

They locked up their weapons in a desk drawer, then went to the third floor and rang the bell at the door to the city jail. Charlie Newman opened the viewing window and then unlocked the big steel door to let them in.

"How you doing, John?" he asked. "And how did you get so lucky to get junior here for a partner?"

Craig shook hands with the sergeant as he replied.

"To tell the truth, Sarge, since he saved my ass at 8th and Broadway last month, I've been wanting to keep him pretty close to me in case it needs saving again."

"Yeah, I heard about that. Good for you, Scott."

McAllister blushed at the compliment.

"Just shows the advantages of having a good training officer, Charlie," he said.

"What's Caldwell up to now, Sarge?" Craig asked.

"I'm not real sure but something has got him fired up. He wants out of here and he wants out bad. He says he can help you on the hooker homicides if you'll get him out. He stopped me this morning when I was back on the cell block and asked me to call you. He was real humble and serious about it, which ain't like Caldwell. Usually, he comes in raising hell, sobers up, dries out and does his time. Couple of times we've had to take him to General Hospital to get a Bellevue Cocktail when he's gone into the D. T.'s but there's no sign of that so far. I think when that fill-in judge gave him ninety days this morning, it really shook him up."

"What's he in for?" McAllister asked.

"He was directing traffic yesterday at 6th and Magnolia with a 3rd District cop's hat on, which he had snaked out of the guy's car while he was in the bar. The cop tried to stop him and get his hat back and Caldwell wasn't ready to quit. It took eight of them to get him under control. Then they had to whip him again at General while they were sewing him up.

So, they were pretty pissed when they booked him. They charged him with everything they could think of, including eight counts of Assault and Battery – Police Officer."

"Even if he had some good information, we'd have a hell of a time getting those charges skinned back, wouldn't we?" Craig asked.

"If you could get ahold of Judge Colson and tell him why, he might set aside the judgment and let him make bond, if the arresting officers went along with it," Newman replied.

"Who are they?" McAllister asked.

"Hank Morrison and a rookie named Evans are the first two on the arrest."

"I know Hank pretty well," Craig said. "Let's see what McFeeny has to say and then we'll figure out if it's worth fooling with."

"Okay, why don't you use my office?" Newman said. "I'll go get Caldwell and bring him in there."

In a few minutes, Newman led the hulking McFeeny into his small office. He was wearing a khaki shirt and pants marked "City Jail" and his head was completely wrapped with a bandage as big as a rajah's turban. There were vivid bruises on both sides of his face and his right eye was swollen shut. McAllister was surprised at the size of the man. Although he and Craig were both big men, McFeeny towered over them both and seemed to fill the room. He glanced at McAllister with suspicion.

"Who's he?" he demanded.

"My partner, Caldwell, Detective McAllister," Craig replied. "He's a good guy. And, he's a good friend of Judge Colson's. He's going to help get you out if what you tell us is any help to us."

The man's demeanor changed completely. He looked at Craig pleadingly.

"I got to get out, Mr. Craig. I can't do no ninety days. I got some things I got to take care of."

"What kind of things, Caldwell?" Craig asked.

"I can't tell. I can't. But it's important. You got to help me, Mr. Craig. You helped me before, back when they said I beat up that woman. You showed them I didn't do it. That's why I asked Sergeant Newman to tell you I wanted to talk to you. You help me this time and I'll help you." The man was becoming more agitated as he spoke. McAllister scanned the office for something to use as a weapon just in case Caldwell decided to go berserk. He decided that the wooden coat tree in the corner was the only thing in sight that might slow McFeeny down.

"How are you going to help me, Caldwell?"

"Get me out of here and I'll tell you," McFeeny replied.

"It doesn't work that way, Caldwell, and you know it. First, you have to tell us what you know. Then we check it out. If it's good information and helps us, we go to the judge and try to get you sprung."

"I got to get out, I tell you. I just got to."

"Then tell us what you know and we'll get started on it. The sooner we check it out, the sooner you're out of here if it's good stuff."

"Caldwell," Sergeant Newman spoke up. "You know you can believe Detective Craig. If he says he'll help you, he'll do it. But you got to give him something to work with. No judge is going to turn you loose from a ninety day sentence unless you give these detectives some good information."

The giant was setting on a metal chair with his head down. He looked up at Craig and there were tears in his eyes.

"All right, I guess I got no choice. I got to get out of here."

"You said you knew something about the man who's been killing these women in town. Do you know who he is?" Craig asked.

McFeeny shook his head.

"I don't know him. I just seen him twice. But I know some things about him."

"When did you see him, Caldwell?" Craig asked.

"The night he left that woman in the park. I seen him get her out of his truck. He drove it right up in the park and put her on the bench. I was up on the stage. There's a room up there where I go sometimes to sleep one off. It was real dark. He couldn't see me. Then he started cuttin' on her. He fucked around with her a long time. He had tape over her mouth so she couldn't yell. He wrote some shit on the wall and then he got in his truck and drove off. At first I thought I was seein' things like I do sometimes. Then I went down to where she was and seen she was dead. He'd split her from asshole to appetite."

"Did you call anybody? Try to get help?" Craig asked.

"What I did was get the hell out of there. I figured if the cops found her with me around, I'd be the number one boy to pin it on. She was dead as a mackerel, anyway. Wasn't nothing nobody could do to help her."

"What did the guy look like, Caldwell?"

"Tall, skinny white guy was all I could tell. Looked like he had on coveralls, like a mechanic."

"That's not much help, Caldwell," Craig said. "I'm not going to be able to convince a judge to let you out, just on that story."

"I know some more about him, Mr. Craig. I know where he keeps his truck."

"The hell you say," Craig replied. "How do you know that?"

"After I seen the woman was dead, I headed to my place. I was unlocking the door when he come down the alley in his truck. I knowed it was the same truck by the writin' on the door. He went on down the alley to an old garage, got out and unlocked it. Then he pulled a big old car out of it and pulled the truck in. He was inside for a while, then come out without the coveralls on. He locked it up and drove off in the car."

Craig was excited. McAllister could tell from watching him, although his demeanor remained calm. He had reason to be excited, if this story turned out to be true.

"Can you show us that garage, Caldwell?" Craig asked.

"Sure can," McFeeny replied. "It's just down the alley from my place. Truck's still there, too, or was yesterday."

"How can you tell if it's in the garage?"

"I pulled the doors far enough apart that I can see in. I check it ever now and then. Sometimes the big car's in there. Sometimes the truck."

"Okay," Craig said, standing up. "Sarge, can you sign Caldwell out in my custody for a while?"

"You bet," Newman replied. "I'll get the release form drawn up."

"Here's the deal, Caldwell. We're going to take you out there and you show us the garage. If it's the truck we're looking for, we'll call the judge and get you sprung. Is that fair enough?"

"That's what I need. I got to get out of here and take care of my ba-. I just got to get out."

"Scott, call the boss and tell him what we're doing. Tell him we'll radio him from the scene yes or no and he can meet us there. We may need Larry and Wallace too."

McAllister was dialing the phone on Newman's desk as Craig spoke.

* * *

Following McFeeny's directions, they pulled into the alley west of 6th Street, just a block from Central Park. This was the Cabbage Patch neighborhood, made up of older, Victorian style homes, many of them with separate carriage houses facing the alley. A number of these had been converted into garages and small apartments.

McFeeny was strapped into the back seat of the detective car with his hands handcuffed to a ring attached to a large leather belt around his waist. The belt was buckled in the back. He was further restrained by leg irons fastened to each ankle and connected by a foot long chain. Having signed him out of jail, Craig was taking no chances on him escaping their custody. The big man was docile as a lamb, however. He seemed to have faith in Craig.

He pointed out a ramshackle single car garage on the west side of the alley. Its double doors were chained together and locked with a large padlock.

"That's the garage, Mr. Craig. That's where he keeps his truck."

Craig pulled into a paved parking space in the rear of a yard two doors down.

"Check it out, Scott. See what you can tell about it from the outside."

McAllister approached the garage and first attempted to peer inside through a small window on the side of the building. It was completely covered from the inside with dark cloth. He then went to the doors and pulled them apart as far as the chain would permit. This opened a gap of about two inches between the two doors. He put his face to this gap and looked into the dim interior.

The outline of a pickup truck was visible. He saw "Chevrolet" on the tailgate and the familiar blue emblem. The garage was too narrow and dark for him to see the sides of the truck. It appeared to be dark green in color. He shined his flashlight through the gap and focused the beam on the license plate. It was a Tennessee tag, heavily covered with mud, rendering the numbers unreadable.

McAllister looked around him and saw a piece of lath sticking out of a trash barrel nearby. When he pulled it out, it was about three feet long. Quickly, he went back to the garage and spread the doors again. Kneeling, he pushed the lath through the gap and began scraping the mud from the license plate, until he could read the numbers.

"MTY604" he muttered to himself. He quickly went back to the car and climbed in.

In response to Craig's quizzical look, he said

"Green Chevy pickup. Tennessee plates, I had to scrape mud off before I could read the numbers."

"What about writing on the doors?" Craig asked.

"It's too dark, John. You can't see the doors. Let's see who it belongs to."

He took the microphone off the dash and called the dispatcher.

"602 Adam to radio. Request stolen and registration on Tennessee license # Mary-Tom-Yankee 604."

"Stand by, 602 Adam," the dispatcher replied.

A few minutes later, she called back.

"Radio to 602 Adam. Be advised that is a stolen license plate. Reported stolen by Franklin, Tennessee PD on February 15, 1968. The plate belongs on a 1965 Ford pickup truck."

Craig nodded in satisfaction.

"That gives us an excuse to get a warrant and search the garage. We'll put what Caldwell told us in the affidavit, too. I'll stretch a point and call him a 'reliable informant'. Call the boss and tell him to meet us and bring 601A. Don't mention anything on the air about what we're doing."

McAllister shot Craig a look of surprise.

"John, I know I'm new at this but I'm not totally dense. I told the boss when I talked to him that we would just tell him to meet us if it looked good."

Craig turned to his partner and made a gesture of apology.

"Scott, I'm sorry. When I get cooking on a case, I just say out loud everything I'm thinking."

"No sweat, partner." McAllister turned back to the radio.

"602 Adam. Advise 610 to meet us at the location."

Garrard's voice came back immediately over the speaker.

"610 is okay. On the way."

In the back seat, McFeeny shifted nervously.

"Mr. Craig, can I go now?" he asked.

"Caldwell, we've got to take you back to jail, get the warrant, get a judge to sign it, check the garage and make sure the truck is the one we want. Then, we go see the judge about letting you out."

"Will I get out today?"

"I think so, probably sometime this afternoon, if it all works out."

"Can we stop at my place? I got to check something."

"I don't think so, Caldwell. We've got a lot of things to take care of."

McFeeny leaned forward in the seat and flexed his arms against the cuffs and the leather belt. McAllister wondered if he were going to pop the cuffs right off the belt.

He reached down beside his side and fingered the strap of his nightstick, lying on the floorboard. If this big bastard went nuts, he wasn't sure he and John could stop him without shooting him. Then, to his surprise, he noticed tears running down McFeeny's cheeks.

"Mr. Craig. I'm beggin' you. Please go by my place. It's right down the alley and it won't take ten minutes. I've got to feed and water my babies or they're gonna die. Then you can take me back to jail if you have to."

Craig looked at McAllister and shrugged his shoulders.

"What do you think, Scott?"

"It looks like he's been straight with us. Let's give him a break. Besides, I want to see what these 'babies' look like."

Craig pulled the car down the alley to an old carriage house that McFeeny pointed out. Most of it had been converted into a garage but there was an area at one side that had formerly been a tack room for the horses. They got out of the car and, unstrapping McFeeny, hoisted him out of the back seat. The man weighed close to three hundred pounds and was as hard as a rock.

"Key's under that brick by the doorstep," he said. Craig turned over the brick and found the key. He put it in the door lock and turned it, opening the door and steeping inside. The room was tidier than he had expected with a narrow bed against one wall, some milk crate shelving, and a small table. Lying beside the table on a pile of rags, a brown and white dog began to whine and wag her tail furiously. Nestled to her were five small puppies, all busily nursing.

"I will be damned," Craig said. "Look at this, Scott. He really does have some babies."

"I told you I did, Mr. Craig, and she ain't been fed since yesterday or had no water either."

The mother, a small collie mix, rose and went to McFeeny, where she sat by his leg and looked anxiously at him. He knelt and began rubbing her head with his shackled hands.

"Unlock me, Mr. Craig, so I can feed her, will you?"

"I can't do that, Caldwell, but show us where the food is and we'll do it."

"In that can in the corner and the water faucet's out in the garage."

"I'll get it, John," McAllister said. He knelt and scratched the little dog behind her ears and was rewarded with a lick on his hand.

"What's her name, Caldwell?" he asked.

"I just call her 'Lady,'" McFeeny replied. "She come in the garage one night and I fed her. So she stayed around and the next thing I know, she's havin' pups."

McAllister filled a bowl with dry dog food and then carried the water dish to the garage and filled it. Lady immediately went to the bowl and began eating. The pups, whose eyes had obviously not been open for long, began exploring their surroundings.

Craig bent down and picked up one of them and began petting it. It reacted with squeals of delight and snuggled into his chest.

"They won't take Lady away from me, will they, Mr. Craig? I mean, I don't have no license for her or nothin'."

"This is between you and us, Caldwell," Craig replied. "Now, that should hold them for awhile. Let's get the rest of our job done, so you can get out of jail and take care of your dogs."

Chapter Twenty-Two

Tuesday, June 4, 1968, 1:15 p. m.

He turned off 7ᵗʰ Street onto Magnolia. He needed to get some things ready for tonight. It was time to send John Craig another memento. He knew just where to find her too. She had flirted with him shamelessly the other night at the bar where she worked. Had let him know she was available. Told him she got off at eight o'clock. He would get her in the parking lot after she left the bar, take her to the new place and dissect her. Send her cunt to Craig like he promised and drop her corpse somewhere downtown, where it would stir up a lot of shit.

The new place was working out well. For one thing, it was a hell of a lot closer to his hunting grounds than the farm. That decreased the chances of him being seen or stopped by the cops with either a live, trussed up whore or a dead body in his truck. Also, it was isolated, which met his needs.

The thought of it made him shiver in anticipation. The fucking shameless whore. She pretended to be a cocktail waitress but she was just another whore. This would be the dress rehearsal for his next and greatest piece of work. He was going to rip the biggest whore of them all. It was going to have to be soon, too. The bitch was really starting to piss him off, with her fucking whining and her demands on him. And when he did it, he'd send her whole carcass to Detective Craig or put it where he'd be sure to be the one to find it.

He started to turn in the alley. Then, he noticed the blue Dodge sedan, parked in one of the pull offs. Blackwall tires, two black guys in the front seat, looking down the alley. Cops, for sure. What were they watching? Could they have found the truck and be waiting for him to come back to it?

He continued straight ahead and turned north on 6th Street. As he went by the next block, he spotted another unmarked car at that end of the alley.

Fuck! They must have found the garage with the truck in it. Why else would they be at both ends of that alley? If they knew about it, how long would it take them to come up with his name? The Tennessee plates wouldn't throw them off for long. They'd run the VIN and eventually get to the fact that its last registered owner had been Libby. That would lead them to Fernwood Farm. From there it could lead back to him. There were some cutouts along the way but once they got in touch with the Army, they might put the pieces together. One thing was certain, the farm was out of the picture now. He didn't dare go near the place anymore.

It would take them some time, though, to find out that Elizabeth Spencer had been dead for three years and then to make the connection to him. So he still had some time. He could just disappear, as he had planned to do. He had plenty of money, thanks to Aunt Libby's will. He'd take up his new identity in another city, Nashville, probably. It had lots of whores. There was plenty of work to be done there. First, however, he needed to take care of his *piece de resistance* here. He would give Craig something to remember for the rest of his life.

He stopped for a red traffic light at 6th and Breckinridge. Then he saw another unmarked police car coming toward him, southbound on 6th Street, with its red grill lights flashing. The car slowed for the light and then went through the intersection. As it went past him, he recognized John Craig as the driver. His new partner, McAllister, was in the passenger seat.

He knew all about McAllister, that he'd just been promoted to detective and assigned to work the Ripper cases. That they would assign a rookie detective the task of trying to stop him made him laugh. The cops had never come close to catching the first Jack the Ripper and these clowns weren't about to catch him.

This McAllister thought he was pretty hot shit, though. The way he acted when he was with Jenny Holcomb showed that. He was obviously besotted with the girl. What a beauty like her saw in a clod like McAllister was beyond him. It meant she was just another whore, just like all the rest of them, better looking than most but a whore just the same.

Then he had an inspiration. He would take care of both of them before he left. It would be talked about and written about for years. It would show that no one was immune from his wrath and his power. First, the biggest whore of them all, then McAllister's little bitch whore. He had plenty of time. He could see clearly how he would accomplish his tasks.

The driver behind him blew his horn. With a start, he realized that the light had changed. He pulled away carefully. He didn't want to get pulled over for a traffic violation. He had too much work to do.

* * *

Craig pulled alongside Lieutenant Garrard's car at the north end of the alley.

"We got the warrant, boss. Anything going on here?"

"No action at all," Garrard replied. "What did you do with Caldwell?"

"Took him back to jail," Craig said. "We told Judge Colson about the truck and I called Hank Morrison. He's spent the day getting deloused. He wasn't real happy about it but he agreed to a bond being set for Caldwell if this all pans out. Judge Colson said to call him if it does and he'll spring Caldwell."

"Okay, let's hit it."

The two cars pulled down to the garage and were joined by Colbert and Wilson, who had been parked at the south end of the alley. McAllister got out with a set of bolt cutters.

"Did we find out who owns this place?" Garrard asked.

"Cohen Realty owns the property," Craig replied. They rent the house to an older couple named Peveler. The garage is rented separately to an Elizabeth Spencer. No record on her. The realty company is looking up the information they have on her and is supposed to call when they find it."

"Okay, everybody got gloves on? Open it up, Scott."

McAllister applied the bolt cutters and snapped the chain holding the doors together. They went into the dark, narrow garage. Colbert snapped a switch by the door and a dim light bulb came on, suspended from the roof beam. There was a truck in the garage, a 1963 Chevrolet painted dark green. Craig quickly moved to examine both doors. There was no lettering visible on either door.

"Shit, there's nothing on the doors," he said. "And it's a lot darker color than either DePaul or Jimmy Mudd described."

"Look here, John," McAllister said, pulling a brown and green canvas and leather bag out from the floorboard. He opened it and shined his light on the contents. A coil of rope and a large roll of wide adhesive tape were on top.

"Hold it, Scott," Garrard commanded. "Larry, get a camera and let's shoot this just as Scott found it. Then we'll shoot the contents as he removes them."

Wilson had been poking around the front of the garage. He came back to the other detectives.

"There's three or four sets of coveralls on the workbench, Lieutenant, along with a couple of pairs of tennis shoes and some cotton work gloves. Could be what he wears when he does a kill. There's a makeup kit there, too, like the ones we were trying to trace."

Colbert had photographed the bag in the floorboard of the truck where it had been found. Now, McAllister had set it on the floor of the garage and, as he removed each article, Colbert photographed it. Pulling the rope and tape out, he revealed two Rapala filet knives in leather sheaths and a small folding saw. Rust colored stains were visible on the saw blade.

Craig had been standing by, watching this process. Then out of the corner of his eye, he caught a glimpse of something on the door of the truck as a flashbulb went off.

"Boss, shine your light at an angle on the door of the truck, there," he said to Garrard.

Garrard did so and the outlines of lettering were made faintly visible under the thick coat of green paint on the door.

"He's had the damn thing painted," Craig shouted. "There is something lettered on the door but it's been painted over."

He knelt beside the door and, holding his flashlight at an angle, traced the outline of the letters with his finger.

"F – E – R-N -W – O. FERNWOOD FARM, that's what it says. Hell, no wonder we couldn't find a farm named after a flower."

"Technically, I guess a fern is a flower, so old Jimmy Mudd wasn't too far off," Colbert said.

"All right, let's get the fingerprint lab boys out here to dust this place real carefully. Larry, you and Wallace photograph and sketch everything, search the place real good, then collect all this paraphernalia and anything else of significance and bring it to the office. We'll tow the truck to the basement after we're done here. We know he hauled at least one of his victims in it. Maybe we can find some trace evidence. John, you and Scott get back to the office and start running down Elizabeth Spencer and Fernwood Farm."

"Okay, boss. All right if I call Judge Colson, too, and get old Caldwell turned loose?"

"By all means. It looks like he's put us on the right track."

The excitement in the garage among the five men was palpable. After three months of fruitless work, they had finally caught a break. Tracing the ownership of the truck and the renter of the garage would surely lead them to the identity of the Ripper. McAllister was tense with anticipation. He found it hard to believe that this case was breaking so fast on his first day as a bona fide homicide detective. Craig seemed to sense what he was thinking.

"Looks like your transfer brought us some luck, Scott," the older detective said.

"What brought us luck, John, was you treating Caldwell McFeeny like a human being two or three years ago. If he hadn't wanted to talk to you this morning, we'd still be chasing our tails," McAllister replied.

"Amen to that, brother," Colbert chimed in. "Big John Craig strikes again."

"Yeah, well, let's save the celebration until we put a name to this asshole and get him locked up," Craig said. "We ain't there yet."

* * *

Back in the Homicide office, McAllister first called the radio room and requested an NCIC check and registration for the VIN number they had taken from the truck. Craig began perusing the lists of farms that they had compiled for Jefferson County and the counties bordering it.

Inexplicably, word had spread through the police department's jungle telegraph that there had been a big break in the Ripper case. Detectives from other squads began drifting in and out of the office to see what was going on. Sergeant Howard shooed them out of the small office and closed the door. Then he turned to Craig.

"What can I do to help, John?" he asked.

"Sarge, we need to locate Jimmy Mudd and run this name 'Fernwood Farm' by him. See if he can verify that's what he saw on the truck that night. He's a bricklayer so he may be on a job someplace. He doesn't answer his phone."

"I'll get Boyette to run him down. He developed a pretty good rapport with him. Why don't we give him two or three names to pick from, like Blossomwood and Sourwood or something like that, so we can be sure we don't influence his recollection?"

"Good idea, Sarge. Can you get that taken care of?"

"Consider it done," Howard replied. "I'll use the captain's office so you guys can have both phones in here."

McAllister, in the meantime, had called Cohen Realty again. After going through two other people, he finally reached the office manager, whose name was Donna Martin. He quickly explained enough of the situation to her to convey a sense of urgency. Somewhat to his surprise, she was helpful.

"Detective, we rented that garage last December to Elizabeth Spencer. We had it listed for rent in the paper, since the tenants living in the house didn't need it. Miss Spencer answered our ad and sends us her rent payment very promptly each month."

"That's very helpful, Miss Martin. Do you recall what Miss Spencer looks like?"

"Actually, it's Mrs. Martin, and I don't believe I've ever met Miss Spencer. All the transactions have been handled by mail."

"Do you have a mailing address for her?" McAllister asked.

"I believe I do," Mrs. Martin replied. "Yes, here it is. It's P. O. Box 12, Goshen, Kentucky."

"Is there a phone number listed or perhaps a street address on her check?"

"Oh, she always pays by money order, Detective, and as I said, very promptly. The rent is $30.00 a month and she is always on time. And, no, we don't have a phone number or a street address for her."

"I see. Well, thank you very much. You've been very helpful."

McAllister hung up the phone and turned to Craig.

"This is kind of screwy, John. The realty company does everything by mail and has never seen the woman. She pays each month by money order."

"Got an address on her?"

"P. O. Box 12, Goshen, Kentucky."

"Oldham County. Call the postmaster there. See if he knows her and where she lives. Ask him if he ever heard of Fernwood Farm."

McAllister called Information and obtained the number for the post office in Goshen, a small rural community about twenty-five miles northeast of Louisville. The postmaster there turned out to be an elderly lady, Mrs. Rossman. She did, indeed, know who Elizabeth Spencer was, or had been, as it turned out.

"She was such a lovely person and so pleasant to deal with. We all miss her."

"Excuse me, ma'am," McAllister said. "Are you saying Elizabeth Spencer is dead?"

"Oh, yes, Officer. She died about three or four years ago, very suddenly. It was such a shame."

"How did she die, ma'am? Do you know?"

"A heart attack, I believe. As I said, it was very sudden."

"Mrs. Rossman, do you still maintain a post office box for her?"

"Well, yes, we do, as a matter of fact. There is still a good bit of mail that comes in for her and for the farm. Her nephew told me to just leave it in her name for the time being."

"I guess this nephew picks the mail up, then. Do you know his name, by any chance?"

"No, I don't believe I do," Mrs. Rossman replied. "He comes in every couple of weeks and gets the mail. I think he lives in Louisville somewhere. His name wasn't Spencer, I do remember that. I think he was her sister's son. Mrs. Spencer's husband died several years ago. They were very well off and didn't have any children. I believe everything went to her nephew."

"You mentioned a farm, Mrs. Rossman. Would that be Fernwood Farm, by any chance?"

"Why, yes, it is. We still get mail addressed to Fernwood Farm. The Spencers raised horses there. I don't believe the nephew does anything with the place. I understood that he was trying to sell it."

"Where is the farm, ma'am?" McAllister asked. He was taking notes rapidly as he talked. Craig had come over to the desk and was reading his notes over his shoulder.

"It's off of Highway 42, Officer, near the river. I'm not exactly sure where you turn off but the Sheriff's office could probably tell you."

"Thank you very much, Mrs. Rossman. You've been a great help. If you should happen to think of the nephew's name, would you give me a call?"

As McAllister ended the call, Craig was on the other line calling the Oldham County Sheriff's Office in LaGrange. He spoke briefly with the deputy on duty and then hung up.

"He never heard of Fernwood Farm so he's going to check with the county clerk's office and see what they have on it or on Elizabeth Spencer. He says they should have a copy of the deed on file that will show the location. He's also going to check and see if a will has been probated. He'll call us back."

Craig began pacing up and down in the narrow office.

"All right, what are we forgetting?" he asked aloud. "And what can we do to speed this up?"

"We're close, John. We're real close," McAllister replied. The phone rang. Craig answered it.

"Homicide, Detective Craig. Hey, Forest. What have you got?"

He scribbled notes on his legal pad, ended the call and turned to McAllister.

"The radio room says the VIN on that truck is a 1963 Chevrolet, owned by Elizabeth Spencer. Last registered in 1966 at P. O. Box 12, Goshen, Kentucky."

"John, this phantom nephew has got to be our boy. He's taken his dead aunt's truck and been using it with stolen plates, keeping it in that garage, which he rents in her name. Then he had it painted. All we need is a name and we've got the bastard," McAllister said.

Lieutenant Garrard had been briefing Captain Hall and the Chief of

Police on the new developments in the case. He walked back in the office as McAllister finished speaking.

"What's happening?" he inquired.

Quickly, the two detectives filled him in on the results of their phone calls. He looked thoughtfully at Craig as he filled his pipe.

"The first two or three cases we had, we know this killer was driving a big car of some type, right?" he asked, striking a kitchen match and puffing away until he got the pipe going to his satisfaction.

"Yes, sir, the first case back in '64, the Sistrunk girl told us she saw Angela Johnson get in a big car, like a Lincoln. Then Sandy Burns saw a big car leaving the scene on Cypress, after the guy shot at him. He also said he thought it was a Lincoln. Sandy was pretty observant," Craig replied.

The mention of Sandy Burns affected all three of the men in the office. McAllister felt a rush of grief at his memory of the young cop lying in his own blood in the middle of 8th Street.

"God rest his soul," Garrard said sincerely. "Now, we also know that most of the killings have occurred where the bodies were found. Isn't that true?"

"All but Doris Purcell," McAllister said. "We don't know where she was killed before he dumped her at the Cathedral."

"She was a bloody mess, though, wrapped up in a tarp, right?"

"Yes, sir, and before her, we had Deborah Brown, who was killed in Central Park. She was brought there in a pick up truck, according to Caldwell. And we know he was driving a truck on May 27th, when he killed Lorraine Carter. I think I know where you're going with this, boss," Craig said.

"So, we are reasonably sure that he has been driving this pickup truck at least since Derby Day. Why did he switch vehicles all of a sudden? Did he know we were looking for a Lincoln or a big car, anyway?

"He could have, boss," Craig replied. "We put out a pickup for a big car, possibly a Lincoln, after Beverly Watson was killed. Then after Lorraine Carter, we put one out for a gray or light green pickup with writing on the doors."

"So, then, he has the truck painted. He also starts sending you body parts, leaving you notes and calling you in the middle of the night. He indicates that he knows about your domestic situation. It seems to me that he has access to a lot more information about our efforts than has ever been reported by the press."

"That's for sure," Craig said. "Do you think he's a cop?"

"Not necessarily," Garrard replied. "He could be somebody that just has contact with the department, a relative of a cop or of a civilian employee."

"Or he could be a civilian employee himself," McAllister said, with a fiendish grin. "Like an assistant safety director or some other political hack who has access to what we do and when."

"You'd like that, wouldn't you, Scott?" Craig said. "Putting cuffs on your boy, Renyard, would boost your morale considerably."

"That would be too good to be true," McAllister replied. "Still, you've got to admit that he fits all the criteria. He damn sure knew what was going on with the investigation as it was happening. He could easily have learned about John's separation. And, didn't he and Major Bishop try real hard to get these killings pinned on Jerome Lewis, even after it was obvious it couldn't have been him? Besides all that, he's such an asshole."

"All good points, Scott," Garrard said. "But it will take a lot more to make a case on him.'

"Just the same, boss, it wouldn't be much trouble to get the lab to check his prints against the prints from the Watson and Carter cases, would it?"

"Probably not, and we'll do that when we run out of more important things to do. Now, if Oldham County calls us back and tells us he was Elizabeth Spencer's nephew, then I'll get excited. What kind of car does he drive, anyway?"

McAllister's face fell.

"A red Corvette," he replied.

Craig and Garrard both burst our laughing at the expression on McAllister's face.

Then the telephone rang. Craig grabbed for it.

"Homicide, Detective Craig."

"Hey, Detective Craig, this is Deputy Noel out in Oldham County. I think I've found what you're looking for. You ready to copy?"

"Let me have it, Deputy."

"Okay, Elizabeth Spencer passed away in October of 1966. She probated a will leaving her entire estate to her nephew, Charles M. Heldrick. The estate included Fernwood Farm, which is 220 acres up near the Trimble County line, right on the river. Her lawyer was Elmer Sawyer, had an office here in LaGrange."

"You say 'had.' Does that mean he's not there any longer?"

"Nope, Elmer kicked the bucket about six months ago. His son's still practicing law here, though. Elmer Jr."

"Have you got an address on Charles Heldrick?" Craig asked.

"Nothing in the clerk's file about him or where he can be located.

Elmer Jr. might have it in his dad's files. I tried to call him but he's gone for the day."

"How about the address of the farm?"

"It doesn't have a regular street address, just the Post Office box that you had, but it's located on Tucker Mill Road. That runs off Highway 42 about two miles before you hit the Trimble County line."

"Deputy Noel, we'll be up there in about 45 minutes. Can you or someone from your office go up to that farm with us? And would you see if you can locate Elmer Jr. and ask him to come back to his office and check that file for us?"

"Sure, I can do that. I'll have the secretary stay over and catch the phones and me and my partner will go up there with you all. I'll try to get Elmer Jr. back to his office before you get here. Guess I'd better call the sheriff at home and fill him in on what's going on, huh?"

"Might be a good idea," Craig said. "We'll see you shortly."

Craig quickly briefed the other two men on the conversation.

"Charles M. Heldrick, has that name come up in any way before?" Garrard asked.

"I never heard it before, boss," Craig replied. "Can you check it out while we head up to LaGrange?"

"Yeah, go ahead and get started. When Larry and Wallace get back in, I'll send them up there to help you."

"Tell them to meet us at the courthouse," Craig said. "We'll call you from there."

The two detectives pulled out of the parking lot into the flow of rush hour traffic on Market Street. Craig flipped on the grill lights and the electronic siren. Its piercing yelp echoed off the walls of the downtown buildings as they forced cars out of their way and sped eastward.

Chapter Twenty Three

Tuesday, June 4, 1968. 4:05 p. m.

Susan Craig was fuming. The realtor had made arrangements to meet her at 3:00. She had left school early in order to keep the appointment. She had been waiting for over an hour and there was no sign of the woman. She paced back and forth in the living room of the house she and John had shared for the past three years. She was rehearsing in her mind the scathing remarks she was going to deliver as soon as the woman did show up. She lit another cigarette and puffed angrily as she walked.

The ringing of the door chimes startled her. She strode quickly to the door and yanked it open, preparing to deliver her tirade. She stopped short when she saw Mark Clayton standing there.

"Why, darling, what a pleasant surprise. Whatever are you doing here?" she asked.

"I need to talk to you, Susan. May I come in?"

"Of course you can. You sound so serious, Mark. Has something happened?"

She stepped to one side as Clayton entered the room. He was carrying a small leather bag. He glanced about the room as he placed the bag on the floor.

"The kids are not here, are they?" he asked casually.

"No, mother is picking them up and keeping them until I finish with this wretched realtor, if she ever gets here."

"She won't be coming, Susan," Clayton said.

"What do you mean? We had an appointment set for 3:00. She's a money hungry bitch. She'll be here."

"No, she won't. I called her and told her you were canceling the appointment. You'd decided not to sell."

"Why on earth did you do that, Mark? I have to get this place on the market and get it sold. We definitely don't want to live here after we're married. We'll get a place in the east end. I need to get this taken care of."

Mark stepped close to her and Susan took an involuntary step backwards. He had an expression on his face she had never seen. It was cold and analytical. She felt as though he was totally detached from her. There was an intense glare in his eyes that caused her to shiver inwardly. He looked – evil.

"Yes, you think everyone has to do everything you want, don't you? The whole world revolves around you, that's what you think. Well, it doesn't. You're just a filthy whore, like all the rest of them."

"What are you talking about, Mark? What do you mean, calling me a whore?"

"Because that's what you are, my dear. You fucked me the first time because you were looking for excitement, but as soon as you found out I had money, you were fucking me to get your hands on that and get the social status you crave so badly. That makes you a whore, a woman who fucks for money."

Clayton reached out and grabbed Susan's arm. Her indignation gave way to fright. She wrenched her arm from his grasp and turned to run. He clubbed her viciously across the back of the neck and knocked her sprawling to the floor. Susan Craig had never been struck by another human being before. The shock of what was happening paralyzed her. She opened her mouth to scream as Clayton grabbed her by the hair and pulled her head backward. Quickly, he wrapped his forearm and bicep around her neck and forced her head forward into the vee of his elbow, choking off her scream in her throat. He applied pressure to her carotid arteries until she lost consciousness.

Clayton moved quickly to his bag and pulled out tape and rope. In a few moments, he had her bound and gagged on the floor. She regained consciousness as he was dragging her into the bedroom. He picked her up bodily and threw her on the bed. She watched helplessly as he donned coveralls and cotton gloves. Then he bound her arms and legs to the bedposts, spreadeagling her on her back.

He pulled a knife with a long thin blade out of his bag and began cutting her clothing away. With quick efficiency, he stripped her naked, the tatters of her clothing underneath her. She twisted and squirmed as she attempted to scream. The wide tape across her mouth made this impossible. Her eyes bulged out with panic as he bent toward her with the knife.

"You don't know how many times I've thought about doing this, Susan. Your incessant bitching and whining has brought me close to it several times. But I wanted to wait until the time was right. Now my work in Louisville is almost done. It's a pity I can't remove your gag, my dear. I would love to hear you scream and squeal like a pig. In fact I'd like to record it so I could send it to your dear husband. But I can't take a chance on your neighbors hearing you. So I'll just leave you gutted for him to find and send him your cunt, as I promised him."

Sweating with excitement, he bent over the helpless woman and brought the razor sharp knife across her abdomen in a long incision. Her body jerked and twitched spasmodically as the blood began to spurt from the gaping wound.

LaGrange, Kentucky. Tuesday, June 4, 1968, 5:10 p. m.

Craig and McAllister sprinted from the car to the door of the courthouse. A short, stocky man with a crew cut, wearing a brown sheriff's uniform met them there. He stuck out his hand and shook each of theirs with a grip of surprising strength.

"Detective Craig?" he asked, looking from one to the other.

"That's me," Craig replied. "This is my partner, Scott McAllister."

"Steve Noel. Glad to meet you both. Come on in the office. Sheriff's waiting in there and Elmer Jr. is on his way back down here."

They followed Noel into the sheriff's office on the first floor. Sheriff Jack Fowler, a tall gray-haired man, shook hands with both of them. The sheriff was of slender build but with a remarkable paunch that extended both over and under his tightly cinched gun belt.

"Tell me what this is all about, fellows. Noel hasn't been this excited since Hamp Johnson's hogs got out of his truck and stampeded down Main Street."

In a few well chosen sentences, Craig explained what they were working on and how the trail had led them to Oldham County. When he finished, the sheriff leaned back in his swivel chair and eyed the two detectives with a quizzical look.

"You say this fellow has killed seven women, now, cut 'em up like beef? How long has this been going on?"

"The first one was in 1964. Then we don't know of any more until

March of this year. There have been six since then. The last one was the night the riot started in Louisville, May 27th," Craig replied."

"And you think your killer is Libby Spencer's nephew, this Heldrick boy?"

"It's beginning to look that way, Sheriff. Do you know Heldrick?" Craig asked.

"I remember him when he was a little kid, coming to visit the Spencers in the summer time. He was Libby's sister's boy. They lived out west, Tucson, I think, or Phoenix. His parents both got killed in a car wreck when he was about sixteen. The last time I talked to Libby about him, she said he was in the Army and going to Viet Nam. She passed away not too long after that."

A short, portly man in a rumpled seersucker suit came bustling through the door of the Sheriff's office. He was perspiring heavily and a few strands of damp black hair made a futile effort to cover his bald head. Seeing the sheriff, he came over to his desk.

"Here I am, Jack. What's the big emergency you needed me to drop everything and get back down here for?"

"Elmer, these here fellows are detectives from Louisville. They need to know about Libby Spencer's will and where to find her nephew."

"Why, they can find him in Louisville. That's where he lives, far as I know."

"Have you got an address in your file for him, Mr. Sawyer?" McAllister asked.

"I'm pretty sure I do. Daddy and I met him there in a lawyer's office to settle the estate and read the will. You know Libby left him everything."

"Can we take a look at that file?" Craig asked.

"Well, I don't know. Attorney-client privilege, you know. I'm not sure I can let you do that."

The sheriff's boots crashed to the floor from his desk.

"Elmer, this boy may have murdered seven women. We ain't got a lot of time for dicking around about attorney-client privilege. Now, I can get Judge Ellingsworth on the phone and get a court order for that file if you insist, but that's gonna take time and this character may kill somebody else while we're waiting."

The lawyer's mouth dropped open in astonishment.

"Seven women. My God, you telling me Libby Spencer's nephew is a mass murderer," he gasped.

"Right now, he's a suspect, Mr. Sawyer, but the sheriff's right. We don't have a lot of time."

Sawyer threw up his hands and turned for the door.

"All right, all right. Let's go across the street to my office and I'll get the file. Jack, you go ahead and call Judge Ellingsworth and tell him what we're doing. I want his blessing on this, even if it's *ex post facto.*"

A few minutes later, they were standing in Sawyer's office examining the skimpy contents of the file. It contained the will, a list of assets, a copy of a letter to Heldrick and a notarized affidavit signed by him to the effect that he had been advised of the provisions of the will and the location of the assets. It listed his address as 325 West Broadway, Louisville, Kentucky.

"Shit!" Craig swore. "That's the address of the Brown Hotel."

"Why, I believe he did say he was staying at a hotel. He was just about to get out of the Army when his aunt died. We sent him a letter to the APO address we found on his letters to Libby. He telephoned my father from Viet Nam and told him that he would be back in the states in a couple of weeks."

"How did you know he was Charles Heldrick, Mr. Sawyer? I understand nobody had seen him since he was a kid," McAllister said.

"That's right but, as I recall, he had his Army I. D. card and a driver's license, California, I think."

"How much was the estate worth?" Craig asked.

"With the farm and all, well over a million dollars. There was about seven hundred and fifty thousand in cash and securities."

"John, look at this," McAllister said. He pointed to the notary's signature at the bottom of the affidavit.

"Michael Renyard," Craig read aloud.

"Yes," Sawyer said. "That was his friend whose office we met in. Like most attorneys, he was a notary so he signed the document. I believe he and Heldrick had been in the Army together at some point."

"I knew that bastard had to be involved in this," McAllister said. "He can tell us where to find Heldrick. Let's go, John."

"Hang on a minute, Scott. We've still got to check that farm out. He may be there right now."

"Oh, I don't think so," Sawyer said. "I don't think anybody's been up there in a couple of years. It's pretty isolated."

"Maybe but we have to check it. I guess Heldrick took possession of all the cash and securities you mentioned."

"Why, yes. There was no reason for him not to. Over the next couple of months, title to all assets was transferred to him."

"Do you know where he has the assets deposited?" Craig asked.

"No, all I know is it's not here. The president of the Bank of Oldham County was pretty upset over losing those accounts."

Sawyer's telephone rang and he answered it, and then turned to Craig.

"Sheriff Fowler wants to speak to one of you," he said.

Craig took the receiver and Fowler's voice crackled over the line.

"Detective Craig, you boys better get back over here. A Lieutenant Garrard just called for you. It looks like all hell is breaking loose back in Louisville."

Louisville, Kentucky. Tuesday, June 4, 1968, 4:50 p. m.

Garrard was impatiently waiting for some of his calls to be returned. When the phone rang, he grabbed it quickly.

"Homicide, Lieutenant Garrard."

"Hey, boss. Boyette here. We finally found Jimmy Mudd. He says Fernwood Farm is the name he saw on that truck. We showed him a list of six names and he picked it right out. Says he don't know why he couldn't remember it before."

"Okay, Jeff. Good job. You and Howard get back in here. This thing may start boiling over any time."

"On the way. We're out off Dixie Highway in Pleasure Ridge Park. Be there shortly."

Garrard had no sooner hung up the phone than it rang again.

"Homicide, Lieutenant Garrard."

"Jim, this is Dave Ferrell," the caller said.

Ferrell was the assistant special agent in charge of the Louisville Field Office of the F. B. I. Garrard had called him earlier and asked him to check on Charles Heldrick.

"Quick response, Dave. I hope you've got something for me."

"We have one Charles M. Heldrick in the national data base. First Lieutenant Charles M. Heldrick, United States Army, as a matter of fact. Home of record is Tucson, Arizona. The strange thing is, he's been missing from his unit in Viet Nam for almost two years."

"Missing in action, you mean?" Garrard asked.

"Well, sort of. I called Army C. I. D. when I learned that his fingerprint file had a flag on it. He was assigned to Headquarters, Military Assistance Command in Saigon, not in a combat assignment. He was a JAG officer. On November 12, 1966, he didn't report for duty. His things were all still in his quarters and no one's seen him since. He had gone out bar hopping the night before and C. I. D. figures he might have been robbed and killed and dumped in the river. It's happened to a few G. I.'s. But they don't know for sure what happened to him. I also asked the lab to compare his prints to the ones from your unsolved homicides. No match. He's not your boy."

"Okay, Dave, thanks for your help. Can you do me one more favor?"

"As long as it doesn't cost me too much," Ferrell replied.

"One or two more phone calls at the most. Can you ask C. I. D. to check for any people in his unit that were reassigned back to the states about the time he disappeared? And, if they come up with any, check their prints against the latents we've got."

"You think maybe one of his buddies killed him and stole his identity?"

"We're pretty sure somebody was using his name around that time. I think it's worth a shot."

"I do, too. I'll call them and get back to you."

Garrard hung up, scribbled a note in his notebook about the conversation, and was reaching for the phone to call Craig and McAllister when it rang again.

"Homicide, Lieutenant Garrard."

A man's voice responded.

"Detective Craig, please."

"Craig's not in right now. Can I take a message?" Garrard replied.

"Why, yes, I guess you can. Tell him I've left a little surprise for him at home. I'm sorry I won't be able to deliver it like I promised him I would. But he'll be able to find it without any trouble."

The man's voice was low pitched and he spoke with a cultured accent. There was something sinister in his tone that made the hair stand up on Garrard's neck. Quickly he pressed the record button on the tape recorder that was attached to the phone.

"Who is this, may I ask?" Garrard said.

"I think you probably know who this is, Lieutenant. You've been wanting to meet me for some time. But I'm afraid I can't linger. I have one more little job to do and I'll be on my way. It's been fun but it's time to go. My compliments, by the way, on finding the garage. It was too late to do you any good but it's caused me to alter my plans somewhat. So, I'll pick up a little insurance policy I've been keeping my eye on and I'll be off. This conversation has gone on long enough, since I'm sure you're trying to trace this call. Goodbye, Lieutenant."

Garrard heard a sharp click on the line. Carefully, he laid his receiver down on the desk. The trap that the telephone company had installed on the police line captured all incoming calls and simplified the process of tracing them, if the line was kept open at the receiving end. He picked up the phone from the other desk and dialed the radio room.

"Carl, Jim Garrard. Get a beat car started to John Craig's house, 912

Kenwood Hill Circle. Also, call 609, Boyette and Howard and head them that way. Something may have happened to Craig's family."

Hanging up, he quickly called the phone company and requested a trace on the open line. He then scrambled through the papers on his desk and found the phone number of the Oldham County Sheriff's Office. With a deep sense of foreboding, he dialed the number.

* * *

Jenny Holcomb squeezed her Corvair into the last available parking space on Cherokee Road. She felt lucky. It was less than a block from her apartment. Gathering the small bag of groceries she had bought, she got out of the car and started down the sidewalk. She intended to fix spaghetti for herself and Scott that evening. Then they were going to talk about wedding plans. They had to decide on a date and start making arrangements. She glanced with pleasure at the diamond engagement ring on her left hand. Marrying Scott would be the culmination of all her girlhood dreams.

Suddenly she heard her name called.

"Jenny. Wait a minute."

She turned around and saw Mark Clayton approaching her. He had a tan windbreaker folded over his arm.

"Hi, Mark. What are you doing in this neighborhood?" she asked.

"Mr. Morgan asked me to stop by on my way home and see if I could catch you. The Bradley case has been moved up on the docket and they need a brief typed tonight. Here, get in my car and I'll run you down there." He gestured toward a Lincoln parked at the curb with the passenger door open.

"I can't do that, Mark. I've got ice cream in this bag and it will melt. I'll run home and drop this stuff off and head to the office in my car."

Clayton pulled the jacket aside and she saw a large handgun in his hand. A cold, sinister expression came over his thin features.

"Get in the car, bitch, or I'll shoot you right here," he hissed. He reached out and grabbed her arm and attempted to pull her toward the car. She jerked away from him and swung the bag of groceries at his head. The weight of a half gallon of ice cream and a quart bottle of orange juice made a solid thud as it struck him. He staggered back and then started after her again. A trickle of blood was running down the side of his face.

"Hold it, mister. What's going on here?" a voice from behind them said.

Clayton turned and saw a motorcycle cop coming toward them. His bike was parked at the curb behind the Lincoln. With a start, Jenny recognized Dave Randall.

"Dave, look out. He's got a gun under that jacket," she screamed.

Randall stopped and then fumbled for the holster at his side. Clayton raised his pistol and fired two shots into his chest before he could react.

The blast of the heavy slugs flung him backwards and to the ground. Then Clayton wheeled and pointed the gun at Jenny's face.

"Get your ass in the car or you're next and now you know I'll do it," he snarled.

Jenny was in shock from seeing someone she knew gunned down in front of her. The fight had gone out of her, at least for the time. Clayton manhandled her to the car and handcuffed her to the inside door handle. They sped away, going north on Cherokee Road.

A middle aged man had seen the entire thing from his front porch across the street. Now, he approached the injured policeman who was lying on his back in a widening pool of blood.

"Use the radio on my bike" the officer muttered through clenched teeth. "Get some help. Tell them – officer down."

The man turned to the motorcycle and spotted the radio microphone clipped to the gas tank. He picked it up and pressed the switch.

"Is anybody there?" he asked.

"Unit calling, repeat," the dispatcher replied.

"This is Dr. Maurice Blanchard of 1016 Cherokee Road," the man said. "There's been a policeman shot in front of my house and he is badly hurt. There was also a young woman taken from here against her will, by the man who shot the policeman."

"Stand by, sir. All cars, at 1016 Cherokee Road, a citizen reports an officer has been shot. Car 103, make the hospital run, code three. Cars 104 and 105 proceed to the scene. First unit arriving, advise. Sir, can you describe the man who shot the officer?"

"He was a tall white man driving a green Lincoln," Dr. Blanchard replied. "Now I've got to see if I can help this officer. You get someone over here as quick as you can."

"Yes, sir. Units are on the way."

Satisfied that help was indeed on the way, Dr. Blanchard turned back to the wounded man. He yelled across the street to his wife, who was standing on their porch.

"Jessica, bring my medical bag. This boy is in a bad way."

He knelt beside Randall and lifted his head, unstrapping and removing his helmet. In the near distance, he could hear the cacophony of sirens. He hoped they arrived in time.

* * *

Garrard turned the corner on two wheels and slammed to a stop near the emergency entrance to General Hospital. Getting out of the car, he looked north as a police station wagon, siren screaming and smoke pouring from its front wheels, turned off Walnut Street and headed toward him. It was closely followed by another police car.

Members of the emergency room staff, notified by the police dispatcher, were waiting by the hospital door with a wheeled gurney. The beat car slowed just enough to make the turn under the overhanging portico and ground to a halt, its depleted brake shoes squealing against the brake drums. Besides the driver, Garrard observed another officer and a civilian in the rear of the car with the stretcher.

Quickly the staff transferred the injured officer's stretcher to the gurney and wheeled it inside. The civilian and the passenger officer followed them. Garrard walked over to the driver, who had pulled the car into a parking slot. The smell of burning brake shoe material filled the air. The driver got out of the car and glanced at the vehicle ruefully. He was a ruddy, heavyset veteran named Simms.

"I think I'll call a wrecker to tow us out of here. Don't think it's got enough brakes left to drive."

"Probably a good idea," Garrard replied. "What did you find on Cherokee Road?"

"Motorcycle cop named Randall. He'd been shot in the chest. The civilian who rode in with us saw the whole thing. He's a doctor, lives across the street. Says the shooter took a girl with him when he drove off. My partner's got more information. He was talking to this doctor all the way here. I couldn't hear it all because of the siren."

Garrard thanked the man and went in search of his partner. He found him in the emergency room charge nurse's office, filling out the hospital run report. He was a young, fresh-faced officer named Givens and he had been a police academy classmate of Dave Randall.

"It doesn't look good, Lieutenant, but he was still conscious. They took him right up to OR. The doctor who found him was working on him when we got there. He saw the whole thing from his front porch. Says this white guy grabbed a girl after she got out of her car. She put up a fight and hit him in the head with a sack she was carrying. Dave evidently was riding by and saw the fight. Here he comes. I'll let him tell you."

A tall, thin man in his sixties walked in the door, wiping his hands with a paper towel. They were quite bloody.

"Doctor Blanchard, this is Lieutenant Garrard. He's in charge of the homicide squad," Givens said.

"How do you do, Lieutenant? I'd offer to shake hands but mine are a little messy right now."

"That's quite all right, sir. Thank you for your help. What would you say are the officer's chances?"

"Well, he was conscious but in shock. He's been shot twice in the chest with a .45 automatic, which makes a damn big hole. But if no vital organs were hit, he could make it."

"Are you sure it was a .45, Doctor?" Garrard asked.

The doctor raised his eyes from wiping his hands and looked at Garrard.

"I was a combat medic with the 101st Airborne at Bastogne, Lieutenant. I know what a .45 looks like and sounds like and what kind of wound it makes."

"Yes, sir. I'll bet you do. Can you give me a rundown on what happened?"

"I had just come out on my front porch to get the evening paper and I noticed the young woman getting out of her car across the street. I see her quite often because she lives in the neighborhood. She's a very attractive young lady, incredible posture. I saw a tall man come up behind her and say something to her. They exchanged words and then he pulled a pistol out from a jacket he was carrying and pointed it at her. Quick as a flash, she hit him in the head with a bag she was carrying. It must have been heavy because it staggered him. The motorcycle officer was coming north on Cherokee Road and must have seen the situation. He got off his wheel and started toward the couple. I heard him ask loudly what was going on. Then the young woman screamed out 'Dave, look out. He's got a gun.' The officer stopped and appeared to being reaching for his weapon. The tall man then shot the officer twice. He fell to the ground. The man then forced the woman in his car and drove away."

"You're sure the girl called the officer 'Dave'", Garrard asked.

"I'm positive. She yelled it loudly."

"Did Randall say anything to you, Givens?" Garrard asked.

"Yes, sir, he did. He said – Givens flipped a page in his notebook and read aloud-

"'Tell Scott it was Jenny. He took Jenny.' Sir, she must have known Dave Randall if she called him by name."

Garrard suddenly felt nauseous. He slumped into a vacant chair as the realization came to him that this was a continuation of the Ripper's crimes and that Scott's fiancée was the insurance policy he had been talking about. Now she was in his hands, if she was alive.

Rick Rovinelli came into the small office with his notebook in his hand.

"I came from the scene, boss. Underwood is covering it and Wallace and Colbert are on the way to help him. We got a pretty good description of the shooter and the car and one woman gave us a license number, J16-714." Rovinelli paused.

"Boss, you all right? You look white as a sheet," he asked.

"This asshole has kidnapped Jenny Holcomb, McAllister's fiancée," Garrard said. "And I'm afraid he's done something to Craig's family."

"Holy shit!" Rovinelli gasped. "I heard 609 get a run to Craig's home address. Is that what that's all about?"

"I'm afraid so. Let's get to work. Who's the car registered to?"

Rovinelli flipped through his notebook.

"Mark Clayton, 829 Rivercrest Court, on a 1967 Lincoln Town Car."

"Okay, get a couple of cars to that address in case he went there. Have you put out a pickup?"

"They're broadcasting it every five minutes," Rovinelli replied. "I told them to make it 'approach with caution', since he had a hostage. I had no idea it was Jenny."

"Thank you very much for your assistance, Doctor Blanchard. Officer Givens will see that you get back home and we'll be in touch," Garrard told the doctor. The man nodded and went out of the office.

"Lieutenant Garrard, call the switchboard," the P. A. system announced. Garrard picked up the phone and dialed, then identified himself. Tom Howard came on the line.

"Lieutenant, this is a slaughterhouse out here. This bastard has cut Susan Craig to pieces. He's got her splayed out on the bed and gutted like a fish."

Garrard was not really surprised.

"Are the kids there?" he asked, dreading the answer.

"They're with her mother. She called here after we arrived, looking for Susan."

"Okay, get a beat car to wherever they are to stay with them. You and Boyette handle the scene there. We've got other problems to deal with."

"Okay. Boss, don't let John Craig come out here. He doesn't need to see this. Hell, I don't need to see it. I don't think I've ever seen anything any worse."

"I understand. Here's the situation."

Quickly, he filled Howard in on the shooting and kidnapping. Hanging up the phone, he went quickly outside to his car and turned on the police radio. As he picked up the microphone, he dreaded with all his soul having to deliver the message that he was about to send.

Chapter Twenty Four

Tuesday, June 4, 1968. 5:40 p. m.

Craig had the speedometer on the Dodge pegged at 110 as they hurtled down the highway from LaGrange. The siren and flashing grill lights cleared the light traffic out of their way. The Jefferson County line flashed by them in a blur. McAllister hung on to the door post as Craig threw the car into a tire-smoking, skidding turn. Over the noise of the siren, the police dispatcher could barely be heard.

"602 Adam, are you calling us, radio?" McAllister shouted into the microphone.

"10-4, 602 Adam. Meet 610 at General Hospital right away."

Craig slowed down to ninety as they got into the heavier traffic of the city. He sped down Brownsboro Road toward downtown. McAllister cringed as an old Plymouth pulled out in front of them from a side street, the elderly driver oblivious to his surroundings and the oncoming police car. With a flick of his wrist, Craig moved into the oncoming lane, passed the Plymouth in an instant and whipped back into his own lane just in time to avoid an oncoming bus. Another screeching turn onto Floyd Street and he brought the car to a smoking, shuddering halt at the emergency room entrance at General. McAllister unfastened his seat belt with trembling hands.

"Jesus Christ, John. That was - was," he stammered, unable to finish the sentence.

Craig looked at him quizzically.

"What?" he demanded.

McAllister waved a hand in surrender.

"Nothing. Forget it. Let's see what the boss has got."

Garrard and Rovinelli were approaching the car quickly. As Craig got out, Garrard went to him and put a hand on his shoulder.

"John, I don't know any easy way to say this. Susan has been murdered by this bastard. And we're afraid he's taken Jenny Holcomb hostage."

"What about my kids?" Craig asked. His outward demeanor was unchanged but his face had turned ashen.

"They're with Susan's mother. We have a beat car with them at her house. He evidently killed her at your place, and then he called me on the phone and left a message for you. That call was made from a pay phone at Eastern Parkway and Bardstown Road. From there, he went to Cherokee Road and snatched Jenny off the street in front of her apartment. Dave Randall was riding by, saw the abduction and tried to stop it. The killer shot him down. He's upstairs in the OR in critical condition."

"Any contact with him or sightings since then?" Craig asked.

"None. He was driving a Lincoln registered to a Mark Clayton on Rivercrest Court. He hasn't shown up there. We've got the bridges and the main routes out of town blocked."

McAllister had been silent during this exchange, totally stunned by Garrard's account. At the mention of Clayton's name, he looked up.

"That son of a bitch!" he said.

"You know him, Scott?" Garrard asked.

"He's in the law firm where Jenny works. John, she told me yesterday that she had seen him having lunch with Susan. I meant to tell you but never got the chance. He's also asshole buddies with that fucking Renyard. They both must be in this with Heldrick. Or maybe Clayton is Heldrick. He may have gone to Renyard's place."

"You may be right," Garrard said. "According to the Feebies, Heldrick has been missing from his unit in Saigon for almost two years. He and Clayton could be the same person."

"Well, Renyard was involved in helping him get his inheritance, so he may very well know where he's gone to," McAllister replied

"If he knows, he'll tell us," Craig said. "Where does he live?"

"In the 800 Apartments," McAllister replied.

"Okay, let's go," Craig said, getting back into the car.

Garrard leaned in the car window.

"John, are you sure you're okay to do this?" he asked. "You've had a shock."

Craig turned and looked him in the face.

"Jim, there is nothing I can do for Susan now but catch her killer. Maybe we can help Jenny but we've got to find her first. Renyard is our best shot. We found enough evidence in LaGrange to tie him into this whole setup with Heldrick or Clayton or whatever the hell his name is. If Renyard knows anything, you know I'll get it out of him."

Garrard stepped back.

"The sheriff in Oldham County called and said they had checked the farm. Clayton wasn't there but they found quite a bit of physical evidence. They're staking it out with the state police in case he shows up. I told them he has a hostage."

"He won't go there," Craig said. "He knows we found the truck and can connect that with the farm. He's on the run. Hopefully he's got another hole he will run to. We've got to find that."

"Let me know what you find out," Garrard replied. "Don't try to take him with just the two of you. If you get a location, we'll all go."

Craig nodded and slammed the gear shift into reverse. He backed up and left the lot with tires smoking. Garrard stood looking after him. Officer Givens came up to him and spoke.

"Loot, you've got a phone call in the nurse's station. FBI guy, says it's important."

Nodding his thanks, Garrard went quickly to the nurse's small office in the emergency room. He picked up the phone and punched the flashing button.

"Lieutenant Garrard."

"Dave Ferrell, Jim. Your hunch was a good one. Mark Winslow Clayton, First Lieutenant, Judge Advocate General's Corps. He left MAC in Saigon two days after Heldrick disappeared, came back to the states and was discharged from the Army in San Francisco. To top it off, the print on that shell casing you sent to the lab matches his right thumb."

"That's good news, Dave. What else do you have on him?"

"White male, DOB April 19th, 1938, born in Framingham, Massachusetts. He's six feet, three inches tall, weighs 185, brown hair, blue eyes. He graduated from Dartmouth, went to law school at the University of Virginia and then took a commission in the JAG Corps to avoid getting drafted. Served three years, including thirteen months in Viet Nam. He was in the same section as Heldrick and they were roommates in Saigon. Oh, he was also stationed at Fort Knox, right after his commission, from November of '63 to May of '64. Then they sent him to Fort Carson, Colorado and from there to Viet Nam."

"While you're resting, Dave, you probably ought to call your office out in Denver and see if they had any murdered prostitutes in that area during his tour at Fort Carson."

"Good idea, Jim. I'll do that. If I learn anything else, I'll call you. I heard your pickup being broadcast for the car he's driving. Did I hear right, that he has a young woman hostage?"

"It looks that way. Listen, Dave, I've got to go. Thanks for your help."

*   *   *

Clayton pulled the Lincoln into a dilapidated shed attached to a larger building and got out of the car. Coming around to the passenger door, he unlocked the handcuff from the door handle and dragged her from the vehicle. She attempted to struggle against him but he was incredibly strong. Quickly he forced her arms behind her and snapped the open cuff onto her wrist. He turned her toward the building and shoved her forward. She stumbled and fell to her knees. He grabbed her roughly by the arms and pushed her through the door of the larger building.

"One sound out of you and I'll put a bullet in your head. Get moving," he said.

Jenny was disoriented and unsure where they were. Somewhere near the river in the west end, she thought. The building seemed to be an abandoned factory of some sort. In the dim light, she could make out the outlines of large pieces of machinery. Clayton steered her across a large room to an interior door. It had a large padlock on it. He pulled a ring of keys from his pocket and unlocked the door. He shoved her into the room and pushed her down to the floor.

"Remember, not a sound if you want to live," he said.

He went out of the room and she heard the padlock snap into place on the door. She sat up and tried to take stock of her situation. The room she was in appeared to have been used as an office. It was fairly large and covered with dust and cobwebs. A couple of dusty desks, a large conference table and several filing cabinets were pushed against the walls. The only light came from two small windows high on the back wall. The place had an unpleasant smell, like rotten pork. She shivered involuntarily. What was she doing here? And what did Clayton intend to do with her?

Clayton had driven through unfamiliar side streets to get there, turning in alleys several times when he saw police vehicles. He talked to himself a lot as he drove and his running commentary made no sense to her. She was totally confused at the turn of events, anyway.

Clayton had always seemed to be a quiet, self effacing presence in the law office, deferential to the senior partners and considerate of the staff. He hadn't seemed to have any close friends other than Mike Renyard. Several of the secretaries had speculated about the possibility of dating him but he had never asked anyone out. Any social life he had evidently took place away from the law firm. Susan Craig was the only woman Jenny had ever seen him with. Seeing him gun Dave Randall down had changed all her impressions of him. There was no doubt he was a killer and no doubt that he intended to kill her.

Jenny began to assess her chances. She was assertive by nature and she didn't intend to meekly submit to whatever Clayton had planned. The cuffs on her wrists were tight but not painful and she didn't think Clayton had double locked them. Scott had shown her his handcuffs one night and explained the double locking process to her. If they weren't double locked, she might be able to loosen them enough to at least get one wrist free. She began twisting her wrists inside the cuffs to determine how much slack there was in them.

She wasn't sure how long Clayton had been gone when he returned. She had been concentrating on loosening the handcuffs for several minutes when she heard the rasp of a key in the padlock. Clayton opened the door. He was wearing work clothes, tennis sneakers and rubber gloves. He had a bandage on the side of his head from the blow she had given him with the orange juice bottle. She was only sorry she hadn't fractured his skull. He was holding a small leather bag which he sat on one of the desks.

"Sorry to keep you waiting, Jenny. I had to secure another car since your boy friend's co-workers have probably sent the description of my Lincoln all over the place. Luckily, the old fellow that runs the junk yard below us here had a truck available, which he won't need any more. So my transportation out of here is provided for. But first you and I will have a little fun. I'll leave you for your boy friend to find, just as I left Craig's whore for him to find. Then I'll be on my way."

"Why do you do this? What have I ever done to you or what has Susan Craig for that matter?"

"Why, you're all whores, my dear girl. Every last one of you. So you have to die. You see, the power is given to some people to determine who lives and who dies. I have that power and I have determined that all you whores must die."

Jenny was trying to keep him talking. If she could just distract him for a moment, she felt that she could get her left wrist free from the handcuff. She had seen a piece of pipe about three feet long lying under a long table against the wall. It might make a weapon.

"Are you saying God is telling you to do this?" she asked.

Clayton laughed shrilly, a sound which sent a shiver down Jenny's spine.

"God? What's God got to do with anything? There is no God. If there were, he would never have allowed my parents to live or to do what they did to me. Why would God put you in my clutches, if he existed? No, God's

243

not here, Jenny, and he won't help you tonight. Feel free to call on him, however, if it makes you feel better."

He turned and opened the bag and removed a coil of rope, a roll of tape and two long thin knives. He picked up one of the knives and ran his thumb along the blade.

"Ah, just right. Let's get you situated and out of that ugly pants suit, shall we? You have beautiful legs, my dear. You should always wear dresses, short dresses that show them off."

As he started toward her, Jenny rolled under the table.

*   *   *

Craig and McAllister entered the lobby of the 800 Building, a high rise apartment complex just south of downtown. A uniformed doorman came out of a small office toward them. He was a heavyset man with the ruddy face and ruptured veins of a chronic drinker. He extended his hand to Craig.

"John Craig, how're you doing? I'm Art Bellows, used to work with you in the Third District."

"Sure, Art. Good to see you. Listen, we're in kind of a hurry. What apartment is Mike Renyard in?"

The old cop's face darkened.

"That asshole. Treats the help around here like dirt. Thinks he's hot shit."

"Yeah, we don't like him either, Art. What apartment?"

"Oh, 1208. Twelfth floor. He's in. I saw him come out of the garage and go to the elevator about twenty minutes ago."

"Thanks, Art. We're going to run up there. Don't bother to call him. We want it to be a surprise."

"You bet, John. Is sonny boy in trouble?"

"You could say that, Art."

"Couldn't happen to a nicer son of a bitch. Need a passkey?"

"Yeah, that would help. Thanks. How's the place laid out?"

"Door opens into a foyer, living room right there, kitchen on the right side, short hall to the bedroom and bathroom on the left. Only other way out is over the balcony and it's a long way down."

Craig took the proffered key and he and McAllister went to the elevator. At the twelfth floor, they paused outside the door and listened. A television or radio could be heard inside the apartment. Craig leaned close to McAllister's ear.

"When I open the door, you go right, I'll go left. Don't shoot him unless you have to and, for God's sake, don't kill him before we can talk to him."

McAllister nodded and pulled his pistol from his holster. Craig slipped the key into the lock and turned it slowly. The lock gave a sharp click as it opened. Craig pushed the door wide and ran into the room, McAllister at his heels. They broke right and left and each fell into a two handed shooting stance.

"Police, don't move!" Craig shouted.

Renyard was stretched out on the sofa in front of the television, a drink on the table beside him. He was wearing a t-shirt and slacks and was barefooted. His mouth fell open in astonishment but his expression quickly changed to rage. He jumped up from the couch and started toward them.

"What the hell do you think-" he started to say but McAllister charged across the room and into him at that point, throwing a shoulder into his chest and knocking him backwards onto the couch. Craig was astride him in an instant, knees on his shoulders, pressing his pistol against his head.

"Your friend Clayton, where is he?" Craig shouted.

"Are you nuts?" Renyard said. "Get the hell off me and get that gun out of my face."

Craig swung the heavy Smith & Wesson against the side of Renyard's head in a vicious swipe. The front sight raked across his scalp and blood spurted from a wide laceration.

"I don't have a lot of time or patience, asshole. Your buddy's murdered my wife and kidnapped Jenny Holcomb. Now, I want to know where he would have taken her. You've got just a few seconds to tell me before I start shooting holes in your kneecaps and work my way up."

Renyard shook his head, causing drops of blood to fly.

"I don't know what you're talking about," he moaned.

"Okay, ace, have it your way."

Craig placed his pistol against Renyard's left knee cap and cocked the hammer back.

"No, wait! I know he has a farm in Oldham County. Maybe he went there. Don't shoot me," Renyard screamed.

"We know about the farm. What about a place in Louisville? If he can't get to the farm, where would he go? Think hard, now."

Renyard hesitated. Craig leaned close to him.

"You sorry ass piece of shit. This bastard has killed my wife and God knows how many other women and you've helped him, ever since he got here. Do you think I will hesitate to blow your fucking brains out? I've got nothing to lose."

His face was flushed and the pure menace in his voice was unmistakable. He raised the pistol to Renyard's head again.

"Wait, wait! He told me about a place he found, down by the river. Said it was an abandoned factory, something like that. It's around the K & I Bridge somewhere. I think he took a girl there before. That's all I can think of. For God's sakes, man, don't shoot me!"

Craig looked at McAllister.

"Does that mean anything to you?" he asked.

"Yeah, the old Chickasaw barrel factory, 31st and Northwestern Parkway. We used to get runs there on kids playing inside."

Craig pulled his handcuffs from his belt. He fastened one cuff to Renyard's right wrist and then dragged him from the couch and over to the balcony door. He opened the door and dragged Renyard on to the balcony and thrust his hands through the balcony rails. Quickly he snapped the other cuff onto his left wrist and stepped back.

"If you've lied to us and this girl dies, I'll kill you myself before the day is over. Enjoy the view. We'll send somebody to get you. Oh, by the way, you're under arrest for fraud and conspiracy to commit murder."

The two detectives ran through the lobby. Bellows came out of his cubbyhole as they did. Craig stopped long enough to tell him to send for help.

"Call the complaint desk. Tell them to call Garrard by phone and tell him it's the Chickasaw Barrel Factory by the K & I Bridge. We're on the way there. Tell them no radio transmissions. Oh, and tell him to send somebody to lock up Renyard. He's handcuffed to the balcony up in his apartment."

The old ex-cop's face broke into a wide grin.

"I'll take care of it, John," he replied.

As they headed west on Broadway, siren screaming, Craig yelled over the noise to McAllister.

"Scott, for all we know this guy has a scanner. If he learns that we're coming, he'll go ahead and kill Jenny before we get there. If we wait for Garrard, we eat up more time. Our best bet is to get down there as quick as we can and hope we're in time to stop him."

"He may try to use her as a hostage," McAllister shouted in reply. "Take 15th Street over to Portland, stay on Portland to 31st. To get there, you have to go under the railroad tracks that lead up on the K & I Bridge."

Their trip through the west end neighborhood of Portland made the ride from LaGrange seem like a Sunday stroll. Craig was a man possessed, weaving in and out of traffic and driving up on the sidewalk two different times. This time it didn't faze McAllister. As far as he was concerned they couldn't go fast enough. If they weren't in time and Jenny died at Clayton's hands, his only goal in life would be to kill the man, slowly and painfully if possible, but kill him any way he could.

At 28th and Portland, McAllister switched the siren off. They turned north on 31st Street, which led to the K & I Railroad Bridge. The bridge carried a double tracked railroad line across the Ohio River. On each side of the railroad tracks, there was a narrow driving lane for cars. There was a toll booth at the entrance to the bridge.

"Turn right before the toll booth and go through that underpass, then bear right up a little hill," McAllister shouted.

They shot through the small underpass at sixty, leaving the toll booth attendant gaping at them. As they pulled up the hill, the bulk of a large factory could be seen. There was no other business in the area, except for a large auto salvage yard next to the river.

"John, hold it," McAllister said. "There's his Lincoln behind that old pickup in that shed."

Craig pulled off the road and, reaching into the back seat, slipped his double barreled, twelve gauge Fox Savage shotgun from its case. The barrels had been sawed off to sixteen inches. He dumped a box of double ought buckshot on the seat and stuffed several shells into his pocket. He had been carrying the shotgun since the first night the Ripper had called him at home. At twenty feet, it was a devastating weapon. McAllister handed Craig one of the two flashlights they kept in the car and stuck the other in his belt.

They quickly ran to the shed, which was attached to the main building. Craig laid his hand on the hood.

"Still warm," he said. "He hasn't been here long."

Raising the hood on the Lincoln, Craig snatched the coil wire from the distributor cap. McAllister similarly disabled the pickup truck.

"What's the setup inside?" Craig said in a whisper.

"A big open area inside the door, with offices at the other end on the north side. There's a loading dock at that end, too. There's still a lot of the old machinery in there. It's dark and hard to see. My best guess is he would be using one of the offices. I'll work my way down the outside and come in from the loading dock if you'll cover this end. Give me five minutes."

"You got it," Craig replied. "Let's be careful we don't catch each other in a cross fire."

"Roger that," McAllister said. He turned and started moving quickly and quietly down the side of the building. He soon came to the old loading dock at the east end of the building. He vaulted up on the dock and crossed to a small door set inside a large overhead door. Carefully he tried the handle. It turned but the door seemed to be bolted from the inside. There was another door at the far end of the dock. He started in that direction and then stopped. He could hear a man's voice yelling inside the building. Putting his ear to the door, he heard footsteps rapidly approaching, then a rattling noise as the bolt holding the door was thrown. Stepping back, McAllister drew his pistol and waited to see who would emerge.

Chapter Twenty Five

Louisville, Kentucky. June 4, 1968. 6:30 p. m.

Lieutenant Garrard returned to the homicide office to run the two scene investigations from there. On the way back from the hospital, he radioed the desk sergeant to begin calling in all off-duty homicide detectives. When he got to the office, he found that they were already there, along with more than twenty detectives from other squads. When the television and radio stations aired the story that a police officer had been shot and seriously wounded, every cop who heard the news put on his gun and started for headquarters. If anything, there was too much help.

Captain Hall was waiting for Garrard when he got to his office.

"Jim, I've assigned two sergeants, Bridemore and Waggoner to get these folks organized who have come in. They've been told to report to you for whatever assignments you need them for."

"Thanks, Captain," Garrard replied. "We'll need some people to canvass the neighborhoods at both scenes. We'll also need some men for an arrest team if and when Craig and McAllister find out where this guy has gone. They're questioning Mike Renyard now."

Hall raised his eyebrows at that.

"Renyard? How did he get involved in this?"

"It's complicated, boss. Let me get some things started and I'll fill you in."

He sat down at his desk and opened his notebook. The phone rang.

"Homicide, Lieutenant Garrard."

"Hey, Lieutenant, this is Art Bellows. Remember me?"

"Of course, Art. Listen, I'm kind of busy right now. Can you-"

"Yeah, I know you are," Bellows cut in. "I work over here at the 800 Building. I've got a message for you from John Craig."

Garrard picked up a pen and began scribbling in his notebook as Bellows recounted what Craig had told him.

"Chickasaw Barrel Factory, by the K & I Bridge. Okay, thanks very much, Art. We'll send a couple of men over to your place to get Renyard."

"Take your time, Lieutenant. He ain't going any place. I'm using the phone in his apartment. Craig left him cuffed to his balcony up here. Apartment 1208 and, by the way, Craig said to tell you 'no radio transmissions.'"

"Thanks again, Art."

Garrard hung up the phone and looked up at Captain Hall who was puffing on his pipe and patiently waiting to learn what was going on.

"Craig and McAllister think that Clayton, the suspect, has taken Jenny Holcomb to the Chickasaw Barrel Factory down by the K & I Bridge. Do you know the place?"

Hall nodded his head.

"It's a big old building down on the other side of the floodwall at 31st and Northwestern. Been vacant for several years. Why do they think he went there?"

"Evidently they got the information from Renyard, who is a friend of Clayton's. He's assisted him in perpetuating some scam that I don't fully understand yet. Clayton has stolen another man's inheritance."

"So Craig thinks Clayton is the Ripper and Renyard has been helping him. That would explain a lot of things, wouldn't it?" Hall said.

"Yes, sir, it would. But right now, we need to get to this barrel factory with some backup. Knowing John Craig, that's where he and McAllister are headed."

"There's a lot of willing bodies back in the squad room," Hall said. "You go round them up. I'll unlock the shotgun rack."

"I'll send a couple of people over to the 800 building to get Renyard."

* * *

Jenny Holcomb was fighting for her life. As Clayton started toward her with a knife, she rolled her body under the long conference table against the office wall. She got as close to the wall as she could and, twisting her wrist back and forth, she succeeded in slipping the handcuff off her left wrist. Quickly, she groped for the piece of pipe she had seen under the table.

"Come out of there, you little bitch," Clayton yelled as he bent down and tried to grab her legs. She drew them back against the wall, forcing him to go to his knees in order to reach her. He snared her ankle in an iron grip and began pulling her from under the table. She grabbed a leg of the heavy table with her left hand and held on as tightly as she could. He continued, inexorably, to pull her toward him, grunting with the exertion and cursing her.

"You're going to pay for this, you cunt. You'll be begging me to kill you before I'm done."

He succeeded in pulling her from under the table but, before he could get to his feet, Jenny swung the pipe with her right hand, striking him on the side of his head, precisely where she had hit him earlier. The pipe was made of lead and it was heavy. Clayton fell backwards and she rolled to her feet and darted past him out the office door into the dark factory.

Looking around quickly, Jenny saw a metal ladder attached to the wall of the factory. Quickly, she ran to it and began to climb. It led to a catwalk that stretched across the main floor of the factory. At the other end of the catwalk, she could make out the outline of a door. Reaching the catwalk, she ran quickly across it. Below her, she could hear Clayton shouting at her.

"Bitch, you can't get away from me."

Looking over her shoulder, she saw him below her, aiming his pistol at her. She ducked into a crouch and kept running, hoping she could reach the door before he shot.

Clayton took aim at the figure of the running girl but the blow to his head had reopened his earlier wound and blood was coursing freely down his forehead and into his eyes. Before he could focus on her, the girl reached the door, jerked it open and was gone from sight.

He knew that the door led to the roof and to the old conveyor belt housing that had been used to load whiskey barrels into railroad cars parked on the adjacent siding. If she used that conveyor housing to get to the ground, she could reach the huge K & I Railroad yard south of the factory and find any one of hundreds of hiding places, or more importantly, get help. He had to stop her. Wiping the blood from his eyes with his handkerchief, he ran toward the loading dock. He kicked the door open and, stepping onto the dock, found himself staring into the muzzle of a pistol held by Scott McAllister.

"Get your hands up, asshole," McAllister hissed. "Behind your head and get down on your knees."

"Okay, okay," Clayton said. "Don't shoot."

He clasped his hands behind his head and, with his fingers, removed the flat throwing dagger from its sheath suspended by a thong around his neck. As quickly as a snake, he flung his right hand forward and threw the razor sharp knife into McAllister's chest. The young cop fell backward off the loading dock. Clayton stepped to the edge of the dock and looked down at him. Derisively, he spit at his prostrate form.

"You weren't quite good enough, McAllister. Now I have to go find your girlfriend and take care of her. She's proving a tougher nut to crack than you were."

Clayton was thankful for the chance encounter with a Vietnamese gangster who had taught him the value of keeping the hidden dagger hanging down his back between his shoulder blades. It had saved him twice now. Still he was concerned as to how McAllister had found this place.

Renyard! It had to be Renyard. Clayton had thoughtlessly told him once about his alternate hideaway. The cops must have squeezed it out of him. But where were the rest of them? Where McAllister was, Craig couldn't be far away. He had to find the girl, finish her and get out of here.

Jenny found herself on the lower roof of the factory. She ran quickly to the edge and tried to judge the distance to the ground in the growing darkness. It looked far, about thirty feet or more. If she jumped, she might break a leg or ankle and would then be completely at Clayton's mercy. Then, to her right, she noticed a long, corrugated metal housing that ran from the upper part of the factory across the driveway to an elevated railroad siding. She could reach the ground if that thing would support her weight. She thanked her stars that she had worn flat heeled shoes to work.

Jenny clambered up on the structure and found that it contained a large conveyor belt. Stepping onto its surface gingerly, she felt it give a little but hold. She ran rapidly down the belt and stepped onto the ground with a sense of relief. Looking back over her shoulder, she saw Clayton come around the back corner of the factory. He was below her and the bulk of the conveyor housing hid her from his view. She ducked down and watched him through a hole in the metal siding. To her dismay, she saw that he was climbing the hill toward her hiding place.

To her rear, she saw bright lights on tall poles and a lot of railroad cars. A locomotive was moving back and forth a few hundred yards away. If she could reach there, she could find help. To stay where she was now was to wait for Clayton to find her and kill her. Summoning her strength, she jumped up and began to run toward the railroad yard.

* * *

John Craig had waited three of the agreed five minutes when he heard a voice from inside the factory. He tried the door leading from the shed and found that it was firmly barred from the inside. He could hear a man's voice shouting inside but couldn't make out the words. He ran out of the shed and to the north side of the building, where a blank wall with no doors or low windows presented itself. Going back to the south side of the building, he was in time to see a slight shadow detach itself from the bulkier shadow of a conveyor housing and run toward the railroad yard. As she passed through a lighted area, he recognized Jenny. Then he saw a tall figure climbing the steep embankment toward the conveyor. The man was taller and thinner than Scott. It had to be Clayton. He started in pursuit, looking toward the back of the factory for his partner who was not to be seen.

By the time he reached the top of the embankment, Craig was wishing he had smoked fewer cigarettes and done more jogging. He was gasping for breath as he reached level ground. Ahead of him, he could see the outlined figures of the girl and her pursuer against the bright lights of the railroad yard. Then Jenny vanished behind a line of boxcars. A few seconds later, Clayton disappeared also.

Craig called up his reserves and began running down the tracks toward the last place he had seen the girl. Where the hell was Scott? Surely he had seen Clayton leaving the factory. Maybe Clayton had waylaid him somehow. The man was pursuing the girl with single-minded intensity, obviously intending to kill her. There was no time to look for McAllister.

Craig reached the point where he had seen the two figures last. The railroad yard widened at that point, expanding into a wide maze of parallel tracks, each containing a long string of freight cars. He could see the headlight of a switch engine several hundred yards to the south, moving strings of cars around to make up a train. The yard was illuminated by large banks of lights on tall poles. The light did not penetrate between the close ranks of freight cars however, and the narrow spaces between the strings of cars were pitch dark. A light rain had started to fall and the low clouds and moisture seemed to soak up the light. He had no idea where the girl had gone from here. Picking a line of cars, he started down the side of them. He paused every few feet to listen for the sound of footsteps crunching on the gravel ballast. All he could hear was the sound of his own raspy breathing. There were dozens of tracks and hundreds of cars in the huge yard. He hoped the girl had succeeded in finding a good hiding spot.

* * *

Raindrops splashing on his face helped revive McAllister. He had hit his head when he fell from the loading dock and it throbbed with intensity. There was a sharp pain in his chest. Struggling to sit up, he looked down and saw the haft of the knife protruding from his chest. A wide bloodstain was spreading over his shirt front. He grabbed the flat handle of the knife and tried to pull it out of his chest. It resisted the effort and he discovered that it had penetrated the leather folds of his badge case in his shirt pocket before entering his body. The knife was razor sharp but the multiple folds of leather had stopped all but a couple of inches of the blade. Otherwise, it would have transfixed his heart. Sheer luck had kept him from becoming Clayton's latest victim.

He gave a convulsive jerk and the knife came free. The wound began to bleed more copiously. McAllister pulled his handkerchief from his hip pocket and, folding it, placed it inside his shirt over the wound. Cautiously, he checked his arms and legs. Everything seemed to work normally. He noticed his pistol lying on the ground a few feet away. He got to his feet and collected his weapon.

McAllister shook his head, trying to recall what he dimly heard Clayton say after he had knifed him. It had been something about finding his girlfriend, so Jenny had escaped. But he had no idea which way they had gone or where Craig was, at this point.

Clayton had been leaving the factory, so they must be outside the building.

He was angry at himself for being caught flatfooted by Clayton. The man was a formidable opponent with lightning reflexes and extremely dangerous. He had thrown that knife into McAllister's chest before he could even think about pulling the trigger. He had to find him before he caught Jenny.

The rain was coming down harder as he started down the drive toward the spot where they had left the police car. At this point, the only option he could think of was to call for help to search the area and to pray that they would be in time. Then he needed to find John. The blood on the handkerchief stuffed in his shirt was beginning to clot and that was slowing the bleeding down. He stripped off his necktie and wadded it up, adding it to his makeshift bandage.

To his left, from the railroad yard, came a sharp report, sounding like a large caliber handgun. It was followed by two loud blasts, unmistakably the sound of Craig's shotgun being fired. As quickly as he could, McAllister scrambled up the embankment and began to run unsteadily toward the sound of the gunfire.

* * *

Jenny ran for some distance alongside a string of boxcars. Then she saw one with a partially open door. She looked inside and saw that the car was empty. Quickly, she hoisted herself up into the car and struggled to push the heavy door closed. The door squealed loudly on rusty rollers but she managed to get it closed, leaving a small crack to see through. Hopefully, Clayton could not find one anonymous boxcar in a sea of hundreds of them.

Struggling to maintain her composure, she crouched in the darkness and waited. Her breathing sounded loudly in her ears and she could feel her pulse racing.

After several minutes, it became stifling hot in the enclosed box car and the rain rattled loudly on the metal roof. Not being able to see or hear unnerved her even further. Common sense told her that her best option was to remain as still and quiet as she could.

However, the uncertainty got the best of her. She reasoned to herself that it would be better to see Clayton coming than to squat blindly in the darkness and wait for him to find her. She put her eye to the crack in the door and peered out into the darkness. She couldn't see anything in the direction she had come from. She shifted her weight and turned her head to look the other way. As she did, the handcuff still attached to her right wrist clinked against the metal sill of the boxcar door.

Suddenly, the door of the car was rolled back and Clayton reached in and grabbed her wrist. With a vicious yank, he jerked her bodily from the boxcar and onto the ground. He bent and grabbed her under the arms and, lifting her erect, pushed her back against the wall of the boxcar. Holding her by the neck with one hand, he drew a long slender knife from a sheath on his waist. With his matted hair plastered to his head and his face partially covered with dried blood, he looked like a ghastly apparition to the stunned girl.

"Know how I found you, Jenny? I can smell you. All you bitches have a scent that hangs in a man's nose, especially when you add perfume to it. And fear, fear compounds it, makes you reek. You are afraid, aren't you, Jenny? You should be. I knew you were there, and then, like a little rabbit, you couldn't be still, you had to move. I took care of your boyfriend a few minutes ago. He thought he had me but he was too slow, way too slow. Now I'm going to cut your guts out and feed them to you very slowly, you little whore. For the pain you caused me, I'm going to make you pay."

Clayton's voice became louder and shriller as he talked. The hand holding the knife to her throat was shaking and his eyes glowed with a lunatic intensity. Jenny attempted to draw back and he grabbed her hair, pulling her toward him.

"Let the girl go, Clayton," a man's voice said from behind them.

Clayton whirled around, using Jenny as a shield. He held her throat in the crook of his right arm with the point of the knife held against her. With his left hand, he pulled an automatic pistol from his waist. John Craig stood fifteen feet away holding a shotgun pointed at him.

"Well, the great Detective Craig rides to the rescue. You're a little late,

Detective, to save this bitch and you were too late to save that cunt you were married to. You make one move and I'll slit her throat right here. Now you back away and put that gun down and Jenny and I are going to walk out of here and take a little trip. If she's lucky and I'm feeling magnanimous, I might let her live when we get to where we're going. But if you try to stop me, she gets the knife. I'll take your car keys, too, since you've probably disabled mine. Do as I say, RIGHT NOW!" Clayton's voice rose to a scream.

"I'll tell you what I'm going to do, asshole," Craig said in a conversational tone. "I'm going to blow your legs out from under you with this double-ought buckshot. A couple of pellets may hit you, Jenny, but he'll get most of it. Then, when you're on the ground, I'm going to put the second barrel in your filthy head. If you cut her before I shoot, I'll kill you anyway. So you see, scumbag, you're dead meat any way it goes. Your only chance to get out of this alive is to turn the girl loose. Any other way, you're dead."

Jenny jerked her head upright and yelled,

"Shoot him, John! Do it!"

Clayton tightened his grip around her neck and raised the pistol in his left hand. Jenny struck like a cobra, sinking her teeth into his right forearm and biting as hard as she could. Involuntarily, he released his grip, uttering a hoarse yell as the girl dived for the ground, her mouth stained with blood. Like a cornered animal, Clayton turned to the immediate threat and fired a shot at Craig, which ricocheted off the boxcar behind him. Almost simultaneously, Craig fired both barrels of the shotgun, pulling to the right to avoid hitting the girl. Part of the shot pattern struck Clayton in the left leg. He let out a high pitched scream and fired two more rounds at Craig, who had taken cover behind the corner of a boxcar on the next track. He broke the shotgun open and punched in two fresh shells.

"Jenny, get under the box car," Craig yelled.

Jenny had already reacted, rolling under the same car Craig was behind.

Four hundred yards to the south of them, a Southern Railway engineer released the brakes and applied the throttle on his four diesel road engines, taking up the slack in a hundred and ten car train that included the car Jenny had hidden in. Slowly, the ponderous weight of the train yielded to the combined horsepower of the locomotives and began to move.

Clayton saw the train moving and seized his chance. He snapped two more shots in Craig's direction and made a limping run to seize the metal grab iron of a box car as it went by. Using his powerful upper body, he swung himself up and around the end of the car, putting the bulk of the car between him and Craig. The train began to pick up speed.

Craig dropped the shotgun and pulled his pistol. Squinting over the sights of the Model 19 Smith & Wesson, he aimed at Clayton's exposed left shoulder. Rain was running down his face but he ignored it. He took in a deep breath, let out half of it and squeezed the trigger like he was shooting a bull's eye target on qualification day. The 190 grain, semi-jacketed, hollow point slug hit Clayton squarely in the shoulder, shattering his collar bone and causing him to lose his grip and fall between the rolling boxcars. A piercing scream escaped from him before the steel wheels of the car passed over his body, severing his head and tangling one of his legs in the air hoses that were coupled between the cars. As Craig watched, the train dragged his decapitated torso down the tracks.

"Have a nice ride to hell, asshole," Craig said aloud.

Then he turned to look for Jenny, who had crossed under the car and was now climbing over the couplers to him. She grabbed him around the neck and began shaking violently and sobbing. Craig clumsily patted her on the back and made reassuring sounds.

"Take it easy, kid. You're all right now. He won't bother you or anybody any more."

"John, he killed Scott. He said he killed Scott and Susan. I've got his filthy blood in my mouth. I feel like I'm going to be sick."

"Honey, you saved your own life when you bit him. That was the gutsiest thing I ever saw. Blood will wash out. Hey, Jenny, look coming here. You can't kill a Scotsman. We're too damn ornery."

Craig took Jenny by the shoulders and turned her around. Scott McAllister was coming down the tracks toward them in a shuffling run. Jenny broke away from Craig and ran to meet him. In the distance, Craig could see flashing red lights around the barrel factory and bobbing flashlights as the cavalry arrived. A little late, perhaps, but welcome none the less.

From force of habit, Craig broke open the loading gate of his pistol and punched out the spent cartridge case. He dropped it in his pants pocket, then fished in his coat pocket and found a loose .357 cartridge and filled the empty chamber. Holstering his weapon, he lit a cigarette and went to find Garrard.

Chapter Twenty-Six

Louisville, Kentucky. Monday, June 10, 1968. 7:50 a. m.

McAllister gingerly took off his sport coat and hung it on the coat rack in the corner of the homicide office. From behind his desk, Lieutenant Garrard eyed him with a skeptical look.

"Aren't you rushing this recovery, Scott?" he asked. "You look like you're moving a little stiffly."

"Boss, if I have to sit at home any longer I'll go nuts. I went to General yesterday and they cleared me to return to duty. I've got a chit from the doctor." He handed Garrard a piece of paper.

"This says light duty. That means I should make you stay in the office and answer the phone," Garrard said.

"Give me a break, Lieutenant. I'll make Craig do all the heavy lifting."

"Have you talked with John lately, Scott?" Garrard asked, changing his tone. "I'm a little concerned about him."

"Yes, sir. He had dinner with Jenny and me Saturday night. He seemed pretty down. Even Jenny couldn't cheer him up and she can usually bring him around. However, he found a house to rent yesterday until he sells his. I think having his kids with him will help a lot."

"I hope so. Knowing your wife was killed in such a horrible manner would have to affect anyone. John is a stronger person than most but I think he blames himself somehow."

"Yes, sir, he does and I can't make him see otherwise. Hell, he saved Jenny's life and God knows how many other women that maniac would have killed if John hadn't stopped him. And we didn't have a decent lead on him until the day it all went down. I don't know how anybody could have done any more."

"How is Jenny doing?" Garrard asked.

"She's fine, sir. She's a very resilient person and she thinks John Craig walks on water."

"Who thinks I walk on water?" Craig asked as he came in the door.

"My fiancé, that's who, and I'm getting a little jealous of all the adoring looks she keeps throwing your way."

"That girl is way too good for your sorry ass and you'd better hope she doesn't come to her senses. What are you doing in here anyway? Aren't you supposed to be convalescing?"

"The doctor said I could come back to work if you would agree to chauffeur me around and wait on me hand and foot."

"What would be different about that?" Craig replied. "Okay, pull up a chair and I'll catch you up on what's been happening."

McAllister dragged a chair over to the desk.

"Did you see Robert Kennedy get shot?" Garrard asked.

"I was still in the hospital when it happened, Lieutenant, but I've seen the film clip about twenty times since then," McAllister replied. "That family has had more than their share of tragedy."

"Yes, they have," Garrard agreed. "And, with all the other things that have happened this year, 1968 has to be one of the most violent years of this century and it's only half over. Well, Major Hall wants to have his first staff meeting, so I'd better shake a leg." He left the office.

"Major Hall?" McAllister asked with a raised eyebrow.

"Yep, they made it official last Friday. He is now the Chief of Detectives," Craig replied.

"Hot damn, things are looking up around here," McAllister said.

"There've been some changes in the squad, too," Craig said. "Rovinelli's been transferred to Burglary and we got Dennis Burton from the First District in his place. And you and I are assigned as regular partners."

"No fooling? That's great, John. Now, tell me what's been going on with our case."

"Okay, I went to the grand jury on Renyard last Wednesday. They indicted him on fraud and conspiracy charges and accessory after the fact of wilful murder. He was arraigned Friday and the judge set $250,000.00 bond. His daddy showed up, put up the old homestead in Lexington, which I understand is worth about 3 million, as surety and he made bond."

"So he's out on the street. Did we get any more out of him?"

"Larry Colbert took a statement from him the night it all went down. He says he met Clayton while they were both in JAG school in the army.

Didn't hear from him for a couple of years and then Clayton contacted him from Viet Nam with the scheme to claim Heldrick's estate. He says Clayton told him Heldrick was killed in action but the body was never found. He supposedly got fifty grand as his part of the deal, with the promise of more later when Clayton sold the farm. He denied knowing anything about the killings. Bishop says he pressured him to focus the investigation on Jerome Lewis, told him he was going to be the safety director and would make Bishop the chief when he got the job. So he was steering things away from Clayton for some reason. Larry says that the one thing that came through real clear was that he hates your guts and he ain't real fond of me. Before we could re-interview him on Tuesday, his daddy got Frank Habeeb to represent him and that was that. No more talking to the police."

"Bishop? Is he charged with anything?" McAllister asked.

Craig made a grimace of disgust.

"They cut a deal with him. He's going to testify against Renyard and they'll allow him to retire quietly. I think it sucks but we'll probably need his testimony to convict Renyard."

"Do we know where Renyard is now?" McAllister asked.

"Since he got out, he's been staying in his apartment. You remember Art Bellows, the retired cop who works there? He's been keeping an eye on Renyard and phoning me with regular reports. He left for a couple of hours yesterday but other than that, he's stayed in."

"What about Clayton? What have we found out about him?"

"Not much. His apartment in River Hills was like a monk's cell, except we did find a little hidden stash behind the stove. Souvenirs from each victim, it looks like. We've had an earring, a bracelet and a locket identified by the families as belonging to some of the victims. There were a lot more than seven items, though. Looks like we may have some victims we don't know about or else he worked in some other cities. The feds are running an NCIC bulletin on him, listing his MO and asking about any unsolveds. They're also digging into his background. The people at the law firm didn't really know much about him. He didn't socialize much. He evidently met Susan when he was a guest lecturer at a night class she took at U of L. The son of a bitch had the locket I gave her with the kids' pictures in it in his pocket when they finally got that train stopped and disentangled his ass or what was left of it." Craig broke off at this point and turned his head. He collected himself and turned back to McAllister.

"Sorry, Scott. I loved her," he said.

"John, you don't ever have to apologize to me," McAllister replied. "I don't know how you've stayed sane through all of this."

"Maybe I haven't. Anyway, there has been lots of trace evidence found at the farm and also the barrel factory. Looks like he killed somebody in each place. We're running lab tests to determine who was killed where. We're not sure we have all the bodies."

The phone rang. Craig answered it.

"Detective Craig? This is Michael Renyard."

"What do you want, Renyard?" Craig answered, waving at McAllister to pick up the extension.

"I want to let you know that the answers to a lot of your questions are here in my apartment. I've written it all out for you. It's here on my desk. I want you to come over here and get it."

"I can't do that until I call your attorney,' Craig said.

"Sure you can. I won't be here. I'm going to take a little flight in just a few minutes.'

"Wait a minute, Renyard. The conditions of your bond say you can't leave Louisville."

"Oh, I know that, Craig. But you see, this will be an unlawful flight. Unlawful flight to avoid prosecution, you might say," Renyard replied with a high, piercing laugh that sounded unhinged. "You come on over, you might even get to watch me leave and, besides, you know you want to see the information that I've left you. It's right here on the desk, all written out for you."

"Don't be a fool, Renyard. We'll find you and next time there won't be a bond."

"Even you can't find me where I'm going, Craig, although I expect I'll see you there some day. Have a nice day, asshole." Renyard hung up the phone.

Craig turned to McAllister who had been listening on the other line.

"What do you think that all means?" he asked.

"Sounds to me like he's getting ready to kill himself," McAllister replied.

"Sounds like it to me, too. Let's get over there."

They headed out the door, stopping at Major Hall's office to tell Garrard what had happened and where they were going. A few minutes later, McAllister pulled their car to a stop across from the entrance to the 800 Building. A small crowd was gathered on the sidewalk, looking up. Joining them, the two detectives saw a man standing on the outside of a balcony rail on one of the top floors. It was Renyard. As they approached, he called out.

"See you in hell!"

Then he let go of the railing with one hand, waved and then launched himself off the balcony in a headlong dive. The crowd let out a collective gasp as he plummeted downward, turning in the air as he fell. He hit the metal marquee canopy over the main entrance feet first with a sickening thud. His body seemed to fold like an accordion, then bounced high and fell off the edge of the canopy to the sidewalk.

Craig knelt by his side and placed two fingers on his neck feeling for a pulse. His legs were twisted in an unnatural manner and blood was running from his nose and mouth.

"He's dead, Scott. Call for a beat car and the coroner," Craig said.

McAllister went back to the police car and made the call. Returning to the sidewalk, he saw Art Bellows standing at the edge of the crowd, most of who were crowding around Craig and the body with ghoulish intensity.

"Art, help me get these people to back up some, so we can establish a crime scene," McAllister said.

"You bet, Detective. Say, that was something, wasn't it. I would never have thought the little bastard had the guts to do something like that."

"Maybe he didn't have the guts to face going to prison and this was the easy way out," McAllister replied. "Come on folks, back up here and give us some working room." He shooed the gawking bystanders away from the area. A Second District car arrived and the two officers began helping him.

A few minutes later, Lieutenant Garrard arrived along with Wilson and Colbert. He called Craig and McAllister to one side.

"Since you two witnessed this, I'm going to have Wallace and Larry do the scene write-up. They'll need interviews from both of you."

"Yes, sir," Craig replied. "When Renyard called me, he said he had left answers to all our questions on his desk. Scott taped most of his call. He pretty much indicated he was going to do himself in. We need to get in that apartment and see what he left behind."

"Well, the suicide does away with the need for a search warrant. Let's take a look. Wallace, are you and Larry okay here?"

Wilson looked up from where he was interviewing one of the bystanders.

"We got it, boss."

Craig called Bellows over and quickly explained the situation to him.

"Still got your pass key, Art?" he asked.

"Sure do, John. Let's go up there and I'll let you all in. Then I've got to call the manager and let him know about this."

The retired cop seemed to relish his involvement in the case. He chattered avidly about Renyard and his dislike for him as they rode up to the twelfth floor in the elevator. McAllister barely heard him as he thought over what Renyard had said on the phone. He had a strong feeling that there was something very strange about the whole scenario.

As they started toward the door to Renyard's apartment, McAllister grabbed Craig by the elbow and pulled him aside.

"John, there's something wrong about this. This clown hated you and me. Why would he want to help us in any way? I don't believe he felt any remorse, so why the phone call? Why not just jump and get it over with?"

Garrard looked back and saw the two detectives talking. He turned and walked back to them. Bellows continued to the apartment door and inserted his pass key in the lock.

"What's the matter, Scott?" Garrard asked.

"Hold on a minute, Art," Craig called, just as the doorman turned the key and pushed the door open.

The blast of a tremendous explosion roared out of the doorway, shredding the door and flinging Bellows backwards into the opposite wall. The force of the blast blew the other three men completely off their feet.

McAllister struggled to stand erect. His ears were ringing and the stench of cordite filled his nostrils. All of the hallway lights had been blown out and the ceiling tiles were torn out of their frames. The entire hallway was filled with smoke and plaster dust. He could barely make out the forms of Craig and Garrard on the floor. As he started toward Craig, the big man struggled up on his elbows. His face was covered with dust and he stared through red-rimmed eyes at McAllister.

"What the fuck happened?"

"Bomb, most likely," McAllister shouted. "Come on, John. We've got to get out of this hallway. There may be a secondary."

He grabbed Craig and helped him to his feet. Craig shook his head and then looked around.

"Where's the boss?" he asked.

"Over here against the wall," McAllister said. "He's out and bleeding from the head. Give me a hand."

Together, they dragged Garrard to the fire door leading to the stairwell and opened it. It was clearer in the stairwell and some light filtered down from fixtures on the floor above them. McAllister went back into the hallway for Bellows. He returned quickly.

"Blown all over the wall," he said in response to Craig's questioning look. "Poor bastard caught the blast head on. What about the lieutenant?"

"Something hit him in the back of the head, probably a piece of the door frame. It's a scalp wound but it's bleeding pretty good. We need to get him out of here."

"Hey, anybody up there," Wilson called out from several floors below.

"Wallace, we're on the twelfth floor. We need a stretcher and a first aid kit," Craig shouted down the stairwell.

"Okay, John. Fire department's on the way. What the fuck happened?"

"We think it was a bomb. The doorman's dead and the lieutenant's been knocked out.

"10-4. I'll get the bomb squad started, too."

Craig leaned against the wall and, with hands that only trembled slightly, fished out his cigarettes and lighter. McAllister laid a hand on his arm.

"Don't light up, John. That blast may have severed the gas lines."

"Shit, you're right. Scott, do me a favor. As long as we ride together, any time you get a hunch about something, let me know, will you?"

* * *

McAllister and Jenny were seated in the nurses' lounge at General Hospital, along with Larry Colbert, who had been taking McAllister's statement. Jenny hung on to his arm and occasionally tried to brush some of the dust from his sport coat. She had a look of concern on her face, mingled with relief. An emergency room doctor had given him a quick once-over and found no new damage. Craig, likewise, had passed inspection except for some scratches. They were all waiting to hear the word on Lieutenant Garrard.

"What did they find in the apartment, Larry?" McAllister asked.

"The bomb squad said it looked like a military fragmentation grenade, maybe with some C-4 wrapped around it and rigged to go off when the door was opened," Colbert replied. "It was taped to the wall of the foyer opposite the door, so that most of the blast and the shrapnel went right through the door. Bellows caught the brunt of it in his face and chest, which was lucky for you guys, unlucky for him."

"Yeah, I didn't know him very well," McAllister said. "Was he married?"

"His wife died three or four years ago," Colbert replied. "No kids that I know of."

"If he hadn't been so anxious to help us, John or I would probably have been the one to open that door, which is what Renyard was counting on, I guess. Was there any evidence in the apartment like what he alluded to on the phone? Any notes or documents?"

"He left a note on his desk, a rambling kind of thing. He blamed you and Craig for all his problems and said he intended to take you both with him. The apartment itself wasn't damaged much, because of that foyer wall forcing the blast out the door. It was just a setup to get you guys over there."

"Nothing about Clayton?"

"Not a word. He just wrote about his situation, how he couldn't face his father and how much he hated the two of you."

Craig entered the room and, going to the coffee pot, poured himself a paper cup of the dark liquid it contained. He brought the cup over to their table and looked at it dubiously.

"This may be what they use to tar the roof," he said. "Anyway, the boss is out of X-Ray and he's alert and talking. He looks like he might have a mild concussion, so they're going to keep him overnight. Boyette brought his wife in from home and she's in the ER with him now. The lobby and the hallway outside the ER are full of reporters and TV cameras, so you might want to sit tight here for awhile."

"Sergeant Howard is working on a statement to give to the press," Colbert said. "I think Major Hall is going to handle that."

"I looked in on Dave Randall while I was upstairs," Craig said. "He is out of the woods, evidently. They've moved him out of ICU and into a private room."

"Oh, thank goodness," Jenny exclaimed. "He was just trying to help me and that – that maniac –"

She broke off and turned her face to McAllister's shoulder. He patted her clumsily. They all turned as the door opened and a slender man in an impeccably tailored suit came in the room. He walked toward Craig and extended his hand.

"Detective Craig, I'm David Ferrell, FBI. We've met before, I think, during a seminar at the Southern Police Institute."

"Sure, I remember you, Mr. Ferrell," Craig replied, shaking the proffered hand. "What can I do for you? And, I didn't throw Renyard out the window, though I would have liked to. There were witnesses."

"No, nothing like that. But I do have some interesting information on your case. I intended to tell it to Jim Garrard but I understand he's indisposed for the time being and that you're the lead detective on the Clayton murders. May I sit down?"

"Sure, have a seat. This is my partner, Detective McAllister, Detective Colbert and Miss Holcomb, Detective McAllister's fiancée."

"Pleased, I'm sure," the federal agent replied. "And, Miss Holcomb, may I say that you're an extraordinary young woman. From what I've been told, you displayed great courage and presence of mind."

Jenny merely smiled and said "Thank you."

"Now concerning the mysterious Mr. Clayton, two interesting facts have come to light. First, there seems to have been a series of homicides of women every place he had been stationed while he was in the Army, starting with your case in 1964 while he was at Fort Knox. From there, he went to Fort Carson, Colorado, and both Denver and Colorado Springs have unsolved cases of prostitutes who were killed and dismembered while he was there, two in Denver and one in Colorado Springs. Then he was shipped to Viet Nam, Saigon to be exact, with the Military Assistance Command. There, it becomes a little more difficult to determine exactly what took place, since the Vietnamese police do not seem to put much emphasis on the murders of prostitutes or much effort into investigating them. But, according to my CID sources, there were at least three women murdered and eviscerated during his thirteen month tour there. And, of course, there is the mysterious disappearance of his roommate, Charles Heldrick, right before Clayton was reassigned to the states and discharged."

Craig was becoming a little impatient with the FBI agent's pontificating manner.

"You mentioned two things, Mr. Ferrell. What's the other one?"

"Yes, that's the most interesting of all," Ferrell replied. "You see, Mr. Clayton isn't really Mr. Clayton."

"Who the hell is he, then?" Colbert said.

"I don't have the slightest idea. You see, when he was commissioned in the Army, a set of fingerprints was taken from him and those prints match the prints that were taken from the body of the individual down in the railroad yard. One of the prints also matched a latent print lifted from a shell casing that I believe was recovered at one of the crime scenes. Additionally, his blood type matches some other physical evidence in your department's possession.

But," Ferrell paused and lifted a finger for effect.

"But," he continued, "when we sent agents to his home of record in Massachusetts, we found that the address he had listed was a non-existent one and no one in that area had ever heard of Mark Clayton. So we ran the record of his social security number and found that it had been issued to Mark Clayton in 1946 in Boston, with the same date of birth that had been given by our Mark Clayton. To make a long story somewhat shorter, as I fear I'm testing your patience, we learned that the Mark Clayton to whom that social security number had been issued, was killed in a fire at his home in Boston, along with his parents in 1952. To make matters more interesting, the Boston Mark Clayton had his fingerprints taken in 1950 as part of a Boy Scout merit badge class and these had been submitted to our civil file. We checked those prints and found that they are of another person entirely."

"Let me get this straight," Craig said. "This fellow was commissioned in the United States Army using a social security number and a date of birth that belonged to a dead person. Is that what you're saying?"

"That's the gist of it. Additionally, he was evidently admitted to Dartmouth and then to the University of Virginia law school, using the same identifiers. His high school record that was sent to Dartmouth has been found to be a forgery, as were his letters of reference. His tuition was paid in full each semester in cash. He was an excellent student, apparently, and qualified for a number of scholarships after his freshman year. But before he entered Dartmouth, his life is a complete mystery."

"Didn't the Army do a background check before they offered him a commission?" McAllister asked.

"Only to the extent that they verified his academic qualifications and, of course, both schools gave him glowing recommendations because of his grades."

"So, who was this guy?" Colbert asked.

The agent stood up and spread his hands.

"We may never know. Tell Jim Garrard I'll send him a write-up on all of this. My congratulations to you all on the successful conclusion of your case."

He turned and walked out of the room. Craig looked at the others with a cynical smile playing around his lips.

"Successful conclusion, my ass. At least nine people dead and we don't have a clue as to the identity of our main suspect. To top that off, the only person we know of that might have given us some answers does a swan dive off a building, killing an innocent victim in the process and nearly succeeding in blowing three of us to kingdom come. I'm not sure I can stand many 'successful conclusions' like this one."

Jenny reached across the table and placed her hand on his arm.

"At least we're all still here, John. And I wouldn't be if it hadn't been for you."

"Amen to that," McAllister said fervently.

At that point, Wallace Wilson opened the door to the lounge.

"Hey, if you heroes have rested enough, I need some help. We've got a shootout between two motorcycle gangs in a bar at 7th and Hill. At least two dead at the scene and a couple more on the way here, according to the beat car."

"We're on the way, Wallace. You and Larry handle it here. Scott and

I will cover the scene," Craig said, gathering up his notebook and pitching his coffee cup into the trash.

"I've got my car, Scott," Jenny said. "I'll see you tonight. Please be careful."

She gave him a quick kiss and bushed some more plaster dust off his coat. In seconds, the nurses' lounge was empty.

About the Author

Edward L. Mercer is a retired law enforcement officer with 40 years of experience. He retired from the Louisville Division of Police as the Chief of Detectives. He then served as the Chief of Investigations for the Kentucky Attorney General's Office and as the Director of Enforcement for the Kentucky Department of Alcoholic Beverage Control. He currently is semi-retired, working as a private investigator and consultant.

He lives and works in Louisville, Kentucky, with his wife, Sharon and their golden retriever, Sarah. He has personally been involved in more than 500 death investigations. The Dead Stroll is his first novel.

CPSIA information can be obtained at www.ICGtesting.com
Printed in the USA
243038LV00006B/83/P